Toyota Tercel Automotive Repair Manual

Dennis S. Yamaguchi
and John H. Haynes Member of the Guild of Motoring Writers

Models covered
Toyota Corolla Tercel, 2-door, 3-door and 4-door models
with 88.6 cu in (1.5 liter) engine. 1980 thru 1982

ISBN 0 85696 636 3

© Haynes Publishing Group 1982

All rights reserved. No part of this book may be reproduced or transmitted in
any form or by any means, electronic or mechanical, including photocopying,
recording or by any information storage or retrieval system, without permission
in writing from the copyright holder.

ABCDE
F

Printed in England

Haynes Publishing Group
Sparkford Nr Yeovil
Somerset BA22 7JJ England

Haynes Publications, Inc
861 Lawrence Drive
Newbury Park
California 91320 USA

CENTENNIAL
D1594990
W
PUBLIC LIBRARY

Acknowledgements

Our thanks are due to the Toyota Motor Sales Company Limited for their assistance with technical information and the supply of certain illustrations. Champion Spark Plug Company supplied the illustrations showing the various spark plug conditions. The bodywork repair photographs used in this manual were provided by Lloyds Industries Limited who supply 'Turtle-Wax', 'Dupli-Color Holts' and other Holts products.

About this manual

Its purpose
The purpose of this manual is to help you get the best value from your vehicle. It can do so in several ways. It can help you decide what work must be done even if you choose to get it done by a dealer service department or a repair shop; it provides information and procedures for routine maintenance and servicing; and it offers diagnostic and repair procedures to follow when trouble occurs.

It is hoped that you will use the manual to tackle the work yourself. For many simpler jobs, doing it yourself may be quicker than arranging an appointment to get the vehicle into a shop and making the trips to leave it and pick it up. More importantly, a lot of money can be saved by avoiding the expense the shop must pass on to you to cover its labor and overhead costs. An added benefit is the sense of satisfaction and accomplishment that you feel after having done the job yourself.

Using the manual
The manual is divided into Chapters. Each Chapter is divided into numbered Sections, which are headed in bold type between horizontal lines. Each Section consists of consecutively numbered paragraphs.

The two types of illustrations used (figures and photographs) are referenced by a number preceding their captions. Figure reference numbers denote Chapter and numerical sequence in the Chapter; i.e. Fig. 12.4 means Chapter 12, figure number 4. Figure captions are followed by a Section number which ties the figure to a specific portion of the text. All photographs apply to the Chapter in which they appear, and the reference number pinpoints the pertinent Section and paragraph.

Procedures, once described in the text, are not normally repeated. When it is necessary to refer to another Chapter, the reference will be given as Chapter and Section number; i.e. Chapter 1/16. Cross references given without use of the word 'Chapter' apply to Sections and/or paragraphs in the same Chapter. For example, 'see Section 8' means in the same Chapter.

Reference to the left or right of the vehicle is based on the assumption that one is sitting in the driver's seat facing forward.

Even though extreme care has been taken during the preparation of this manual, neither the publisher nor the author can accept responsibility for any errors in, or omissions from, the information given.

Introduction to the Toyota Corolla Tercel

The Tercel is one of Toyota's entries into the small economy car field.

The engine is located conventionally on a front-to-rear axis and drives the front wheels through a transaxle, which powers independently-sprung driveaxles.

The transaxle unit is the core of the front drive system used on the Tercel and allows it to have its flat floor passenger compartment, along with the traction and efficiency long attributed to other front wheel drive cars.

The body comes in 2-, 3- and 4-door versions with three trim levels. The SR-5 is the top-of-the-line Tercel and comes equipped with such items as a tachometer and a higher grade of interior trim.

The Tercel has four-wheel independent suspension for good ride and handling qualities. Rack and pinion steering is another desirable engineering feature provided on this automobile.

The engine offered in the Tercel is a single overhead cam, 4-cylinder powerplant. Emissions control variations, along with compression ratio, carburetion and ignition differences, are required by the varying geographic areas in which the car is sold.

Transmissions offered are a 4-speed and a 5-speed manual as well as a fully automatic 3-speed model.

Contents

1980 Toyota Tercel 2-door

1981 Toyota Tercel 4-door

General dimensions, capacities and weights

Overall length
    1980 .... 160.0 in (4065 mm)
    1981 and 1982 .... 161.2 in (4095 mm)
Overall width
    1980 .... 61.0 in (1550 mm)
    1981 and 1982 .... 61.2 in (1555 mm)
Overall height
    1980 .... 53.9 in (1370 mm)
    1981 and 1982 .... 53.1 in (1350 mm)
Wheelbase .... 98.4 in (2500 mm)
Front track .... 52.4 in (1330 mm)
Rear track .... 51.8 in (1315 mm)
Turning circle
    1980 .... 32.2 ft (9.8 m)
    1981 and 1982 .... 33.5 ft (10.2 m)
Total vehicle capacity (occupants and luggage)
    1980 .... 700 lb (318 kg)
    1981 .... 800 lb (363 kg)
Fuel tank capacity .... 11.9 gal (9.9 Imp Gal/45 Litres)

Note: *For other capacities, see Chapter 1.*

Spare parts and vehicle identification numbers

Buying spare parts

Spare parts are available from many sources, which generally fall into one of two categories – authorized dealer parts departments and independent retail auto parts stores. Our advice concerning spare parts is as follows:

Authorized dealer parts department: This is the best source for parts which are peculiar to your vehicle and not generally available elsewhere (i.e. major engine parts, transmission parts, trim pieces, etc). It is also the only place you should buy parts if your vehile is still under warranty, as non-factory parts may invalidate the warranty. To be sure of obtaining the correct parts, have your vehicle's engine and chassis numbers available and, if possible, take the old parts along for positive identification.

Retail auto parts stores: Good auto parts stores will stock frequently needed components which wear out relatively fast (i.e. clutch components, exhaust systems, brake parts, tune-up parts, etc.). These stores often supply new or reconditioned parts on an exchange basis, which can save a considerable amount of money. Discount auto parts stores are often very good places to buy materials and parts needed for general vehicle maintenance (i.e. oil, grease, filters, spark plugs, belts, touch-up paint, bulbs, etc.). They also usually sell tools and general accessories, have convenient hours, charge lower prices, and can often be found not far from your home.

Vehicle identification numbers

Regardless from which source parts are obtained, it is essential to provide correct information concerning the vehicle model and year of manufacture plus the engine serial number and the vehicle ident-ification number (VIN). The VIN can be found on the dashboard edge as you look into the windshield on the driver's side. A data plate including the date of manufacture can be found on the latch post of the driver's door. Emissions hose routing and tune-up information are located on the underside of the hood.

Typical VIN plate as seen from outside of the vehicle looking through the lower left corner of the windshield

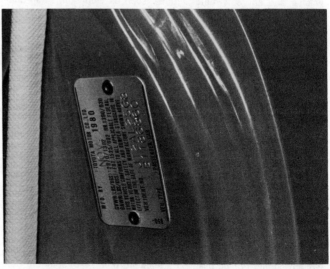

Typical Warranty plate located on the post above the driver's door latch

Maintenance techniques, tools and working facilities

Basic maintenance techniques

There are a number of techniques involved in maintenance and repair that will be referred to throughout this manual. Application of these techniques will enable the home mechanic to be more efficient, better organized and capable of performing the various tasks properly, which will ensure that the repair job is thorough and complete.

Fasteners

Fasteners, basically, are nuts, bolts, studs and screws used to hold two or more parts together. There are a few things to keep in mind when working with fasteners. Almost all of them use a locking device of some type; either a lock washer, locknut, locking tab or thread adhesive. All threaded fasteners should be clean and straight, with undamaged threads and undamaged corners on the hex head where the wrench fits. Develop the habit of replacing damaged nuts and bolts with new ones. Special locknuts with nylon or fiber inserts can only be used once. If they are removed, they lose their locking ability and must be replaced with new ones.

Rusted nuts and bolts should be treated with a penetrating fluid to ease removal and prevent breakage. Some mechanics use turpentine in a spout-type oil can, which works quite well. After applying the rust penetrant, let it "work" for a few minutes before trying to loosen the nut or bolt. Badly rusted fasteners may have to be chiseled or sawed off or removed with a special nut breaker, available at tool stores.

If a bolt or stud breaks off in an assembly, it can be drilled and removed with a special tool commonly available for this purpose. Most automotive machine shops can perform this task, as well as other repair procedures (such as repair of threaded holes that have been stripped out).

Flat washers and lock washers, when removed from an assembly should always be replaced exactly as removed. Replace damaged washers with new ones. Always use a flat washer between a lock washer and any soft metal surface (such as aluminum), thin sheet metal or plastic.

Fastener sizes

For a number of reasons, automobile manufacturers are making wider and wider use of metric fasteners. Therefore, it is important to be able to tell the difference between standard (sometimes called U.S., English or SAE) and metric hardware, since thay cannot be interchanged.

All bolts, whether standard or metric, are sized according to diameter, thread pitch and length. For example, a standard $\frac{1}{2}$ – 13 x 1 bolt is $\frac{1}{2}$ inch in diameter, has 13 threads per inch and is 1 inch long. An M12 – 1.75 x 25 metric bolt is 12 mm in diameter, has a thread pitch of 1.75 mm (the distance between threads) and is 25 mm long. The 2 bolts are nearly identical, and easily confused, but they are not interchangeable.

In addition to the differences in diameter, thread pitch and length, metric and standard bolts can also be distinguished by examining the bolt heads. To begin with, the distance across the flats on a standard bolt head is measured in inches, while the same dimension on a metric bolt is measured in millimeters (the same is true for nuts). As a result, a standard wrench should not be used on a metric bolt and a metric wrench should not be used on a standard bolt. Also, standard bolts have slashes radiating out from the center of the head to denote the grade or strength of the bolt (which is an indication of the amount of

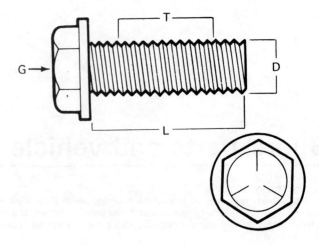

Standard (SAE) bolt dimensions/grade marks

G   Grade marks (bolt strength)
L   Length (in inches)
T   Thread pitch (number of threads per inch)
D   Nominal diameter (in inches)

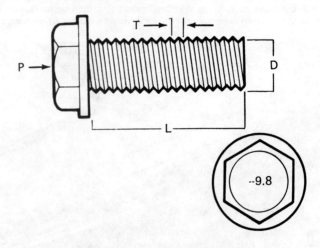

Metric bolt dimensions/grade marks

P   Property class (bolt strength)
L   Length (in millimeters)
T   Thread pitch (distance between
    threads; in millimeters)
D   Nominal diameter (in millimeters)

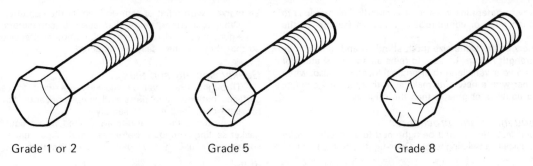

SAE system bolt identification (slash marks indicate strength rating; increasing number of marks means higher strength)

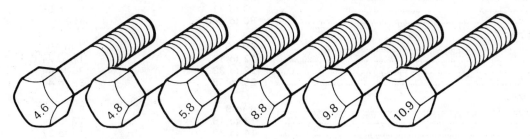

Metric system bolt identification (numbers correspond to bolt strength; the higher the number the greater the strength)

Grade	Identification	Class	Identification
Hex Nut Grade 5	3 Dots	Hex Nut Property Class 9	Arabic 9
Hex Nut Grade 8	6 Dots	Hex Nut Property Class 10	Arabic 10

SAE system hex nut identification (increasing dots represent an increasing strength rating)

Metric system hex nut identification (the higher the number, the greater the strength rating)

torque that can be supplied to it). The greater the number of slashes, the greater the strength of the bolt (grades 0 through 5 are commonly used on automobiles). Metric bolts have a property class (grade) number, rather than a slash, molded into their heads to indicate bolt strength. In this case, the higher the number the stronger the bolt (property class numbers 8.8, 9.8 and 10.9 are commonly used on automobiles).

Strength markings can also be used to distinguish standard hex nuts from metric hex nuts. Standard nuts have dots stamped into one side, while metric nuts are marked with a number. The greater the number of dots, or the higher the number, the greater the strength of the nut.

Metric studs are also marked on their ends according to property class (grade). Larger studs are numbered (the same as metric bolts), while smaller studs carry a geometric code to denote grade.

It should be noted that many fasteners, especially Grades 0 through 2, have no distinguishing marks on them. When such is the

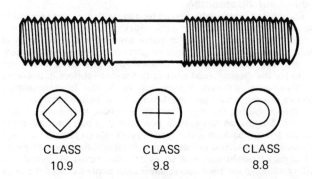

CLASS 10.9   CLASS 9.8   CLASS 8.8

Metric stud identification (large studs are marked with strength rating numbers which increase as strength increases; smaller studs are marked with a geometric code)

case, the only way to determine whether it is standard or metric is to measure the thread pitch or compare it to a known fastener of the same size.

Since fasteners of the same size (both standard and metric) may have different strength ratings, be sure to reinstall any bolts, studs or nuts removed from your vehicle in their original locations. Also, when replacing a fastener with a new one, make sure that the new one has a strength rating equal to or greater than the original.

Tightening sequences and procedures

Most threaded fasteners should be tightened to a specific torque value (torque is basically a twisting force). Over-tightening the fastener

Metric thread sizes
M-6	
M-8	
M-10	
M-12	
M-14	

Pipe thread sizes
$\frac{1}{8}$	
$\frac{1}{4}$	
$\frac{3}{8}$	
$\frac{1}{2}$	

U.S. thread sizes
$\frac{1}{4}$ - 20	
$\frac{5}{16}$ - 18	
$\frac{5}{16}$ - 24	
$\frac{3}{8}$ - 16	
$\frac{3}{8}$ - 24	
$\frac{7}{16}$ - 14	
$\frac{7}{16}$ - 20	
$\frac{1}{2}$ - 13	

can weaken it and lead to eventual breakage, while under-tightening can cause it to eventually come loose. Bolts, screws and studs, depending on the materials they are made of and their thread diameters, have specific torque values (many of which are noted in the Specifications Section at the beginning of each Chapter). Be sure to follow the torque recommendations closely. For fasteners not assigned a specific torque, a general torque value chart is presented here as a guide. As was previously mentioned, the sizes and grade of a fastener determine the amount of torque that can safely be applied to it. The figures listed here are approximate for Grade 2 and Grade 3 fasteners (higher grades can tolerate higher torque values).

Fasteners laid out in a pattern (i.e. cylinder head bolts, oil pan bolts, differential cover bolts, etc.) must be loosened and tightened in a definite sequence to avoid warping the component. Initially, the bolts or nuts should be assembled finger-tight only. Next, they should be tightened one full turn each, in a criss-cross or diagonal pattern. After each one has been tightened one full turn, return to the first one and tighten them all one half turn, following the same pattern. Finally, tighten each of them one-quarter turn at a time until they all have been tightened to the proper torque value. To loosen and remove them the procedure would be reversed.

Component disassembly

Component disassembly should be done with care and purpose to help ensure that the parts go back together properly. Always keep track of the sequence in which parts are removed. Make note of special characteristics or markings on parts that can be installed more than one way (such as a grooved thrust washer on a shaft). It is a good idea to lay the disassembled parts out on a clean surface in the order that they were removed. It may also be helpful to make simple sketches or take instant photos of components before removal.

When removing fasteners from an assembly, keep track of their locations. Sometimes threading a bolt back in a part, or putting the washers and nut back on a stud, can prevent mixups later. If nuts and bolts cannot be returned to their original locations, they should be kept in a compartmented box or a series of small boxes. A cupcake or muffin tin is ideal for this purpose, since each cavity can hold the bolts and nuts from a particular area (i.e. oil pan bolts, valve cover bolts, engine mount bolts, etc.). A pan of this type is especially helpful when working on assemblies with very small parts (such as the carburetor, alternator, valve train or interior dash and trim pieces). The cavities can

be marked with paint or tape to identify the contents.

Whenever wiring looms, harnesses or connectors are separated, it's a good idea to identify them with numbered pieces of masking tape so that they can be easily reconnected.

Gasket sealing surfaces

Throughout any vehicle, gaskets are used to seal the mating surfaces between two parts and keep lubricants, fluids, vacuum or pressure contained in an assembly.

Many times these gaskets are coated with a liquid or paste-type gasket sealing compound before assembly. Age, heat and pressure can sometimes cause the two parts to stick together so tightly that they

ft-lb	Nm
6 to 9	9 to 12
14 to 21	19 to 28
28 to 40	38 to 54
50 to 71	68 to 96
80 to 140	109 to 154
5 to 8	7 to 10
12 to 18	17 to 24
22 to 33	30 to 44
25 to 35	34 to 47
6 to 9	9 to 12
12 to 18	17 to 24
14 to 20	19 to 27
22 to 32	30 to 43
27 to 38	37 to 51
40 to 55	55 to 74
40 to 60	55 to 81
55 to 80	75 to 108

are very difficult to separate. Often the assembly can be loosened by striking it with a soft-faced hammer near the mating surfaces. A regular hammer can be used if a block of wood is placed between the hammer and the part. Do not hammer on cast parts or parts that could be easily damaged. With any particularly stubborn part, always recheck to see that every fastener has been removed.

Avoid using a screwdriver or bar to pry apart an assembly, as they can easily mar the gasket sealing surfaces of the parts (which must remain smooth). If prying is absolutely necessary, use an old broom handle, but keep in mind that extra clean-up will be necessary if the wood splinters.

After the parts are separated, the old gasket must be carefully scraped off and the gasket surfaces cleaned. Stubborn gasket material can be soaked with rust penetrant or treated with a special chemical to soften it so that it can be easily scraped off. A scraper can be fashioned from a piece of copper tubing by flattening and sharpening one end. Copper is recommended because it is usually softer than the surfaces to be scraped, which reduces the chance of gouging the part. Some gaskets can be removed with a wire brush, but regardless of the method used, the mating surfaces must be left clean and smooth. If for some reason the gasket surface is gouged, then a gasket sealer thick enough to fill scratches will have to be used upon reassembly of the components. For most applications, a non-drying (or semi-drying) gasket sealer should be used.

Hose removal tips

Caution: If equipped with air conditioning, do not ever disconnect any of the a/c hoses without first de-pressurizing the system.

Hose removal precautions closely parallel gasket removal precautions. Avoid scratching or gouging the surface that the hose mates against or the connection may leak. This is especially true for radiator hoses. Because of various chemical reactions, the rubber in hoses can bond itself to the metal spigot that the hose fits over. To remove a hose, first loosen the hose clamps that secure it to the spigot. Then, with slip joint pliers, grab the hose at the clamp and rotate it around the spigot. Work it back and forth until it is completely free, then pull it off (silicone or other lubricants will ease removal if they can be applied between the hose and the spigot). Apply the same lubricant to the inside of the hose and the outside of the spigot to simplify installation.

If a hose clamp is broken or damaged, do not re-use it. Do not reuse hoses that are cracked, split or torn.

Tools

A selection of good tools is a basic requirement for anyone who plans to maintain and repair his or her own vehicle. For the owner who has few tools, if any, the initial investment might seem high, but when compared to the spiraling costs of professional auto maintenance and repair, it is a wise one.

To help the owner decide which tools are needed to perform the tasks detailed in this manual, the following tool lists are offered: *Maintenance and minor repair, Repair and overhaul* and *Special*. The newcomer to practical mechanics should start off with the *Maintenance and minor repair* tool kit, which is adequate for the simpler jobs performed on a vehicle. Then, as his confidence and experience grow, he can tackle more difficult tasks, buying additional tools as they are needed. Eventually the basic kit will be expanded into the *Repair and overhaul* tool set. Over a period of time, the experienced do-it-yourselfer will assemble a tool set complete enough for most repair and overhaul procedures and will add tools from the *Special* category when he feels the expense is justified by the frequency of use.

Maintenance and minor repair tool kit

The tools in this list should be considered the minimum for performance of routine maintenance, servicing and minor repair work. We recommend the purchase of combination wrenches (box end and open end combined in one wrench); while more expensive than open-ended ones, they offer the advantages of both types of wrench.

Combination wrench set ($\frac{1}{4}$ in to 1 in or 6 mm to 19 mm)
Adjustable wrench – 8 in
Spark plug wrench (with rubber insert)
Spark plug gap adjusting tool
Feeler gauge set
Brake bleeder wrench
Standard screwdriver ($\frac{5}{16}$ in x 6 in)
Phillips screwdriver (No.2 x 6 in)
Combination pliers – 6 in
Hacksaw and assortment of blades
Tire pressure gauge
Grease gun
Oil can
Fine emery cloth
Wire brush
Battery post and cable cleaning tool
Oil filter wrench
Funnel (medium size)
Safety goggles
Jack stands (2)
Drain pan

Note: *If basic tune-ups are going to be a part of routine maintenance, it will be necessary to purchase a good quality stroboscopic timing light and a combination tachometer/dwell meter. Although they are included in the list of Special tools, they are mentioned here because they are absolutely necessary for tuning most vehicles properly.*

Repair and overhaul tool set

These tools are essential for anyone who plans to perform major repairs and are in addition to those in the *Maintenance and minor repair tool kit.* Included is a comprehensive set of sockets which, though expensive, will be found invaluable because of their versatility (especially when various extensions and drives are available). We recommend the $\frac{1}{2}$ in drive over the $\frac{3}{8}$ in drive. Although the larger drive is bulky and more expensive, it has the capability of accepting a very wide range of large sockets (ideally, the mechanic would have a $\frac{3}{8}$ in drive set and a $\frac{1}{2}$ in drive set).

Socket set(s)
Reversible ratchet
Extension – 10 in
Universal joint
Torque wrench (same size drive as sockets)
Ball pein hammer – 8 oz
Soft-faced hammer (plastic/rubber)
Standard screwdriver ($\frac{1}{4}$ in x 6 in)
Standard screwdriver (stubby – $\frac{5}{16}$ in)
Phillips screwdriver (No.3 x 8 in)
Phillips screwdriver (stubby – No.2)
Pliers – vise grip
Pliers – lineman's
Pliers – needle nose
Pliers – spring clip (internal and external)
Cold chisel – $\frac{1}{2}$ in
Scriber
Scraper (made from flattened copper tubing)
Center punch
Pin punches ($\frac{1}{16}$, $\frac{1}{8}$, $\frac{3}{16}$ in)
Steel rule/straight edge – 12 in
Allen wrench set ($\frac{1}{8}$ to $\frac{3}{8}$ in or 4 mm to 10 mm)
A selection of files
Wire brush (large)
Jack stands (second set)
Jack (scissor or hydraulic type)

Note: *Another tool which is often useful is an electric drill motor with a chuck capacity of $\frac{3}{8}$ in (and a set of good quality drill bits).*

Special tools

The tools in this list include those which are not used regularly, are expensive to buy, or which need to be used in accordance with their manufacturer's instructions. Unless these tools will be used frequently, it is not very economical to purchase many of them. A consideration would be to split the cost and use between yourself and a friend or friends. In addition, most of these tools can be obtained from a tool rental shop on a temporary basis.

This list contains only those tools and instruments widely available to the public, and not those special tools produced by vehicle manufacturers for distribution to dealer service departments. Occasionally, references to the manufacturer's special tools are included in the text of this manual. Generally, an alternative method of doing the job without the special tool is offered. However, sometimes there is no alternative to their use. Where this is the case, and the tool cannot be purchased or borrowed, the work should be turned over to the dealer, a repair shop or an automotive machine shop.

Valve spring compressor

Valve spring compressor   **Piston ring compressor**   **Universal hub puller**

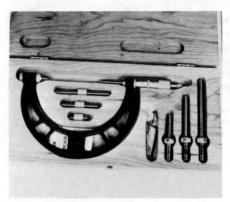

Micrometer set

Dial caliper

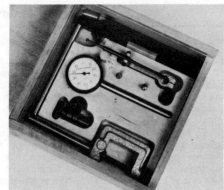

Dial gauge set

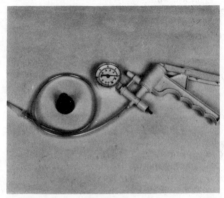

Vacuum pump

Brake shoe spring tool

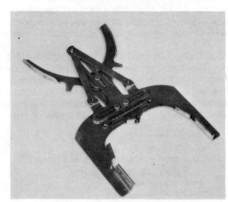

Piston ring expander

Piston ring groove cleaner

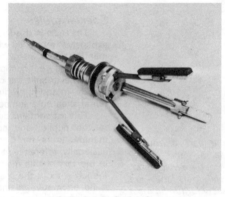

Cylinder surfacing hone

Cylinder ridge reamer

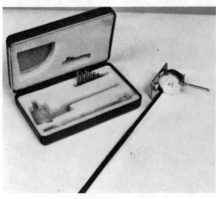

Cylinder bore gauge

Piston ring groove cleaning tool
Piston ring compressor
Piston ring installation tool
Cylinder compression gauge
Cylinder ridge reamer
Cylinder surfacing hone
Cylinder bore gauge
Micrometer(s) and/or dial calipers
Hydraulic lifter removal tool
Balljoint separator
Universal-type puller
Impact screwdriver
Dial indicator set
Stroboscopic timing light (inductive pickup)
Hand-operated vacuum/pressure pump
Tachometer/dwell meter
Universal electrical multi-meter
Cable hoist
Brake spring removal and installation tools
Floor jack

Buying tools

For the do-it-yourselfer who is just starting to get involved in vehicle maintenance and repair, there are a couple of options available when purchasing tools. If maintenance and minor repair is the extent of the work to be done, the purchase of individual tools is satisfactory. If, on the other hand, extensive work is planned, it would be a good idea to purchase a modest tool set from one of the large retail chain stores. A set can usually be bought at a substantial savings over the individual tool prices (and they often come with a tool box). As additional tools are needed, add-on sets, individual tools and a larger tool box can be purchased to expand the tool selection. Building a tool set gradually allows the cost of the tools to be spread over a longer period of time and gives the mechanic the freedom to choose only those tools that will actually be used.

Tool stores will often be the only source of some of the special tools that are needed, but regardless of where tools are bought, try to avoid cheap ones (especially when buying screwdrivers and sockets) because they won't last very long. The expense involved in replacing cheap tools will eventually be greater than the initial cost of quality tools.

Care and maintenance of tools

Good tools are expensive, so it makes sense to treat them with respect. Keep them in a clean and usable condition and store them properly when not in use. Always wipe off any dirt, grease or metal chips before putting them away. Never leave tools lying around in the work area. Upon completion of a job, always check closely under the hood for tools that may have been left there (so they don't get lost during a test drive).

Some tools, such as screwdrivers, pliers, wrenches and sockets, can be hung on a panel mounted on the garage or workshop wall, while others should be kept in a tool box or tray. Measuring instruments, gauges, meters, etc. must be carefully stored where they cannot be damaged by weather or impact from other tools.

When tools are used with care and stored properly, they will last a very long time. Even with the best of care, tools will wear out if used frequently. When a tool is damaged or worn out, replace it; subsequent jobs will be safer and more enjoyable if you do.

For those who desire to learn more about tools and their uses, a book entitled *How to Choose and Use Car Tools* is available from the publishers of this manual.

Working facilities

Not to be overlooked when discussing tools is the workshop. If anything more than routine maintenance is to be carried out, some sort of suitable work area is essential.

It is understood, and appreciated, that many home mechanics do not have a good workshop or garage available, and end up removing an engine or doing major repairs outside (it is recommended that the overhaul or repair be completed under the cover of a roof).

A clean, flat workbench or table of suitable working height is an absolute necessity. The workshop should be equipped with a vise that has a jaw opening of at least 4 inches.

As mentioned previously, some clean, dry storage space is also required for tools, as well as the lubricants, fluids, cleaning solvents, etc. which soon become necessary.

Sometimes waste oil and fluids, drained from the engine or transmission during normal maintenance or repairs, present a disposal problem. To avoid pouring oil on the ground or into the sewage system, simply pour the used fluids into large containers, seal them with caps and deliver them to a local recycling center or disposal facility. Plastic jugs (such as old anti-freeze containers) are ideal for this purpose.

Always keep a supply of old newspapers and clean rags available. Old towels are excellent for mopping up spills. Many mechanics use rolls of paper towels for most work because they are readily available and disposable. To keep the area under the vehicle clean, a large cardboard box can be cut open and flattened to protect the garage or shop floor.

Whenever working over a painted surface (such as when leaning over a fender to service something under the hood), always cover it with an old blanket or bedspread to protect the finish. Vinyl covered pads, made especially for this purpose, are available at auto parts stores.

Jacking and towing

Jacking

The jack supplied with the vehicle should only be used for raising the car for changing a tire or placing jackstands under the frame. *Under no circumstances should work be performed beneath the vehicle or the engine started while this jack is being used as the only means of support.*

All vehicles are supplied with a scissors-type jack which fits into a flange located between two notches in the vertical rocker panel closest to the wheel being changed.

The car should be on level ground with the wheels blocked and the transmissions in Park (automatic) or Reverse (manual). Pry off the hub cap (if equipped) using the tapered end of the lug wrench. Loosen the wheel nuts one half turn and leave them in place until the wheel is raised off the ground.

Place the jack under the side of the car at the jacking point. Use the handle supplied and insert it into the jack. Turn the jack handle clockwise until it contacts the body. Check the jack to see that it is properly positioned. Raise the car until the wheel clears the ground. Remove the lug nuts and remove the wheel. Check the face of the brake drum or hub for corrosion. Clean the face of the brake drum or hub and the mating surface of the spare wheel if any material has collected on them.

Install the wheel onto the axle studs and install the wheel nuts, with the beveled side in, finger tight. Make sure the wheel is on correctly and the tire has adequate air pressure. Lower the vehicle by turning the jackscrew counterclockwise. Remove the jack and tighten the nuts in a diagonal fashion. Replace the hubcap by placing it into position and using the heel of your hand or a rubber mallet to seat it.

Towing

A vehicle with manual transmission can be towed with all four wheels on the ground provided speeds do not exceed 30 mph and the distance is not over 50 miles, otherwise transmission damage can result. Under no circumstances should a vehicle with an automatic transmission be towed with the front wheels on the ground.

Towing equipment specifically designed for this purpose should be used and should be attached to the main structural members of the car and not the bumper or brackets.

Safety is a major consideration when towing and all applicable state and local laws must be obeyed. A safety chain system must be used for all towing.

While towing, the parking brake should be fully released and the transmission should be in Neutral. The steering must be unlocked (ignition switch in the Off position). Remember that power brakes will not work with the engine off.

Always position the jack on the underbody lip between the two notches when jacking the vehicle

Automotive chemicals and lubricants

A number of automotive chemicals and lubricants are available for use in vehicle maintenance and repair. They represent a wide variety of products ranging from cleaning solvents and degreasers to lubricants and protective sprays for rubber, plastic and vinyl.

Contact point/spark plug cleaner is a solvent used to clean oily film and dirt from points, grime from electrical connectors and oil deposits from spark plugs. It is oil free and leaves no residue. It can also be used to remove gum and varnish from carburetor jets and other orifices.

Carburetor cleaner is similar to contact point/spark plug cleaner but it is a stronger solvent and may leave a slight oily residue. It is not recommended for cleaning electrical components or connections.

Brake system cleaner is used to remove grease or brake fluid from brake system components (where clean surfaces are absolutely necessary and petroleum-based solvents cannot be used); it also leaves no residue.

Silicone based lubricants are used to protect rubber parts such as hoses, weatherstripping and grommets, and are used as lubricants for hinges and locks.

Multi-purpose grease is an all purpose lubricant used whenever grease is more practical than a liquid lubricant such as oil. Some multi-purpose grease is colored white and specially formulated to be more resistant to water than ordinary grease.

Bearing grease/wheel bearing grease is a heavy grease used where increased loads and friction are encountered (i.e. wheel bearings, universal joints, etc.).

High temperature wheel bearing grease is designed to withstand the extreme temperatures encountered by wheel bearings in disc brake equipped vehicles. It usually contains molybdenum disulfide, which is a 'dry' type lubricant.

Gear oil (sometimes called gear lube) is a specially designed oil used in differentials, manual transmissions and manual gearboxes, as well as other areas where high friction, high temperature lubrication is required. It is available in a number of viscosities (weights) for various applications.

Motor oil, of course, is the lubricant specially formulated for use in the engine. It normally contains a wide variety of additives to prevent corrosion and reduce foaming and wear. Motor oil comes in various weights (viscosity ratings) of from 5 to 80. The recommended weight of the oil depends on the seasonal temperature and the demands on the engine. Light oil is used in cold climates and under light load conditions; heavy oil is used in hot climates and where high loads are encountered. Multi-viscosity oils are designed to have characteristics of both light and heavy oils and are available in a number of weights from 5W-20 to 20W-50.

Oil additives range from viscosity index improvers to slick chemical treatments that purportedly reduce friction. It should be noted that most oil manufacturers caution against using additives with their oils.

Gas additives perform several functions, depending on their chemical makeup. They usually contain solvents that help dissolve gum and varnish that build up on carburetor and intake parts. They also serve to break down carbon deposits that form on the inside surfaces of the combustion chambers. Some additives contain upper cylinder lubricants for valves and piston rings.

Brake fluid is a specially formulated hydraulic fluid that can withstand the heat and pressure encountered in brake systems. Care must be taken that this fluid does not come in contact with painted surfaces or plastics. An opened container should always be resealed to prevent contamination by water or dirt.

Undercoating is a petroleum-based tar-like substance that is designed to protect metal surfaces on the under-side of a vehicle from corrosion. It also acts as a sound deadening agent by insulating the bottom of the vehicle.

Weatherstrip cement is used to bond weatherstripping around doors, windows and trunk lids. It is sometimes used to attach trim pieces as well.

Degreasers are heavy duty solvents used to remove grease and grime that accumulate on engine and chassis components. They can be sprayed or brushed on and, depending on the type, are rinsed with either water or solvent.

Solvents are used alone or in combination with degreasers to clean parts and assemblies during repair and overhaul. The home mechanic should use only solvents that are non-flammable and that do not produce irritating fumes.

Gasket sealing compounds may be used in conjunction with gaskets, to improve their sealing capabilities, or alone, to seal metal-to-metal joints. Many gaskets can withstand extreme heat, some are impervious to gasoline and lubricants, while others are capable of filling and sealing large cavities. Depending on the intended use, gasket sealers either dry hard or stay relatively soft and pliable. They are usually applied by hand, with a brush, or are sprayed on the gasket sealing surfaces.

Thread cement is an adhesive locking compound that prevents threaded fasteners from loosening because of vibration. It is available in a variety of types for different applications.

Moisture dispersants are usually sprays that can be used to dry out electrical components such as the distributor, fuse block and wiring connectors. Some types can also be used as treatment for rubber and as a lubricant for hinges, cables and locks.

Waxes and polishes are used to help protect painted and plated surfaces from the weather. Different types of paint may require the use of different types of wax or polish. Some polishes utilize a chemical or abrasive cleaner to help remove the top layer of oxidized (dull) paint in older vehicles.

Safety first!

Regardless of how enthusiastic you may be about getting on with the job at hand, take the time to ensure that your safety is not jeopardized. A moment's lack of attention can result in an accident, as can failure to observe certain simple safety precautions. The possibility of an accident will always exist, and the following points should not be considered a comprehensive list of all dangers. Rather, they are intended to make you aware of the risks and to encourage a safety conscious approach to all work you carry out on your vehicle.

Essential DOs and DON'Ts

DON'T rely on a jack when working under the vehicle. Always use approved jackstands to support the weight of the vehicle and place them under the recommended lift or support points.

DON'T attempt to loosen extremely tight fasteners (i.e. wheel lug nuts) while the vehicle is on a jack — it may fall.

DON'T start the engine without first making sure that the transmission is in Neutral (or Park where applicable) and the parking brake is set.

DON'T remove the radiator cap from a hot cooling system — let it cool or cover it with a cloth and release the pressure gradually.

DON'T attempt to drain the engine oil until you are sure it has cooled to the point that it will not burn you.

DON'T touch any part of the engine or exhaust system until it has cooled sufficiently to avoid burns.

DON'T siphon toxic liquids such as gasoline, antifreeze and brake fluid by mouth, or allow them to remain on your skin.

DON'T inhale brake lining dust — it is potentially hazardous (see *Asbestos* below).

DON'T allow spilled oil or grease to remain on the floor — wipe it up before someone slips on it.

DON'T use loose fitting wrenches or other tools which may slip and cause injury.

DON'T push on wrenches when loosening or tightening nuts or bolts. Always try to pull the wrench toward you. If the situation calls for pushing the wrench away, push with an open hand to avoid scraped knuckles if the wrench should slip.

DON'T attempt to lift a heavy component alone — get someone to help you.

DON'T rush or take unsafe shortcuts to finish a job.

DON'T allow children or animals in or around the vehicle while you are working on it.

DO wear eye protection when using power tools such as a drill, sander, bench grinder, etc. and when working under a vehicle.

DO keep loose clothing and long hair well out of the way of moving parts.

DO make sure that any hoist used has a safe working load rating adequate for the job.

DO get someone to check on you periodically when working alone on a vehicle.

DO carry out work in a logical sequence and make sure that everything is correctly assembled and tightened.

DO keep chemicals and fluids tightly capped and out of the reach of children and pets.

DO remember that your vehicle's safety affects that of yourself and others. If in doubt on any point, get professional advice.

Asbestos

Certain friction, insulating, sealing, and other products — such as brake linings, brake bands, clutch linings, torque converters, gaskets, etc. — contain asbestos. *Extreme care must be taken to avoid inhalation of dust from such products since it is hazardous to health.* If in doubt, assume that they *do* contain asbestos.

Fire

Remember at all times that gasoline is highly flammable. Never smoke or have any kind of open flame around when working on a vehicle. But the risk does not end there. A spark caused by an electrical short circuit, by two metal surfaces contacting each other, or even by static electricity built up in your body under certain conditions, can ignite gasoline vapors, which in a confined space are highly explosive. Do not, under any circumstances, use gasoline for cleaning parts. Use an approved safety solvent.

Always disconnect the battery ground (–) cable *at the battery* before working on any part of the fuel system or electrical system. Never risk spilling fuel on a hot engine or exhaust component.

It is strongly recommended that a fire extinguisher suitable for use on fuel and electrical fires be kept handy in the garage or workshop at all times. Never try to extinguish a fuel or electrical fire with water.

Fumes

Certain fumes are highly toxic and can quickly cause unconsciousness and even death if inhaled to any extent. Gasoline vapor falls into this category, as do the vapors from some cleaning solvents. Any draining or pouring of such volatile fluids should be done in a well ventilated area.

When using cleaning fluids and solvents, read the instructions on the container carefully. Never use materials from unmarked containers.

Never run the engine in an enclosed space, such as a garage. Exhaust fumes contain carbon monoxide, which is extremely poisonous. If you need to run the engine, always do so in the open air, or at least have the rear of the vehicle outside the work area.

If you are fortunate enough to have the use of an inspection pit, never drain or pour gasoline and never run the engine while the vehicle is over the pit. The fumes, being heavier than air, will concentrate in the pit with possibly lethal results.

The battery

Never create a spark or allow a bare light bulb near the battery. The battery normally gives off a certain amount of hydrogen gas, which is highly explosive.

Always disconnect the battery ground (–) cable *at the battery* before working on the fuel or electrical systems.

If possible, loosen the filler caps or cover when charging the battery from an external source. Do not charge at an excessive rate or the battery may burst.

Take care when adding water and when carrying a battery. The electrolyte, even when diluted, is very corrosive and should not be allowed to contact clothing or skin.

Always wear eye protection when cleaning the battery to prevent the caustic deposits from entering your eyes.

Household current

When using an electric power tool, inspection light, etc., which operates on household current, always make sure that the tool is correctly connected to its plug and that, where necessary, it is properly grounded. Do not use such items in damp conditions and, again, do not create a spark or apply excessive heat in the vicinity of fuel or fuel vapor.

Secondary ignition system voltage

A severe electric shock can result from touching certain parts of the ignition system (such as the spark plug wires) when the engine is running or being cranked, particularly if components are damp or the insulation is defective. In the case of an electronic ignition system, the secondary system voltage is much higher and could prove fatal.

Troubleshooting

Contents

1 Engine will not rotate when attempting to start

1   Battery terminal connections loose or corroded. Check the cable terminals at the battery; tighten or clean corrosion as necessary.
2   `Battery discharged or faulty. If the cable connectors are clean and tight on the battery posts, turn the key to the On position and switch on the headlights and/or windshield wipers. If these fail to function, the battery is discharged.
3   Automatic transmission not fully engaged in 'Park'.
4   Broken, loose or disconnected wiring in the starting circuit. Inspect all wiring and connectors at the battery, starter solenoid (at lower left side of engine) and ignition switch (on steering column).
5   Starter motor pinion jammed on flywheel ring gear. If manual transmission, place gearshift in gear and rock the vehicle to turn the engine manually. Remove starter (Chapter 5) and inspect pinion and flywheel at earliest convenience.
6   Starter solenoid faulty (Chapter 5).
7   Starter motor faulty (Chapter 5).
8   Ignition switch faulty (Chapter 10).

2 Engine rotates but will not start

1   Fuel tank empty.
2   Battery discharged (engine rotates slowly). Check the operation of electrical components as described in previous Section (see Chapter 1).
3   Battery terminal connections loose or corroded. See previous Section.
4   Carburetor flooded and/or fuel level in carburetor incorrect. This will usually be accompanied by a strong fuel odor from under the hood. Wait a few minutes, depress the accelerator pedal all the way to the floor and attempt to start the engine.
5   Choke control inoperative (Chapter 6).
6   Fuel not reaching carburetor. With ignition switch in Off position, open hood, remove the top plate of air cleaner assembly and observe the top of the carburetor (manually move choke plate back if necessary). Have an assistant depress accelerator pedal fully and check that fuel spurts into carburetor. If not, check fuel filter (Chapters 1 and 4), fuel lines and fuel pump (Chapter 4).
7   Excessive moisture on, or damage to, ignition components (Chapter 5).
8   Worn, faulty or incorrectly adjusted spark plugs (Chapter 1).
9   Broken, loose or disconnected wiring in the starting circuit (see previous Section).
10 Distributor loose, thus changing ignition timing. Turn the distributor body as necessary to start the engine, then set ignition timing as soon as possible (Chapter 5).
11 Ignition condenser faulty (3A engines only) (Chapter 5).
12 Broken, loose or disconnected wires at the ignition coil, or faulty coil (Chapter 5).

3 Starter motor operates without rotating engine

1   Starter pinion sticking. Remove the starter (Chapter 5) and inspect.
2   Starter pinion or engine flywheel teeth worn or broken. Remove the inspection cover (automatic) or starter (manual) to inspect.

4 Engine hard to start when cold

1   Battery discharged or low. Check as described in Section 1.
2   Choke control inoperative or out of adjustment (Chapter 4).
3   Carburetor flooded (see Section 2).
4   Fuel supply not reaching the carburetor (see Section 2).
5   Carburetor worn and in need of overhauling (Chapter 4).

5 Engine hard to start when hot

1   Choke sticking in the closed position (Chapter 4).
2   Carburetor flooded (see Section 2).
3   Air filter in need of replacement (Chapter 1).

4   Fuel not reaching the carburetor (see Section 2).

6 Starter motor noisy or excessively rough in engagement

1   Pinion or flywheel gear teeth worn or broken. Remove the inspection cover (automatic trans) or starter (manual trans) and inspect.
2   Starter motor retaining bolts loose or missing.

7 Engine starts but stops immediately

1   Loose or faulty electrical connections at distributor, coil or alternator.
2   Insufficient fuel reaching the carburetor. Disconnect the fuel line at the carburetor (Chapter 1). Place a container under the disconnected fuel line. Observe the flow of fuel from the line. If little or none at all, check for blockage in the lines and/or replace the fuel pump (Chapter 4).
3   Vacuum leak at the gasket surfaces or the intake manifold and/or carburetor. Check that all mounting bolts (nuts) are tightened to specifications and all vacuum hoses connected to the carburetor and manifold are positioned properly and are in good condition.

8 Engine 'lopes' while idling or idles erratically

1   Vacuum leakage. Check mounting bolts (nuts) at the carburetor and intake manifold for tightness. Check that all vacuum hoses are connected and are in good condition. Use a stethoscope or a length of fuel line hose held against your ear to listen for vacuum leaks while the engine is running. A hissing sound will be heard. A soapy water solution will also detect leaks. Check the carburetor and intake manifold gasket surfaces.
2   Leaking EGR valve or plugged PCV valve (see Chapter 6).
3   Air cleaner clogged and in need of replacement (Chapter 1).
4   Fuel pump not delivering sufficient fuel to the carburetor (see Section 7).
5   Carburetor out of adjustment (Chapter 4).
6   Leaking head gasket. If this is suspected, take the vehicle to a repair shop or dealer where this can be pressure checked without the need to remove the head.
7   Timing belt worn and in need of replacement (Chapter 2).
8   Camshaft lobes worn, necessitating the removal of the camshaft for inspection (Chapter 2).

9 Engine misses at idle speed

1   Spark plugs faulty or not gapped properly (Chapter 1).
2   Faulty spark plug wires (Chapter 1).
3   Carburetor choke not operating properly (Chapter 4).
4   Sticking or faulty emissions systems (see Troubleshooting in Chapter 6).
5   Clogged fuel filter and/or foreign matter in fuel. Remove the fuel filter (Chapter 1) and inspect.
6   Vacuum leaks at carburetor, intake manifold or at hose connections. Check as described in Section 8.
7   Incorrect idle speed or idle mixture (Chapter 1).
8   Incorrect ignition timing (Chapter 1).
9   Uneven or low cylinder compression. Remove plugs and use compression tester as per manufacturer's instructions.

10 Engine misses throughout driving speed range

1   Carburetor fuel filter clogged and/or impurities in the fuel system (Chapter 1). Also check fuel output at the carburetor (see Section 7).
2   Faulty or incorrectly gapped spark plugs (Chapter 1).
3   Incorrectly set ignition timing (Chapter 1).
4   Check for a cracked distributor cap, disconnected distributor wires or damage to the distributor components (Chapter 5).
5   Leaking spark plug wires (Chapter 1).
6   Emission system components faulty (Chapter 6).
7   Low or uneven cylinder compression pressures. Remove spark

plugs and test compression with gauge.
8 Vacuum leaks at carburetor, intake manifold or vacuum hoses (see Section 8).

11 Engine stalls

1 Carburetor idle speed incorrectly set (Chapter 4).
2 Carburetor fuel filter clogged and/or water and impurities in the fuel system (Chapter 4).
3 Choke improperly adjusted or sticking (Chapter 4).
4 Distributor components damp, points out of adjustment or damage to distributor cap, rotor etc. (Chapter 5).
5 Emission system components faulty (Troubleshooting Section, Chapter 6).
6 Faulty or incorrectly gapped spark plugs (Chapter 1). Also check spark plug wires (Chapter 1).
7 Vacuum leak at the carburetor, intake manifold or vacuum hoses. Check as described in Section 8.
8 Valve clearance incorrectly set (Chapter 1).

12 Engine lacks power

1 Incorrect ignition timing (Chapter 1).
2 Excessive play in distributor shaft. At the same time check for worn or maladjusted contact points, faulty distributor cap, wires, etc. (Chapter 1).
3 Faulty or incorrectly gapped spark plugs (Chapter 1).
4 Carburetor not adjusted properly or excessively worn (Chapter 4).
5 Weak coil or condensor (Chapter 5).
6 Brakes adjusted too tightly (Chapter 9).
7 Automatic transmission fluid level incorrect, causing slippage (Chapter 1).
8 Manual transmission clutch slipping (Chapter 8).
9 Fuel filter clogged and/or impurities in the fuel system (Chapter 1).
10 Emission control system not functioning properly (Chapter 6).
11 Use of sub-standard fuel. Fill tank with proper octane fuel.
12 Low or uneven cylinder compression pressures. Test with compression tester, which will also detect leaking valves and/or blown head gasket.

13 Engine backfire

1 Emission system not functioning properly (Chapter 6).
2 Ignition timing incorrect (Section 4).
3 Carburetor in need of adjustment or worn excessively (Chapter 4).
4 Vacuum leak at carburetor, intake manifold or vacuum hoses. Check as described in Section 8.
5 Valve clearance incorrectly set, and/or valves sticking (Chapter 1).
6 Emissions control system operating improperly (Chapter 6).

14 Pinging or knocking engine sounds on hard acceleration or uphill

1 Incorrect grade of fuel. Fill tank with fuel of the proper octane rating.
2 Ignition timing incorrect (Chapter 1).
3 Carburetor in need of adjustment (Chapter 4).
4 Improper spark plugs. Check plug type with that specified on tune-up decal located inside engine compartment. Also check plugs and wires for damage (Chapter 1).
5 Worn or damaged distributor components (Chapter 5).
6 Faulty emission system (Chapter 6).
7 Vacuum leak. (Check as described in Section 8).

15 Engine 'diesels' (continues to run) after switching off

1 Idle speed too fast (Chapter 1).
2 Electrical solenoid(s) at side of carburetor not functioning properly (not all models, see Chapter 6).
3 Ignition timing incorrectly adjusted (Chapter 1).

4 Air cleaner valve not operating properly (Chapter 6).
5 Excessive engine operating temperatures. Probable causes of this are: malfunctioning thermostat, clogged radiator, faulty water pump (see Chapter 3).

Engine electrical

16 Battery will not hold a charge

1 Alternator drivebelt defective or not adjusted properly (Chapter 1).
2 Electrolyte level too low or too weak (Chapter 1).
3 Battery terminals loose or corroded (Chapter 1).
4 Alternator not charging properly (Chapter 5).
5 Loose, broken or faulty wiring in the charging circuit (Chapter 5).
6 Short in vehicle circuitry causing a continual drain on battery.
7 Battery defective internally.

17 Ignition light fails to go out

1 Fault in alternator or charging circuit (Chapter 5).
2 Alternator drivebelt defective or not properly adjusted (Chapter 11).

18 Warning lights fail to come on when key is turned

1 Warning light bulbs faulty (Chapter 11).
2 Alternator faulty (Chapter 5).
3 Fault in the printed circuit, dash wiring or bulb holder (Chapter 11).

Engine fuel system

19 Excessive fuel consumption

1 Dirty or choked air filter element (Chapter 1).
2 Incorrectly set ignition timing (Chapter 1).
3 Choke sticking or improperly adjusted (Chapter 4).
4 Emission system not functioning properly (Chapter 6).
5 Carburetor idle speed and/or mixture not adjusted properly (Chapter 4).
6 Carburetor internal parts excessively worn or damaged (Chapter 4).
7 Low tire pressure or incorrect tire size (Chapter 1).

20 Fuel leakage and/or fuel odor

1 Leak in a fuel feed or vent line (Chapter 4).
2 Tank overfilled. Fill only to automatic shut-off.
3 Evaporative emissions canister faulty (Chapter 1).
4 Vapor leaks from system lines (Chapter 4).
5 Carburetor internal parts excessively worn or out of adjustment (Chapter 4).

Engine cooling system

21 Overheating

1 Insufficient coolant in system (Chapter 3).
2 Fan belt defective or not adjusted properly (Chapter 1).
3 Radiator core blocked or radiator grille dirty and restricted (Chapter 3).
4 Thermostat faulty (Chapter 3).
5 Electric cooling fan inoperative (Chapter 3).
6 Radiator cap not maintaining proper pressure. Have cap pressure tested by gas station or repair shop.
7 Ignition timing incorrect (Chapter 1).

22 Overcooling

1   Thermostat faulty (Chapter 3).
2   Inaccurate temperature gauge (Chapter 10).

23 External water leakage

1   Deteriorated or damaged hoses. Loose clamps at hose connections (Chapter 3).
2   Water pump seals defective. If this is the case, water will drip from the 'weep' hole in the water pump body (Chapter 3).
3   Leakage from radiator core or header tank. This will require the radiator to be professionally repaired (see Chapter 3 for removal procedures).
4   Engine drain plugs or water jacket freeze plugs leaking (see Chapters 1 and 3).

24 Internal water leakage

Note: *Internal coolant leaks can usually be detected by examining the oil. Check the dipstick and inside of valve cover for water deposits and an oil consistency like that of a milkshake.*
1   Faulty cylinder head gasket. Have the system pressure-tested professionally or remove the cylinder head (Chapter 2) and inspect.
2   Cracked cylinder bore or cylinder head. Dismantle engine and inspect (Chapter 2).

25 Water loss

1   Overfilling system (Chapter 3).
2   Coolant boiling away due to overheating (see causes in Section 21).
3   Internal or external leakage (see Sections 23 and 24).
4   Faulty radiator cap. Have the cap pressure tested.

26 Poor coolant circulation

1   Inoperative water pump. A quick test is to pinch the top radiator hose closed with your hand while the engine is idling, then let it loose. You should feel a surge of water if the pump is working properly (Chapter 3).
2   Restriction in cooling system. Drain, flush and refill the system (Chapter 1). If it appears necessary, remove the radiator (Chapter 3) and have it reverse-flushed or professionally cleaned.
3   Fan drivebelt defective or not adjusted properly (Chapter 1).
4   Thermostat sticking (Chapter 3).

Clutch

27 Fails to release (pedal pressed to the floor – shift lever does not move freely in and out of gear)

1   Improper linkage adjustment (Chapter 8).
2   Clutch disc warped, bent or excessively damaged (Chapter 8).

28 Clutch slips (engine speed increase with no increase in road speed)

1   Clutch cable in need of adjustment (Chapter 8).
2   Clutch disc oil soaked or facing worn. Remove disc (Chapter 8) and inspect.
3   Clutch disc not seated in. It may take 30 or 40 normal starts for a new disc to seat.

29 Grabbing (juddering) on take-up

1   Oil on clutch disc facings. Remove disc (Chapter 8) and inspect. Correct any leakage source.

2   Worn or loose engine or transmission mounts. These units may move slightly when clutch is released. Inspect mounts and bolts.
3   Worn splines on clutch disc. Remove clutch components (Chapter 8) and inspect.
4   Warped pressure plate or flywheel. Remove clutch components and inspect.

30 Squeal or rumble with clutch fully engaged (pedal released)

1   Improper adjustment; no lash (Chapter 8).
2   Release bearing binding on transmission bearing retainer. Remove clutch components (Chapter 8) and check bearing. Remove any burrs or nicks, clean and relubricate before reinstallation.
3   Weak cable return spring. Replace the spring.

31 Squeal or rumble with clutch fully disengaged (pedal depressed)

1   Worn, faulty or broken release bearing (Chapter 8).
2   Worn or broken pressure plate springs (or diaphragm fingers) (Chapter 8).

32 Clutch pedal stays on floor when disengaged

1   Bind in cable or release bearing. Inspect cable or remove clutch components as necessary.
2   Clutch pressure plate weak or broken. Remove and inspect clutch pressure plate (Chapter 8).

Manual transmission
Note: *All the following Sections contained within Chapter 7 unless noted.*

33 Noisy in Neutral with engine running

1   Input shaft bearing worn.
2   Damaged main drive gear bearing.
3   Worn countergear bearings.
4   Excessive countergear clearance.

34 Noisy in all gears

1   Any of the above causes, and/or:
2   Insufficient lubricant (see checking procedures in Chapter 1).

35 Noisy in one particular gear

1   Worn, damaged or chipped gear teeth for that particular gear.
2   Worn or damaged synchronizer for that particular gear.

36 Slips out of high gear

1   Transmission retaining bolts loose.
2   Shift mechanism not working freely.
3   Damaged mainshaft pilot bearing.
4   Dirt between transmission housing and engine or misalignment of transmission (Chapter 7).
5   Worn or improperly adjusted linkage (Chapter 7).

37 Difficulty in engaging gears

1   Clutch not releasing fully (see clutch adjustment, Chapter 8).
2   Loose, damaged or maladjusted shift linkage. Make a thorough inspection, replacing parts as necessary. Adjust as described in Chapter 8.

38 Fluid leakage

1 Excessive amount of lubricant in transmission (see Chapter 1 for correct checking procedures. Drain lubricant as required).
2 Gaskets leaking between case and housing or rear cover.
3 Oil seal or speedometer oil seal in need of replacement (Chapter 7).

Automatic transmission

Note: *Due to the complexity of the automatic transmission, it is difficult for the home mechanic to properly diagnose and service this component. For problems other than the following, the vehicle should be taken to a reputable mechanic.*

39 Fluid leakage

1 Automatic transmission fluid is a deep red color, and fluid leaks should not be confused with engine oil which can easily be blown by air flow to the transmission.
2 To pinpoint a leak, first remove all built-up dirt and grime from around the transmission. Degreasing agents and/or steam cleaning will achieve this. With the underside clean, drive the vehicle at low speeds so that air flow will not blow the leak far from its source. Raise the vehicle and determine where the leak is coming from. Common areas of leakage are:

a) Fluid pan: tighten mounting bolts and/or replace pan gasket as necessary (see Chapter 7)
b) Rear cover: tighten bolts and/or replace oil seal as necessary (Chapter 7)
c) Filler pipe: replace the rubber oil seal where pipe enters transmission case
d) Transmission oil lines: tighten connectors where lines enter transmission case and/or replace lines
e) Vent pipe: transmission over-filled and/or water in fluid (see checking procedures, Chapter 7)
f) Speedometer connector: replace the O-ring where speedometer cable enters transmission case

40 General shift mechanism problems

1 Chapter 7 deals with checking and adjusting the shift linkage on automatic transmissions. Common problems which may be attributed to maladjusted linkage are:

a) Engine starting in gears other than 'P' (Park) or 'N' (Neutral)
b) Gearshift lever situated in a gear other than the one the car is actually in
c) Vehicle will not hold firm when in 'P' (Park) position
Refer to Chapter 7 to adjust the manual linkage.

41 Transmission will not downshift with accelerator pedal pressed to the floor

1 Chapter 7 deals with adjusting the downshift linkage to enable the transmission to downshift properly.

42 Engine will start in gears other than 'P' (Park) or 'N' (Neutral)

1 Chapter 7 deals with adjusting the Neutral start switches used with automatic transmissions.

43 Transmission slips, shifts rough, is noisy or has no drive in forward or reverse gears

1 There are many probable causes for the above problems, but the home mechanic should concern himself only with one possibility: fluid level.

2 Before taking the vehicle to a specialist, check the level of the fluid and condition of the fluid as described in Chapter 1. Correct fluid level as necessary or change the fluid and filter if needed. If problem persists, have a professional diagnose the probable cause.

Driveshaft (drive axles)

44 Leakage of fluid at front of bellhousing

1 Defective transmission oil seal. See Chapter 7 for replacing procedures. While this is done, check the splined yoke for burrs or a rough condition which may be damaging the seal. If found, these can be dressed wth crocus cloth or a fine dressing stone.

45 Knock or clunk when transmission is under initial load (just after transmission is put into gear)

1 Loose front end components. Check all mounting bolts and bushings (Chapter 11).
2 Worn or damaged driveaxle joints. Test for wear (Chapter 8).

46 Metallic grating sound consistent with road speed

1 Pronounced wear in the driveaxle joints. Check for wear (Chapter 8).

47 Vibration

Note: *Before it can be assumed that the driveaxles are at fault, make sure the tires are perfectly balanced and perform the following test.*
1 Install a tachometer inside the vehicle to monitor engine speed as the vehicle is driven. Drive the vehicle and note the engine speed at which the vibration (roughness) is most pronounced. Now shift the transmission to a different gear and bring the engine speed to the same point.
2 If the vibration occurs at the same engine speed (rpm) regardless of which gear the transmission is in, the driveaxles are NOT at fault since the driveaxle speed varies.
3 If the vibration decreases or is eliminated when the transmission is in a different gear at the same engine speed, refer to the following probable causes.
4 Bent driveaxle(s). Inspect and replace as necessary (Chapter 8).
5 Undercoating or built-up dirt, etc, on the driveaxle(s). Clean the shafts throroughly and test.
6 Worn driveaxle joints (see Chapter 8).

Differential

48 Noise – same when in Drive as when vehicle is coasting

1 Road noise. No corrective procedures available.
2 Tire noise. Inspect tires and tire pressures (Chapter 1).
3 Front wheel bearings loose, worn or damaged (Chapter 11).

49 Vibration

1 See probable causes under Section 47. Proceed under the guidelines listed for the driveaxles. If the problem persists, check the rear wheel bearings by raising the rear of the vehicle and spinning the wheels by hand. Listen for evidence of rough (noisy) bearings. Remove and inspect (Chapter 11). Do the same for the front wheel bearings.

50 Oil leakage

1 Pinion oil seal damaged (Chapter 7).
2 Axle shaft oil seals damaged (Chapter 7).

3   Differential cover leaking. Tighten mounting bolts or replace the gasket as required (Chapter 7).

Brakes

Note: *Before assuming a brake problem exists, check: that the tires are in good condition and are inflated properly (see Chapter 10); the front end alignment is correct; and that the vehicle is not loaded with weight in an unequal manner.*

51 Vehicle pulls to one side under braking

1   Defective, damaged or oil contaminated disc pad on one side. Inspect as described in Chapter 9.
2   Excessive wear of brake pad material or disc on one side. Inspect and correct as necessary.
3   Loose or disconnected front suspension components. Inspect and tighten all bolts to specifications (Chapter 11).
4   Defective caliper assembly. Remove caliper and inspect for stuck piston or damage (Chapter 9).

52 Noise (high-pitched squeak without brake applied)

1   Front brake components excessively worn or damaged. Inspect all brake parts immediately (Chapter 1, Section 18).

53 Excessive brake pedal travel

1   Partial brake system failure. Inspect entire system (Chapter 9) and correct as required.
2   Insufficient fluid in master cylinder. Check (Chapter 9) and add fluid and bleed system if necessary.
3   Rear brakes not adjusting properly. If adjustment (Chapter 9) does not correct the situation remove drums and inspect self-adjusters (Chapter 9).

54 Brake pedal feels spongy when depressed

1   Air in hydraulic lines. Bleed the brake system (Chapter 9).
2   Faulty flexible hoses. Inspect all system hoses and lines. Replace parts as necessary.
3   Master cylinder mountings insecure. Inspect master cylinder bolts (nuts) and torque-tighten to specifications.
4   Master cylinder faulty (Chapter 9).

55 Excessive effort required to stop vehicle

1   Power brake servo not operating properly (Chapter 9).
2   Excessively worn linings or pads. Inspect and replace if necessary (Chapter 9).
3   One or more caliper pistons (front wheels) or wheel cylinders (rear wheels) seized or sticking. Inspect and rebuild as required (Chapter 9).
4   Brake linings or pads contaminated with oil or grease. Inspect and replace as required (Chapter 9).
5   New pads or linings fitted and not yet 'broken in'. It will take a while for the new material to seat against the drum (or rotor).

56 Pedal travels to floor with little resistance

1   Little or no fluid in the master cylinder reservoir caused by; leaking wheel cylinder(s); leaking caliper piston(s); loose, damaged or disconnected brake lines. Inspect entire system and correct as necessary.

57 Brake pedal pulsates during brake application

1   Wheel bearings not adjusted properly or in need of replacement (Chapter 11).

2   Caliper not sliding properly due to improper installation or obstructions. Remove and inspect (Chapter 9).
3   Rotor not within specifications. Check the rotor for excessive lateral run-out and parallelism. Have the rotor professionally machined or replace it with a new one (Chapter 9).

Suspension and steering

58 Vehicle pulls to one side

1   Tire pressures uneven (Chapter 1).
2   Defective tire (Chapter 11).
3   Excessive wear in suspension or steering components (Chapter 11).
4   Front end in need of alignment. Take vehicle to a qualified specialist.
5   Front brakes dragging. Inspect braking system as described in Chapter 9.

59 Shimmy, shake or vibration

1   Tire or wheel out of balance or out of round. Have professionally balanced.
2   Loose, worn or out of adjustment wheel bearings (Chapter 11).
3   Shock absorbers and/or suspension components worn or damaged (Chapter 11).

60 Excessive pitching and/or rolling around corners or during braking

1   Defective shock absorbers. Replace as a set (Chapter 11).
2   Broken or weak springs and/or suspension components. Inspect as described in Chapter 11.

61 Excessively stiff steering

1   Lack of lubricant in steering box (manual) (Chapter 11).
2   Incorrect tire pressures (Chapter 1).
3   Binding steering joints or internal problems in the steering box.
4   Front end out of alignment (Chapter 11).

62 Excessive play in steering

1   Loose wheel bearings (Chapter 11).
2   Excessive wear in suspension or steering components (Chapter 11).

63 Excessive tire wear (not specific to one area)

1   Incorrect tire pressures (Chapter 1).
2   Tires out of balance. Have professionally balanced.
3   Wheels damaged. Inspect and replace as necessary.
4   Suspension or steering components excessively worn (Chapter 11).

64 Excessive tire wear on outside edge

1   Inflation pressures not correct (Chapter 1).
2   Excessive speed on turns.
3   Front end alignment incorrect (excessive toe-in). Have professionally aligned.
4   Suspension arm bent or twisted.

65 Excessive tire wear on inside edge

1 Inflation pressures incorrect (Chapter 11).
2 Front end alignment incorrect (toe-out). Have professionally aligned.
3 Loose or damaged steering components (Chapter 11).

66 Tire tread worn in one place

1 Tires out of balance. Balance tires professionally.
2 Damaged or buckled wheel. Inspect and replace if necessary.
3 Defective tire.

Chapter 1 Tune-up and routine maintenance

Contents

Specifications

Note: *Additional specifications can be found in the individual Chapters.*

Recommended lubricants and capacities

Engine oil type .... API service SE or better
Viscosity
    -20°F to 50°F (-29°C to 10°C) 5W-30
    -10°F to 100°F (-24°C to 36°C) 10W-30, 10W-40, 10W-50
    10°F to 100°F (-14°C to 36°C) 20W-40, 20W-50
    10°F to 60°F (-14°C to 16°C) 20W
    40°F to 100°F (4°C to 36°C) 30W
Oil capacity (with filter) .... 3.7 US qt (3.1 Imp qt/3.5 liter)
Manual transaxle fluid type .... Hypoid gear oil API GL-5
Manual transaxle fluid weight
    Above 0°F .... SAE 80W-90 or 90W
    Below 0°F .... SAE 80W-90 or 80W
Manual transaxle capacity .... 3.5 US qt (2.9 Imp qt/3.3 liter) (includes differential)
Differential fluid type (with AT) .... Hypoid gear oil API GL-5
Differential fluid capacity (with AT) .... 1.0 US qt (0.8 Imp qt/0.95 liter)
Differential fluid viscosity (with AT)
    Above 0°F .... SAE 80W-90 or 90W
    Below 0°F .... SAE 80W-90 or 80W
Automatic transmission fluid type .... Type F
Automatic transmission capacity
    Dry fill .... 4.8 US qt (4.0 Imp qt/4.5 liter)
    Drain and refill .... 2.3 US qt (1.9 Imp qt/2.2 liter)
Brake fluid type .... DOT 3 or SAE J1703
Wheel bearing grease .... High temperature wheel bearing grease
Engine coolant type .... Ethylene glycol
Coolant capacity .... 5.5 US qt (4.6 Imp qt/5.2 liter)

Ignition system

Spark plug type	
1A-C	ND W20ET-S/ND W20ETR-S
1A-C (Canada models)	ND W20ETR-S
3A (Canada models)	ND W16EXR-U
3A-C (California models)	ND W16EXR-U11
3A-C (US Federal models)	ND W16EXR-U11 or ND W14EXR-U11
3A	ND W16EXR-U or ND W14EXR-U
Spark plug gap	
1A-C	0.039 in (1.0 mm)
3A-C	0.043 in (1.1 mm)
1A and 3A	0.031 in (0.8 mm)
Rubbing block gap (3A engine)	0.018 in (0.45 mm)
Dwell angle (3A engine)	52°
Ignition timing	
1A-C	5°BTDC @ 900 rpm max (with sub-vacuum advancer off)
3A-C	5°BTDC @ 950 rpm max (with vacuum advancer off)
3A	5°BTDC @ 900 rpm max
Spark plug firing order	1–3–4–2
Distributor direction of rotation	Counterclockwise
Battery electrolyte specific gravity (fully charged)	1.260

Cooling system

Thermostat rating	180°F
Drivebelt tension	
New belts	125 ± 25 lb (56 ± 11 kg)
Used belts	80 ± 20 lb (36 ± 9 kg)

Valves

Valve clearance (engine hot)	
Intake	0.008 in (0.20 mm)
Exhaust	0.012 in (0.30 mm)

Clutch

Clutch pedal free travel	0.08 to 1.1 in (2 to 28 mm)

Brakes

Pedal height	6.437 to 6.476 in (163.5 to 164.5 mm)
Pedal minimum clearance when depressed	2.36 in (60 mm)
Pedal free play	0.16 to 0.28 in (4 to 7 mm)
Parking brake adjustment	2 to 5 clicks with 33 lb (15 kg) pull
Disc	
Brake pad minimum thickness	0.039 in (1.0 mm)
Rotor minimum thickness	0.354 in (9.0 mm)
Drum brake shoe minimum thickness	0.039 in (1.0 mm)

Torque specifications

	ft-lb	(m-Kg)
Oil pan drain plug	15 to 21	(2.0 to 3.0)
Spark plugs	11 to 15	(2.0 to 3.0)
Manual transaxle drain plugs		
Transmission case	26.8 to 32.6	(3.7 to 4.5)
Extension housing	18.1 to 25.3	(2.5 to 3.5)
Manual transaxle fill plug	26.8 to 32.6	(3.7 to 4.5)
Automatic transmission drain plug	19.5 to 23.9	(2.7 to 3.3)
Automatic transmission oil pan bolts	4.3 to 6.5	(0.6 to 0.9)
Differential drain plug (with automatic transmission)	19.5 to 23.9	(2.7 to 3.3)
Differential filler plug (with automatic transmission)	26.8 to 32.6	(3.7 to 4.5)
Valve cover bolts	3 to 5	(0.4 to 0.8)
Wheel nuts	66 to 86	(9 to 12)

1 Introduction

This Chapter was designed to help the home mechanic maintain his (or her) vehicle for peak performance, economy, safety and longevity.

On the following pages you will find a maintenance schedule along with Sections which deal specifically with each item on the schedule. Included are visual checks, adjustments and item replacements.

Servicing your vehicle using the time/mileage maintenance schedule and the sequenced Sections will give you a planned program of maintenance. Keep in mind that it is a full plan, and maintaining only a few items at the specified intervals will not give you the same results.

You will find as you service your vehicle that many of the procedures can, and should, be grouped together due to the nature of the job at hand. Examples of this are as follows:

If the vehicle is fully raised for a chassis lubrication, for example, this is the ideal time for the following checks: manual transaxle fluid, exhaust system, suspension, steering and the fuel system.

If the tires and wheel are removed, as during a routine tire rotation, go ahead and check the brakes and wheel bearings at the same time.

If you must borrow or rent a torque wrench, it would be advisable to service the spark plugs and repack (or replace) the wheel bearings all in the same day to save time and money.

The first step of this or any maintenance plan is to prepare yourself before the actual work begins. Read through the appropriate Sections for all work that is to be performed before you begin. Gather together all necessary parts and tools. If it appears you could have a problem during a particular job, don't hesitate to ask advice from your local parts man or dealer service department.

Routine maintenance intervals

The following recommendations are given with the assumption that the vehicle owner will be doing the maintenance or service work. They are based on factory service/maintenance recommendations. However, certain lubrication-related items (such as oil changes) could be done on a more frequent basis in the interest of extended longevity of wear-related components.

If the vehicle is subjected to severe use conditions listed below, the service intervals should be cut in half to ensure that wear factors on the vehicle do not become exceedingly high.

Severe conditions:
Repeated short trips
Driving on rough and/or non-existent roads
Driving on dusty and/or muddy roads
Operating in extremely cold weather and/or driving in areas using road salt

Every 250 miles or weekly – whichever comes first

Check the engine oil level (Section 3)
Check the engine coolant level (Section 3)
Check the windshield washer fluid level (Section 3)
Check the battery water level (if equipped with removable vent caps) (Section 3)
Check the tires and tire pressures (Section 4)
Check the automatic transmission fluid level, if so equipped (Section 23)

Every 10 000 miles (16 000 km) or 8 months

Change engine oil and filter

Every 15 000 miles or 12 months – whichever comes first

Check and/or adjust, if necessary, the engine valve clearances (Specifications will appear on the information label under the hood)
Inspect the engine exhaust pipes and mountings
Check and/or adjust, if necessary, the fuel idle speed and fast idle speed*
Inspect and correct or replace as necessary, the fuel throttle positioner system*
Set ignition timing (Canada only)
Replace ignition spark plugs (US Federal and Canada)
Inspect and replace as necessary, transmission and differential oil
Inspect and replace as necessary, automatic transmission fluid
Inspect brake pedal travel and parking brake, brake lining and drums, brake pads and discs, brake line pipes and hoses and brake fluid level
Inspect clutch pedal, steering linkage, gear box and steering wheel

free play. Also driveshaft boots, balljoint and dust cover, bolts and nuts on chassis and body

Every 30 000 miles or 24 months – whichever comes first

Note: *In addition to the 15 000 mile maintenance procedures, do the following:*
Replace or lubricate or adjust drivebelts (including air conditioner drivebelt)
Replace engine coolant
Inspect and correct or replace as necessary, vacuum fittings, hoses and connections
Inspect and correct or replace exhaust pipes and mountings
Inspect and correct or replace as necessary, choke system
Replace air filter
Inspect and correct or replace as necessary, fuel lines and connections
Inspect and correct or replace as necessary, fuel filler cap*
Set ignition timing*
Replace spark plugs
Inspect ignition wiring and correct or replace as necessary (US Federal and Canada). (In areas where salt is used on roads, inspection and cleaning of the distributor cap and ignition wiring should be performed each year just after snow season)
Inspect and correct or replace as necessary, spark control system*
Inspect PCV system. Replace only the PCV valve (US Federal and Canada)
Inspect air injection (California only), or air suction (US Federal and Canada only) system*
Inspect or replace as necessary, the charcoal canister and fuel evaporative emission control system, hoses and connections*
Inspect and replace as necessary, the transmission and differential oil and automatic transmission fluid
Inspect the brake pedal free play and parking brake, brake lining and drums, brake pads and discs, brakeline pipes and hoses and brake fluid level
Inspect the clutch pedal, steering linkage, gearbox and steering wheel free play, driveshaft boots, balljoint and dust cover
Service wheel bearings

Every 60 000 miles or 48 months – whichever comes first

Note: *In addition to the 30 000 mile maintenance procedures, do the following:*
Inspect and replace as necessary, the cooling and heating system hoses and connections
Replace fuel filter
Replace fuel filler cap gasket
Recommended maintenance items for California vehicles, but are required maintenance items for US Federal and Canada.

2   Fluid levels check

1   There are a number of components on a vehicle which rely on the use of fluids to perform their job. Through the normal operation of the vehicle, these fluids are used up and must be replenished before damage occurs. See the Recommended Lubricants Section in the specifications for the specific fluid to be used when adding is required. When checking fluid levels, it is important that the vehicle is on a level surface.

Engine oil

2   The engine oil level is checked with a dipstick which is located at the right front of the engine block. This dipstick travels through a tube and into the oil pan at the bottom of the engine.
3   The oil level should be checked preferably before the vehicle has been driven, or about 15 minutes after the engine has been shut off. If the oil is checked immediately after driving the vehicle, some of the oil will remain in the upper engine components, thus giving an inaccurate reading on the dipstick.
4   Pull the dipstick from its tube and wipe all the oil from the end with a clean rag (photo). Insert the clean dipstick all the way back into the oil pan and pull it out again. Observe the oil at the end of the

2.4 Checking the engine oil level with the dipstick

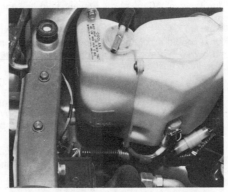

2.9 Engine coolant (left) and windshield washer (right) reservoirs

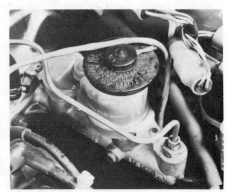

2.22 Brake fluid reservoir

dipstick. At its highest point, the level should be between the 'Low' and 'Full' marks.

5   It takes approximately 1 quart of oil to raise the level from the 'Low' mark to the 'Full' mark on the dipstick. Do not allow the level to drop below the 'Low' mark, as this may cause engine damage due to oil starvation. On the other hand, do not overfill the engine by adding oil above the 'Full' mark, as this may result in oil-fouled spark plugs, oil leaks or oil seal failures.

6   Oil is added to the engine after removing a twist-off cap located on the rocker arm cover. An oil can spout or funnel will reduce spills as the oil is poured in.

7   Checking the oil level can also be an important preventative maintenance step. If you find the oil level dropping abnormally, it is an indication of oil leakage or internal engine wear which should be corrected. If there are water droplets in the oil, or if it is milky-looking, this also indicates component failure and the engine should be checked immediately. The condition of the oil can also be checked along with the level. With the dipstick removed from the engine, take your thumb and index finger and wipe the oil up the dipstick, looking for small dirt particles or engine filings which will cling to the dipstick. This is an indication that the oil should be drained and fresh oil added (Section 4).

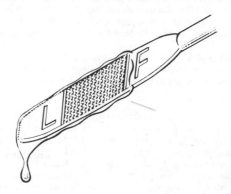

Fig. 1.1 Checking the engine oil level with the dipstick (Sec 2)

Engine coolant

8   Most vehicles are equipped with a pressurized coolant recovery system which makes coolant level checks very easy. A clear or white coolant reservoir, attached at the right front corner of the engine compartment, is connected by a hose to the radiator cap (do not confuse this reservoir with the windshield washer fluid container which is located in the same corner but slightly to the rear, towards the passenger compartment). As the engine heats up during operation, coolant is forced from the radiator, through the connecting tube and into the reservoir. As the engine cools, this coolant is automatically drawn back into the radiator to keep the level correct.

9   The coolant level should be checked when the engine is cold. Merely observe the level of fluid in the reservoir, which should be between the 'Low' and the 'Full' marks on the side of the reservoir (photo). If the system is completely cooled, also check the level in the radiator by removing the cap.

10   If your particular vehicle is not equipped with a coolant recovery system, the level should be checked by removing the radiator cap. However, the cap should not under any circumstances be removed while the system is hot, as escaping steam could cause serious injury. Wait until the engine has completely cooled, then wrap a thick cloth around the cap and turn it to its first stop. If any steam escapes from the cap, allow the engine to cool further. Then remove the cap and check the level in the radiator. It should be about 1 in below the bottom of the filler neck.

11   If only a small amount of coolant is required to bring the system up to the proper level, regular water can be used. However, to maintain the proper antifreeze/water mixture in the system, both should be mixed together to replenish a low level. High-quality antifreeze offering protection to -20° should be mixed with water in the proportion specified on the container. Do not allow antifreeze to come in contact with your skin or painted surfaces of the car. Flush contacted areas immediately with plenty of water.

12   On systems with a recovery tank, coolant should be added to the

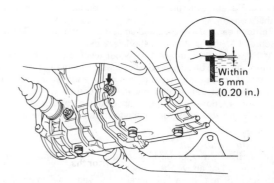

Fig. 1.2 Checking the manual transaxle oil level (Sec 2)

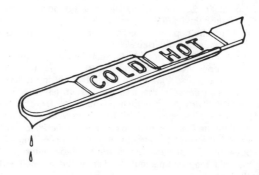

Fig. 1.3 Checking the automatic transmission fluid level (Sec 2)

reservoir after removing the cap at the top of the reservoir. Coolant should be added directly into the radiator on systems without a coolant recovery check.

13 As the coolant level is checked, observe the condition of the coolant. It should be relatively clear. If the fluid is brown or a rust color, this is an indication that the system should be drained, flushed and refilled (Section 11).

14 If the cooling system requires repeated additions to keep the proper level, have the radiator pressure cap checked for proper sealing ability. Also check for leaks in the system (cracked hoses, loose hose connections, leaking gaskets, etc).

Windshield washer

15 The fluid for the windshield washer system is located in the right front corner of the engine compartment directly behind the engine coolant bottle in a similar white plastic reservoir (photo). *Do not confuse the two* as the fluid requirements are entirely different, and substitution of the wrong type of fluid could result in damage to the car's exterior finish or internal engine components. The level inside the reservoir should be maintained at the 'Full' mark. Some cars are additionally equipped with a rear window washer and wiper system and the fluid container can be found in the left rear corner of the cargo area.

16 A good quality washer solvent should be added through the plastic cap whenever replenishing is required. Do not use plain water alone in this system, especially in cold climates where the water could freeze.

Battery

17 There are certain precautions to be taken when working on or near the battery: a) Never expose a battery to open flame or sparks which could ignite the hydrogen gas given off by the battery; b) Wear protective clothing and eye protection to reduce the possibility of the corrosive surface acid solution inside the battery harming you; if the fluid is splashed or spilled, flush the contacted area immediately with plenty of water); c) Remove all metal jewelry which could contact the positive terminal and another grounded metal source, thus causing a short circuit; d) Always keep batteries and battery acid out of the reach of children.

18 If equipped with a maintenance-type battery, the caps on the top of the battery should be removed periodically to check for a low water level. This check will be more critical during the warm summer months.

19 Remove each of the caps and add distilled water to bring the level of each cell to the split ring in the filler opening.

20 At the same time the battery water level is checked, the overall condition of the battery and its related components should be inspected. If corrosion is found on the cable ends or battery terminals, remove the cables and clean away all corrosion using a baking soda/water solution or a wire brush cleaning tool designed for this purpose. See Section 29 for complete battery care and servicing.

Brake fluid reservoir

21 The brake fluid reservoir is located on the left side of the engine compartment, just above the fender well.

22 Check that the brake fluid level is between the upper and lower level markings on the reservoir (photo). If it is low, you will have to add brake fluid to bring it up to the proper level.

23 Before removing the cap on the reservoir, use a rag to clean all dirt and grease from around the cap area. If any foreign matter enters the reservoir with the cap removed, blockage in the brake system lines can occur. Also, make sure all painted surfaces around the reservoir are covered, as brake fluid will ruin paintwork.

24 Carefully lift the cap off the cylinder and set it aside, taking care not to set it on a painted surface.

25 Carefully pour the specified brake fluid into the reservoir to bring it up to the proper level. Be careful not to spill the fluid on painted surfaces. Be sure the specified fluid is used, as mixing different types of brake fluid can cause damage to the system (see *Recommended Lubricants and Fluids* or your owner's manual). **Note:** *Change the brake fluid every 2 years (30 000 miles) as described in Chapter 9.*

26 At this time the fluid and reservoir can be inspected for contamination. Normally, the braking system will not need servicing other than noted above, but if rust deposits, dirt particles or water droplets are seen in the fluid, the system should be dismantled, drained and refilled with fresh fluid.

27 Reinstall the reservoir cap. Make sure the lid is properly seated to prevent fluid leakage and/or system pressure loss.

28 The brake fluid in the reservoir will drop slightly as the brake shoes or pads at each wheel wear down during normal operation. If it requires repeated replenishing to keep it at the proper level, this is an indication of leakage in the brake system which should be corrected immediately. Check all brake lines and their connections, along with the wheel cylinders and booster (see Chapter 9 for more information).

29 If upon checking the reservoir fluid level you discover that one or both reservoirs is empty or nearly empty, the braking system should be bled (Chapter 9). When the fluid level gets low, air can enter the system and should be removed by bleeding the brakes.

Manual transmission

30 Manual transmissions do not have a dipstick. The fluid level is checked by removing a plug in the left side of the transmission case under the car. If you raise the car with a jack or jackstands, make sure the car is level before you check the fluid. Use a rag to clean the plug and the surrounding area before removal.

31 With the vehicle components cold, remove the plug. If fluid immediately starts leaking out, thread the plug back into the transmission because the fluid level is all right. If there is no fluid leakage, completely remove the plug and place your little finger inside the hole. The fluid level should be within 0.20 in (5 mm) of the bottom of the hole.

32 If the transmission needs more fluid, use a syringe to squeeze the appropriate lubricant into the plug hole to bring the fluid up to the proper level.

33 Thread the plug back into the transmision and tighten it securely. Drive the vehicle and check for leaks around the plug.

Automatic transmission

34 The fluid level in the automatic transmission may be checked with the transmission cold (car has not been driven for over five hours and the fluid temperature ranges from 70° to 85°F or 20° to 30°C). This cold temperature check may be used for reference only and must be followed with a normal operating temperature reading. To check the transmission fluid level when cold, start the engine and shift the transmission selector from Park through the entire range to Low and back to Park. With the engine still running in Park, remove the transmission dipstick, wipe it clean and re-insert it all the way back into the dipstick tube. Withdraw the dipstick, and read the fluid level on the marks. If the level is below the cold notch (last mark), add ATF fluid type F, a half-pint at a time, rechecking the reading after each addition. Once the cold reading is reached, proceed with the normal operating temperature transmission fluid check sequence.

35 A normal operating temperature transmission fluid check is started by driving the vehicle for several miles, making frequent starts and stops to allow the transmission to shift through all the gears. Park the vehicle on a level surface. With the parking brake engaged and the engine idling, select each gear momentarily, ending with the selector lever in the Park position.

36 Remove the transmission dipstick (located on the right side, near the firewall) and wipe all the fluid from the end of the dipstick with a clean rag.

37 Push the dipstick back into the transmission as far as it will go. Remove the dipstick and observe the fluid in relation to the marks on the stick. Be sure to hold the dipstick horizontal as the fluid runs quickly and can give a misreading if held vertically. The fluid should be somewhere between the two 'hot' notches on the dipstick.

38 If the fluid is below the second notch (the cold side) of the dipstick, add sufficient fluid, a small amount at a time, through the dipstick tube with a funnel. Check with the dipstick wiped clean, allowing approximately a minute after filling for the fluid to circulate into the transmission.

39 It is important that the transmission is not overfilled. Under no circumstances should the fluid level be above the top 'Hot' notch on the dipstick as this could cause internal damage to the transmission. The best way to prevent overfilling is to add fluid in small amounts and then either drive the car or at least move the selector through the entire range slowly to ensure proper circulation of the added fluid. Be sure to add only ATF fluid type F from a quality manufacturer.

40 The condition of the fluid should also be checked along with the level. If the fluid showing on the end of the dipstick is a dark reddish-brown color, or if the fluid has a burnt smell, the transmission fluid should be changed. If you are in doubt about the condition of the fluid, compare it with new fluid on a clean (preferably white) rag for color

and smell. If the color or smell differs from new fluid in any way or if tiny dot-like particles show up, the transmission oil pan should be removed for closer examination of the fluid and the visible components of the transmission.

Differential

41 Like the manual transmission, the differential has an inspection and fill plug which must be removed to check the fluid level. This is an under-car operation and care must be taken that the car is sitting level no matter what means are used to gain underside access.

42 Remove the plug which is located on the left side of the differential directly behind the inner-left driveaxle flange. Use a finger to reach inside the differential housing to feel the level of the fluid. It should be at the bottom of the plug hole.

43 If this is not the case, add the proper lubricant through the plug hole. A special suction pump or squeeze bottle with tube designed for this purpose is the best method for filling the differential. Make certain the correct hypoid gear oil and not automatic transmission oil is used to fill the differential.

44 Tighten the plug securely and check for leaks after the first few miles of driving.

3 Tires – pressure check and rotation

1 Periodically inspecting the tires can not only prevent you from being stranded with a flat tire, but can also give you clues as to possible problems with the steering and suspension systems before major damage occurs.

2 Proper tire inflation adds miles to the lifespan of the tires, allows the car to achieve maximum miles per gallon figures, and helps the overall riding comfort of the car.

3 When inspecting the tire, first check the wear on the tread. Irregularities in the tread pattern (cupping, flat spots, more wear on one side than the other) are indications of front end alignment and/or balance problems. If any of these conditions are found you would do best to take the car to a competent repair shop which can correct the problem.

4 Also check the tread area for cuts or punctures. Many times a nail or tack will imbed itself into the tire tread and yet the tire will hold its air pressure for a short time. In most cases, a repair shop or gas station can repair the punctured tire.

5 It is also important to check the sidewalls of the tire, both inside and outside. Check for the rubber being deteriorated, cut or punctured. Also inspect the inboard side of the tire for signs of brake fluid leakage, indicating a thorough brake inspection is needed immediately (Section 18).

6 Incorrect tire pressure cannot be determined merely by looking at the tire. This is especially true for radial tires. A tire pressure gauge must be used. If you do not already have a reliable gauge, it is a good idea to purchase one and keep it in the glove box. Built-in pressure gauges at gas stations are often unreliable. If you are in doubt as to the accuracy of your gauge, many repair shops have 'master' pressure gauges which you can use for comparison purposes.

7 Always check tire inflation when the tires are cold. Cold, in this case, means the car has not been driven more than one mile after sitting for three hours or more. It is normal for the pressure to increase 4 to 8 pounds or more when the tires are hot.

8 Unscrew the valve cap protruding from the wheel or hubcap and firmly press the gauge onto the valve stem. Observe the reading on the gauge and check this figure against the recommended tire pressure listed on the tire placard. This tire placard is usually found attached to the glove box door.

9 Check all tires and add air as necessary to bring all tires up to the recommended pressure levels. Do not forget the spare tire. Be sure to reinstall the valve caps which will keep dirt and moisture out of the valve stem mechanism.

10 The tires should be rotated at the specified intervals and whenever uneven wear is noticed. Since the vehicle will be raised and the tires removed anyway, this is a good time to check the brakes (Section 18) and/or repack the wheel bearings (Section 25). Read over these Sections if this is to be done at the same time.

11 The location for each tire in the rotation sequence depends on the type of tire used on your vehicle. Tire type can be determined by reading the raised printing on the sidewall of the tire.

12 See the information in *Jacking and Towing* at the front of the

manual for the proper procedures to follow in raising the vehicle and changing a tire; however, if the brakes are to be checked do not apply the parking brake as stated. Make sure the tires are blocked to prevent the vehicle from rolling.

13 Preferably, the entire vehicle should be raised at the same time. This can be done on a hoist or by jacking up each corner of the vehicle and then lowering it onto jack stands placed under the frame rails. Always use four jack stands and make sure the vehicle is firmly supported all around.

14 After rotation, check and adjust the tire pressures as necessary and be sure to check wheel nut tightness.

4 Engine oil and filter change

1 Frequent oil changes may be the best form of preventative maintenance available for the home mechanic. When engine oil ages, it gets diluted and contaminated which ultimately leads to premature parts wear.

2 Although some sources recommend oil filter changes every other oil change, we feel that the minimal cost of an oil filter and the relative ease with which it is installed dictates that a new filter be used whenever the oil is changed.

3 The tools necessary for a normal oil and filter change are: a wrench to fit the drain plug at the bottom of the oil pan; an oil filter wrench to remove the old filter; a container with at least a six-quart capacity to drain the old oil into; and a funnel or oil can spout to help pour fresh oil into the engine.

4 In addition, you should have plenty of clean rags and newspapers handy to mop up any spills. Access to the underside of the car is greatly improved if the car can be lifted on a hoist, driven onto ramps or supported by jack stands. Do not work under a car which is supported only by a bumper, hydraulic or scissors-type jack.

5 If this is your first oil change on the car, it is a good idea to crawl underneath and familiarize yourself with the locations of the oil drain plug and the oil filter (photo). Since the engine and exhaust components will be warm during the actual work, it is best to figure out any potential problems before the car and its accessories are hot.

6 Allow the car to warm up to normal operating temperature. If the new oil or any tools are needed, use this warm-up time to gather everything necessary for the job. The correct type of oil to buy for your application can be found in *Recommended Lubricants* near the front of this Chapter.

7 With the engine oil warm (warm engine oil will drain better and more built-up sludge will be removed with the oil), raise the vehicle for access beneath. Make sure the car is firmly supported. If jack stands are used they should be placed towards the front of the frame rails which run the length of the car.

8 Move all necessary tools, rags and newspapers under the car. Position the drain pan under the drain plug. Keep in mind that the oil

4.5 Engine oil filter location

4.9 Removing the engine oil drain plug

5.1 Locating the steering stops (arrow) for lubrication

will initially flow from the pan with some force, so place the pan accordingly.

9   Being careful not to touch any of the hot exhaust pipe components, use the wrench to remove the drain plug near the bottom of the oil pan (photo). Depending on how hot the oil has become, you may want to wear gloves while unscrewing the plug the final few turns.

10   Allow the old oil to drain into the pan. It may be necessary to move the pan further under the engine as the oil flow reduces to a trickle.

11   After all the oil has drained, clean the drain plug thoroughly with a clean rag (photo). If equipped, be sure to use a new drain plug gasket and make sure the old gasket is removed from the drain plug or oil pan.

12   Clean the area around the drain plug opening and reinstall the drain plug. Tighten the plug securely with your wrench. If a torque wrench is available, the torque setting is 20 ft-lb.

13   Move the drain pan in position under the oil filter.

14   Now use the filter wrench to loosen the oil filter (photo). Chain or metal band-type filter wrenches may distort the filter canister, but don't worry too much about this as the filter will be discarded anyway.

15   Sometimes the oil filter is on so tight it cannot be loosened, or it is positioned in an area which is inaccessible with a filter wrench. As a last resort, you can punch a metal bar or long screwdriver directly through the bottom of the canister and use this as a T-bar to turn the filter. If this must be done, be prepared for oil to spurt out of the canister as it is punctured.

16   Completely unscrew the old filter. Be careful, it is full of oil. Empty the old oil inside the filter into the drain pan.

17   Compare the old filter with the new one to make sure they are of the same type.

18   Use a clean rag to remove all oil, dirt and sludge from the area where the oil filter mounts to the engine. Check the old filter to make sure the rubber gasket is not stuck to the engine mounting surface. If this gasket is stuck to the engine (use a flashlight if necessary), remove it.

19   Open one of the cans of new oil and fill the new filter with fresh oil. Also smear a light coat of this fresh oil onto the rubber gasket of the new oil filter.

20   Screw the new filter to the engine following the tightening directions printed on the filter canister or packing box. Most filter manufacturers recommend against using a filter wrench due to possible overtightening or damage to the canister.

21   Remove all tools, rags, etc from under the car, being careful not to spill the oil in the drain pan. Lower the car off its support devices.

22   Move to the engine compartment and locate the oil filler cap on the engine. In most cases there will be a screw-off cap on the rocker arm cover.

23   If an oil can spout is used, push the spout into the top of the oil can and pour the fresh oil through the filler opening. A funnel placed into the opening may also be used.

24   Pour about 3 qts of fresh oil into the engine. Wait a few minutes to allow the oil to drain to the pan, then check the level on the oil dipstick (see Section 2 if necessary). If the oil level is at or near the 'Low' mark, start the engine and allow the new oil to circulate.

25   Run the engine for only about a minute and then shut it off. Immediately look under the car and check for leaks at the oil pan drain plug and around the oil filter. If either is leaking, tighten with a bit more force.

26   With the new oil circulated and the filter now completely full, recheck the level on the dipstick and add enough oil to bring the level to the 'Full' mark on the dipstick.

27   During the first few trips after an oil change, make a point to check for leaks and also the oil level.

28   The old oil drained from the engine cannot be reused in its present state and should be disposed of. Oil reclamation centers, auto repair shops and gas stations will normally accept the oil which can be refined and used again. After the oil has cooled, it can be drained into a suitable container (capped plastic jugs, topped bottles, milk cartons, etc) for transport to one of these disposal sites.

5   Chassis and body lubrication

1   The chassis and undercarriage of the Tercel does not have any grease fittings at any of the key suspension links. There is one area, however, which requires the constant application of a heavy grade of chassis lube to insure quiet, trouble-free operation of the steering system, particularly when the steering is turned to the full-lock positions. These steering stops are located outboard of the front suspension arms directly under the outer axle joints (photo). They appear as a concave cavity and a generous amount of chassis grease should be applied whenever the front of the car is elevated for maintenance or inspection. Since these stops are exposed and are composed of two plates making metal-to-metal contact, any car which encounters a suspension jolt while making a full turn (such as backing out of a driveway or alleyway) will soon wear off the grease. The resulting 'creaking' or 'groaning' sound is usually very disconcerting to the driver.

2   In addition, door hinges and latching hardware need a periodic application of grease or light oil to ensure quiet, wear-free operation. The rubber seals around the door and cargo hatches will benefit from an occasional application of silicone spray to maintain their supple, sealing qualities. Be sure to wipe off any excess spray after application as it is easy for the driver or passengers to rub against these seals and ruin articles of clothing.

6   Suspension and steering system check

1   Whenever the front of the vehicle is raised for service it is a good idea to check the suspension and steering components for wear.

2   Indications of a fault in these systems are: excessive play in the steering wheel before the front wheels react; excessive sway around

corners or body movement over rough roads; binding at some point as the steering wheel is turned.

3   Before the vehicle is raised for inspection, test the shock absorbers by pushing downward to rock the vehicle at each corner. If you push the vehicle down and it does not come back to a level position without one or two bounces, the shocks are worn and need to be replaced. As this is done, check for squeaks and strange noises from the suspension components. Information on shock absorber and suspension components can be found in Chapter 11.

4   Now raise the front end of the vehicle and support it firmly on jack stands placed under the frame rails. Because of the work to be done, make sure the vehicle cannot fall from the stands.

5   Grab the top and bottom of the front tire with your hands and rock the tire/wheel on its spindle. If there is movement of more than 0.059 in, the wheel bearings should be serviced (see Section 25).

6   Crawl under the vehicle and check for loose bolts, broken or disconnected parts and deteriorated rubber bushings on all suspension and steering components. Look for grease or fluid leaking from around the steering box. Check the balljoints for wear (see Chapter 11).

7   Have an assistant turn the steering wheel from side to side and check the steering components for free movement, chafing or binding. If the steering does not react with the movement of the steering wheel, try to determine where the slack is located.

7   Cooling system check

1   Many major engine failures can be attributed to a faulty cooling system. If equipped with an automatic transmission, the cooling system also plays an integral role in transmission longevity.

2   The cooling system should be checked with the engine cold. Do this before the car is driven for the day or after it has been shut off for one or two hours.

3   Remove the radiator cap and thoroughly clean the cap (inside and out) with clean water. Also clean the filler neck on the radiator. All traces of corrosion should be removed.

4   Carefully check the upper and lower radiator hoses along with the smaller diameter heater hoses. Inspect their entire length, replacing any hose which is cracked, swollen or shows signs of deterioration. Cracks may become more apparent if the hose is squeezed.

5   Also check that all hose connections are tight. A leak in the cooling system will usually show up as white or rust colored deposits on the areas adjoining the leak.

6   Pay particular attention to the area surrounding the thermostat housing, as this is often a source of leakage. It is essential to have a clean engine for leak checks of this type. Fluids tend to move from their point of origin due to gravity and under-hood air currents and can hide their source on a dirty engine.

7   Use compressed air or a soft brush to remove bugs, leaves, etc, from the front of the radiator or air conditioning condenser. Be careful not to damage the delicate cooling fins, or cut yourself on the sharp fins.

8   Finally, have the cap and system tested for proper pressure. If you do not have a pressure tester, most gas stations and repair shops will do this for a minimal charge.

8   Exhaust system check

1   With the exhaust system cold (at least three hours after being driven), check the complete exhaust system from its starting point at the engine to the end of the tailpipe. This is best done on a hoist where full access is available.

2   Check the pipes and their connections for signs of leakage and/or corrosion indicating a potential failure. Check that all brackets and hangers are in good condition and are tight.

3   At the same time, inspect the underside of the body for holes, corrosion, open seams, etc, which may allow exhaust gases to enter the passenger compartment. Seal all body openings with silicone or body putty.

4   Rattles and other driving noises can often be traced to the exhaust system, especially the mounts and hangers. Try to move the pipes and muffler. If the components can come into contact with the body or driveline parts, secure the exhaust system with new mountings.

5   This is also an ideal time to check the running condition of the engine by inspecting the very end of the tailpipe. The exhaust deposits here are an indication of engine tune. If the pipe is black and sooty or bright white deposits are found here, the engine is in need of a tune-up including a thorough carburetor inspection and adjustment.

9   Air filter replacement

1   At the specified intervals, the air filter should be replaced with a new one. A thorough program of preventative maintenance would call for the filter to be inspected periodically between changes.

2   The air filter is located inside the air cleaner housing on the top of the engine. To remove the filter, unscrew the wing nut at the top of the air cleaner, unsnap the four spring-type clamps, and lift off the top plate.

3   While the top plate is off, be careful not to drop anything down into the carburetor.

4   Lift the air filter out of the housing.

5   To check the filter, hold it up to strong sunlight, or place a flashlight or droplight on the inside of the ring-shaped filter. If you can see light coming through the paper element, the filter is all right. Check all the way around the filter.

6   Wipe the inside of the air cleaner clean with a rag.

7   Place the old filter (if in good condition) or the new filter (if specified interval has elapsed) back into the air cleaner housing. Make sure it seats properly in the bottom of the housing.

8   Reinstall the top plate with the four clamps and wing nut. Be sure to align the arrow stamped on the plate with the arrow stamped on the snorkel tube (photo).

10   Fuel filter replacement

Caution: *Keep in mind that any fuel system work is potentially dangerous so work in a well ventilated area with no adjoining source of flame or spark.*

1   The fuel filter is located in the engine compartment on the left inner fenderwell directly under the end of the brake master cylinder and across from the starter. In some cars, the air conditioner hoses or miscellaneous cables and wires may hide it from view. It appears from the top as a small white cylinder with two hoses protruding from the top (photo).

2   The two rubber hoses are the first items to be removed. Loosen or remove the hose clamps and, with a 'twisting' motion, slide the two hoses off the old filter. A small empty tin can or similar container placed under the filter will help catch the small amount of fuel dropping out of the hoses and filter. Remove the hoses slowly as the fuel is under slight pressure and can spray out momentarily.

3   The fuel filter is retained by a spring clip and is readily replaced by pulling up to remove and pushing the new filter back in to install.

9.8 Aligning the arrows when installing the air cleaner plate

10.1 Fuel filter location (arrow)

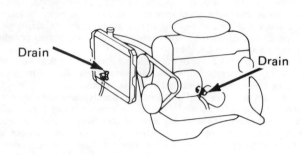

Fig. 1.4 Engine and radiator coolant plug locations (Sec 11)

4   After the new filter is in place, the hoses are reinserted taking care that the direction of flow is followed. An arrow is usually provided on the filter to indicate the proper direction. A rotating motion is again best for installing the hoses since the fuel filter is usually plastic and can be damaged by rough handling. New hose clamps are advisable and should be installed $\frac{1}{8}$ to $\frac{1}{4}$ inch back from the ends. Relocate any hoses or lines which were moved to gain access to the filter. Start the engine and check for leaks.

11 Cooling system – servicing, draining, flushing and refilling

1   Periodically, the cooling system should be drained, flushed and refilled to replenish the antifreeze mixture and prevent the formation of rust and corrosion which can impair the performance of the cooling system and ultimately cause engine damage.
2   At the same time the cooling system is serviced, all hoses and the radiator pressure cap should be inspected and replaced if faulty (see Section 7).
3   As antifreeze is a poisonous solution, take care not to spill any of the cooling mixture on the vehicle's paint or your own skin. If this happens, rinse immediately with plenty of clear water. Also, it is advisable to consult your local authorities about the dumping of antifreeze before draining the cooling system. In many areas reclamation centers have been set up to collect automobile oil and drained antifreeze/water mixtures rather than allowing these liquids to be added to the sewage and water facilities.
4   With the engine cold, remove the radiator pressure cap.
5   Move a large container under the radiator to catch the water/antifreeze mixture as it is drained.
6   Drain the radiator by opening the drain petcock at the bottom of the radiator.
7   Open the engine drain plug at the left side of the engine. This will allow the coolant to drain from the engine itself.
8   Disconnect the overflow tube and remove the coolant reserve system reservoir. Flush it out with clean water.
9   Place a cold water hose (a common garden hose is fine) in the radiator filler neck at the top of the radiator and flush the system until the water runs clear at all drain points.
10   In severe cases of contamination or clogging of the radiator, remove it (see Chapter 3) and reverse flush it. This involves simply inserting the cold pressure hose in the bottom radiator outlet to allow the clear water to run against the normal flow, draining through the top. A radiator repair shop should be consulted if further cleaning or repair is necessary.
11   Where the coolant is regularly drained and the system refilled with the correct antifreeze/inhibitor mixture there should be no need to employ chemical cleaners or descalers.
12   To refill the system, tighten the drain plug securely in the engine. Install the reserve system reservoir and the overflow hose. Close the radiator drain.

13   Fill the radiator to the base of the filler neck and then add more coolant to the coolant reservoir system reservoir until it reaches the 'FULL' mark.
14   Run the engine until normal temperature is reached and with the engine idling, add coolant up to the correct level (see Section 2). Install the reservoir cap.
15   Always refill the system with a mixture of high quality ethylene glycol-based antifreeze and water in the proportion called for on the antifreeze container or in your owner's manual. Chapter 3 also contains information on antifreeze mixtures.
16   Keep a close watch on the coolant level and the various cooling hoses during the first few miles of driving. Tighten the hose clamps and/or add more coolant mixture as necessary.

12 Spark plug replacement

1   The spark plugs are located on the left side of the engine and are easily accessible for servicing.
2   In most cases the tools necessary for a spark plug replacement job are: a plug wrench or spark plug socket which fits onto a ratchet wrench (this special socket will be insulated inside to protect the porcelain insulator) and a feeler gauge to check and adjust the spark plug gap.
3   The best policy to follow when replacing the spark plugs is to purchase the new spark plugs beforehand, adjust them to the proper gap and then replace each plug one at a time. When buying the new spark plugs it is important that the correct plug is purchased for your specific engine. This information can be found in the Specifications Section of this Chapter, but should be checked against the information found on the tune-up decal located under the hood of your vehicle or in the factory owner's manual. If differences exist between these sources, purchase the spark plug type specified on the tune-up decal as this information was printed for your specific engine.
4   Inspect the new spark plugs for defects and observe the end that the spark plug wire attaches to. In some cases it will be necessary to screw on the special plug tip which will be packaged separately in the new spark plug container. At this time, the new plugs should also be gapped.
5   The gap is checked by inserting the proper thickness plug gap gauge between the electrodes at the threaded end of the plug. 1A-C engines have dual-side electrodes converging on a common center electrode. Both side gaps must be checked and a wire-type plug gapping gauge is the only type used on these side-gap plugs. 3A and 3A-C engines have the more common center gap type of spark plugs and either type (wire or wedge) of gapping tool may be used. In either type of plug, the gap between electrodes should be the same as that given in the Specifications or on the tune-up decal. Make sure the correct gap specification is used for the type of plug your engine has. The gapping tool should just touch each of the electrodes. If the gap is incorrect, use the notched adjuster on the feeler gauge body to bend

the curved side electrode slightly until the proper gap is achieved. If the side electrode is not centered directly over the center electrode in the case of the center gap (3A and 3A-C engine) plugs, the notched adjuster should be used to align the two. If a used spark plug is being re-gapped, it is important to check for cracks in the ceramic portion of the spark plug body. If any defects are found, or if the electrodes are burnt away any appreciable amount, new spark plugs should be used.

6 Cover the fenders of the vehicle to prevent damage to exterior paint.

7 With the engine cool, remove the spark plug wire from one spark plug. Do this by grabbing the boot at the end of the wire, not the wire itself. Sometimes it is necessary to use a twisting motion while the boot and plug wire is pulled free. Using a plug wire removal tool is the easiest and safest method.

8 If compressed air is available, use this to blow any dirt or foreign material away from the spark plug area. A common bicycle pump will also work. The idea here is to eliminate the possibility of material falling into the engine cylinder as the spark plug is removed.

9 Now place the spark plug wrench or socket over the plug and remove it from the engine by turning in a counterclockwise motion.

10 Compare the spark plug with those shown in Chapter 5 to get an indication of the overall running condition of the engine.

11 Carefully insert one of the new plugs into the spark plug hole, making sure that you have screwed a new sealing gasket (sometimes found separately in the new spark plug container) onto the threaded portion of the plug. Also make sure the sealing ring from the old spark plug is not clinging to the outer edge of the spark plug hole. Since the cylinder head on your engine is aluminum, special care should be taken to ensure the spark plug is not cross-threaded into the hole. It is a wise idea to coat the threads of the new spark plug with a special anti-seizure compound, since aluminum and steel tend to react with heat to 'weld' themselves together. If resistance is felt as you thread the spark plug in by hand, back it out and start again. If the plug refuses to start into the threads properly, it may be necessary to 'chase' the threads using a special tap designed for this purpose. If this operation is necessary, be sure to clean out all of the resulting aluminum shavings so as not to damage the engine internally. Do not, under any circumstances, force the spark plug into the hole with a wrench or socket.

12 Finally tighten the spark plug with the wrench or socket. It is best to use a torque wrench for this to ensure the plug is seated correctly. The correct torque figure is given in Specifications.

13 Before pushing the spark plug wire onto the end of the plug, inspect it following the procedures outlined in Section 21.

14 Install the plug wire to the new spark plug, again using a twisting motion on the boot until it is firmly seated on the spark plug. Make sure the wire is routed away from the hot exhaust manifold.

15 Follow the above procedures for the remaining spark plugs, replacing each one at a time to prevent mixing up the spark plug wires.

13 Ignition points – replacement and dwell adjustment (3A engine only)

1 When performing the operation of ignition point replacement, take care to assemble all of the parts in the exact same order they came apart. For instance, certain washers and insulators on the pigtail wire leading to the points can become easily grounded to the distributor which will prevent the engine from running. In addition, the small screws which hold down the points themselves could easily drop into the base of the distributor, thus necessitating a complete distributor disassembly.

2 Remove the distributor cap by opening the two spring clips which hold the cap to the distributor body. A screwdriver placed between the cap and the clip works well for this task and care should be exercised so as not to crack the cap.

3 Next, remove the rotor, dustproof cover, and sealing gasket. The points are now exposed to view.

4 Unscrew the nut which holds the coil-to-distributor wire along with the condenser lead. If the condenser is replaced (always a good idea when points are changed) unscrew it from the distributor and unplug the terminal leading to the coil wire lead.

5 Loosen, but do not remove the two point hold-down screws. The points plate should now slide out due to the slotted construction of its base plate.

6 Reassembly is the reverse of disassembly. Before tightening the

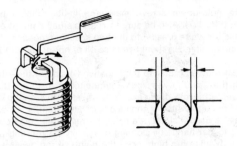
Fig. 1.5 Checking the gap on side gap spark plug (Sec 12)

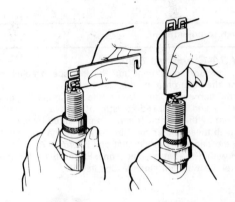
Fig. 1.6 Checking the gap on center gap spark plug (Sec 12)

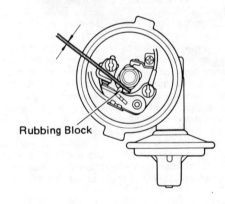
Rubbing Block

Fig. 1.7 The distributor rubbing block gap adjustment can be made after loosening the point hold-down screws (Sec 13)

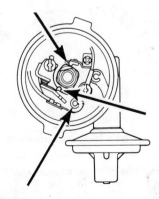
Fig. 1.8 Apply lubricant to the points shown (arrows) (Sec 13)

point plate hold-down screw, make the initial rubbing block gap adjustment (Fig. 1.7). Also be sure to apply a small amount of rubbing block grease (or white grease) to the two specified locations (Fig. 1.8). Under no circumstances should you use oil or normal automotive-type grease.

7   Connect a dwell meter to the negative (-) side of the ignition coil along with the usual power source connections to the battery. Have someone seated in the driver's seat to assist in this operation (if you are familiar enough with the engine electrical system, a remote starter button may be used instead of a helper). Crank the engine over, being careful not to get hands or clothing caught in the rotating pulleys or belts. If the dwell is too high, open the points, if the dwell is too low, close the points until the proper reading is obtained.

8   Complete the job by installing the remaining gaskets, cover, rotor and cap making sure the cap is seated securely in its locating notch before closing the spring clips.

14 Idle mixture adjustment

1A-C and 3A-C engines only

1   The idle mixture adjustment and the idle speed adjustment are related, since the 'lean drop' method is used. However, these cannot be done by the home mechanic. Due to the laws regarding emissions, the idle mixture and idle speed adjustment screws have limiter caps placed on them by the manufacturer. It is prohibited by law to tamper in any way with these limiter caps unless you are an approved service center with the necessary equipment and information to make these adjustments within the set specifications. For further information, see the carburetor Section contained in Chapter 4.

3A engine

2   Before adjusting the idle speed and the idle mixture make certain that the ignition dwell and timing are set to the proper specifications. Warm the engine thoroughly and make sure the choke is fully open. Leave all vacuum lines connected, put the transmission in Neutral, and turn all accessories off including the engine cooling fan. Check the float level through the sight glass in the carburetor. The float level should be between the two facing tangs at the center of the glass.

3   Turn the idle mixture screw to achieve the highest engine speed. You may have to experiment with this setting at first and allow a minute to elapse between each change for the engine to stabilize to the new setting. Do not turn the screw more than $\frac{1}{4}$-turn each time.

4   Set the idle speed by turning the idle speed adjusting screw until the specified engine speed is reached. For engine specifications, consult the underhood decal of the car or, if no decal exists, see Specifications at the front of this Chapter.

5   Go back to the idle mixture adjusting screw and again adjust for the maximum engine speed. Continue back and forth between the two adjustments until the maximum engine speed will rise no farther no matter how much adjustment is made to the idle mixture adjusting screw.

6   At this time the final idle speed is set by turning in the mixture screw until rpms drop to the specified speed. You have now completed the 'lean drop' method of adjusting idle mixture and speed.

15 Ignition timing – check and adjustment

1   Prior to making any ignition timing adjustments or checks, the following conditions must exist: The engine must be idling at normal operating temperature with the transmission in Neutral. The choke must be fully open with all accessories switched off.

2   Make sure the engine is idling at the specified rpm by using a tachometer. On 1A-C and 3A-C engines, which have electronic ignition, be sure that the tachometer used is compatible with this type of system, as an incorrect hook-up instrument can damage costly components. On 3A engines, make sure the dwell setting is correct before proceeding with the new step.

3   On 1A-C engines only, disconnect the vacuum hose leading to the distributor sub-diaphragm which has the check valve in-line. Plug this vacuum hose. On 3A-C engines only, disconnect both of the vacuum hoses leading to the distributor sub-diaphragm and main diaphragm. Plug the ends of both hoses.

4   Connect a stroboscopic-type timing light to the engines, utilizing the number 1 spark plug lead as the source of triggering impulse (in addition, most timing lights have two connections to the positive and negative terminals of the battery).

5   Read the ignition timing on the scale found on the lower left front of the engine next to the crankshaft pulley. An easy way to locate this scale is to draw an imaginary straight line down the front of the engine along the left side of the camshaft drivebelt cover. Extreme caution should be exercised in looking for this marker since it is in direct line-of-sight with several of the drivebelts. Under no circumstances should you reach into this area with the hand or fingers while the engine is running. If grease or oil has covered the scale and rendered it unreadable, turn the engine off first and make sure there is no chance that a helper can accidentally start the engine while you are reaching into this location. This same precaution holds true for the mark on the crankshaft pulley if it needs to be wiped off. You may need to 'bump' the engine around to the mark on the pulley with short on/off clicks of the ignition key or a remote starter switch. Notice that the numbers reading to the left of 'O' on the scale are the before-top-dead-center (BTDC) readings and the number to the right of the 'O' is an after-top-dead-center (ATDC) reading. If the correct number does not correspond to the specification, loosen the distributor bolt and turn the distributor until the mark on the pulley lines up (photo). Retighten the distributor bolt and readjust the idle speed if necessary.

6   If the timing setting was incorrect, and had to be changed, it will be necessary to go back and readjust the idle mixture and idle speed of the engine. In some areas, the emissions from the exhaust system will have to be checked after adjusting the timing also.

Idle Mixture Adjusting Screw

Fig. 1.9 Carburetor idle mixture adjusting screw location – 3A engine (Sec 14)

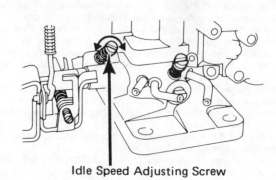

Idle Speed Adjusting Screw

Fig. 1.10 Carburetor idle speed adjusting screw location – 3A engine (Sec 14)

16 PCV (Positive Crankcase Ventilation) valve – replacement

1 The PCV valve is located on the rocker arm cover. There is a hose connected to the valve which runs to the carburetor (photo). Notice that there are two hoses and the PCV valve is located under the forward hose.

2 When purchasing a replacement PCV valve, make sure it is for your particular vehicle, model year and engine series. In some cases, a difference will exist, depending on whether the car was intended for 49-state or California emissions requirements.

3 Pull the valve from its rubber grommet after sliding back the clamp

and removing the rubber hose. Note carefully the valve's installed position (large end down).

4 Compare the old valve with the new one to ensure that they are the same.

5 Inspect the rubber grommet in the cover for cracks or damage and replace it with a new one if necessary.

6 Push the new valve into the rubber grommet using a slight twisting motion to help it go in. Be sure to note the direction the valve is facing.

7 Resecure the hose and clamp to the PCV valve. More information on the PCV system can be found in Chapter 6.

15.5 Loosening the distributor hold down bolt to adjust timing

16.1 Removing the positive crankcase ventilation valve

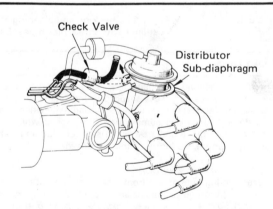

Fig. 1.11 Remove and plug the hose leading to the distributor sub-diaphragm when checking ignition timing (Sec 15)

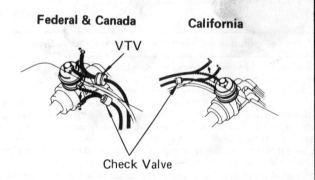

Fig. 1.12 Remove and plug both hoses leading to the distributor sub-diaphragm when checking ignition timing on 3A – engines (Sec 15)

Fig. 1.13 Ignition timing scale (Sec 15)

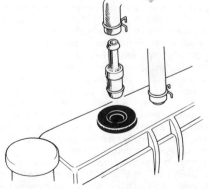

Fig. 1.14 Correct PCV valve installation direction (Sec 16)

18.5 Measuring the front brake pads for wear

18.18 Examining the rear wheel brake cylinder for fluid leakage under the dust cap

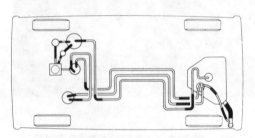

Fig. 1.15 Fuel system hose and line locations
(Sec 17)

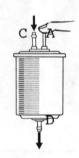

Fig. 1.16 Checking and cleaning
charcoal canister (Sec 17)

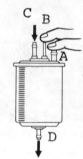

Fig. 1.17 Checking and cleaning charcoal
canister with three inlet pipes (Sec 17)

17 Fuel evaporative emission control system – inspection

1   There are two main areas for examination when inspecting the fuel evaporative emission control system. For a more detailed explanation of the operation and checking of this system, see Chapter 6.
2   Inspect the system hoses and connections, paying particular attention to the rubber hoses as they are the most likely area for deterioration and/or cracking. It will be necessary to remove the fuel tank cover at the rear of the car's interior to check the hoses connected to the fuel tank. The fuel tank should also be checked from under the car for deformation, fuel leakage, tank retaining strap looseness, and damage. If a leak is found in one of the rubber hoses, it would be wise to replace all the rubber hoses, as their deterioration rate would be approximately the same. If a leak is found in the fuel tank, it will be necessary to remove it completely from the car and have it repaired by an outside specialist such as a radiator repair shop. Do not attempt any repairs of the fuel tank while in the car and use great caution as this is one of the most dangerous flammable areas in a motor vehicle. Don't forget to check the large filler neck and vent line hoses in this inspection. For more information see Chapter 4.
3   The other major component to inspect in the evaporative emission control system is the charcoal canister. This canister may be found in the engine compartment on the right side of the firewall next to the fender-well. It appears as a black canister with hoses coming out of the top. To check and clean the canister, remove all of the hoses from the top and bottom after first carefully marking their respective locations. Do not mix them up! Blow a gentle stream of air (40 psi or 3 kg/cm^2) through pipe C while plugging pipe A (Fig. 1.16) and pipe B in some engine applications (Fig. 1.17) with your fingers. Air should blow out the bottom pipe with no resistance. No charcoal should come out of pipe D during this operation. If air does not flow freely or if charcoal emits through pipe D, the canister will have to be replaced as it is a sealed and non-serviceable unit. Reconnect all of the hoses and tighten the clamps carefully.

18 Brake check

1   The brakes should be inspected every time the wheels are removed or whenever a fault is suspected. Indications of a potential braking system fault are: the car pulls to one side when the brake pedal is depressed; noises coming from the brakes when they are applied; excessive brake pedal travel; pulsating pedal; and leakage of fluid usually seen on the inside of the tire or wheel.

Front disc brake inspection
2   Loosen the lug nuts on the front wheels but do not remove them.
3   Raise the front end of the car and support it with jackstands. Be sure the parking brake is set (see *Jacking and Towing* in the front of this book).
4   Remove the front wheels.
5   Turn the front steering all the way to the right to observe the brake inspection hole of the left brake system. The inspection hole appears as an oval shaped 'window' squarely in the center of the brake caliper bracket. We recommend that the brake pads be replaced if any difference in wear is apparent between the two brake pads (one on either side of the brake rotor) or if the pad is worn less than 0.10 in (2.54 mm) (photo). You may allow the brake pads to wear down to the factory recommended limit, however, due to the complexity and expense involved in replacing the brake discs, the extra margin of caution would be a wise move.
6   If there is doubt about whether to replace the pads or not, a more accurate measurement can be made by removing the pads as described in Chapter 9. Remember, disc brake pads are relatively inexpensive and easy to replace, other brake parts such as discs are not.
7   Perform the same inspection on the right front brake system after turning the steering all the way to the left for better viewing access. If any deviation is noted between the four front brake pads (two per side), all of the pads should be replaced at the same time. Do not mix

different types of replacement pads or use pads of a different material type than original equipment.

8   While checking the pad linings, also inspect the rotor surface for scoring or 'hot spots' indicated by small discolored blemishes. Light scoring is acceptable but if the damage is excessive, the rotor should be resurfaced or replaced with a new one.

9   Before installing the wheels, check for any leakage around the brake hose connections leading to the caliper or damage (cracking, splitting, etc) to the brake hose. Replace the hose or fittings as necessary, referring to Chapter 9.

Rear brakes inspection

10   Loosen the lug nuts on the rear wheels, but do not remove them. Chock the front wheels.

11   Raise the rear end of the car and support it with jackstands. Be sure the parking brake is released.

12   Remove the rear wheels.

13   Remove in order the dust cap, cotter key, castellated locknut, spindle nut, washer, and outer wheel bearing.

14   Pull the drum straight off the spindle. If the drum is stuck due to the shoes having worn a groove in the drums, the self-adjusters will have to be backed off as described in Chapter 9.

15   Clean the dirt and dust from the inside of the drum by wiping with a damp cloth. Do not blow the dust out with compressed air as the brake dust contains asbestos and can be very hazardous to your health. Remove the rear seal and inner bearing. A small pry bar can be used to pull out the seal.

16   Inspect the inside surface of the brake drum. If any scoring, deep scratching or heat damage is evident, or if new brake shoes are being installed, have the drums resurfaced at an automotive machine shop. If the drum is cracked it must be replaced. **NOTE:** *If the drum is grooved but the brake linings are only slightly worn, the drum should be polished with fine emery cloth. Roughing up the surface of the brake shoes in this circumstance would deglaze the linings and help them to perform their job better. A medium grade of emery cloth works well for this purpose.*

17   Observe the thickness of both the front and rear brake shoe lining material. Measure it with a rule or micrometer and replace the shoes if they are less than the minimum given in the Specifications listed in the front of this Chapter. The shoes should also be replaced if they are cracked, glazed (shiny surface) or wet with brake fluid or grease. Refer to Chapter 9 for replacement procedures.

18   Inspect the wheel cylinders for any sign of leakage and overhaul or replace them if any wetness is evident (photo).

19   Inspect all brake lines for leakage, cracking, or other damage and be sure all brake lines, hoses and connectors are tight.

20   Install the brake drums, making sure the bearings are lubed properly and seals are in place and in good condition. Tighten the spindle nut to the prescribed setting found in Section 25 of this Chapter.

21   Install the remaining attaching parts in the opposite order of removal and use a new cotter key before installing the dust cap.

22   Install the rear wheels and tighten the lug nuts to the specified torque. Recheck the lug nut torque after lowering the car to the ground.

Parking brake check and adjustment

23   Before attempting to adjust the parking brake, make sure the rear brake shoes are in good condition and that the brake shoe clearance is properly set (refer to Chapter 9).

24   Pull the parking brake lever up slowly all the way and count the notches (or clicks) through the whole lever travel. It should fall within the range listed in the specification table. If not, tighten or loosen the adjusting nut on the equalizer bar under the car. Make sure both cables are pulling evenly and that no kinks prevent the cables from traveling freely.

19   Brake pedal free play check

1   The first step in checking the brake pedal free play is to depress the brake pedal with the engine running and ensure that the pedal travels in a smooth arc with no hard spots or catches. The pedal should come to a firm point which will hold the car from moving and should not sink any further from this spot when held at a steady pressure.

2   The pedal height from the floor should be within 6.437 to 6.476

in (163.5 to 164.5 mm) when measured from the face of the pedal pad in a straight line to the floor of the pedal area. If the pedal height is incorrect, adjust it before going on (see Chapter 9).

3   Stop the engine and leave the car in gear or in Park if automatic transmission equipped. Release the parking brake. Depress the brake pedal several times to relieve the pressure accumulated in the vacuum booster.

4   Press down on the pedal with the fingers until the initial resistance is felt. The amount of travel between this point of resistance and the initial pedal height when released is the correct pedal free play.

5   The brake pedal minimum clearance should also be inspected at this time. With the engine running, have someone step down hard on the brake pedal to the point of full application. Measure the distance from the face of the pedal to the floor while this position is held. The minimum distance under this condition should be more than 2.36 inches (60 mm) at 110 lbs (50 kg) of pressure. If the distance is less than this amount, adjust the rear brake shoe clearance as described in Chapter 9.

6   The brake vacuum booster can also be checked at this time. With the engine off, press on and off the brake pedal several times. The distance of travel should not change after the first few applications.

7   While holding the brake pedal in the full on position, start the engine. The pedal should sink a *slight* amount when the engine starts.

8   Again, while holding the brake pedal in the full on position, turn the engine off. Hold the pedal for about 30 seconds. The pedal shouldn't change position.

9   With the brake pedal released, start the engine and run it for about one minute. Turn the engine off and firmly apply the brake several times. The pedal travel should decrease a little each time the brake is applied.

20   Clutch pedal free play check and adjustment

1   With the clutch pedal released, measure the distance from the face of the pedal to the floor. It should be 6.65 in (169 mm)

2   Press down and release the clutch pedal several times to check its motion for lack of binding and smooth cable operation. Press on the pedal with the fingers to the point where resistance is felt. The distance between this point and the position of the pedal in its full release position is the clutch pedal free play. The specification for this distance is 0.08 to 1.1 in (2 to 28 mm).
mm).

3   If the free play is not within the specified amount the cable will have to be adjusted at the point it exits the firewall on the passenger side. Turning the adjustment nut clockwise increases the free play measurement while turning the adjustment nut counterclockwise decreases the free play. If the adjustment will not produce the proper free play, the cable has stretched beyond its useful limit and will have to be replaced. See Chapter 8 for this procedure.

21   Spark plug wiring inspection

1   The spark plug wires should be checked at the recommended intervals or whenever new spark plugs are installed.

2   The wires should be inspected one at a time to prevent mixing up the order which is essential for proper engine operation.

3   Disconnect the plug wire from the spark plug. A removal tool can be used for this, or you can grab the rubber boot, twist slightly and then pull the wire free. Do not pull on the wire itself, only on the rubber boot.

4   Inspect inside the boot for corrosion, which will look like a white, crusty powder. Some vehicles use a conductive white grease which should not be mistaken for corrosion.

5   Now push the wire and boot back onto the end of the spark plug. It should be a tight fit on the plug end. If not, remove the wires and use a pair of pliers to carefully crimp the metal connector inside the wire boot until the fit is secure.

6   Now using a clean rag, clean the wire its entire length. Remove all built-up dirt and grease. As this is done, inspect for burns, cracks or any other form of damage.

7   Disconnect the wire at the distributor (again, pulling and twisting only on the rubber boot). Check for corrosion and a tight fit in the same manner as the spark plug end.

8   Check the remaining spark plug wires in the same way, making sure they are securely fastened at the distributor and spark plug.

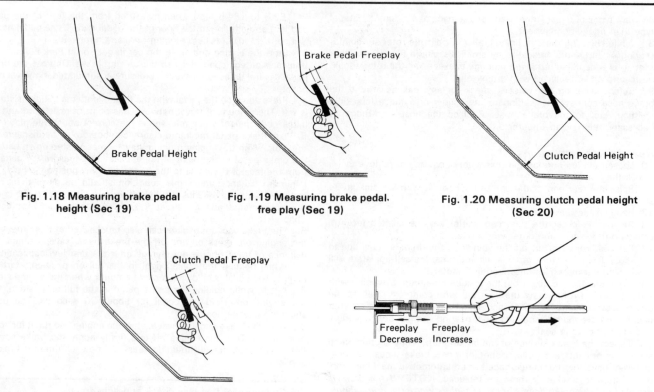

Fig. 1.18 Measuring brake pedal height (Sec 19)

Fig. 1.19 Measuring brake pedal. free play (Sec 19)

Fig. 1.20 Measuring clutch pedal height (Sec 20)

Fig. 1.21 Measuring clutch pedal free play (Sec 20)

Fig. 1.22 Adjusting the clutch pedal free play (Sec 20)

9 A visual check of the spark plug wires can also be made. In a darkened garage (make sure there is ventilation), start the engine and observe each plug wire. Be careful not to come into contact with any moving engine parts. If there is a break or fault in the wire, you will be able to see arcing or a small spark at the damaged area.

10 If it is decided the spark plug wires are in need of replacement, purchase a new set for your specific engine model. Wire sets can be purchased which are pre-cut to the proper size and with the rubber boots already installed. Remove and replace each wire individually to prevent mix-ups in the firing sequence.

22 Automatic transmission fluid change

1 The factory recommends changing the automatic transmission fluid only under severe conditions. However, it is more cost-effective in the long run to change the fluid at least every 30 000 miles (48 000 km). The cost of changing the fluid and filter is quite low when compared to the cost of major transmission work or an overhaul. If the decision is made not to change the fluid, it is very important to monitor its condition at periodic intervals to ascertain the quality of the lubricant. Smelling the fluid and feeling its quality from the dipstick are two important tests as is checking the color and transparency. Fluid should closely resemble fluid in a new can. If any deviation from similarity to new fluids is noted, a change of the fluid and filter is in order.

2 Thoroughly warm the transmission fluid by driving at least 15 minutes, preferably in city stop-and-go type driving. Backing the car up in reverse gear will also ensure the fluid is thoroughly warm and circulated throughout the entire transmission.

3 Elevate the car on a suitable lift or use four jack stands to maintain a level attitude of the vehicle (see jacking instructions at the front of the book). Place a large drain pan directly under the automatic transmission pan and remove the drain plug. Note the drain plug gasket.

4 Fully drain the transmission and replace the drain plug in the transmission pan. Remove the transmission oil pan retaining bolts by loosening all bolts a small amount and then withdrawing all but the corner fasteners. While supporting the pan with one hand, remove the remaining corner bolts and drop the pan from the transmission. Care should be taken in this step because the thin metal construction of the pan makes it susceptible to warpage.

5 Carefully check for any sediment in the bottom of the pan, paying close attention to the material trapped by the magnets located at each end of the pan sump. These magnets are placed in the pan to trap any metallic particles floating in the transmission fluid. If any sediment is found or if the magnets have trapped a significant amount of metallic particles, further work on the transmission may be necessary. An analysis by a speciality automatic transmission shop or dealership would be a wise decision if any material is present in the pan.

6 The transmission oil strainer can be found by looking up into the transmission from under the car. It appears as a rectangular pan with an oval slot and six retaining screws. Remove the retaining screws and pull the oil strainer and gasket from the transmission. Once again, check thoroughly for any sediment stuck in the screen mesh of the strainer.

7 Clean all gasket surfaces and replace the strainer and gasket. Insert the six screws finger-tight and in small increments, with a diagonal pattern, torque them to a final setting of 35 to 60 in-lb (0.4 to 0.7 kg/m). Clean the pan and make sure the magnets are repositioned at either end of the sump.

8 Glue a new gasket to the pan and put it back on the transmission with the corner bolts. Draw them up finger-tight and insert the rest of the bolts. Tighten the bolts in small increments all the way around the pan until a final reading of 53 to 78 in-lb (0.6 to 0.9 kg/m) is obtained. Be careful not to overtighten, as the pan is easily deformed and leakage will result. Retorque the drain plug and use a new drain plug gasket.

9 Refill the transmission through the dipstick tube (using a long funnel) with the proper fluid and amount shown in the front of this Chapter.

10 Run the engine, check for leaks, shift the transmission several times throughout the entire range and recheck the fluid level before attempting to drive the car. After making sure the fluid is filled to the proper height and that all gaskets are leak free, road test the car as described in the fluid levels section at the front of this Chapter. Again, recheck the fluid level, as air pockets sometimes develop when performing this maintenance operation.

23 Transmission (manual) and/or differential – fluid change

1 The transmission and differential use the same fluid and are drained and filled in the same way in manual transmission equipped

23.4a Manual transaxle drain plugs (arrows)

23.4b Removing the drain plug for the differential (automatic transmission-equipped cars)

cars. The differential only, is drained and filled according to the following procedure on automatic transmission equipped cars. Do not confuse the two, as serious damage can result from filling the automatic transmission with manual transmission (hypoid) gear oil or the reverse.

2   Drive the car for at least 15 minutes in city-type stop-and-go traffic. Use all of the gears including reverse to ensure the oil is sufficiently warm to drain completely.

3   Raise the car to a level position using either a suitable lift or four stands (see jacking instructions in the front of this book).

4   Remove all three drain plugs (manual transmission equipped cars) or just the differential drain plug (automatic equipped cars) (photos). Allow the oil to drain completely. Remove the two filler plugs (manual) or one filler plug (automatic).

5   After all of the oil has drained, replace and re-torque the differential drain plug. Replace and re-torque the drain plug on the manual transmission and replace but leave loose the extension housing drain plug.

6   Using the proper grade and type of hypoid gear oil, refill the differential (all cars) and the transmission (manual transmission equipped cars only) until fluid runs out of the filler hole(s).

7   Tighten the extension housing drain plug to the proper torque and replace the two filler plugs (manual) or plug (automatic) to the torque setting listed in the front of the Chapter.

24 Driveaxles and axle boots – check

1   Raise the front of the car and support it on jack stands according to the instructions given in the front of the book. Make sure the parking brake is engaged and the transmission is in the neutral position.

2   Carefully inspect the driveaxles for any signs of damage or wear caused by road hazards. Rotate the wheel on each side, checking for signs of looseness or unevenness due to a bent axle or worn parts.

3   Pay particular attention in this inspection procedure to the driveaxle boots, watching for clamp looseness, grease leakage or damage. As is the car in any front wheel drive car, the condition of these boots is critical, as they contain the necessary lubricant as well as keeping wear-producing dirt out. If any problem is noted, refer to Chapter 8 for more detailed inspection and checking procedures.

25 Wheel bearings – servicing

1   Due to the complexity of the procedure involved in repacking the front wheel bearings, it is not included in this Section. You will find instructions in Chapter 11, Section 9.

2   Rear wheel bearings can be repacked according to the factory recommended procedure. However, a special spring scale with a range of 0 to 3 lb (0 to 1.361 Kg) will be needed. A hand held fish scale will usually work.

3   Remove the rear wheels after raising the rear of the car according

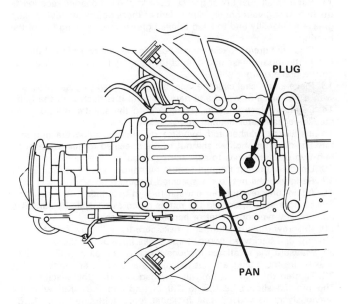

Fig. 1.23 Automatic transmission pan and drain plug location (Sec 22)

PLUG

PAN

Fig. 1.24 Torquing the fasteners for automatic transmission oil strainer (Sec 22)

to the jacking instructions found at the front of this book. Release the parking brake.

4   Remove in order the hub cover, cotter key, castellated locknut, spindle nut, washer, and outer wheel bearing.

5   Remove the brake drum and wipe out the brake dust carefully (do not breathe the asbestos dust).

6   Use a screwdriver or pry bar to pry out the seal on the rear of the the hub. Note how it is installed. The inner bearing can now be removed from the hub.

7   Use clean parts solvent to remove all traces of the old grease from the bearings and spindle. Do not wash the hub in solvent, as the brake drum will transfer the solvent to the brake shoes, lowering their effectiveness. Carefully clean out the inner hub and race area with rags. Be careful not to spread grease or solvent onto the brake drums. Allow the parts to air dry.

8   Carefully inspect the bearings for cracks, heat discoloration, bent rollers, etc. Check the bearing races inside the hub for cracks, scoring or uneven surfaces. If the bearing races are in need of replacement, the job is best left to a repair shop which can press the new races into position.

9   Use an approved high temperature wheel bearing grease to pack the bearings. Work the grease fully into the bearings, forcing the grease between the rollers, cone and cage.

10   Apply a thin coat of grease to the spindle at the outer bearing seat, inner bearing seat, shoulder and seal seat.

11   Put a small quantity of grease inboard at each bearing race inside the hub. Using your finger, form a dam at these points to provide extra grease availability and to keep thinned grease from flowing out of the bearing.

12   Place the grease-packed inner bearing into the rear of the hub and put a little more grease outboard of the bearing. Do not get any grease on the brake drum.

13   Place a new seal over the inner bearing and tap the seal into place with a flat piece of wood and hammer until it is flush with the hub.

14   Carefully place the hub assembly onto the spindle and push the grease-packed outer bearing into position.

15   Install the washer and spindle nut. While rotating the hub in a forward direction, tighten the nut to the specified torque. Rotate the hub two or three times to seat the bearings.

16   Unscrew the nut enough to turn by hand.

17   Retighten the nut to the specified torque.

18   Again, unscrew the nut enough to turn by hand.

19   Using a socket, tighten the nut as much as possible by hand. Do not use any type of ratchet or handle on the socket.

20   Unscrew the nut $\frac{1}{2}$ turn and make sure there is play. Turn the hub forward and backward two or three times in each direction.

21   Measure the rotational frictional force of the oil seal (Fig. 1.27). Make sure the brakes are not touching the drum at any time.

22   Tighten the hub nut until the preload is within the specification. The preload should be 0.8 to 1.9 lb (0.35 to 0.87 Kg) with the previously measured oil seal frictional force subtracted (Fig. 1.28). Make sure the hub turns smoothly and the bearings are tight.

23   Replace the castellated locknut, install a new cotter key and reinstall the hub cover.

24   Adjust the rear brakes through the adjuster slot in the rear backing plate until the shoes almost touch the drums. See Chapter 9, Section 9.

25   Install the wheels, and lower the car to the ground. Tighten the wheel lug nuts to the specified torque.

26   Pump the brakes several times to ensure that a good pedal is felt before attempting to drive the car.

26 Valve clearance adjustment

1   The valve adjustment is one of the most critical maintenance items of an internal combustion engine. It must be done with care and accuracy because misadjusted valves can result in serious damage to the inside of the engine (burning of valves or accelerated wear on valve gear) as well as poor running and fuel economy losses. Read through this Section and understand thoroughly the entire procedure before attempting this job. If you do not think your skills are up to the level required, it would be best to let a professional mechanic handle this task.

2   Run the engine until normal operating temperature is reached. Be

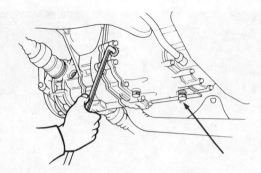

Fig. 1.25 Filling the manual transaxle (Sec 23)

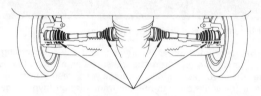

Fig. 1.26 Location of the driveaxle boots (arrows) (Sec 24)

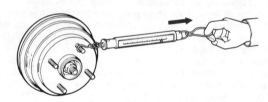

Fig. 1.27 Checking the frictional force of the wheel bearing oil seal (Sec 25)

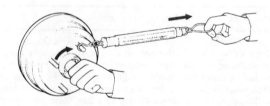

Fig. 1.28 Measuring the wheel bearing preload (Sec 25)

careful when working on the engine as many of the parts will be hot and could cause serious injury.

3   With the engine stopped, remove the air cleaner assembly (see Section 27) and the throttle cable. Remove both vent hoses from the top of the valve cover and anchor them out of the way without kinking them. Remove the single top camshaft belt cover bolt and the clamp held beneath it. Note the location of all of these components so they can be replaced properly. Remove the spark plug wires and mark them if there is any doubt which cylinder they belong to. Remove the spark plugs.

4   Remove the valve cover after removing the two top bolts retaining it. You may have to angle the cover or turn it slightly but have patience so as not to pull any hoses or wiring out of their respective sockets.

5   Turn the engine to the compression stroke of the number one cylinder. This can be verified by checking the timing mark on the

26.7 Adjusting valve clearances

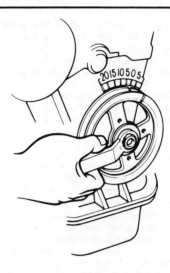

Fig. 1.29 Rotating the crankshaft with the pulley bolt (Sec 26)

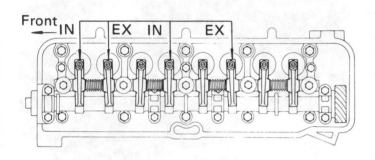

Fig. 1.30 Location of the four valves to be adjusted in the first sequence (Sec 26)

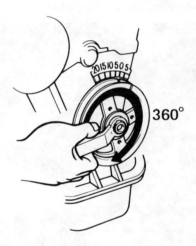

Fig. 1.31 Rotating the crankshaft 360° for second sequence of valve adjustment (Sec 26)

crankshaft in relation to the timing scale, and by ensuring that both valves of the number 1 cylinder have play. This can be checked by grasping the rocker arm over the first two valves and moving them up and down. A slight clearance should be felt and both valves should be in their released (or up) position. The engine can be turned by rotating it with the bolt on the front of the crankshaft pulley.

6   Four of the engine's eight valves can now be adjusted. Both valves of number 1 cylinder, the intake valve of number 2 cylinder, and the exhaust valve of number 3 cylinder. Check that all of these valves have a little play in them before adjustment (Fig. 1.30).

7   Attempt to slide the correct feeler gauge under the first valve (note that the intake and exhaust valves have different clearances). If the gauge slides through with no drag or if it won't fit at all, the valve will have to be adjusted. To adjust the valve, loosen the locknut (photo). Next, turn the adjuster with a correct size feeler gauge in place. Carefully tighten the screw (if the valve was too tight you may have to back the adjustment screw off in order to insert the feeler gauge) until you can feel a slight drag on the feeler gauge as it is withdrawn from between the stem and adjusting screw.

8   Hold the adjusting screw with the screwdriver to keep it from turning and tighten the locknut. Recheck the clearance to make sure it hasn't changed.

9   Repeat the procedure to adjust the remaining three valves of this sequence.

10 Rotate the crankshaft exactly 360° (one full revolution). The timing mark on the crankshaft will again line up at top-dead-center. Confirm that the proper four remaining valves have clearance by grasping the rocker tips and feeling for play. Adjust these remaining four valves using the same method listed in step 8 above.

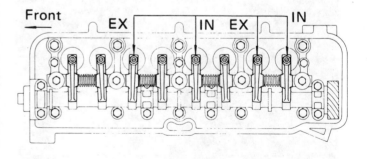

Fig. 1.32 Location of the four valves to be adjusted in the second sequence (Sec 26)

11 Reinstall the valve cover and use a new valve cover gasket. Reinstall the spark plugs, wires, cam belt cover top bolt, and both vent hoses.

12 Start and run the engine. It should run smoothly with no unusual noises. If the engine runs rough you may have to recheck the valve clearance for one that is too tight. (First check for any disconnected vacuum hoses or improperly placed spark plug cables). If a metallic tapping noise is present, a valve may be too loose and again will have to be rechecked. Also check for oil leakage between the valve cover and cylinder head.

27 Carburetor and choke system – inspection

Carburetor check

1   The first step in inspection of the carburetor is the removal of the air cleaner. The instructions provided cover cars marketed in the US. If the car you are working on was originally marketed in Canada or general countries, certain steps may be omitted due to the lack of emissions controls normally found on US cars.

2   Remove the wing nut in the center of the top cover. Remove the clamp and rubber air intake hose from the air cleaner snorkel. Remove the clamp and flexible 'stove pipe' hose from the bottom of the air cleaner snorkel (photo). Be careful in this step if the engine is warm as

this hose is used to duct hot air from the exhaust manifold area up to the carburetor.

3   Remove the clamp and hose from the front area of the air cleaner (near the snorkel) which leads to the air suction system (49-state cars) or to the air control valve (California cars). This will usually be a rubber hose approximately one inch in diameter which leads downward and to the rear of the engine (photo).

4   Remove the hose from the bottom of the air cleaner which leads to the air injection pump (California cars only).

5   Remove the crankcase vent hose from the air cleaner (hose closest to the firewall if the car is equipped with two hoses). Remove the two bolts holding the air cleaner tabs to the valve cover (photo).

6   Lift the air cleaner assembly up on the side closest to the valve cover and remove the small vacuum line which feeds the HIC valve (white plastic cylindrical valve on the underside of the air cleaner) (photo).

7   Lift the air cleaner assembly straight up and the rest of the way off the carburetor. **Note:** *Make sure that the inlet gasket either remains with the air cleaner or stays on the inlet flange of the carburetor. It sometimes can come loose and fall into the engine or carburetor intake as the air cleaner is removed.*

8   Once the air cleaner has been removed, a visible inspection of the carburetor is possible. The main item to look for is decaying and/or leaking hoses. It is not necessary to remove any hoses to check their condition but flexing them with the fingers will usually reveal tell-tale

27.2 Removing hot air inlet hose and clamp from air cleaner snorkel

27.3 Removing air suction (or air control valve) hose from air cleaner

27.5 Removing the air cleaner hold-down bolts

27.6 Removing the vacuum line from the HIC valve

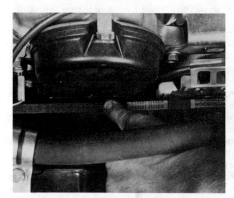

28.4 Checking the drivebelt deflection

28.6 Loosening alternator bolts prior to drive-belt adjustment

28.7 Moving alternator to adjust drivebelt tension

cracks or splits. Check the carburetor body itself for any signs of leakage and if a great deal of residue (either oil or gasoline) has built up on the body and linkages, cleaning of the entire area with a commercially available carburetor cleaner is advised. If a leak is suspected but not readily identifiable, clean the entire area and then prepare to run the car without the air cleaner. **Note:** *Do not drive the car in this condition as the engine is heavily dependent on filtered air for its continued service. This is a test procedure and should be done only long enough to pinpoint any leaks which may occur under pressure or with the engine running.* Before starting the engine, plug the small vacuum hose which leads to the HIC valve and make sure that the other hoses which have been disconnected are out of the way of the belts and pulleys.

9   Check the accelerator pump linkages and the cable which operates the throttle. A helper working the throttle from the driver's position will allow close observation of the moving parts. Do this procedure with the engine off. Have an assistant slowly depress the accelerator to its full travel then allow it to return while observing the cable and attending moving parts. Lubricating these parts can be accomplished at the same time. Use a lightweight penetrating-type oil for the cable.

10   If any major leaks or problems are noticed in the carburetor, refer to Chapter 4 for further information. **Note:** *Always use caution to see that nothing is dropped or lost into the carburetor air intake, as it will eventually end up in the engine and cause serious damage.*

Choke system check

11   The choke only operates when the engine is cold, so this check can be performed before the vehicle has been started for the day.

12   The air cleaner need not be removed for this check, but the top plate must be opened up. To take the top plate off, remove the wing nut and unclamp the four clamp levers around the perimeter of the air cleaner assembly. Place the top plate and wing nut aside, out of the way of moving engine components.

13   Look at the top of the carburetor at the center of the air cleaner housing. You will notice a flat plate at the carburetor opening.

14   Have an assistant press the accelerator pedal to the floor. The plate should close fully. Start the engine while you observe the plate at the carburetor. Do not position your face directly over the carburetor, as the engine could backfire, causing serious burns. When the engine starts, the choke plate should open slightly.

15   Allow the engine to continue running at an idle speed. As the engine warms up to operating temperature, the plate should slowly open, allowing more air to enter through the top of the carburetor.

16   After a few minutes, the choke plate should be fully open to the vertical position.

17   You will notice that the engine speed corresponds with the plate opening. With the plate fully closed, the engine should run at a fast idle speed. As the plate opens, the engine speed will decrease.

18   If during the above checks a fault is detected, refer to Chapter 4 for specific information on adjusting and servicing the choke components.

28 Drivebelts – inspection and adjustment

1   The drivebelts, or V-belts as they are sometimes called, at the

front of the engine play an important role in the overall operation of the car and its components. Due to their function and material make-up, the belts are prone to failure after a period of time and should be inspected and adjusted periodically to prevent major engine damage.

2   The number of belts used on a particular car depends on the accessories installed. Drivebelts are used to turn: the alternator, air injection smog pump, water pump, and air conditioning compressor. Depending on the pulley arrangement, a single belt may be used for more than one of these ancillary components.

3   With the engine off, open the hood and locate the various belts at the front of the engine. Using your fingers (and a flashlight if necessary) move along the belts checking for cracks or separation. Also check for fraying and for glazing which gives the belt a shiny appearance. Both sides of the belts should be inspected, which means you will have to twist the belt to check the underside.

4   The tension of each belt is checked by pushing on the belt at a distance halfway between the pulleys. Push firmly with your thumb and see how much the belt moves downward (deflects) (photo). A rule of thumb, so to speak, is that if the distance (pulley center to pulley center) is between 7 inches and 11 inches the belt should deflect $\frac{1}{4}$ inch. If the belt is longer and travels between pulleys spaced 12 inches to 16 inches apart, the belt should deflect $\frac{1}{2}$ in.

5   If it is found necessary to adjust the belt tension, either to make the belt tighter or looser, this is done by moving the belt-driven accessory on its bracket.

6   For each component there will be an adjustment or strap bolt and a pivot bolt. Both bolts must be loosened slightly to enable you to move the component (photo).

7   After the two bolts have been loosened, move the component away from the engine (to tighten the belt) or toward the engine (to loosen the belt) (photo). Hold the accessory in this position and check the belt tension. If it is correct, tighten the two bolts until snug, then recheck the tension. If it is alright, fully tighten the two bolts.

8   It will often be necessary to use some sort of pry bar to move the accessory while the belt is adjusted. If this must be done to gain the proper leverage, be very careful not to damage the component being moved, or the part being pried against.

29 Battery – cleaning, checking and charging

1   Certain precautions must be followed when checking or servicing the battery. Hydrogen gas, which is highly flammable, is always present in the battery cells so keep lighted tobacco or any other open flames away from the battery. The electrolyte inside the battery is actually diluted sulfuric acid, which can be hazardous to your skin and cause damage if splashed in the eyes. It will also ruin clothes and painted surfaces. Also, see *Safety first* near the front of this manual.

2   Check the battery case for cracks and evidence of leakage.

3   To check the electrolyte level in the battery, see Section 2 of this Chapter.

4   Periodically check the specific gravity of the electrolyte with a hydrometer. This is especially important during cold weather. If the reading is below the specification, the battery should be recharged.

5   Check the tightness of the battery terminals to ensure good electrical connections. The terminals can be cleaned with a stiff wire brush. Corrosion can be kept to a minimum by applying a layer of

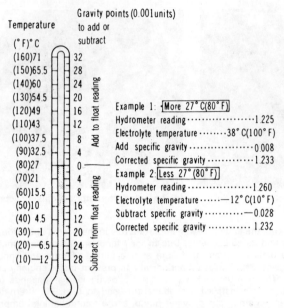

**Fig. 1.33 Hydrometer reading temperature correction chart
(Sec 29)**

Example 1: More 27° C(80° F)
Hydrometer reading · · · · · · · · · · · · · · · · · 1.225
Electrolyte temperature · · · · · · · 38° C(100° F)
Add specific gravity · · · · · · · · · · · · · · · · 0.008
Corrected specific gravity · · · · · · · · · · 1.233

Example 2: Less 27° (80° F)
Hydrometer reading · · · · · · · · · · · · · · · · · 1.260
Electrolyte temperature · · · · · · −12° C(10° F)
Subtract specific gravity · · · · · · · · · · · −0.028
Corrected specific gravity · · · · · · · · · · · 1.232

petroleum jelly or grease to the terminal and cable connectors after they are assembled.

6   Inspect the entire length of the battery cables for corrosion, cracks and frayed conductors.

7   Check that the rubber protector over the positive terminal is not torn or missing. It should completely cover the terminal.

8   Make sure that the battery is securely mounted.

9   The battery case and caps should be kept clean and dry. If corrosion is evident, clean the battery by referring to the following instructions in this Section.

10 If the vehicle is not being used for an extended period, disconnect the battery cables and have it charged approximately every six weeks.

11 Corrosion on the battery hold down components and inner fender panels can be removed by washing with a solution of water and baking soda. Once the area has been thoroughly cleaned, rinse it with clear water.

12 Corrosion on the battery case and terminals can also be removed with a solution of water and baking soda and a stiff brush. Be careful not to get any of the solution in the battery cells.

13 As was mentioned before, if the battery's specific gravity is below the specified amount, the battery must be recharged.

14 If the battery is to remain in the vehicle during charging, disconnect the cables from the battery to prevent damage to the electrical system.

15 When batteries are being charged, hydrogen gas, which is very explosive and flammable is produced. Do not smoke or allow an open flame near a charging or a recently charged battery. Also, do not plug in the battery charger until the connections have been made at the battery posts.

16 The average time necessary to charge a battery at the normal rate is from 12 to 16 hours (sometimes longer). Always charge the battery slowly. A quick charge or boost charge is hard on a battery and will shorten its life. Use a battery charger that is rated at no more than 3½ amperes.

17 Remove all of the vent caps and cover the vent holes with a clean cloth to prevent the spattering of electrolyte. Hook the battery charger leads to the battery posts (positive to positive, negative to negative), then plug in the charger. Make sure it is set at 12 volts if it has a selector switch.

18 Watch the battery closely during charging to make sure that it does not overheat.

19 The battery can be considered fully charged when it is gassing freely and there is no increase in specific gravity during three successive readings taken at hourly intervals.

20 Overheating of the battery during charging at normal charging rates, excessive gassing and continual low specific gravity readings are an indication that the battery should be replaced with a new one.

30 Cylinder compression check

1   A compression check will tell you what mechanical condition the engine is in. Specifically, it can tell you if the compression is down due to leakage caused by worn piston rings, defective valves and seats or a blown head gasket.

2   Begin by cleaning the area around the spark plugs before you remove them. This will keep dirt from falling into the cylinders while you are performing the compression test.

3   Remove the coil high-tension lead from the distributor and ground it on the engine block. Block the throttle and choke valves wide open.

4   With the compression gauge in the number one cylinder's spark plug hole, crank the engine over at least four compression strokes and observe the gauge (the compression should build up quickly in a healthy engine). Low compression on the first stroke, followed by gradually increasing pressure on successive strokes, indicates worn piston rings. A low compression reading on the first stroke, which does not build up during successive strokes, indicates leaking valves or a defective head gasket. Record the highest gauge reading obtained.

5   Repeat the procedure for the remaining cylinders and compare the results to the specifications. Compression readings 10% above or below the specified amount can be considered normal.

6   Pour a couple of teaspoons of engine oil (a squirt can works great for this) into each cylinder, through the spark plug hole, and repeat the test.

7   If the compression increases after the oil is added, the piston rings are definitely worn. If the compression does not increase significantly, the leakage is occurring at the valves or head gasket.

8   If two adjacent cylinders have equally low compression, there is a strong possibility that the head gasket between them is blown. The appearance of coolant in the combustion chambers or the crankcase would verify this condition.

9   If the compression is higher than normal, the combustion chambers are probably coated with carbon deposits. If that is the case, the cylinder head should be removed and decarbonized.

10 If compression is way down, or varies greatly between cylinders, it would be a good idea to have a 'leak-down' test performed by a reputable automotive repair shop. This test will pinpoint exactly where the leakage is occuring and how severe it is.

Chapter 2 Engine

Contents

Specifications

General

Type	In-line, liquid-cooled, 4-cylinder, overhead-cam. Aluminium head with case iron block.
Displacement	88.6 cu in (1452 cc)
Bore and stroke	3.05 x 3.03 in (77.5 x 77.0 mm)
Compression ratio	
3A and 3A-C engine	9.0 to 1
1A-C engine	8.7 to 1
Compression pressure	128 to 177 psi (9.0 to 12.5 kg/cm^2)

Engine block

Cylinder bore	
Diameter	3.0512 to 3.0524 in (77.50 to 77.53 mm)
Taper limit	0.0008 in (0.02 mm)
Out-of-round limit	0.0008 in (0.02 mm)
Deck warpage limit	0.002 in (0.05 mm)

Pistons and rings

Piston diameter	3.0468 to 3.0480 in (77.39 to 77.42 mm)
Piston oversizes available	+0.019, 0.029, 0.039 in (+0.50, 0.75, 1.00 mm)
Piston-to-cylinder bore clearance	0.0039 to 0.0047 in (0.10 to 0.12 mm)
Piston pin installation temp	68°F (20°C)
Piston ring-to-groove clearance	
Top ring	0.0016 to 0.0031 in (0.04 to 0.08 mm)
2nd ring	0.0012 to 0.0028 in (0.03 to 0.07 mm)
Piston ring end gap (Riken rings)	
Top ring	0.0079 to 0.0138 in (0.20 to 0.35 mm)
2nd ring	0.0059 to 0.0118 in (0.15 to 0.30 mm)
Oil ring	0.0118 to 0.0354 in (0.30 to 0.90 mm)

Piston ring end gap (TP rings)
    Top ring .... 0.0079 to 0.0157 in (0.20 to 0.40 mm)
    2nd ring .... 0.0059 to 0.0138 in (0.15 to 0.35 mm)
    Oil ring .... 0.0039 to 0.0236 in (0.10 to 0.60 mm)

Crankshaft and flywheel

Crankshaft end play .... 0.0008 to 0.0073 in (0.02 to 0.185 mm)
    Main journal diameter .... 1.8892 to 1.8898 in (47.985 to 48.000 mm)
    Taper limit .... 0.0008 in (0.02 mm)
    Out-of-round limit .... 0.0008 in (0.02 mm)
Main bearing oil clearance
    Standard .... 0.0005 to 0.0019 in (0.012 to 0.049 mm)
    Service limit .... 0.0031 in (0.08 mm)
Connecting rod journal
    Diameter .... 1.5742 to 1.5748 in (39.985 to 40.000 mm)
    Taper limit .... 0.0008 in (0.02 mm)
    Out-of-round limit .... 0.0008 in (0.02 mm)
Connecting rod bearing oil clearance
    Standard .... 0.0008 to 0.0020 in (0.020 to 0.051 mm)
    Service limit .... 0.0031 in (0.08 mm)
Connecting rod side clearance .... 0.0059 to 0.0098 in (0.15 to 0.25 mm)
Flywheel clutch face runout limit .... 0.0039 in (0.10 mm)

Camshaft

Bearing journal diameter .... 1.1015 to 1.1022 in (27.979 to 27.995 mm)
Bearing oil clearance
    Standard .... 0.0015 to 0.0029 in (0.037 to 0.073 mm)
    Service limit .... 0.004 in (0.1 mm)
Lobe height (USA – 4-speed M/T only)
    Standard (Intake and exhaust) .... 1.5366 to 1.5530 in (39.03 to 39.04 mm)
    Service limit (Intake and exhaust) .... 1.5248 in (38.73 mm)
Lobe height (all others)
    Standard (Intake and exhaust) .... 1.5526 to 1.5530 in (39.44 to 39.45 mm)
    Service limit (Intake and exhaust) .... 1.5409 in (39.14 mm)
Runout limit .... 0.0024 in (0.06 mm)
End play
    Standard .... 0.0031 to 0.0071 in (0.08 to 0.18 mm)
    Service limit .... 0.0098 in (0.25 mm)

Cylinder head and valve train

Head warpage limit .... 0.0020 in (0.05 mm)
Manifold warpage limit .... 0.012 in (0.3 mm)
Valve seat angle .... 45°
Valve seat width (Intake and exhaust) .... 0.047 to 0.063 in (1.2 to 1.6 mm)
Valve seat refacing angle .... 30°, 45°, 60°
Valve face angle .... 44.5°
Valve overall length (standard)
    Intake .... 4.2079 in (106.88 mm)
    Exhaust .... 4.2039 in (106.78 mm)
Valve overall length (limit)
    Intake .... 4.1882 in (106.38 mm)
    Exhaust .... 4.1842 in (106.28 mm)
Valve stem diameter
    Intake .... 0.2744 to 0.2750 in (6.970 to 6.985 mm)
    Exhaust .... 0.2742 to 0.2748 in (6.965 to 6.980 mm)
Valve guide diameter .... 0.2760 to 0.2768 in (7.01 to 7.03 mm)
Valve stem-to-guide clearance
    Intake:
        Standard .... 0.0010 to 0.0024 in (0.025 to 0.060 mm)
        Service limit .... 0.0031 in (0.08 mm)
    Exhaust:
        Standard .... 0.0012 to 0.0026 in (0.030 to 0.065 mm)
        Service limit .... 0.0039 in (0.10 mm)
Valve spring free length (Intake and exhaust) .... 1.756 in (44.6 mm)
Valve spring installed height (Intake and exhaust) .... 1.520 in (38.6 mm)
Valve spring out-of-square limit .... 0.079 in (2.0 mm)
Valve spring pressure (lbs/in; kg/mm)
    Standard .... 52.0 at 1.520 in (23.6 at 38.6 mm)
    Service limit .... 46.3 at 1.520 in (21.0 at 38.6 mm)
Valve clearance (hot)
    Intake .... 0.0079 in (0.20 mm)
    Exhaust .... 0.0118 in (0.30 mm)
Rocker arm-to-shaft oil clearance
    Standard .... 0.0004 to 0.0019 in (0.010 to 0.048 mm)
    Limit .... 0.0024 in (0.06 mm)

Oil pump

Outer rotor-to-housing clearance	0.0023 to 0.0122 in (0.058 to 0.310 mm)
Inner rotor-to-housing clearance	0.0040 to 0.0100 in (0.102 to 0.253 mm)
Rotor end clearance	0.0014 to 0.0033 in (0.035 to 0.085 mm)
Gear-to-housing clearance	0.0039 to 0.0075 in (0.100 to 0.191 mm)

Torque specifications

	ft-lb	m-kg
Cylinder head retaining bolt	40 to 47	(5.4 to 6.6)
Rocker arm shaft retaining bolt	17 to 19	(2.3 to 2.7)
Camshaft bearing cap retaining bolts	8 to 10	(1.1 to 1.5)
Manifold-to-cylinder head retaining bolts	15 to 21	(2.0 to 3.0)
Timing belt idler retaining bolt	22 to 32	(3.0 to 4.5)
Oil pump retaining bolts	13 to 18	(1.75 to 2.60)
Oil strainer-to-oil pump retaining nuts	14 to 18	(1.75 to 2.60)
Oil strainer support bracket-to-block retaining bolts	6 to 8	(0.8 to 1.1)
Oil pan-to-block retaining bolts and nuts	3 to 3.5	(0.4 to 0.5)
Crankshaft bearing cap retaining bolts	40 to 47	(5.4 to 6.6)
Camshaft timing belt pulley retaining bolt	29 to 39	(4.0 to 5.5)
Crankshaft pulley retaining bolt	80 to 94	(11.0 to 13.0)
Flywheel-to-crankshaft retaining bolts	55 to 61	(7.5 to 8.5)
Distributor drive gear-to-camshaft retaining bolt	20 to 23	(2.7 to 3.3)
Connecting rod cap-to-connecting rod retaining nuts	26 to 32	(3.5 to 4.5)

1 General description

Tercels are equipped with a 4-cylinder, overhead camshaft, cast iron block engine of 88.6 cubic inch (1452 cc) displacement. The cylinder head is made of aluminium alloy with pressed-in valve guides and seats.

The camshaft is driven by a toothed rubber belt running on two sprockets with a spring-loaded tensioner. Rocker arms operate directly from the camshaft on their own shaft and activate the valves directly. Valve adjustment is handled through threaded adjusters in the rocker arms.

The crankshaft is supported by five main bearings and drives the oil pump directly off the front of the shaft. The engine is mounted front to rear (conventionally) and it drives the front wheels through the transaxle assembly.

The engine comes in 1A-C, 3A-C and 3A versions which vary according to carburetion, camshaft specifications, ignition systems and emission controls. The basic engine assembly is the same for all of these versions. Engine application depends on the year manufactured and geographic location where the vehicle was intended to be sold.

2 Repair operations possible with the engine in the vehicle

1   Many major repair operations can be accomplished without removing the engine from the vehicle.
2   It is a very good idea to clean the engine compartment and the exterior of the engine with some type of pressure washer before any work is begun. A clean engine will make the job easier and will prevent the possibility of getting dirt into internal areas of the engine.
3   Remove the hood and cover the fenders to provide as much working room as possible and to prevent damage to the painted surfaces.
4   If oil or coolant leaks develop, indicating a need for gasket or seal replacement, the repairs can generally be made with the engine in the vehicle. The cylinder head gasket, intake and exhaust manifold gaskets, timing belt case gaskets and the front and rear crankshaft oil seals are accessible with the engine in place. In the case of the rear crankshaft oil seal, the transaxle. the clutch components and the flywheel must be removed first.
5   Exterior engine components, such as the starter motor, the alternator, the distributor, the fuel pump and the carburetor, as well as the intake and exhaust manifolds, are easily removed for repair with the engine in place.
6   Since the cylinder head can be removed without pulling the engine, valve servicing can also be accomplished with the engine in the vehicle.
7   Repairs to or inspection of the camshaft, the timing belt assembly, rocker shaft and arms and the oil pump are all possible with the engine in place.

3 Engine removal

Note: *If equipped with air conditioning, have the system de-pressurized by a professional.*
1   Disconnect the windshield washer supply hose.
2   Scribe a mark around the hood hinge retaining bolts to maintain the adjustment during installation. Remove the four hood retaining bolts. A helper would be beneficial in this process.
3   Remove the hood.
4   Disconnect the negative cable from the battery.
5   Drain the cooling system at the two drain points (Chapter 1).
6   Remove the vacuum brake booster hose bracket from the firewall. Note that the ground strap is also attached to this same connection (photo).
7   Disconnect the vacuum brake booster hose from the brake booster assembly.
8   Disconnect the distributor electrical harness at the connector.
9   Disconnect the secondary wiring from the spark plugs, distributor and the coil. Remove the distributor cap along with the secondary wiring.
10 Disconnect the connectors from the temperature switches (two) located on the front of the engine and the inlet pipe. Remove this loom from the left side of the engine and place it out of the way.
11 Remove the small electrical ground lead secured by the bolt and clamp assembly located behind the alternator on the engine block.
12 Remove the bolt securing the negative battery cable to the block.
13 Disconnect the clutch cable (if the car is equipped with a manual

3.6 Removing the brake booster hose and ground strap

transmission) and remove it from the bellhousing (refer to Chapter 8).

14 Disconnect the clip connector from the oil pressure switch located under the alternator.

15 Disconnect the air conditioning compressor clutch switch connector located to the rear of the alternator (if so equipped).

16 Unplug the two connectors at the rear of the alternator.

17 Remove the alternator (Chapter 5).

18 Release the tension on the air conditioning idler pulley (if so equipped) and remove the drive belt. Remove the four compressor through-bolts from the bracket, then move the compressor and the compressor sub-bracket to the side and remove the five compressor mounting bolts. Note the bolt on the bottom. Remove the air conditioning compressor mounting bracket. Secure the air conditioning compressor off to the side to prevent damage.

19 Loosen the tension and remove the air pump drive belt (if so equipped).

20 Remove the alternator drive belt.

21 Remove the air cleaner (see description in Chapter 1).

22 Remove the radiator (see description in Chapter 3).

23 Remove the cold air intake snorkel.

24 Remove the emissions control system hoses as necessary (refer to Chapter 6 for information and diagram).

25 Disconnect the emissions control systems electric connectors. Disconnect the oxygen sensor electrical harness located directly below the air suction valve (if so equipped).

26 Disconnect the hose between the air injection pump and the air suction valve (if so equipped).

27 Disconnect the heater outlet hose from the heater outlet pipe (note the location directly beneath the fuel pump).

Caution: *Before performing the next step observe all precautions pertaining to gasoline as the fuel lines will probably leak gasoline under pressure.*

28 Remove the two fuel lines from the top of the fuel pump and plug them.

29 Remove the heater outlet hose (note this is the hose with the T-fitting and control valve on it).

30 Disconnect the throttle cable. Remove it and set it off to the side, out of the way.

31 Remove the forward facing 10 mm bolt from the clutch cover (refer to Chapters 7 and 8 for location information).

Note: *If the car is equipped with automatic transmission, remove the transmission throttle linkage and the transmission cooler lines as described in Chapter 7. Remove the transmission cooler line pipe clamp.*

32 Raise the vehicle as described in Chapter 1 and support it securely on jackstands.

33 Wrap the driveshaft boots with shop towels.

34 Drain engine oil.

35 Remove the front exhaust pipe (refer to Chapter 4).

36 Remove the engine stiffener plates (refer to Chapter 7).

37 Disconnect the ground strap from the driver's side of the bellhousing.

38 Disconnect the engine shock absorber link bolt.

39 Disconnect the engine mount lower nuts.

40 Remove the starter (Chapter 5).

41 Support the transaxle assembly with a jack.

42 Attach an engine sling or chain to the hooks provided on the corners of the engine. Attach the sling or chain to an approved engine hoisting device. Mobile engine lifts are preferred.

43 Remove the torque converter cover and the transmission output line (automatic transmission equipped vehicles only).

44 Remove the torque converter housing bolts (automatic transmission equipped vehicles only).

45 Raise the engine high enough to clear the motor mount studs.

46 Support the transaxle assembly with a jack or other suitable device.

Note: *Caution should be used in the following steps to ensure the proper removal of the engine and to prevent damage to the transmission input connector.*

47 Remove the two remaining bellhousing bolts. Carefully separate the engine from the bellhousing. **Caution:** *Do not lift the engine until the engine and bellhousing are separated by at least 2 to 5 inches. This prevents the input shaft of the transmission from being damaged by upward force being applied to it.*

48 If the engine and bellhousing cannot be separated by jiggling motion, a soft faced pry bar may be used. Notice that the clutch will

3.49 Lifting the engine up and moving it forward to clear the transmission (note how the chain is attached)

come out with the engine on manual transmission equipped vehicles or that the torque converter will come out on automatic transmission equipped vehicles. Take care not to pry against either of these assemblies.

49 Once the engine has cleared the transmission input shaft, lifting may begin. It may be necessary to lift the engine a short distance and then pull it forward (clear of the vehicle's firewall) before it can be lifted directly out of the engine bay (photo). Be very careful at this point to hold the engine steady and not to scrape either the body or the many lines, wires, components and hoses that are anchored to the vehicle. A heavy engine assembly can easily damage fragile but important items like brake lines.

50 Lift the engine high enough to clear the front radiator support and pull it away from the vehicle.

51 Leave the jack under the transaxle assembly while the engine is out of the car or support the front of the assembly with a sling and crossbar if the jack must be removed. Don't allow the assembly to hang freely.

4   Engine dismantling – general note

1   The best job can be performed with the least effort by using an engine stand to support the engine while dismantling and rebuilding it. These are available as rentals or they can be purchased. If it is impossible to use an engine stand, a strong workbench will place the engine at a comfortable, manageable working height.

2   Keep the internal engine components clean during dismantling as well as rebuilding. Clean the exterior of the engine thoroughly with a commercial engine cleaner before taking it apart. These cleaners are available in both brush-on and spray-on form. Follow the instructions for cleaning and rinse thoroughly after the process is completed. An especially dirty engine may require scrubbing with brushes or rags but the end result will provide a cleaner and easier engine to work on.

3   As you remove each part from the engine, clean it in a bath of parts cleaner. The best method is a commercial solvent sink available from many sources. Always use a solvent that is non-flammable and observe all cautions involving chemicals used in closed places and around open flames.

4   Never immerse parts which have internal oil passages in solvent (such as the crankshaft or rocker shaft) but wipe them carefully with a solvent soaked rag. Clean the passageways with a small brush and blow them dry with compressed air. If you don't have the facilities to clean these parts correctly, it would be best to take them to a machine shop and have them properly cleaned. The cost is minimal and the end result is much better.

5   Clean all gasket surfaces of old material and save the old gaskets to use as comparisons for the new ones. Never re-use old gaskets as they will leak (they are not designed for more than one usage).

6   Whenever possible, replace nuts, bolts and washers finger-tight in their original locations. This helps avoid loss and mix-ups. If they cannot be replaced, lay them out in an orderly fashion to clearly define where they came from.

7   If you are not familiar with the interior layout of your engine, refer to the Figures and photos and study them carefully before you take the engine apart. If you feel you are unclear about certain areas of the order of parts, draw a picture, make notes or take pictures (Polaroid cameras work well for this). The time to figure out the assembly order is before you take the engine apart. One misplaced washer or shim can ruin an engine overhaul job. Be careful and plan ahead.

5   Engine – external component removal

1   The Sections in this Chapter deal with removal, installation, overhaul and inspection of the various engine components. Reference should be made to appropriate Chapters for removing and servicing the ancillary engine accessories. These parts include the alternator, air pump, carburetor, etc.
2   If the engine is removed from the vehicle for a major overhaul, the entire engine should be stripped of its components. The exact order in which the engine parts are removed is to some degree a matter of personal preference, however, the following sequence can be used as a guide.
3   Remove the flywheel (Sec 17).
4   Remove the two bolts securing the engine end plate and remove the engine end plate.
5   Place the engine on an engine stand or suitable work and assembly device.
6   Remove the distributor adjusting bolt and distributor (Chapter 5).
7   Remove the spark plugs (Chapter 1).
8   Withdraw the two bolts retaining the combination alternator bracket, engine lifting hook and wiring harness assemblies. Remove these assemblies.
9   Remove the engine block coolant drain fitting.
10 Remove the engine oil pressure sender from the block.
11 Remove the three nuts and one bolt securing the left side engine mount and combination accessory mount. Remove this assembly as a single unit.
12 Remove the water pump (Chapter 3).
13 Remove the front accessory drive pulley from the crankshaft (if so equipped).
14 Remove the center pulley retainer bolt and front crankshaft pulley. Use a suitable puller to pull this part off.
15 Remove the dipstick tube and dipstick.
16 Remove the coolant temperature sensor from the front of the cylinder head.
17 Remove the passenger side combination motor mount and accessory brackets secured by three nuts and washers.
18 Remove the oxygen sensor from the base of the exhaust manifold (if so equipped).
19 Using two wrenches, remove the EGR transfer tube.
20 Remove the carburetor (Chapter 4).
21 Remove the brake vacuum booster supply line from the intake manifold and the brake vacuum booster.
22 Remove the intake manifold (Sec 6).
23 Remove the exhaust manifold (Chapter 4).
24 Remove the heater hose coolant transfer tube (Chapter 3). Remove the rear heater hose connecting tube from the rear of the cylinder head.
25 Remove the fuel pump and shield (Chapter 4).
26 Remove the rocker cover.
27 Rotate the engine to top dead center for number one cylinder.
28 Remove the camshaft covers, the belt and the tensioner (Sec 11).
29 Remove the rocker arm assembly (Sec 12).
30 Remove the camshaft (Sec 13).
31 Remove the oil filter (Chapter 1).
32 With these components removed, the general engine sub-assemblies can be removed, serviced and installed using the following Sections in this Chapter.
33 At the appropriate times, refer to Section 19, which deals with general inspection procedures and Section 29, describing the engine reassembly steps.
34 If at any time during the dismantling procedure damage is found to any of the major engine components (cylinder heads, cylinder block, crankshaft etc.), consider the possibility of purchasing new or rebuilt assemblies as described in Section 20. This decision will in most cases alter your particular rebuilding sequence as dismantling, inspection and assembly will not be required.

6   Intake and exhaust manifolds – removal and installation

Intake manifold

1   Remove the negative battery cable from the battery.
2   Remove the air cleaner (Chapter 1).
3   Remove the carburetor (Chapter 4).
4   If the vehicle is equipped with an automatic transmission, disconnect the throttle link from the carburetor.
5   Remove the brake vacuum booster hose from the manifold port.
6   Remove the throttle cable retaining bracket.
7   Remove the four inter-connecting bolts between the intake manifold and the exhaust manifold. Notice that the two longer bolts are positioned closest to the engine.
8   Note the locations of the emission control system tube brackets and other hardware secured by the intake manifold-to-head retaining bolts. Remove the intake manifold-to-head retaining bolts. Anchor the emissions control system brackets, engine hook and other hardware out of the way.
9   Remove the intake manifold.
10 Make sure the mating surfaces of the intake manifold and head are clean and straight. Use new sealing gaskets and install the manifold in the reverse order of removal.
11 Tighten the intake manifold retaining bolts to the prescribed torque, starting with the center bolts and working outward.

Exhaust manifold

12 Refer to Chapter 4 for details on this procedure.

7   Cylinder head – removal and installation

Note: *If equipped with air conditioning, have the system de-pressurized by a professional.*

Removal

1   If you are removing the cylinder head as part of a total engine overhaul procedure, you may skip steps through 32.
2   Remove the negative battery cable from the battery.
3   Remove the air cleaner (Chapter 1).
4   Drain the coolant out of both the radiator and the engine drain fittings (Chapter 1).
5   Disconnect the heater inlet hose from the cylinder head rear plate.
6   Remove the fuel hoses from the fuel pump.
7   Remove the vent hose which connects the emissions control canister to the carburetor.
8   Remove the vacuum hose leading from the vacuum switching valve (on vehicles equipped with factory air conditioning).
9   Identify the location of all emissions control vacuum hoses leading to the carburetor by means of tags, drawings, Polaroid photos or any other suitable means. Remove these hoses leading to the carburetor (Chapter 6).
10 Unplug the wiring connectors in the wires from the carburetor to the wiring loom.
11 Remove the small ground wire leading from the upper rear intake manifold retaining bolt to the firewall.
12 Remove the connector from the distributor wiring loom.
13 Remove the coil wire leading from the center of the distributor cap to the coil.
14 Remove the temperature sender connecting wire.
15 Remove the thermo-sensor wire from the upper coolant outlet.
16 Disconnect the throttle linkage from the carburetor. Remove the throttle cable from its retaining brackets.
17 Disconnect the throttle link from the carburetor (if the vehicle is equipped with an automatic transmission).
18 Disconnect the down pipe from the exhaust manifold (Chapter 4).
19 Disconnect the oxygen sensor wire from the manifold (if so equipped).
20 Disconnect the radiator outlet hose.
21 Remove the drive belts from the front of the engine.
22 Remove the alternator and alternator upper bracket from the cylinder head (Chapter 5).
23 Remove the water outlet housing from the cylinder head (Chapter 3).
24 Remove the distributor (Chapter 5).
25 Remove the spark plugs (Chapter 1).

26 Remove the cylinder head rocker cover and gasket. Remove the half moon shaped plug at the rear of the cylinder head.
27 Remove the air suction component parts (if so equipped) (Chapter 6).
28 Remove the air conditioner idler pulley and bracket (if so equipped).
29 Remove the upper and lower timing belt covers (Sec 10).
30 Remove the timing belt and drive gears (Sec 11).
31 Remove the exhaust manifold support bolt from the lower front of the exhaust manifold.
Caution: *Remove the cylinder head bolts in the exact sequence shown in Fig. 2.1, as the head can be warped or cracked by incorrect removal procedure.*
32 Remove the head bolts by loosening them all a little at a time.
33 Lift the cylinder head from the alignment dowels and place it on wooden blocks.
34 If the cylinder head is difficult to remove, pry on the tang provided directly above the water pump. Do not pry at any other point and make sure all of the fasteners are removed.

Installation
35 Locate the number one piston at top-dead center.
36 Position the new head gasket on the cylinder block. Notice that there is an oval opening at the front of the head gasket water passageways and a double opening at the rear (photo).
37 Install the head onto the cylinder block. Position the head carefully over the alignment dowels.
38 Install the 10 cylinder head retaining bolts using the proper torque sequence (Fig. 2.2).
39 Start the tightening procedure at 35 ft-lbs and move up in 5 lb increments to the final torque.
40 Follow steps 2 through 32 in reverse numerical order.

7.37 Proper positioning of the cylinder head gasket

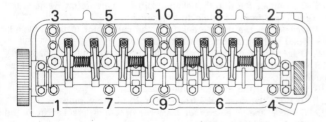

Fig. 2.1 Head bolt removal sequence (Sec 7)

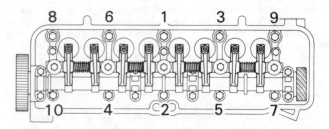

Fig. 2.2 Head bolt tightening sequence (Sec 7)

8 Cylinder head – disassembly and inspection

Note: *Refer to Fig. 2.3 for the following procedure.*
1 Thoroughly clean the cylinder head. The cylinder head is made of aluminium and it would be best to have it cleaned out by a commercial process available at a machine shop.
2 Using a straight-edge, check the manifold mating surface for flatness. Notice that it should be measured in several directions (lines) to ensure total surface flatness.
3 Measure the cylinder head-to-block mating surface for flatness.
4 Using a valve spring compressor, remove the valve spring keepers, retainer, spring, spring seats and valves (photo). Make sure that all of the components are kept in order and store each individual valve assembly components separately (photo).
5 Clean the valves and seats with a wire brush.
6 Measure the inside diameter of the valve guide in several positions. Check for maximum variation and compare it to the specifications. If the guide is worn beyond the specified limit, it must be replaced with a new one by a machine shop.
7 Measure the valve stem in several positions, again checking it against the specification listed (photo).
8 Subtract the smallest valve stem outside measurement from the largest valve guide inside diameter measurement and compare the results to the Specifications. If the clearance exceeds the specified amount, the guide must be replaced with a new one. The valve may also need to be replaced if this clearance cannot be achieved.
9 Check the valve spring for squareness. If it exceeds the limit, replace the valve spring with a new one.
10 Measure the valve spring free length (photo). Replace the spring with a new one if the length does not meet the specification.
11 Repeat the inspection procedure for each of the remaining valves and related components. If excessive wear is noted, the valve train components should be reassembled and the head should be taken to an automotive machine shop for service.
12 Inspect the cam bearing surfaces in the head and caps for flaking, galling, scoring or excessive wear patterns, Replace the head with a new one if any of these conditions exist.
13 If the head exhibits normal valve and seat wear but is otherwise sound, send it to a machine shop for a valve job. A proper valve job requires specialized shop equipment for the grinding processes, and the head can be cleaned thoroughly and examined for cracks or other damage at the same time.

9 Cylinder head reassembly

1 Coat the upper flange of the valve guide with oil and install the new valve guide seal.
2 Place the valve spring seat into position next to the cylinder head.
3 Install the valve spring into position over the shim.
4 Install the valve through the guide after coating it with oil and making sure that the valve seat and mating surface of the valve face are clean.
5 Install the valve retainer.
6 Using a valve spring compressor, compress the valve spring in order to install the valve keepers. Use a soft-faced hammer to tap the end of the valve stem several times to ensure that the valve keepers are properly seated in their locked positions.

8.4A Compressing the valve spring to remove the related valve components

8.4B Valve spring components in order of removal from right to left

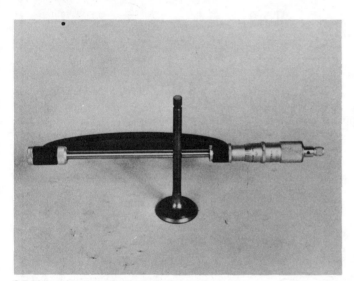

8.7 Measuring the valve stem diameter

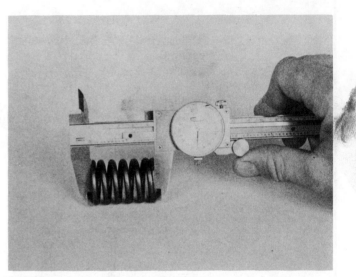

8.10 Measuring the valve spring free length

10 Timing belt covers – removal and installation

Note: *Refer to Fig. 2.5 for the following steps.*
1   Disconnect the negative battery cable from the battery.
2   Remove the alternator, air pump and air conditioning (if so equipped) drive belts. Refer to the appropriate Chapters for removal procedures.
3   Remove the water pump drive pulley from the water pump.
4   Remove the accessory drive pulley (if so equipped) from the front of the crankshaft pulley.
5   Prevent the engine from rotating by putting the transmission in gear (with the parking brake on) if the engine is in the vehicle and equipped with a manual transmission. The flywheel will have to be held stationary if the engine is out of the vehicle or if it is equipped with an automatic transmission.
6   Remove the front pulley retaining bolt. Use a suitable puller to remove the pulley from the crankshaft.
7   Remove the five bolts retaining the upper timing belt cover. Remove the two remaining bolts retaining the lower timing belt cover. Remove both covers. Remove the gasket from the upper cover.
8   Installation is the reverse of removal. Tighten the front pulley retaining bolt to the specified torque. Make sure nothing has dropped inside of the timing belt area and that the covers are on straight and not interfering with the operation of the timing belt or pulleys. When installing the lower belt cover, use a new gasket. Install three of the

four retaining bolts leaving the bolt at the 11 o'clock position out until the top cover is installed.

11 Timing belt, tensioner and gears – removal, inspection and installation

Note: *Refer to Fig. 2.6 for the following steps.*
Removal
1   Remove the timing covers (Sec 10).
2   Rotate the engine until the number one piston is at TDC (on the compression stroke). Both the timing belt and camshaft drive gear alignment marks should be pointing straight up.
3   Loosen the idler pulley set bolt and retract the idler pulley to its loosest position. The timing belt will have maximum deflection in this position. Retighten the set bolt to hold the idler at this spot.
4   Slide the timing belt guide off the nose of the crankshaft. Mark the timing belt for direction of rotation and place match marks on the belt and pulleys if they are to be reused.
5   Slide the timing belt simultaneously off both the upper and lower timing gears. Do not pry on the belt with any tools and don't kink the belt. Do not allow oil to contaminate the belt.
6   Pull the lower pulley off the key and the nose of the crankshaft. It may be a tight fit but no puller should be necessary.
7   Hold the camshaft with a wrench on the special flat provided for this purpose (photo).

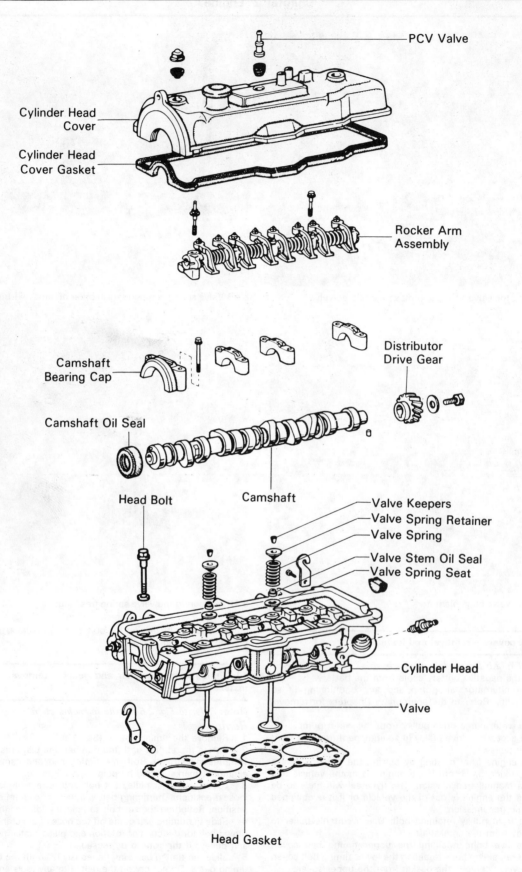

PCV Valve

Cylinder Head
Cover

Cylinder Head
Cover Gasket

Rocker Arm
Assembly

Camshaft
Bearing Cap

Distributor
Drive Gear

Camshaft Oil Seal

Head Bolt

Camshaft

Valve Keepers
Valve Spring Retainer
Valve Spring

Valve Stem Oil Seal
Valve Spring Seat

Cylinder Head

Valve

Head Gasket

Fig. 2.3 Cylinder head assembly components — exploded view
(Sec 8)

11.16 Aligning the mark on the lower pulley with the dot on the oil pump (arrows)

11.17 Holding the tensioner in its retracted position while tightening the hold down bolt

11.19 Tightening the camshaft sprocket bolt

11.20 Hole in the camshaft gear aligned with the mark on the bearing cap (arrow)

11.21 Match marks on the camshaft pulley and belt must be aligned

Fig. 2.4 Checking block and manifold mating surfaces on the cylinder head for flatness (Sec 8)

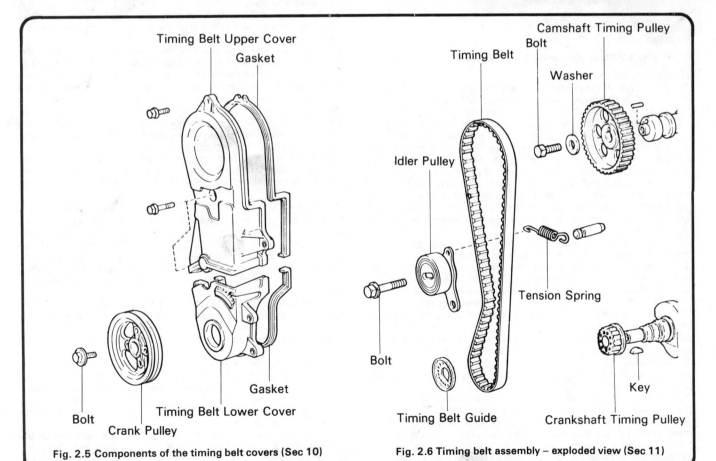

Fig. 2.5 Components of the timing belt covers (Sec 10)

Timing Belt Upper Cover
Gasket
Bolt
Crank Pulley
Gasket
Timing Belt Lower Cover

Fig. 2.6 Timing belt assembly – exploded view (Sec 11)

Camshaft Timing Pulley
Bolt
Washer
Timing Belt
Idler Pulley
Bolt
Tension Spring
Timing Belt Guide
Key
Crankshaft Timing Pulley

8   Remove the bolt from the camshaft drive gear.

9   Remove the camshaft drive gear.

10   Remove the tensioner spring from the idler pulley.

11   Remove the bolt retaining the idler pulley. Remove the idler pulley.

Inspection

12   Inspect the camshaft gear and the crankshaft gear for damage, excessive wear or broken teeth. Replace both gears if any signs of the above are present.

13   Check the camshaft drive belt idler pulley for roughness or binding when turned. Check the idler face for any damage or excessive wear. Check the tensioner spring for deformation or signs of fatigue. If any of these conditions exist, replace the idler pulley assembly.

14   Check the timing belt for damage on both sides. If the belt is broken or teeth are sheared off, make sure the camshaft is not locked or binding. If there is damage to the belt face, make sure the face of the idler pulley is not damaged or worn. If one edge is worn, check the pulleys for alignment. If oil is present on the belt, check both the crankshaft (oil pump) and camshaft oil seals. If any of the above conditions exist, find the cause, remedy it and replace the timing belt with a new one.

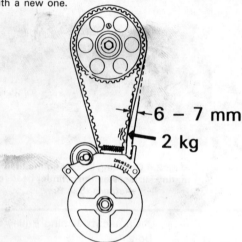

6 – 7 mm

2 kg

Fig. 2.7 Checking camshaft drivebelt tension (Sec 11)

Replacement

Note: *Clean all of the pulleys and idler thoroughly as grease or water on the belt can seriously affect its life and performance.*

15   Make sure the number one piston is at top-dead-center.

16   Install the crankshaft drive pulley onto the crankshaft nose. Align the mark on the pulley with the mark on the oil pump (photo).

17   Install the idler pulley and the tensioner spring. Push the pulley to its fully retracted position with a wooden hammer handle or other similar soft tool (photo). Tighten the idler pulley in this position.

18   Install the camshaft gear with the slot in the gear lined up with the key on the camshaft. Install the retaining bolt and washer.

19   Tighten the camshaft gear retaining bolt to the specified torque (photo). Hold the camshaft stationary with a wrench on the lug provided for this purpose.

20   Turn the camshaft gear so the small hole aligns with the mark on the bearing cap and is pointed straight up (photo).

21   If the old belt is being re-used, install the belt over the pulleys with the direction and indexing marks positioned as planned in step four (photo). Make sure the belt is positioned squarely over both pulleys and the teeth and grooves are matched together properly.

22   Loosen the timing belt idler pulley and allow the spring to tension the pulley and the belt.

23   Temporarily install the crankshaft lower pulley bolt and use it to rotate the crankshaft and engine two full revolutions clockwise back to top-dead-center.

24   Recheck the camshaft and crankshaft timing marks to ensure proper alignment.

25   Tighten the idler pulley retaining bolt to the specified torque.

26   Measure the timing belt tension on the long (driver's) side using a fish scale or other similar device to gauge tension. (Fig. 2.7). If the measurement is less than shown in the illustration, readjust the idler pulley to achieve the correct setting. It may be necessary to 'help' the tensioning spring with the hammer handle reversed from the direction it was in in Step 17.

27   Remove the temporarily installed crankshaft pulley retaining bolt. Do not turn the engine backwards while performing this step.

28   Install the timing belt guide over the nose of the crankshaft pulley and key, with the cupped side facing out.

29   Refer to Sec 10 and install the timing belt covers.

12 Rocker arm assembly – removal, inspection and installation

Removal

1   Disconnect the negative battery cable from the battery.

2   Remove the air cleaner (Chapter 1).

3   Remove the throttle cable from the carburetor and anchor it out of the way.

4   Remove the PCV hoses and valve from the top of the camshaft cover (Chapter 6).

5   Remove the front top timing belt cover retaining bolt and wire clamp.

6   Remove the three camshaft cover retaining bolts and remove the cover.

7   Loosen the rocker arm retaining bolts sequentially, prior to removal (Fig. 2.8).

8   Completely loosen and remove all but the end two bolts retaining the rocker arm assembly. Remove the rocker arm assembly with the end bolts in place.

Inspection

9   Check the clearance between the rocker arm and shaft by rotating the arm side to side (opposite the normal up and down motion it has on the shaft) and straight up and down (as opposed to rocking back and forth). If any excessive play is felt, the rocker arms and shaft will have to be disassembled for further measurement.

10   The rocker arms are under spring tension provided by the locating springs between the rocker arms and the rocker stands, so perform the following step carefully to prevent parts from propelling themselves off the rocker arm shaft.

11   Remove one of the end bolts and carefully remove the rocker arm stand, rocker arm and spring. Lay these parts out in order to ease reassembly.

12   Use a dial caliper to measure the inside diameter of the rocker arm. Use a micrometer to measure the outside diameter of the shaft at each rocker arm position (photo). Measure the shaft in the vertical or "as installed" position as the wear will be more pronounced this way. Subtract the shaft diameter from the rocker arm diameter and the difference will be the oil clearance. Do this at each rocker arm position and with each individual rocker arm. Check the clearance against the specification listed at the beginning of this Chapter. Replace the rocker arm and/or the shaft if the clearance is excessive.

13   Check the valve stem contact surface of the rocker arm for excessive wear or galling. If either of these conditions exist, the rocker arm should be replaced or resurfaced by an automotive machine shop.

Installation

14   Coat the rocker arm shaft and the inner bore surfaces of the rocker arms with oil. Assemble the rocker arms, springs and stands on the shaft in the exact order and direction as they were removed. The oil holes on the rocker arm shaft face to the sides and bottom (Fig. 2.9).

15   Loosen the valve adjusting locknuts and adjusters before installing the rocker arm assembly. Insert the two end bolts into the rocker arm stands to keep the assembly together.

16   Notice that there are three different types of rocker arm assembly retaining bolts. The long bolts fit in the middle and end holes of the rocker arm stands. The short bolts fit onto the valve side of the rocker arm stands and the intermediate bolts fit in the two remaining middle holes.

17   Position the complete rocker arm assembly on the cylinder head and make certain that all of the rocker arms are seated squarely over their respective valves and camshaft lobes. Make sure the five rocker arm locating stands are seated squarely on the cylinder head and make sure none of the rocker arms or the shaft are binding or interfering with any other valve train gear.

18   Start all of the retaining bolts by hand and gradually tighten the bolts in the sequence shown in Fig. 2.10. Start the tightening procedure at five ft-lb (0.7 kg-m) and increase the settings in five lb (0.7 kg) increments until the final torque is achieved.

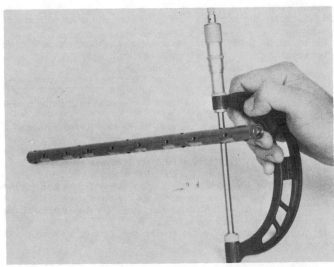

12.12 Using a micrometer to measure the rocker arm shaft diameter

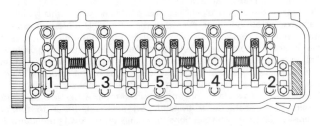

Fig. 2.8 Rocker arm retaining bolt loosening sequence (Sec 12)

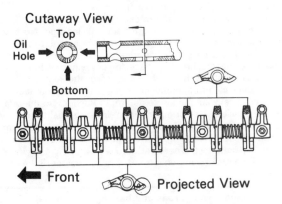

Fig. 2.9 Direction and position of rocker arm shaft during installation (Sec 12)

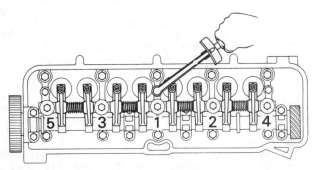

Fig. 2.10 Rocker arm assembly retaining bolt tightening sequence (Sec 12)

19 The valve clearance will need to be set after the rocker arm assembly is installed (Chapter 1).
20 Follow in reverse order steps one through six of this Section for the remaining assembly procedure.

13 Camshaft – removal, inspection and installation

Removal

1   Remove the air cleaner assembly (Chapter 1).
2   Remove the fuel pump (Chapter 4).
3   Remove the distributor (Chapter 5).
4   Remove the front timing belt covers (Sec 10).
5   Remove the timing belt and camshaft gear (Sec 11).
6   Remove the rocker arm assembly (Sec 12).
7   This step is optional. The distributor drive gear only needs to be removed if it or the camshaft are worn or damaged to the point of needing replacement. Loosen the distributor drive gear by holding the flat provided on the camshaft with a wrench and loosening the retaining bolt at the rear of the camshaft.
8   Measure the camshaft thrust clearance before removing the camshaft. Gently pry the camshaft to its most rearward position (photo). Set the dial indicator up as shown in the photo and zero the gauge. Now pry the camshaft to its most forward position. The reading on the dial indicator is the camshaft thrust clearance. If it exceeds the maximum specification, the cylinder head will have to be replaced.
9   Remove the camshaft retaining caps in the order shown in Fig. 2.11. Notice that the bearing caps are marked for direction and order. Always keep the caps in order to ensure correct replacement.
10 Remove the camshaft by pulling it straight up and off the head.

Inspection

11 Inspect the camshaft for galling or excessive wear characteristics on the bearing surfaces as well as the lobes. Replace the camshaft with a new one if any excessive wear is present. Inspect the distributor drive gear for damaged teeth or excessive wear.
12 Measure the camshaft lobes with a micrometer (photo). If the lobe height is less than the specification, replace the camshaft with a new one. Notice that the specifications vary, depending on what transmission the vehicle is equipped with.
13 Place the camshaft on V-blocks or a roller block assembly. Most home mechanics are not equipped with this tool so this inspection step may need to be carried out by a local automotive machine shop or repair facility. Measure the runout of the center journal with a dial indicator while rotating the camshaft in the V-blocks. If the runout exceeds the maximum specification, the camshaft must be replaced with a new one.
14 Measure the center journal diameter with a micrometer. Replace the camshaft with a new one if the journal is smaller than the minimum specification.

13.7 Checking the camshaft thrust clearance with a dial indicator

13.11 Measuring the camshaft lobes with a micrometer

15 Measure the camshaft journal oil clearance using the Plastigage method described in Section 26. Tighten the caps in the sequence show in Fig. 2.12 and make sure the caps are positioned correctly and face the right direction (arrow). If the clearance is greater than the maximum allowable tolerance, the head will need to be replaced with a new one.

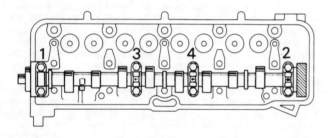

Fig. 2.11 Camshaft retaining cap removal sequence (Sec 13)

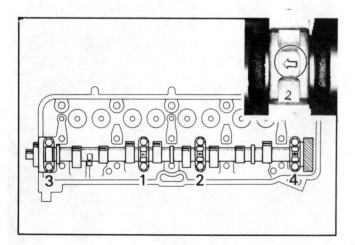

Fig. 2.12 Camshaft bearing cap installation sequence (Sec 13)

Installation

16 Lubricate the camshaft bearing surfaces and lobes with engine assembly lube.
17 Install the distributor drive gear, retainer bolt and washer if it has been removed.
18 Place the camshaft into the cylinder head.
19 Install bearing caps two, three and four onto each journal facing the proper direction.
20 Apply grease to the inner lip of the front oil seal. Apply gasket sealer to the front oil seal outer lip.
21 Install the oil seal over the nose of the camshaft and position it squarely in the recess at the front of the head.
22 Install bearing cap number one over the oil seal. Make sure the seal stays straight and seats squarely in its recess.
23 Tighten the bearing caps in the order shown in Fig. 2.13, starting at about half of the specified torque figure. Incrementally increase the torque up to the final specification in two or three stages.
24 The remainder of the reassembly steps are the reverse of the removal procedures starting with step 8.
25 When installing the rocker arm assembly, be sure to follow the exact procedure described in Section 12.

14 Rear crankshaft seal – removal, inspection and installation

1   The rear crankshaft seal is contained in its own housing bolted to the rear of the engine block. The seal contained within this housing is easily replaced; however, access to the housing is difficult due to the many major components which must be removed. The transmission, clutch or torque converter, flywheel or flex-plate, bellhousing, differential housing assembly and rear engine plate must be removed. Another alternative is to remove the engine for access to the seal. Either way, it is obviously a long, multi-step procedure to replace a defective or leaking seal. It would be advantageous to replace the seal as part of a clutch replacement or transmission overhaul. Refer to the appropriate Chapters and Sections for details on removal procedures for the various sub-assemblies.
2   After removing the assemblies listed in Step 1, remove the six retaining bolts holding the seal and retainer to the engine block.
3   Remove the retainer and gasket.
4   Remove the seal from the retainer with an approved pusher tool.
5   Inspect the seal and housing for signs of leakage. **Note:** *Always replace the seal with a new one as part of an engine overhaul or if a clutch or transmission job is performed.*
6   Examine the crankshaft surface for any signs of burrs or ridges which would damage the flexible inner lip of the seal.
7   Push the seal into the retainer, taking care not to damage it in any way. Be especially careful not to deform it. Push it into the retainer as evenly as possible. Use an appropriate driver or pusher tool.
8   Coat the inner lip of the seal with a light lithium-based grease.
9   Install the retainer on the block using a new gasket and tighten the six retaining bolts to the specified torque.
10 Install the major components in the reverse order of their removal.

15 Pistons, connecting rods and bearings – removal

1   Remove the oil pan, oil pickup and cylinder head as described in this Chapter.
2   Before the piston assemblies can be forced up through the top of the engine block, a ridge reamer should be used to remove the ridge and/or carbon deposits at the top of each cylinder (photo). Working on one cylinder at a time, turn the engine so the piston is at the bottom of its stroke. Then place a rag on top of the piston to catch the cuttings. After the ridge is removed, crank the engine until the piston is at the top of the cylinder and remove the cloth and cuttings. Failure to remove this ridge may cause damage to the piston rings, pistons or cylinder walls.
3   Inspect the connecting rods and connecting rod caps for cylinder identification. If these components are not plainly marked, identify each using a small punch to make the appropriate number of indentations.
4   Working in sequence, remove the nuts on the connecting rod stud and lift the cap (with bearing inside) off the crankshaft. Place the connecting rod cap and bearing on a clean work surface marked cylinder 1, 2, 3, etc.

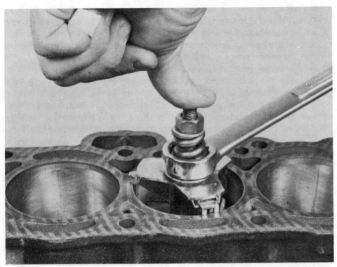

15.2 Removing the ridge at the top of the cylinder bore with a ridge reamer

5   Push a piece of rubber or plastic tubing over the connecting rod studs to completely cover the studs. This is important as these studs could easily damage the crankshaft or cylinder wall when the piston assembly is removed.

6   Push the piston/connecting rod assembly out through the top of the cylinder. Place the piston with its connecting rod next to its rod cap on the sequenced work area.

7   Repeat these procedures for the remaining three cylinders, turning the crankshaft as necessary to gain access to the connecting rod nuts. Reuse the rubber or plastic tubing for each assembly.

8   Remove the bearings from the connecting rods and the connecting rod caps. This is easily done with a small screwdriver. If the engine has many miles, it is false economy to reuse the bearings, but if they are to be reinstalled place them in a numbered rack.

9   If a piston ring expanding tool is available, use this to remove each of the rings from the piston. An alternative method is to expand the ring just enough to clear the lands of the piston body. Then place strips of tin (about $\frac{1}{4}$ in wide) under the ring at equal distances around the piston. Using a slight twisting motion, 'walk' the ring up the piston and off the top.

10   Place the rings, in their 'installed' order adjacent to the piston/connecting rod on your numbered work area.

11   Separating the connecting rod from the piston requires the removal of the piston pin. This job is best left to a dealer or automotive machine shop equipped with the proper support tools and an arbor press.

12   Do not take the time to clean and inspect the piston/rod assemblies at this time as they may have to be replaced with new units depending on the condition of the cylinder block and/or crankshaft.

16 Crankshaft and main bearings – removal

1   The crankshaft and main bearings should only be removed with the engine out of the vehicle.

2   The engine should be completely stripped of its components as described in the previous Sections of this Chapter.

3   Check that each of the five main bearing caps is marked in respect to its location in the engine block. If not, use a punch to make small indentations in the same fashion as for the connecting rods and caps. The main bearing caps must be reinstalled in their original positions.

4   Loosen each of the main bearing cap bolts $\frac{1}{4}$ of a turn at a time, in sequence, starting at the center of the engine, until they can be removed by hand.

5   Gently tap the main bearing caps with a soft-faced hammer, then remove them from the engine block. If necessary, use the main bearing cap bolts as levers to remove the caps. Try not to drop the bearing shell, if it comes out with the cap. Remove the two half-circle thrust bearings from their position on the center main bearing journal.

6   Carefully lift the crankshaft out of the engine. With the bearing

inserts in place in the engine block and the main bearing caps, return the caps to their respective location on the engine block and tighten the bolts finger-tight.

17 Flywheel – removal, inspection and installation

1   Mark the flywheel and the crankshaft end with a pin punch or similar device to ensure it is installed in the same position.

2   Prevent the crankshaft from turning by inserting a shaft or tool in an open hole and locking the flywheel against a boss at the rear of the block. Make sure the locking tool is not prying against a surface that it will damage or bend (such as the oil pan). Another method for preventing crankshaft rotation would be to hold the front pulley retaining bolt with a socket and handle. This method will probably require the aid of a helper.

3   Support the flywheel before performing the following step as it could fall off and be damaged or cause injury.

4   Remove the six flywheel retaining bolts from the back of the crankshaft.

5   Remove the flywheel by pulling it straight back from the rear of the crankshaft.

6   Inspect the flywheel-to-clutch disc mating surface for scoring, heat marks, cracks and warpage. If any of these conditions exist, the flywheel should be taken to an automotive machine shop to be resurfaced on a special grinder. If the flywheel is cracked, however, it should be replaced with a new one.

7   Installation is the reverse of removal. The six retaining bolts should be coated with a thread locking compound. Tighten the six bolts in a criss-cross pattern until all are tightened to the prescribed torque specification.

18 Oil pan and oil pump – removal and installation

1   The oil pump can be removed with the engine in the car, however, the oil pan and pickup assembly must also be removed. If the oil pump is being removed as part of an engine overhaul, you may omit steps two through nine, as they will have already been done as part of the engine removal and dismantling process.

2   Raise and support the front of the vehicle.

3   Drain the engine oil.

4   Drain the coolant from the engine and radiator drain valves (Chapter 1).

5   Remove the radiator (Chapter 3).

6   Remove the engine front splash shield.

7   Remove the four stabilizer bracket retaining bolts and lower the stabilizer bar.

8   Remove the left and right engine stiffener plates.

9   Remove the engine rear under plate and seal (if the vehicle is equipped with an automatic transmission).

10   Remove the four retaining nuts and seventeen bolts holding the oil pan to the block. Remove the oil pan and gasket.

11   Remove the two bolts and two nuts holding the oil strainer to the pump and block. Remove the oil strainer-to-pump gasket.

12   Remove the timing covers (Sec 10), timing belt and lower belt drive gear (Sec 11).

13   Remove the dipstick tube (it is retained by one bolt). Remove the dipstick. Remove the O-ring from the base of the dipstick tube.

14   Remove the six bolts retaining the oil pump to the block.

15   Tap the pump loose, if necessary, with a plastic or other type of soft-faced hammer. Remove the pump by pulling it straight forward over the nose of the crankshaft.

16   Remove the old oil pump-to-block gasket and clean all mating surfaces.

17   Using RTV silicone gasket sealer, attach a new oil pump-to-block gasket to the block.

18   Install the oil pump over the nose of the crankshaft and align the spline teeth of the oil pump drive gear with the large spline groove on the crankshaft (Fig. 2.13).

19   Install the six oil pump retaining bolts and tighten them to the specified torque.

20   Coat a new sealing O-ring with oil and position it on the dipstick tube. Install the dipstick tube into the oil pump and secure the mounting bolt to the block.

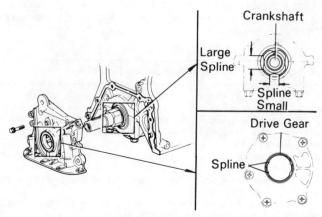

Fig. 2.13 Alignment of the oil pump drive gear with the crankshaft splines (Sec 18)

21 Using RTV silicone gasket sealer, attach a new oil pickup-to-oil pump gasket to the oil pump. Install the oil strainer assembly and tighten the two nuts and two bolts to the proper torque.

22 Install a new oil pan gasket to the block with a silicone type gasket sealer. Install the oil pan over the alignment studs on the block and secure it with the seventeen bolts and four nuts. Tighten all fasteners a little at a time, in many steps until the final torque is reached.

23 To complete the procedure, follow the process in reverse order.

19 Engine block – cleaning and inspection

1   Remove the soft plugs from the engine block. To do this, knock the plugs into the block (using a hammer and punch), then grasp them with large pliers and pull them back through the hole.

2   Using a gasket scraper, remove all traces of gasket material from the engine block. Be very careful not to nick or gouge the gasket sealing surfaces.

3   Remove the main bearing caps and separate the bearing shells from the caps and the engine block. Tag the bearing shells according to which cylinder they were removed from (and whether they were in the cap or the block) and set them aside if they are to be re-used.

4   Using a hex wrench of the appropriate size, remove the threaded oil gallery plugs from the front and back of the block.

5   If the engine is extremely dirty, it should be taken to an automotive machine shop to be steam cleaned or hot tanked.

6   After the block is returned, clean all oil holes and oil galleries one more time (brushes for cleaning oil holes and galleries are available at most auto parts stores). Flush the passages with warm water (until the water runs clear), dry the block thoroughly and wipe all machined surfaces with a light rust-preventative oil. If you have access to compressed air, use it to speed the drying process and to blow out all of the oil holes and galleries.

7   If the block is not extremely dirty or sludged up, you can do an adequate cleaning job with warm soapy water and a stiff brush. Take plenty of time to do a thorough job. Regardless of the cleaning method used, be very sure to thoroughly clean all oil holes and galleries, dry the block completely and coat all machined surfaces with light oil.

8   The threaded holes in the block must be clean to ensure accurate torque readings during reassembly. Run the proper size tap into each of the holes to remove any rust, corrosion, thread sealant or sludge and to restore any damaged threads. If possible, use compressed air to clear the holes of debris produced by this operation. Now is a good time to thoroughly clean the threads on the head bolts and the main bearing cap bolts as well.

9   Reinstall the main bearing caps and tighten the bolts finger-tight.

10 After coating the sealing surfaces of the new soft plugs with a good quality gasket sealer, install them in the engine block (photo). Make sure they are driven in straight and seated properly, or leakage could result. Special tools are available for this purpose, but equally good results can be obtained using a large socket (with an outside diameter slightly smaller than the outside diameter of the soft plug) and a large hammer.

11 Double-check to make sure that the ridge at the top of the cylinders has been completely removed.

12 Visually check the block for cracks, rust and corrosion. Look for stripped threads in the threaded holes. It is also a good idea to have the block checked for hidden cracks by an automotive machine shop that has the special equipment to do this type of work. If defects are found, have the block repaired, if possible, or replaced.

13 Check the cylinder bores for scuffing and scoring.

14 Using the appropriate precision measuring tools, measure each cylinder's diameter at the top (just under the ridge), center and bottom of the cylinder bore, parallel to the crankshaft axis (photos). Next, measure each cylinder's diameter at the same 3 locations across the crankshaft axis. Compare the results to the specifications. If the cylinder walls are badly scuffed or scored, or if they are out-of-round or tapered beyond the limits given in the specifications, have the engine block rebored and honed at an automotive machine shop (photo). If a rebore is done, oversized pistons and rings will be required as well.

15 If the cylinders are in reasonably good condition and not worn to the outside of the limits, and if the piston-to-cylinder clearances can be maintained properly, then they do not have to be rebored; honing is all that is necessary.

16 Before honing the cylinders, install the main bearing caps (without the bearings) and tighten the bolts to the specified torque.

17 To perform the honing operation, you will need the proper size flexible hone (with fine stones), plenty of light oil or honing oil, some rags and an electric drill motor. Mount the hone in the drill motor, compress the stones and slip the hone into the first cylinder (photo). Lubricate the cylinder thoroughly, turn on the drill and move the hone up and down in the cylinder at a pace which will produce a fine cross-hatch pattern on the cylinder walls (with the cross-hatch lines intersecting at approximately a 60° angle). Be sure to use plenty of lubricant, and do not take off any more material than is absolutely necessary to produce the desired finish. Do not withdraw the hone from the cylinder while it is running. Instead, shut off the drill and continue moving the hone up and down in the cylinder until it comes to a complete stop, then compress the stones and withdraw the hone. Wipe the oil out of the cylinder and repeat the procedure on the remaining cylinders. Remember, do not remove too much material from the cylinder wall. If you do not have the tools or do not desire to perform the honing operation, most automotive machine shops will do it for a reasonable fee.

18 If a sharp edge exists at the top edge of each cylinder, it can be carefully removed using a small file. A slight chamfer will ease piston installation.

19 Check the cylinder head mating surface (top deck) of the block using a straight edge and a feeler gauge. Have the deck surface of the block machined if the clearance exceeds the specification (photo).

20 Next, the entire engine block must be thoroughly washed again with warm, soapy water to remove all traces of the abrasive grit produced during the honing operation. Be sure to run a brush through all oil holes and galleries and flush them with running water. After rinsing, dry the block and apply a coat of light rust preventative oil to all machined surfaces. Wrap the block in a plastic trash bag to keep it clean and set it aside until reassembly.

20 Engine – rebuilding alternatives

1   At this point in the engine rebuilding process the home mechanic is faced with a number of options for completing the overhaul. The decision to replace the cylinder block, piston/rod assemblies and crankshaft depend on a number of factors with the number one consideration being the condition of the cylinder block. Other considerations are: cost, competent machine shop facilities, parts availability, time available to complete the project and experience.

2   Some of the rebuilding alternatives are as follows:

Individual parts – If the inspection procedures prove that the engine block and most engine components are in reusable condition, this may be the most economical alternative. The block, crankshaft and piston/rod assemblies should all be inspected carefully. Even if the block shows little wear, the cylinder bores should receive a finish hone; a job for a machine shop.

Master kit (crankshaft kit) – This rebuild package usually consists of a reground crankshaft and a matched set of pistons and connecting rods. The pistons will come already installed with new piston pins to the connecting rods. Piston rings and the necessary bearings may or may not be included in the kit. These kits are commonly available for

19.10 Installing the soft plugs in the engine block using a socket and hammer

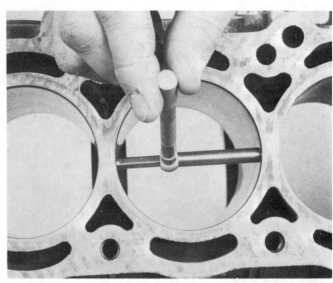

19.14A Determining the internal bore size with a telescoping gauge

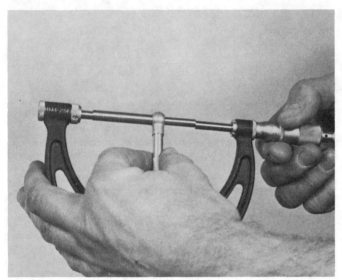

19.14B Measuring the telescoping gauge with a micrometer

19.14C Cylinder taper being measured with a taper gauge

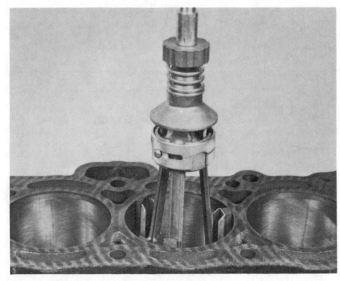

19.17 Honing the cylinder with a cylinder surfacing hone (notice the cross-hatch pattern in the two adjacent cylinders)

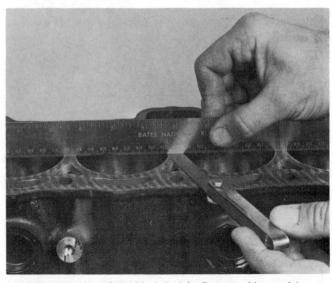

19.19 Checking the cylinder block deck for flatness with a straight edge and a feeler gauge

standard cylinder bores, as well as for engine blocks which have been bored to a regular oversize.

Short block – A short block consists of a cylinder block with a crankshaft and piston/rod assemblies already installed. All new bearings are incorporated and all clearances will be within tolerances. Depending on where the short block is purchased, a guarantee may be included. The existing camshaft, valve mechanism, cylinder heads and ancillary parts can be bolted to this short block with little or no machine shop work necessary for the engine overhaul.

Long block – A long block consists of a short block plus oil pump, oil pan, cylinder head, valve cover, camshaft and valve mechanism, camshaft gear, timing belt and crankcase front cover. All components are installed with new bearings, seals and gaskets incorporated throughout. The installation of manifolds and ancillary parts is all that is necessary. Some form of guarantee is usually included with purchase.

3   Give careful thought to which method is best for your situation and discuss the alternatives with local machine shop owners, parts dealers or dealership partsmen.

21 Oil pump – disassembly, inspection and reassembly

Note: *Refer to Figure 2.14 for component details in reference to the following steps.*
1   Remove the snap-ring retaining the relief valve keeper, spring and piston.
2   Remove the five screws retaining the oil pump cover to the oil pump body.
3   Remove the cover.
4   Remove the drive and driven gears.
5   The crankshaft seal can be pried out of the cover with a screwdriver.
6   Thoroughly clean all parts with solvent and dry them with compressed air.
7   Inspect the gears, cover plate and housing for excessive wear patterns, cracks or damage (photo).
8   Inspect the relief valve piston for excessive wear or damage.
9   Measure the clearance between the drive gear and the body using a feeler gauge (photo).

21.9 Checking clearance between the drive gear and the body with a feeler gauge

21.10 Checking the clearance between the driven gear and the body with a feeler gauge

21.12 Checking the distance between the outside of the driven gear and the pump body

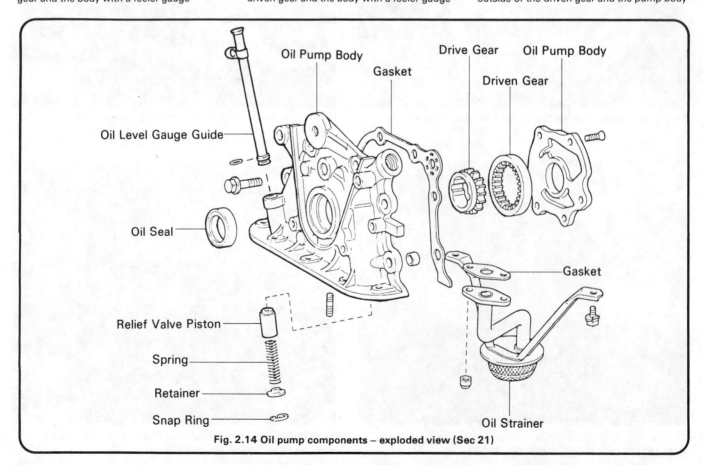
Fig. 2.14 Oil pump components – exploded view (Sec 21)

Oil Pump Body

Drive Gear   Oil Pump Body

Gasket

Driven Gear

Oil Level Gauge Guide

Oil Seal

Gasket

Relief Valve Piston

Spring

Retainer

Snap Ring

Oil Strainer

10 Measure the clearance between the driven gear and the body using a feeler gauge (photo).
11 Use a straight edge and a feeler gauge to measure the rotor-to-cover clearance.
12 Measure the distance between the outside of the driven gear and the pump body (photo).
13 Lightly lubricate all of the moving parts with clean 10 weight oil.
14 Insert the parts into the housing.
15 Place the cover onto the housing and secure it with the five bolts.
16 **Caution:** *Before attempting this procedure, secure the oil pump in a soft-jawed vise. Use protective eye gear, as the spring is under tension.* Insert the piston, spring and retainer into the relief valve bore.
17 Install the retainer clip with the proper tool.
18 Using an approved pusher tool (slightly smaller than the outer diameter of the seal), install the crankshaft oil seal. Make sure it is situated squarely in its seat.

22 Crankshaft and bearings – inspection and servicing

1 Examine the crankpin and main journal surfaces for scoring, scratches or corrosion. If evident, then the crankshaft will have to be reground professionally.
2 Using a micrometer, test each journal and crankpin at several different points for ovality (photo). If this is found to be more than 0.0008 inch then the crankshaft must be reground. Undersize bearings are available to suit the recommended reground diameter, but normally your dealer will supply the correct matching bearings with the reconditioned crankshaft.
3 After high mileage, the main bearings and the connecting rod bearings may have worn to give an excessive running clearance. The correct running clearance for the different journals is given in the Specifications.
    The clearance is best checked using a product such as 'Plastigage' having installed the original bearings and caps and tightened the cap bolts to the torque specified in Specifications. *Never attempt to correct excessive running clearance by filing the caps but always fit new shell bearings, having first checked the crankshaft journals and crankpins for ovality and to establish whether their diameters are of standard or reground sizes.*
    It is good practice to check the running clearance of main bearings even if new bearings are installed. The use of 'Plastigage' is described in Section 26.
4 If the crankshaft needs to be reground or if it has slight blemishes on its surfaces, it is a good idea to send it to an automotive machine shop specializing in crankshaft work. The crankshaft can be polished or reground if necessary and it receives a thorough cleaning as well as careful examination. The warpage of the crankshaft can only be checked with special roller blocks which the average home mechanic doesn't have. The crankshaft is the heart of the engine, so a little extra care and attention to detail in its preparation will result in a smoother, longer lasting engine.
5 Install the crankshaft and bearings with no oil. Do not turn the crankshaft. Check the thrust clearance of the crankshaft by prying the crankshaft to the rearmost position. Now set a dial indicator up at the nose of the crank and zero it (photo). Pry the crankshaft to its forward position. Read the clearance on the dial indicator. The clearance can also be checked with a feeler gauge inserted between the thrust bearing and the thrust surface on the journal although this is a less accurate method. If the thrust clearance measures up to the Specifications listed at the front of this Chapter, go ahead to the next step. If the clearance is more or less than the Specification listed, a new thrust bearing set must be substituted to achieve the proper clearance.
6 If the vehicle is equipped with a manual transmission, check the end of the crankshaft for the pilot bearing. Rotate it and assure that it has smooth movement and no excessive play. If any of these conditions exist, remove the pilot bearing and replace it with a new one. This procedure requires the use of a special puller specifically designed for this purpose. Push in the new bearing with a proper drive tool. A socket may be used in this process, however, it is easier to damage the new bearing this way, so use care with this method.

23 Pistons, connecting rods and bearings – inspection

1 Before the inspection process can be carried out, the piston/connecting rod assemblies must be cleaned and, if not already done, the old piston rings removed from the pistons.
2 Using a piston ring installation tool, carefully remove the rings from the pistons. Do not nick or gouge the pistons in the process.
3 Scrape all traces of carbon from the top (or crown) of the piston. A hand-held wire brush or a piece of fine emery cloth can be used once the majority of the deposits have been scraped away. Do not, under any circumstances, use a wire brush mounted in a drill motor to remove deposits from the pistons. The piston material is soft and will be eroded away by the wire brush.
4 Use a piston ring groove cleaning tool to remove any carbon deposits from the ring grooves (photo). If a tool is not available, a piece broken off the old ring will do the job. Be very careful to remove only the carbon deposits. Do not remove any metal and do not nick or scratch the sides of the ring grooves.
5 Once the deposits have been removed, clean the piston/rod assemblies with solvent and dry them thoroughly. Make sure that the oil hole in the big end of the connecting rod and the oil return holes in the back side of the ring groove are clear.
6 If the pistons are not damaged or worn excessively, and if the engine block is not rebored, new pistons will not be necessary. Normal piston wear appears as even vertical wear on the piston thrust surfaces and slight looseness of the top ring in its groove. New piston rings, on the other hand, should always be used when an engine is rebuilt.

22.2 Measuring the crankshaft journals with a micrometer

22.5 Checking the crankshaft thrust clearance with a dial indicator

23.4 Cleaning the piston ring grooves with a piston ring groove cleaning tool

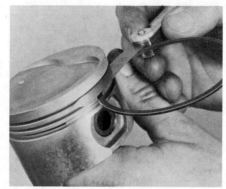

23.10 Checking the piston ring side clearance

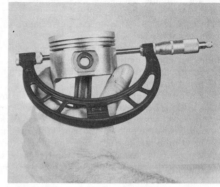

23.11 Measuring the piston diameter with a micrometer

7   Carefully inspect each piston for cracks around the skirt, at the pin bosses and at the ring lands.

8   Look for scoring and scuffing (on the thrust faces of the skirt), holes (in the piston crown) and burned areas (at the edge of the crown). If the skirt is scored or scuffed, the engine may have been suffering from overheating and/or abnormal combustion, which caused excessively high operating temperatures. The cooling and lubrication systems should be checked thoroughly. A hole in the piston crown, an extreme to be sure, is an indication that abnormal combustion (preignition) was occurring. Burned areas at the edge of the piston crown are usually evidence of spark knock (detonation). If any of the above problems exist, the causes must be corrected or the damage will occur again.

9   Corrosion of the piston (evidenced by pitting) indicates that coolant is leaking into the combustion chamber and/or the crankcase. Again, the cause must be corrected or the problem may persist in the rebuilt engine.

10 Measure the piston ring side clearance by laying a new piston ring in the ring groove and slipping a feeler gauge in beside it (photo). Check the clearance at three or four locations around the groove. Be sure to use the correct ring for each groove; they are different. If the side clearance is greater than specified, new pistons will have to be used and the block rebored to accept them.

11 Check the piston-to-bore clearance by measuring the bore (see Section 19) and the piston diameter (photo). Make sure that the pistons and bores are correctly matched. Measure the piston across the skirt, on the thrust faces (at a 90° angle to the piston pin), about 0.100 in (2 mm) up from the bottom of the skirt. Subtract the piston diameter from the bore diameter to obtain the clearance. If it is greater than specified, the block will have to be rebored and new pistons and rings installed. Check the piston pin-to-rod clearance by twisting the piston and rod in opposite directions. Any noticeable play indicates that there is excessive wear, which must be corrected. The piston/connecting rod assemblies should be taken to an automotive machine shop to have new piston pins installed and the pistons and connecting rods rebored.

12 If the pistons must be removed from the connecting rods, such as when new pistons must be installed, or if the piston pins have too much play in them, they should be taken to an automotive machine shop. While they are there, it would be convenient to have the connecting rods checked for bend and twist, as automotive machine shops have special equipment for this purpose.

13 Check the connecting rods for cracks and other damage. Temporarily remove the rod cap, lift out the old bearing inserts, wipe the rod and cap bearing surfaces clean and inspect them for nicks, gouges and scratches. After checking the rods, replace the old bearings, slip the caps in place and tighten the nuts finger-tight. Unless new pistons or connecting rods must be installed, do not disassemble the pistons from the connecting rods.

14 Even though the connecting rod bearings should be replaced with new ones during the engine overhaul, the old bearings should be retained for close examination, as they may reveal valuable information about the condition of the engine. Bearing failure occurs mainly because of lack of lubrication, the presence of dirt or other foreign particles, overloading the engine and/or corrosion. Regardless of the cause of bearing failure, it must be corrected before the engine is reassembled to prevent it from happening again.

15 When examining the bearings, remove them from the connecting rods and the rod caps and lay them out on a clean surface in the same general position as their location in the engine. This will enable you to match any noted bearing problems with the corresponding crankshaft journal.

16 Dirt and other foreign particles get into the engine in a variety of ways. It may be left in the engine during assembly, or it may pass through filters or breathers. It may get into the oil, and from there into the bearings. Metal chips from machining operations and normal engine wear are often present. Abrasives are sometimes left in engine components after reconditioning, especially when parts are not thoroughly cleaned using the proper cleaning methods. Whatever the source, these foreign objects often end up embedded in the soft bearing material and are easily recognized. Large particles will not embed in the bearing and will score or gouge the bearing and shaft. The best prevention for this cause of bearing failure is to clean all parts thoroughly and keep everything spotlessly clean during engine assembly. Frequent and regular changes of engine oil, and oil filters, is also recommended.

17 Lack of lubrication (or lubrication breakdown) has a number of interrelated causes. Excessive heat (which thins the oil), overloading (which squeezes the oil from the bearing face) and oil leakage or throw-off (from excessive bearing clearances, worn oil pump or high engine speeds) all contribute to lubrication breakdown. Blocked oil passages, which usually are the result of misaligned oil holes in a bearing shell, will also oil-starve a bearing and destroy it. When lack of lubrication is the cause of bearing failure, the bearing material is wiped or extruded from the steel backing of the bearing. Temperatures may increase to the point where the steel backing turns blue from overheating.

18 Driving habits can have a definite effect on bearing life. Full-throttle low-speed operation (or 'lugging' the engine) puts very high loads on bearings, which tends to squeeze out the oil film. These loads cause the bearings to flex, which produces fine cracks in the bearing face (fatigue failure). Eventually the bearing material will loosen in pieces and tear away from the steel backing. Short-trip driving leads to corrosion of bearings, as insufficient engine heat is produced to drive off the condensed water and corrosive gases produced. These products collect in the engine oil, forming acid and sludge. As the oil is carried to the engine bearings the acid attacks and corrodes the bearing material.

19 Incorrect bearing installation during engine assembly will lead to bearing failure as well. Tight-fitting bearings, which leave insufficient bearing oil clearance, result in oil starvation. Dirt or foreign particles trapped behind a bearing insert result in high spots on the bearing which lead to failure.

24 Pistons and piston rings – assembly

1   The piston should be attached to its appropriate connecting rod. As mentioned previously, this is a job for a professional equipped with the proper supports and an arbor press.

2   The new piston rings should be comparable in size to the piston being used.

3   The installation of the piston rings on the piston is critical to the overall performance of the rebuilt engine.

4   Measure the ring end gap of each ring before it is installed in the piston. This is done as follows:

   a)   Arrange the piston rings into sets for each piston. The set will contain a top ring, 2nd ring and a three-piece oil control ring (two rails and a spacer).

   b)   Slip the top ring into the appropriate cylinder bore. Push the ring into the cylinder bore about $\frac{1}{4}$ inch below the upper limit of ring travel (a total of about 1 inch below block deck). Push the ring down into position with the top of a piston to make sure the ring is square with the cylinder wall

   c)   Using a feeler gauge, measure the gap between the ends of the ring (photo). If the gap is less than specified (see Specifications), remove the ring and try another top ring for fit

   d)   Check all top rings in the same manner and if necessary use a fine file to remove a slight amount of material from the ends of the ring(s). If inadequate end gap is used, the rings will break during operation

   e)   Measure the end gap of each 2nd ring and oil control ring as described above

5   Check the fit of each piston ring into its groove by holding the ring next to the piston and then placing the outer surface of the ring into its respective groove. Roll the ring entirely around the piston and check for any binding. If the binding is due to a distorted ring, replace the ring with a new one. Perform this check for the top and 2nd rings of each piston.

6   Install the piston rings as follows:

   a)   Study Fig. 2.15 thoroughly to understand exactly where each ring gap should be located in relation to the piston and other rings. The location of each ring gap is important

   b)   If a piston ring expander tool is available, use this to install the rings (photo). If not, small lengths of tin can be used to prevent the rings from entering the wrong groove (see Section 15 on piston ring removal)

   c)   Install the bottom oil ring spacer in its groove and insert the anti-rotation tang in the oil hole. Hold the spacer ends butted and install the lower steel oil ring rail with the gap properly located. Install the upper steel oil ring rail and properly set its gap. Flex or squeeze the oil ring assembly to make sure it is free in the groove. If not, dress the groove with a file or replace the oil control ring assembly as necessary

   d)   Install the end ring and properly locate its gap

   e)   Install the top ring with gap properly positioned

   f)   Repeat the above procedures for all piston assemblies

25 Engine assembly – general information

1   Before assembling any parts to the engine block, the block should have all necessary machine work completed and the engine block should be thoroughly cleaned.

2   Clean and examine all bolts, nuts and fasteners. Replace any that are damaged with new ones.

3   Clean and cover all engine components to keep dirt and dust away from them until they can be installed.

4   Have assembly lube and an oil can filled with engine oil handy to lubricate parts as they are installed.

5   Lay out all necessary tools and a reliable torque wrench on a clean work table for easy retrieval.

6   New gaskets and seals must be used throughout. These are commonly available together in a master rebuild gasket set.

7   In almost all cases, parts to be replaced during a major overhaul include: camshaft bearings, connecting rod bearings, main bearings, piston rings, camshaft drive belt, spark plugs and oil filter. These are in addition to any parts found damaged or excessively worn during dismantling or the various inspection processes.

26 Main bearings and rod bearings – checking clearances

1   **Note:** *There are three precautions to take when working with Plastigage. These are:*

   a)   *Plastigage is soluble in oil, so all oil and grease should be*

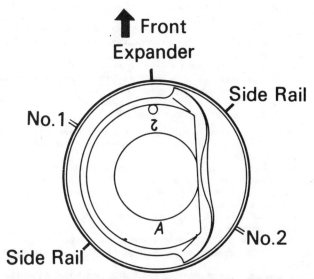

Fig. 2.15 Proper location of ring end gaps on the piston (Sec 24)

24.4 Measuring the piston ring end gap

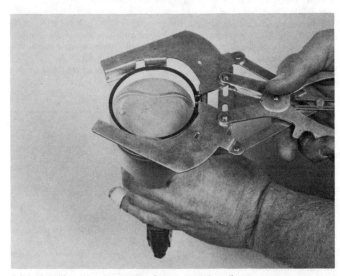

24.6 Installing the piston rings (note special tool)

removed from the crankshaft and bearing surfaces while the testing is done

b)   *Do not rotate the crankshaft while the Plastigage is installed in the engine as this may cause damage to the crankshaft or bearing surfaces*

c)   *Remove all traces of the Plastigage when testing is complete. Be very careful not to harm the crankshaft or bearing surfaces as the Plastigage is removed. Do not use sharp tools or abrasive cleaners, instead, remove the used Plastigage with your fingernail or a blunt wood stick*

2   Whenever an engine is overhauled the bearing clearances should be checked. This should be done for reused bearings as well as for new bearings.

3   The procedure is basically the same for both the main bearings and the connecting rod bearings.

4   With the crankshaft set into the engine block, install the main bearings into the engine block and the main bearing caps.

5   Remove all oil, grime and foreign materials from the crankshaft and bearing surfaces.

6   Place a piece of Plastigage (available at most auto supply shops) along the length of each main bearing journal on the crankshaft (photo).

7   Install each main bearing cap and tighten the attaching bolts to specifications. The arrow on each cap should face toward the front of the engine.

8   Now remove each bearing cap and measure the width of the Plastigage strip which will have flattened out when the caps were tightened. A scale is provided on the Plastigage envelope for measuring the width of the Plastigage strip, and thus, bearing clearance (photo).

9   If the Plastigage is flattened more at the ends than in the middle, or vice versa, this is an indication of journal taper which can be checked in the Specifications Section.

10   To test for an out of round condition, remove all traces of the Plastigage (be careful not to damage the crankshaft or bearing surfaces) and rotate the crankshaft 90 degrees. With the crankshaft rotated to this point, use the Plastigage to check the clearances again. Compare these measurements with those taken previously to arrive at eccentricity or out-of-round.

11   To check connecting rod bearing clearances, install each piston/rod assembly (Section 28) and use the Plastigage as described above.

12   If the bearings have shown to be within all tolerances, they may be installed following the steps outlined in the appropriate Sections.

13   If not within specifications, the bearings should be replaced with the correctly sized bearings. Upper and lower bearings should always be replaced as a unit.

14   Connecting rod side clearance can also be checked at this time. Side clearance can be checked with the piston/rod assemblies temporarily installed for bearing clearance checking.

15   With the piston/rod assemblies installed and the bearing caps tightened to specifications, use feeler gauges to check the clearance between the sides of the connecting rods and the crankshaft (photo).

16   If the clearance at this point is below the minimum tolerance, the rod may be machined for more clearance at this area.

17   If the clearance is too excessive, a new rod must be used or the crankshaft must be reground or replaced with a new one.

27   Crankshaft and main bearings – installation

1   Crankshaft installation is generally one of the first steps in engine reassembly; it is assumed at this point that the engine block and crankshaft have been cleaned and inspected and repaired or reconditioned.

2   Position the engine so that the bottom is facing up.

3   Remove the main bearing cap bolts and lift out the caps. Lay them out in the proper order to help ensure they are installed correctly.

4   If they are still in place, remove the old bearing inserts from the block and the main bearing caps. Wipe the main bearing surfaces of the block and caps with a clean, lint-free cloth (they must be kept spotlessly clean).

5   Clean the back side of the new main bearing inserts and lay one bearing half in each main bearing saddle (in the block) and the other bearing half from each bearing set in the corresponding main bearing

cap. Make sure the tab on the bearing insert fits into the recess in the block or cap. Also, the oil holes in the block and cap must line up with the oil holes in the bearing insert. Do not hammer the bearing into place and do not nick or gouge the bearing faces. No lubrication should be used at this time.

6   The thrust bearing must be installed in the number 3 (center) cup and saddle (photo).

7   Clean the faces of the bearings in the block and the crankshaft main bearing journal with a clean, lint-free cloth. Check or clean the oil holes in the crankshaft, as any dirt here can only go one way – straight through the new bearings.

8   Once you are certain that the crankshaft is clean, carefully lay it in position (an assistant would be very helpful here) in the main bearings with the counterweights lying sideways.

9   Before the crankshaft can be permanently installed, the main bearing oil clearance and thrust clearance must be checked. See Sec 22 and 26 for this procedure.

10   If the clearance is not correct, double-check to make sure that you have the right size bearing inserts. Also, recheck the crankshaft main bearing journal diameters and make sure that no dirt or oil was between the bearing inserts and the main bearing caps or the block when the clearance was measured.

11   Carefully scrape all traces of the Plastigage material off the main bearing journals and/or the bearing faces. Do not nick or scratch the bearing faces.

12   Carefully lift the crankshaft out of the engine. Clean the bearing faces in the block, then apply a thin, uniform layer of clean, high-quality multi-purpose grease (or engine assembly lube) to each of the bearing faces. Be sure to coat the thrust flange faces as well as the journal face of the thrust bearing in the number 3 (center) main. Make sure the crankshaft journals are clean, then carefully lay it back in place in the block.

13   Install the thrust bearing shells into the recess provided in the block at the center journal. Note that the oil recesses fit toward the crankshaft.

14   Install the center-lower crankshaft bearing and cap. Tighten it to the specified torque and rotate the crankshaft to check for free movement.

15   Clean the faces of the bearings in the caps, then apply a thin, uniform layer of clean, high-quality multi-purpose grease to each of the bearing faces and install the caps in their respective positions with the arrows pointing toward the front of the engine. Install the bolts and tighten them to the specified torque, starting with the center main and working out toward the ends. Work up to the final torque in 3 steps.

16   Rotate the crankshaft a number of times by hand and check for any obvious binding.

28   Piston/connecting rod assembly – installation

1   Before installing the piston/connecting rod assemblies, the cylinder walls must be perfectly clean, the top edge of each cylinder must be slightly chamfered, and the crankshaft must be in place.

2   Remove the connecting rod cap from the end of the number 1 connecting rod. Remove the old bearing inserts and wipe the bearing surfaces of the connecting rod and cap with a clean, lint-free cloth (they must be spotlessly clean).

3   Clean the back side of the new upper bearing half, then lay it in place in the connecting rod. Make sure that the tab on the bearing fits into the recess in the rod. Also, the oil holes in the rod and bearing insert must line up. Do not hammer the bearing insert into place, and be very careful not to nick or gouge the bearing face. Do not lubricate the bearing at this time.

4   Clean the back side of the other bearing insert half and install it in the rod cap. Again, make sure the tab on the bearing fits into the recess in the cap, and do not apply any lubricant. It is critically important to ensure that the mating surfaces of the bearing and connecting rod are perfectly clean and oil-free when they are assembled together.

5   Position the piston ring gaps as shown, then slip a section of plastic or rubber hose over the connecting rod cap bolts.

6   Lubricate the piston and rings with clean engine oil and install a piston ring compressor on the piston. Leave the skirt protruding about $\frac{1}{4}$ in to guide the piston into the cylinder. The rings must be compressed as far as possible.

26.6 Placing a strip of Plastigage on the main bearing journal

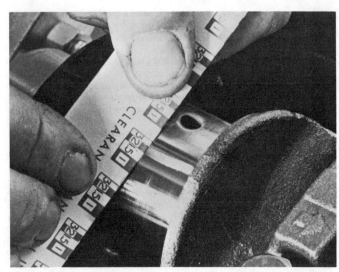

26.8 Measuring the flattened Plastigage strip with the scale provided on the package

26.15 Using a feeler gauge to check the connecting rod side clearance

27.6 Thrust bearing half in place on the number three crankshaft journal

7   Rotate the crankshaft so that the number 1 connecting rod journal is as far from the number 1 cylinder as possible (bottom dead center), and apply a uniform coat of engine oil to the number 1 cylinder walls.

8   With the dot on top of the piston pointing to the front of the engine, gently place the piston/connecting rod assembly into the number 1 cylinder bore and rest the bottom edge of the ring compressor on the engine block. Tap the top edge of the ring compressor to make sure it is contacting the block around its entire circumference.

9   Clean the number 1 connecting rod journal on the crankshaft and the bearing faces in the rod.

10 Carefully tap on the top of the piston with the end of a wooden hammer handle or a soft faced hammer while guiding the end of the connecting rod into place on the crankshaft journal (photo). The piston rings may try to pop out of the ring compressor just before entering the cylinder bore, so keep some downward pressure on the ring compressor. Work slowly, and if any resistance is felt as the piston enters the cylinder, stop immediately, find out what is hanging up and fix it before proceeding. Do not, for any reason, force the piston into the cylinder, as you will break a ring and/or piston.

11 Once the piston/connecting rod assembly is installed, the connecting rod bearing oil clearance must be checked before the rod cap is permanently bolted in place. Check the clearance as described in Section 26. Compare it to the specifications to make sure the clearance is correct. If the clearance is not correct, double-check to

28.10 Tapping the piston rod assembly into the cylinder bore with a soft-faced hammer (note the ring compressor being used)

make sure that you have the correct size bearing inserts. Also, recheck the crankshaft connecting rod journal diameter and make sure that no dirt or oil was between the bearing inserts and the connecting rod or cap when the clearance was measured.

12 Carefully scrape all traces of the Plastigage material off the rod journal and/or bearing face (be very careful not to scratch the bearing). Make sure the bearing faces are perfectly clean, then apply a uniform layer of clean, high quality multi-purpose grease (or engine assembly lube) to both of them. You will have to push the piston into the cylinder to expose the face of the bearing insert in the connecting rod; be sure to slip the protective hoses over the rod bolts first.

13 Slide the connecting rod back into place on the journal, remove the protective hoses from the rod cap bolts, install the rod cap and tighten the nuts to the specified torque. Again, work up to the torque in 3 steps.

14 Without turning the crankshaft, repeat the entire procedure for the number 4 piston/connecting rod assembly. Keep the back sides of the bearing inserts and the inside of the connecting rod and cap perfectly clean when assembling them. Make sure you have the correct piston for the cylinder and that the dot on the piston points to the front of the engine when the piston is installed. Remember, use plenty of oil to lubricate the piston before installing the ring compressor, and be sure to match up the mating marks on the connecting rod and rod cap. Also, when installing the rod caps for the final time, be sure to lubricate the bearing faces adequately.

15 After completing the procedure for piston number 4, turn the crankshaft 180° and repeat the entire operation for pistons number 2 and 3.

29 Engine – assembly sequence

1   Follow all of the assembly steps if you are assembling the engine from a bare block. If you are starting with a short block (Sec 20), begin with step 5. If you have a used or rebuilt 'long' block such as might come from a wrecking yard or engine rebuild shop, begin with step 12.
2   Clean and prepare the block (Sec 19 and Sec 25).
3   Install the crankshaft and main bearings (Sec 27).
4   Install the pistons, connecting rods and bearings (Sec 28).
5   Install the cylinder head (Sec 7).
6   Install the oil pump, and pickup assembly and oil pan (Sec 18).
7   Install the camshaft (Sec 13).
8   Install the timing belt, gears and tensioner (Sec 11).
9   Install the rocker arm assembly (Sec 12).
10   Install the lower timing belt cover (Sec 10).
11   Install the crankshaft pulley.
12   Adjust the valves (Chapter 1).
13   Install the crankshaft rear seal (Sec 14).
14   Install the flywheel if the vehicle is manual transmission equipped or the flex plate if automatic transmission equipped.
15   Install the engine oil filter if the engine is not being immediately lowered into the car. The filter will keep dust and debris out of the internal engine oil passages. Remove the filter immediately before beginning the engine installation procedure.
16   Install the cam cover gasket into the cam cover.
17   Install the camshaft cover onto the cylinder head.
18   Install the three sealing grommets over the camshaft cover retaining studs.
19   Install the retaining nuts over the camshaft cover studs. Tighten them to the proper torque.
20   Install the fuel pump and the fuel pump shield using new gaskets (Chapter 4).
21   Install the rear coolant tube onto the rear area of the cylinder head using a new gasket, gasket sealer and the two bolts (Chapter 3).
22   Install the front-to-rear heater transfer tube to the side of the block (Chapter 3).
23   Inspect the mating surfaces of the exhaust and intake manifold as described in Chapter 4.
24   Install a new gasket for the intake and exhaust manifold. Notice that it fits properly in only one direction. **Note:** *If the exhaust manifold was separated from the intake manifold on disassembly, the following procedures should be used. Notice that the lifting hook and ground wire are attached to the rear manifold stud.*
25   Loosely install the exhaust manifold using the four retaining bolts.
26   Install the intake manifold. Loosely install the intake manifold retaining bolts.

27   Loosely install the intake-to-exhaust manifold connecting bolts.
28   Tighten the exhaust manifold bolts.
29   Tighten the intake manifold retaining bolts.
30   Tighten the intake manifold-to-exhaust manifold clamping bolts.
31   Tighten the manifold retaining bolts to the specified torque, starting from the center and working outward in a pattern from side-to-side.
32   Install a new gasket between the intake manifold and the carburetor heat shield. Install the carburetor heat shield over the carburetor hold-down studs. Install the PCV adapter plate over the carburetor hold-down studs. Install the carburetor. Make sure that any brackets that need to be retained over the carburetor hold-down studs are positioned in place at this time, then install the carburetor hold-down nuts. Tighten them to the prescribed torque.
33   Attach the retaining bracket to air injection feed pipe (if so equipped).
34   Install the accelerator cable retainer bracket to the rear runner of the intake manifold, using one bolt and one nut.
35   Install the throttle return spring from the above mentioned bracket to the throttle linkage.
36   Coat the EGR valve tube flare nuts with anti-sieze compound. Install the EGR tube. Tighten both fitting nuts (use a flare nut wrench if possible).
37   Install the heat transfer duct onto the flange of the exhaust manifold. Install the oxygen sensor into the exhaust manifold (if so equipped).
38   Install the combination right side motor mount and air pump assembly.
39   Install the three nuts and washers retaining the right hand motor mount air pump assembly to the stud on the lower right front of the block.
40   Install the bolt retaining the support strap locating the air pump to the exhaust manifold.
41   Secure the air pump in its inner-most retracted position.
42   Install the exhaust manifold-to-block support bracket. Install both retaining bolts to the bracket. Tighten the bolts by hand and finally tighten them starting with the bolt on the exhaust manifold and ending with the bolt on the engine block.
43   Install the coolant temperature sending unit in the front of the cylinder head.
44   Install the water pump utilizing the procedure described in Chapter 3.
45   Install new O-rings on the by-pass pipe which connects the water outlet housing to the water pump. Install the water outlet housing and the by-pass pipe using a new gasket and silicone sealing material behind the water outlet housing.
46   Install the thermostat and housing.
47   Install the dipstick tube using a new O-ring and tighten the bolt. Install the dipstick.
48   Install the upper timing cover using a new gasket. Notice that the top bolt of the five retaining bolts also secures a wiring harness.
49   Install the auxiliary drive pulley onto the crankshaft pulley (if so equipped). Tighten the pulley retaining bolts to the prescribed torque.
50   Install the block drain using teflon-type sealer on the threads. **Note:** *Omit the following step if the engine is being immediately installed in a vehicle with factory air conditioning.*
51   Install the left-hand motor mount and accessory mounting bracket assembly using three bolts and a washer.
52   Install the oil pressure sender using teflon coating on the threads.
53   Install the spark plugs in the cylinder head.
54   Install the upper alternator bracket and engine hook onto the tab on the left-front area of the cylinder head.
55   Install the distributor as described in Chapter 5.
56   Install the clutch if the vehicle is equipped with a manual transmission or install the torque converter if it is automatic transmission equipped.
57   Install the rear flywheel dust cover. The pan gasket may interfere slightly so a small amount of trimming may be necessary around the lip of the oil pan.

30 Engine installation

1   Support the transaxle assembly with a jack.
2   Attach a sling to the two engine lifting hooks, making sure that the engine is balanced at a nearly level position. The following steps are

best performed with a two man team of installers.

3   Raise the engine to a height which will enable it to clear the front radiator support.

4   Center the engine over the engine compartment both side-to-side and front-to-rear. **Note:** *If the vehicle is equipped with air conditioning and you have left the air conditioning compressor hooked-up and supported at the left inner fender well, the left motor mount will have to be removed at this point in order for the engine to drop into its proper position.*

5   Slowly lower the engine into the engine compartment bay, watching carefully for all clearances front-to-rear and left-to-right.

6   Lower the engine into place until it is directly in line with the mating surface of the bellhousing or transmission torque converter cover.

7   Carefully guide the engine backwards onto either the splines of the input shaft (if manual transmission equipped) or onto the splines of the front transmission shaft (if automatic transmission equipped).

8   Take care to use a gentle motion when engaging the engine to the transmission during the last inch of movement. As the transmission shaft enters the rear of the pilot bearing, there may be slight interference and turning of the front crankshaft pulley could possibly help.

9   Insert the four large bellhousing-to-engine block retaining bolts and tighten them incrementally to the proper torque.

10 Insert the left-hand motor mount back into position if the vehicle is equipped with the air conditioning compressor.

11 Gradually lower the jack supporting the transaxle assembly.

12 Gradually lower the engine hoist, using the helper to guide both motor mounts into their respective holes in the crossmember.

13 Install the washers and nuts which retain the lower part of the engine motor mounts.

14 Install the lower link of the engine shock absorber using the bolt, washer and nut.

15 Attach the ground lead to the bellhousing using the bolt and nut. Notice this ground lead is attached at the 7 o'clock position as you look toward the front of the vehicle.

16 Attach the small bolt which retains the dust shield to the bellhousing at the 12 o'clock position as you look toward the front of the vehicle. Notice that this bolt faces toward the rear of the vehicle and is threaded into the bellhousing.

17 Install the left-hand engine stiffener plate using three bolts. Notice that there is a ground strap attached to this plate.

18 Install the right-hand engine stiffener plate using four bolts.

19 Install two new sealing gaskets onto the exhaust down pipe.

20 Install the exhaust down pipe to the exhaust manifold using three nuts. Tighten the nuts to the specified torque.

21 Install the headpipe support bracket using one bolt.

22 Install the remaining pieces of the exhaust system as described in Chapter 4.

23 Install the starter, which is retained by two bolts.

24 If the vehicle is equipped with a manual transmission, connect the clutch cable to the clutch actuating arm. Refer to Chapter 8 for the clutch cable installation procedure.

25 Connect the throttle linkage cable to the hold-down and to the carburetor linkage.

26 Install the brake vacuum booster supply line along with its accompanying clamp. Notice that the clamp also retains the ground strap.

27 Reconnect the wiring which leads from the alternator harness to the engine ground.

28 Connect the positive battery lead to the starter post.

29 Connect the starter switch lead to the solenoid with the quick connect clip.

30 Connect the ground lead, which is secured by one bolt directly ahead of the starter.

31 Connect the push-on connector for the oil pressure switch.

32 Install the air conditioning compressor (if so equipped) to the engine according to the instructions found in Chapter 3.

33 Install the air conditioner idler pulley bracket, which is retained by two bolts.

34 Install the alternator.

35 Connect the wiring to the alternator.

36 Connect the push-on wiring connector to the water temperature sender and to the sensor on the water outlet housing (if so equipped).

37 Install the engine oil filter.

38 Install the drivebelts on front pulleys of the engine. The number and size of the belts will vary depending on what accessories the vehicle is equipped with. For information regarding tightening procedures, refer to Chapter 1.

39 Connect the diverter valve air hose to the air pump.

40 Connect the quick release wiring connectors to the emissions control devices on the right-hand side of the engine compartment near the inner fender well.

41 Connect the oxygen sensor connector located directly beneath the diverter valve (if so equipped).

42 Connect both heater hoses to the coolant transfer tubes near the rear of the engine. Tighten the clamps on all water connections.

43 Install the heater control retainer bracket.

44 Connect the fuel lines to the fuel pump.

45 Install the radiator.

46 Attach the connector to the coolant sensor at the bottom of the radiator.

47 Connect the ground wire to the top of the radiator.

48 Install the lower radiator hose and tighten the clamps.

49 Install the coolant overflow hose at the top outlet on the radiator.

50 Install the upper radiator hose and tighten the clamps.

51 Attach the various hoses and lines for the emissions control devices as per the diagram or Figures from Chapter 6.

52 Install the heater control cable retainer bracket located in the center of the firewall.

31 Valves – adjustment

Refer to Chapter 1, Section 26 for the valve adjustment procedure.

32 Engine – start-up after major repair or overhaul

1   With the engine in place in the vehicle and all components connected, make a final check that all pipes and wiring have been connected and that no rags or tools have been left in the engine compartment.

2   Connect the negative battery cable. If it sparks or arcs, power is being drawn from someplace and all accessories and wiring should be checked.

3   Fill the cooling system with the proper mixture and amount of coolant (Chapter 1).

4   Fill the crankcase with the correct quantity and grade of oil (Chapter 1).

5   Check the tension of all drive belts (Chapter 1).

6   Disconnect the distributor at the harness loom connector, (Chapter 5) to prevent the engine from starting. Now crank the engine over for about 15 to 30 seconds. This will allow the oil pump to distribute oil and the fuel pump to start pumping fuel to the carburetor.

7   Now reconnect the harness connector at the distributor and start the engine. Immediately check all gauges and warning lights for proper readings and check for leaks of coolant or oil.

8   If the engine does not start immediately, check to make sure fuel is reaching the carburetor. This may take a while.

9   After allowing the engine to run for a few minutes at low speed, turn it off and check the oil and coolant levels.

10 Start the engine again and check the ignition timing, emission control settings and carburetor idle speeds (Chapter 1).

11 Run the vehicle easily during the first 500 to 1000 miles (break-in period) then check the torque settings on all major engine components, particularly the cylinder heads. Tighten any bolts which may have loosened.

12 The valve clearance adjustment should also be reset at this time.

Chapter 3 Cooling, heating and air conditioning

Contents

Specifications

Thermostat

Opening temperature

    Starts to open at .... 176° to 183°F (80° to 84°C)

    Fully open at .... 203°F (95°C)

Valve travel .... 0.31 in (8 mm)

Coolant

Capacity

    Manual transmission .... 5.4 US qts (5.1 liters)

    Automatic transmission .... 5.5 US qts (5.2 liters)

Coolant type .... Ethylene glycol

Fan

Amperage draw

    Automatic transmission .... 8 to 11 amps

    Manual transmission .... 3.8 to 5.4 amps

Activation temperatures

    High temperature (fan comes on) .... 194°F (90°C)

    Low temperature (fan comes on) .... 181°F (83°C)

Radiator cap opening pressure .... 10.7 to 14.9 psi (0.75 to 1.05 kg/cm²)

---

1 Cooling system – general description

The cooling system used on the Tercel is conventional in design. It utilizes a vertical-flow radiator, an engine-driven, vane-type water pump and a thermostatically-controlled electric cooling fan mounted ahead of the radiator. An in-line thermostat controls warm-up temperature.

The water pump is mounted at the front of the engine and driven by the front pulley through a flexible drive belt.

The heater uses the heat from the circulated engine coolant by drawing air through a passenger compartment-mounted heater core (similar to a small radiator). Flow to the heater core is controlled from the passenger compartment by a cable connected to an engine compartment mounted valve.

Air conditioning is an available option. Most of the air conditioning components are mounted in the engine compartment except for the controls and the cooling unit. Special refrigerant lines transfer the freon back and forth between the interior and engine compartment components.

2   Antifreeze and inhibiting solutions

1   It is recommended that the cooling system be filled with a water/ethylene glycol based antifreeze solution which will give protection down to at least − 20°F at all times. This provides protection against corrosion and increases the coolant boiling point. When handling antifreeze, take care that it is not spilled on the vehicle paintwork, since it will invariably cause damage if not removed immediately.

2   The cooling system should be drained, flushed and refilled every alternate Fall. The use of antifreeze solutions for periods of longer than two years is likely to cause damage and encourage the formation of rust and scale due to the corrosion inhibitors gradually losing their efficiency.

3   Before adding antifreeze to the system, check all hose connections and check the tightness of the cylinder head bolts.

4   The exact mixture of antifreeze to water which you should use depends upon the relative weather conditions. The mixture should contain at least 50 percent antifreeze, offering protection to −34°F. Under no circumstances should the mixture contain more than 70 percent antifreeze.

3   Cooling system – draining, flushing and refilling

1   As part of regular routine maintenance, the coolant should be drained and the system completely flushed. Refer to Chapter 1 for the procedure to follow.

2   Always use a mixture of 50% soft water and 50% ethylene glycol based antifreeze when refilling the cooling system. Many of the engine parts are made of aluminium, which requires the corrosion protection offered by this type of antifreeze.

4   Thermostat – removal, inspection and installation

1   Drain the cooling system at the radiator and engine block drain points.

2   Disconnect the wire for the coolant switch located at the lower part of the radiator. Disconnect the coolant reservoir tube and then remove the lower radiator hose at the thermostat housing.
Note: *The thermostat housing is in an unconventional location on the right side of the water pump. See Fig. 3.1 for details.*

3   Remove the two nuts securing the thermostat housing to the water pump.

4   Remove the thermostat housing.

5   Remove the thermostat. **Note**: *It may remain in the water pump housing after the outlet housing is removed.*

6   Note the number on the thermostat which will indicate the temperature at which the valve is supposed to open. Emerge the thermostat in water and heat the water gradually using a thermometer to indicate temperature. Check the temperature at which the valve opens and see that it opens the correct amount. If the opening temperature and/or valve lift are not within the specifications, replace the thermostat with a new one. Check that the valve spring is tight when the thermostat is fully closed.

7   Clean the inlet housing and the mating surface on the water pump to remove old gasket material.

8   Install a new gasket on the inlet housing and install the thermostat making sure it is facing the correct direction (Fig. 3.1).

9   Install the housing and thermostat onto the water pump using the two nuts.

10 Connect the lower radiator hose to the housing.

11 Close the drain plugs and fill the radiator with a 50/50 solution of water and approved coolant.

12 Connect the coolant reservoir tube.

13 Connect the wire for the coolant temperature switch at the lower part of the radiator.

14 Check for leaks before running the engine. Warm the engine and observe the temperature gauge to ensure that the thermostat is operating correctly.

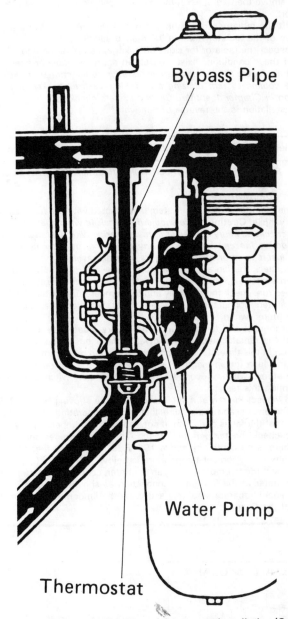

Fig. 3.1 Location and direction of thermostat installation (Sec 4)

5   Radiator – removal, inspection and installation

1   Disconnect the negative battery cable. Drain the cooling system at the two drain points shown in Chapter 1.

2   Remove the front lower splash shield.

3   Disconnect the electrical wire to the coolant temperature switch.

4   Disconnect the lower radiator hose at the radiator.

5   Disconnect the lower radiator hose at the water pump and remove it from the vehicle.

6   Disconnect the upper radiator hose from the radiator and from the engine water adapter.

7   Remove the upper radiator hose.

8   If the vehicle is equipped with an automatic transmission, disconnect the two transmission cooler lines at the lower part of the radiator.
Note: *The lines will leak transmission fluid and should be plugged.*

9   Bend the tab securing the coolant temperature switch wiring harness to the side of the radiator and release the wiring harness.

10 Remove the coolant recovery hose from the radiator filler neck.

11 Disconnect the air conditioning suction hose bracket (if so equipped) from the radiator upper support. Move the suction hose to the side of the engine compartment to facilitate radiator removal.

12 Remove the two upper retaining bolts securing the radiator to the support.
13 Lift the radiator straight up and out of the vehicle. Note that the bottom of the radiator fits in a 'U' shaped saddle.
14 Inspect the radiator for signs of leakage, deterioration and rust. If any of these conditions exist, consult an approved radiator specialist for repair. **Note**: *The radiator can be tested in conjunction with the rest of the cooling system utilizing a radiator pressure checker. See the Section in Chapter 1 entitled Cooling system checking.*
15 Installation is the reverse of removal.

6 Electric cooling fan – removal, inspection and installation

Note: *Refer to Fig. 3.2 when performing the following procedures.*

Fan inspection

1 The electric cooling fan system is inspected with the fan installed in the vehicle. **Caution**: *Care should be exercised while making any of these checks as injury can result from interfering with the fan's motion. The cooling fan can come on at any time when it is connected, so never insert tools or hands within its area of travel.*
2 To check the fan at a temperature below 181°F (83°C), turn the ignition switch on. The fan should not run at this temperature. If the fan does run, check the fan relay and the temperature switch. Look for a separated connector or severed wires between the relay and temperature switch.
3 Disconnect the temperature switch wire located at the bottom side of the radiator next to the lower radiator hose. The fan should come on at this time. If it does not, check the fan relay, motor, ignition relay and fuse for an electrical short between the fan relay and the temperature switch. Reconnect the temperature switch wire after performing this test.
4 To inspect the fan at a vehicle temperature above 194°F (90°C), start the engine and make sure that it is at operating temperature. Check that the fan is operating. If not, replace the temperature switch.
5 To check the temperature switch, use an ohmmeter and check that there is no continuity above 194°F (90°C). Check that there is continuity when coolant temperature is below 180°F (83°C).
6 Inspect the fan motor. Using an ammeter, connect the battery and the ammeter to the fan motor connection as shown in Fig. 3.3. The motor should operate smoothly and draw the amperage listed at the front of the Chapter.

Removal and installation

7 Remove the grille as described in Chapter 12.
8 Disconnect the negative cable at the battery.
9 Disconnect the electrical wire leading to the fan at the connector located directly below the passenger side headlight. Release the wiring by opening the metal tab located at the eight o'clock position on the fan housing.
10 Remove the three fan motor mount bolts.
11 Remove the nut and two washers which attach the fan to the cooling fan motor. This is accomplished by reaching around to the front of the fan (next to the radiator) and unthreading the nut.
12 Remove the fan motor from its mount. Note that the fan will remain in its same relative position while this step is being performed.
13 Installation is the reverse of removal.

7 Water pump – removal, inspection and installation

1 Disconnect the negative battery cable, then drain the radiator and engine block at the drain cock.
2 Remove the radiator as described in Section 5.
3 Loosen the pivot and adjusting bolts for the alternator (see Chapter 5) and remove the alternator drive belt from the alternator pulley.
4 If the vehicle is equipped with an air pump, loosen the adjusting and pivot bolts for the air pump and remove the air pump drive belt from its pulley.
5 Separate the pulley from the front of the water pump by removing the four bolts.
6 Remove the water outlet fitting from the backside of the pump.
Note: *There are two bolts securing the water outlet and a combination of vacuum hoses connected to the switches on the water outlet.*
7 Remove the thermostat and thermostat housing (Section 4).
8 Remove the front upper timing belt cover which is secured by five bolts.
9 Remove the two nuts securing the heater outlet hose to the water pump.
10 Remove the dipstick and dipstick tube secured by one bolt. Temporarily plug the hole with a rag or suitable plug.
11 Remove the three bolts securing the water pump to the front of the engine (photo).
12 Remove the water pump.
13 Check the seal drain hole for signs of leakage.

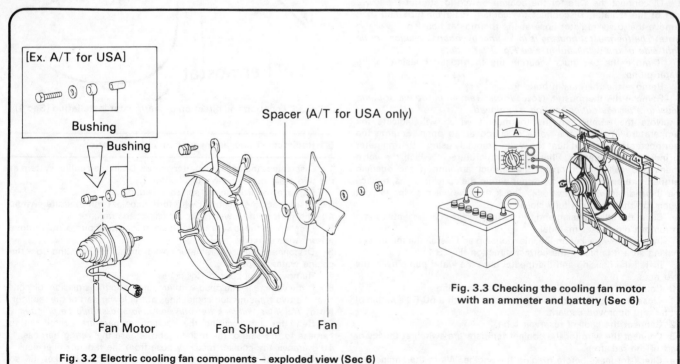

[Ex. A/T for USA]

Bushing

Bushing

Spacer (A/T for USA only)

Fan Motor   Fan Shroud   Fan

Fig. 3.2 Electric cooling fan components – exploded view (Sec 6)

Fig. 3.3 Checking the cooling fan motor with an ammeter and battery (Sec 6)

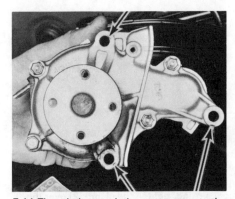

7.11 Three bolts attach the water pump to the engine block

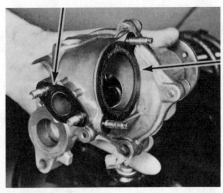

7.19 Be sure to use new gaskets on the outlet housing and heater connecting tube of the water pump

8.16 Push the heater valve to the Off position and attach the cable

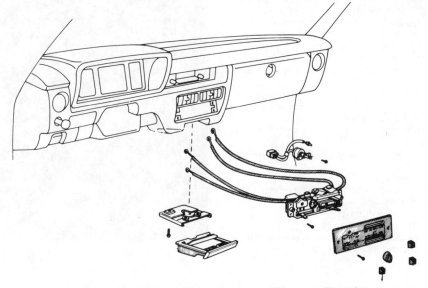

Fig. 3.4 Components of the heater control system (Sec 8)

14 Turn the shaft in the pump and feel for roughness or excessive looseness.

15 Check the sealing surfaces of the gaskets for signs of leakage.

16 If any of the above conditions exist, replace the water pump with a new one.

17 If the water pump is to be replaced, remove the four bolts securing it to the back plate.

18 Clean all gasket mating surfaces, replace the gasket and secure the back mounting plate with the four bolts.

19 Install a new heater outlet pipe gasket onto the water pump (photo).

20 Replace the O-ring in the front of the engine block which seals the water pump. Use a lithium based grease to hold the O-ring in position while installing the pump.

21 Installation is basically the reverse of removal.

22 When installing belts, be sure to adjust the free play to the specified amount listed in Chapter 1 specifications.

8 Heater controls – removal, checking and installation

Note: *Refer to Fig. 3.4 thru 3.7 for components and locations related to the following steps.*

Removal

1 Remove the negative battery cable from the battery.

2 Remove the ash tray. Remove the three screws retaining the ash tray bracket.

3 Pull the knobs off the front of the control panel.

4 Remove the screws retaining the heater control panel face. Remove the heater control panel face.

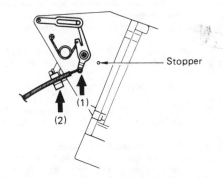

Fig. 3.5 With the damper (1) set to the fresh air position, clamp the cable (2) in position (Sec 8)

5 Disconnect the cable at the air inlet damper.

6 Disconnect the cable leading to the water control valve.

7 Disconnect the air mix damper cable.

8 Disconnect the mode select damper cable.

9 Remove the screws from the heater blower switch. Disconnect the heater blower switch connector.

10 Remove the heater control assembly by pulling it straight out.

Checking

11 Check that all the cables move freely and are not kinked.

12 Lubricate the cables with a penetrating oil. Lubricate the pivot points on the heater control levers.

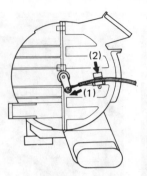

Fig. 3.6 With the mode select damper (1) set to the vent position, tighten the clamp (2) over the cable (Sec 8)

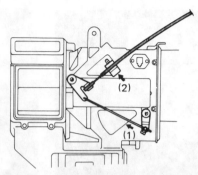

Fig. 3.7 With the air mix damper (1) positioned as shown, and the air mix lever on the cool setting, tighten the clamp (2) over the cable (Sec 8)

Installation

13 Set the air inlet damper to the fresh air side. Set the air control lever to the fresh air setting. Install the air inlet damper cable on the control pivot and clamp the cable.
14 Set the mode select damper to the vent side. Set the air control to vent. Install the cable end onto the damper lever and clamp the cable.
15 Set the air mix damper to the cool side. Set the control panel to cool also. Install the cable onto the damper lever and clamp the cable in place.
16 Set the heater valve to the Off position. Set the temperature control to the Cool position. Connect the cable end to the temperature control lever and clamp the cable into place (photo).
17 Connect the blower control switch and install the switch into the dash with the retaining screws.
18 Install the heater control assembly into the dash and tighten the hold down screws.
19 Push the knobs onto the levers.
20 Test the operation of all of the levers and see that they move their full length of travel in a smooth manner.
21 Install the ash tray bracket and ash tray.
22 Install the negative battery cable.
23 Test the air flow operation with the blower on to ensure that the controls are hooked up properly and all modes of the heating system function properly.

9.14 Loosening the heater core retaining screw

9 Heater core – removal, inspection and installation

1   Remove the heater controls as described in the previous Section.
2   Drain the engine and radiator at their respective drain spigots (see Chapter 1).
3   Remove the heater rear duct (if the car is so equipped).
4   Remove the left-hand air duct that is secured by one bolt.
5   Remove the dash under tray (if so equipped).
6   Remove the glove compartment.
7   Remove the right-hand air duct.
8   Remove the fresh air intake connecting duct (this duct may be replaced with the air conditioning connecting module on cars so equipped).
9   Remove the radio as described in Chapter 10.
10   Remove the heater clamps, hoses and grommets from the heater core spigots. Be careful when pulling on these spigots as they are fragile and can easily be twisted off the heater core.
11   Remove the connecting transfer duct (photo).
12   Remove the right-hand upper airflow duct.
13   Remove the heater core housing assembly after unbolting it from the firewall.
14   The heater core will pull out of the housing assembly after loosening the retaining screw and swiveling the keeper to the side (photo).
15   Check for evidence of leaks and other damage. Repair and cleaning of the core should be handled by a radiator repair shop. If the heater core is in questionable condition, replace it with a new one.
16   Installation is the reverse of removal. Be sure the heater hoses are properly seated on the heater core inlet and outlet spigots, and tighten the clamps securely. Do not over-tighten the clamps as they can distort the heater spigots and cause a leak.
17   Adjust the control cables as described in Section 8.

10 Air conditioning – general servicing information

1   Because of the special tools, equipment and skills required to service air conditioning systems, and the differences between the various systems that may be installed on vehicles, air conditioner servicing cannot be covered in this manual.
2   We will cover component removal, as the home mechanic may realize a substantial savings in repair costs if he removes components himself, takes them to a professional for repair, and/or replaces them with new ones.
3   The Tercel uses air conditioning available from a number of different sources. This and the following Sections will deal with the factory installed system only. Air conditioning systems are available as dealer-installed Toyota brand as well as from many independent manufacturers.
4   Determine what type of system is on your car by looking at the data plate usually found on the compressor. If you can't find the type of system, it would be best to consult an air conditioning specialty shop for repair information, or help. Problems in the air conditioning system should be diagnosed, and the system refrigerant evacuated, by an air conditioning technician. **Note:** *If any component of the air conditioning system needs to be removed, the system must be depressurized first. Do not attempt to disconnect any part yourself as the system contains freon gas under very high pressure. This could result in serious physical injury as well as damage to the system.*
5   Once the new or reconditioned component has been installed, the system should then be charged and checked by an air conditioning technician.
6   Before indiscriminately removing air conditioning system components, get more than one estimate of repair costs from reputable air conditioning service centers. You may find it to be cheaper and less trouble to let the entire operation be performed by someone else.

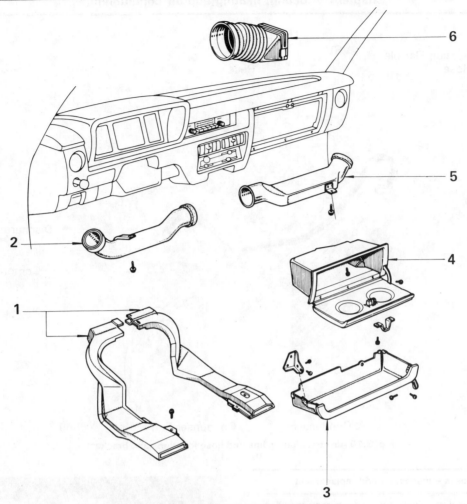

Fig. 3.8 Lower dash components and locations:
(1) Heater rear duct (optional), (2) left side
air duct, (3) underdash tray (optional), (4) glove
compartment, (5) right side air duct, (6) fresh air
intake connecting duct

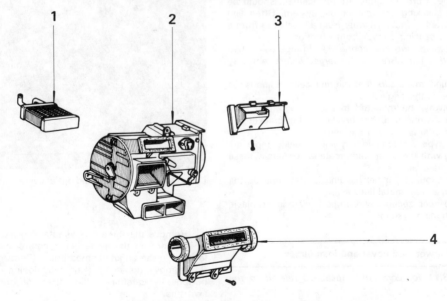

Fig. 3.9 Heater core related components:
(1) heater core, (2) heater module, (3) center defroster connecting
duct, (4) connecting transfer duct

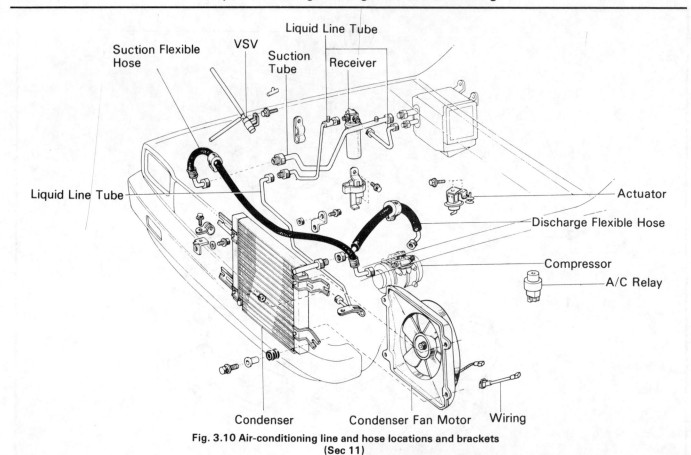

**Fig. 3.10 Air-conditioning line and hose locations and brackets
(Sec 11)**

11 Air conditioning hoses – inspection and replacement

1   If the air conditioning system has become discharged and a line is suspected, the system will need to be recharged and a dye inserted with the recharge for proper leak detection.

2   If you are not familiar with recharging air conditioning systems, this work would be best left to an air conditioning technician.

3   Once a line has been proved faulty, its replacement should be considered only after checking the rest of the system. Often line breakage can be attributed to frictional wear from a bracket or from a loosened mounting part causing a crack from vibration.

4   Remove a line from its two end connecting fittings using two wrenches. *Make sure that the system is discharged before removing any lines.*

5   When replacing a line, make sure that the replacement line is the exact length and shape as the original.

6   Metal lines will always be mounted in such a way that their movement is contained within a rubber bracket. If the bracket has worn, replace the bracket(s) along with the line.

7   If a flexible hose type air conditioning line is being replaced, always replace it along with the outer lining material. Generally these hoses come with this material.

8   The procedure for mounting a flexible line is the same as the procedure for mounting a rigid metal line.

9   After all lines have been secured and properly clamped in place, recharge the air conditioning system.

12 Air conditioning blower – removal and installation

Note: *Refer to Fig. 3.11 for component locations related to the following Section.*

Removal

1   Remove the glove box assembly.

2   Remove the right-hand air conditioning connecting tube (photo).

3   Remove the right-hand air conditioning outlet, secured by one screw at the top, from the inside of the dash (photo).

12.2 Remove the right-hand outlet connecting tube

4   Remove the three screws retaining the ash tray support plate.

5   Disconnect the heater valve control cable from the heater valve located in the engine compartment (Section 8).

6   Remove the heating air conditioning control switch knobs and buttons by carefully pulling them off their respective levers and switches.

7   Remove the heating/air conditioning control plate retained by two Phillips head screws.

8   Remove the four control unit retaining screws and push the unit back into the dash.

9   Remove the wiring harness retaining strap affixed to the left center dash support.

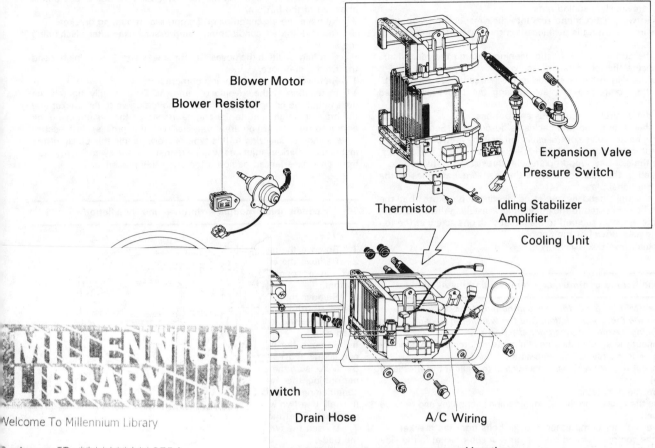

Air-conditioning system components and locations
(Sec 12)

Welcome To Millennium Library

Customer ID: **********9534

Title: Toyota Tercel automotive repair manu
ID: 33097039750218
Due: 24 May 2011

Total items: 1
22 May 2011

Overdue fines:
Adult items .40 cents/day per item
Children's items .20 cents/day per item

Visit Us Online At: Winnipeg.ca/Library or call
Telecirc at 986-4657

12.10 Unplug the two wiring connectors (arrows) for the air conditioning system and blower

12.15 Two mounting lugs (arrows) attach the top of the blower module box

valve control cable through the firewall.
13 Remove the heater/air conditioning control unit and cables from the rear of the dashboard.
14 Remove the adapter from the blower module. It is retained by one screw.
15 Remove the two nuts from the mounting lugs on top of the blower module box (photo).
16 Remove the blower module box assembly.
17 Remove the blower from the blower module box. It is secured by three screws.

Installation

18 Install the blower motor onto the blower housing. Make sure that the lugs that fit the three locating holes in the motor adapter are placed in position before tightening the screws. This is critical for blower alignment.
19 Screw the adapter to the blower module box.
20 Secure the module and adapter into place utilizing the two mounting lugs at the top to locate the unit.
21 Install, but do not tighten, the two nuts on the top mounting lugs.
22 Remove the screw which secures the adapter to the blower box. This allows you to move the adapter plate sufficiently to install the mounting tabs.
23 Reinsert the screw which connects the adapter to the blower module.

24 Complete the installation by installing the remaining bolt, then tighten the previously installed nuts.

25 Plug the two plastic connectors into their respective receptacles and make sure the wiring is positioned on the upper bulkhead side of the dash.

26 Insert the control unit into the opening through the rear of the dash and secure the four retaining screws.

27 Secure the wiring harness strap to the left center dash support.

28 Install the control cover plate utilizing the two Phillips head screws.

29 Install the control switch knobs and buttons.

30 Install the three air control cables as described in Section 8.

31 Push the heater valve control cable through the firewall and attach it to the heater valve as described in Section 8.

32 Secure the ash tray support plate with three screws. The two front screws attach to the dashboard while the rear screw attaches to the heater control panel plate.

33 Install the right-hand air outlet connecting tube. Note that the elbow must be connected to the outlet before installing the cross tube. Note that the elbow is secured to the outlet with one screw at the top and an alignment dowel at the bottom.

34 Install the glove box assembly.

13 Air conditioning compressor – removal and installation

Note: *Refer to Fig. 3.12 for the components and their locations described in the following Section. See the warning in Section 10 on air conditioning system charging and discharging.*

1 Disconnect the air conditioning compressor clutch switch connector located near the rear of the alternator.

2 Disconnect the two wiring connections at the rear of the alternator (Chapter 5).

3 Remove the alternator.

4 Release the tension on the air conditioning idler pulley and remove the drive belt.

5 Remove the four compressor through bolts from the bracket.

6 Move the compressor and the compressor sub-bracket to the side and remove the five compressor mounting bolts. Note that one bolt is attached to the bottom.

7 Remove the air conditioning compressor mounting bracket.

8 Remove the air conditioning compressor hoses after discharging the system.

9 Carefully position the hoses out of the way and do not kink or bend the fixed metal hose.

10 Remove the air conditioning compressor.

11 Installation is the reverse of removal. Do not fully tighten the hoses until the compressor is securely bolted down to its bracket and the bracket is tightened to the engine. Recharge the system using the approved method. If you are unfamiliar with this process, it is best to have a shop specializing in this type of work handle this phase of the installation. Serious injury as well as damage to the system can result from an inexperienced person attempting this procedure.

14 Air conditioning module – removal and installation

Removal

1 Remove the left-hand air conditioning and bi-level air duct.

2 Remove the central air flow diffuser located between the heater box and air conditioning ducts by withdrawing the two screws at the bottom.

3 Remove the center air flow diffuser held in place by two screws on the rear of the dash panel.

4 Remove the lower heat diffuser retained by two screws and one snap clip.

5 Remove the heater box-to-defroster connecting link retained by one screw and two lock tabs.

6 Make sure the air conditioning system is totally discharged before performing this next step (see Section 10). Remove the two air conditioning line fittings on the engine compartment side of the firewall. Use two wrenches for this task. Remove the insulating rubber grommets from these lines (photo).

7 Loosen the two bolts and one nut retaining the heater module to the body.

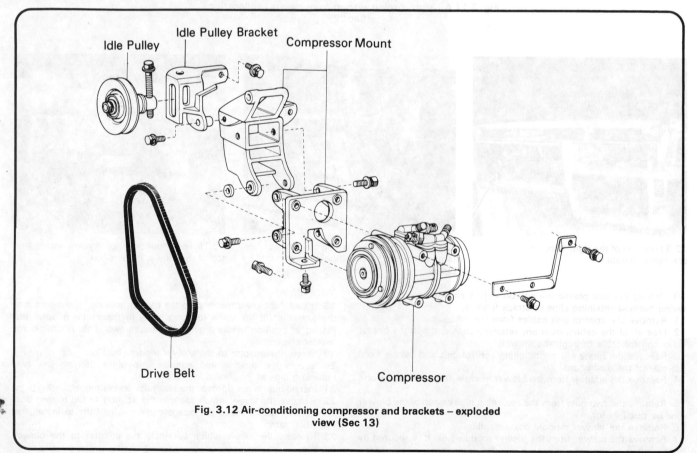

Fig. 3.12 Air-conditioning compressor and brackets – exploded view (Sec 13)

14.6 Remove the air conditioning line fittings and insulating grommets

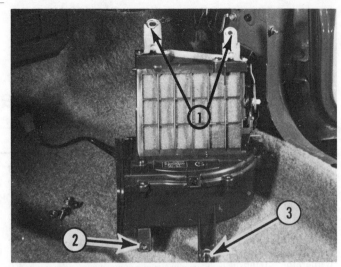

14.8 Two nuts (1), one screw (2) and one bolt (3) attach the air conditioning module to the car body

8   Remove the two nuts, one bolt and one screw retaining the air conditioning module to the body (photo).
9   Carefully withdraw the air conditioning module and pay special attention to the two lines as they come through the firewall.

Installation

10 After attaching the heater core box to the body and loosely installing the two bolts and one nut, insert the air conditioning module. While inserting the air conditioning module, push the drain hose through the hole in the floor pan.
11 Next, carefully push the fittings through the firewall holes while an assistant guides the rubber grommets and the fittings onto their receiving lines.
12 From the interior, loosely install the two nuts and one attaching bolt.
13 Tighten the air conditioning line fittings.
14 Now fully tighten the three fasteners for the module.
15 Place the carpeting into position and make sure the velcro fasteners are engaged.
16 Tighten the three heater module fasteners.
17 Attach the heater box to the defroster connecting link by inserting the two tabs into the accompanying grooved slots of the defroster duct.
18 Insert the one screw and two lock tabs retaining the intermediate link.
19 Install the lower heat diffuser using two screws and one snap-lock.
20 Install the center air conditioner diffuser duct utilizing the two screws which are inserted from the rear of the dash panel.
21 Install the central air flow diffuser between the heater box and air conditioning ducts. Note the alignment tab which mates with the lug on this connecting junction.
22 Insert and tighten the two screws at the bottom of this connecting link.
23 Now install and tighten the left-hand air conditioning and bi-level air duct. When locating this piece, be sure that it is properly positioned to mate up with the left-hand air conditioning duct and the center intermediate connecting junction.

Chapter 4 Fuel and exhaust systems

Contents

Specifications

General

Fuel tank capacity	11.9 US gallons/9.9 Imp gallons (45 liters)
Fuel pump pressure	4.6 to 6 psi (32 to 42 KPa)
Catalytic converter outer surface dent limit	0.79 in (20 mm)

Carburetor

Type	Downdraft, 2 barrel
Applications	**Part number**
1A-C and 3A-C (Fed. 4-speed)	21100-15080
1A-C and 3A-C (Fed. 4-speed w/HAC)	21100-15130
1A-C and 3A-C (Fed. 5-speed)	21100-15090
1A-C and 3A-C (Fed. 5-speed w/HAC)	21100-15140
1A-C and 3A-C (Fed. A/T)	21100-15100
1A-C and 3A-C (Fed. A/T w/HAC)	21100-15150
1A-C and 3A-C (California)	21100-15120
3A (M/T)	21100-15040
3A (A/T)	21100-15050
Float level	
Raised position	0.283 in (7.2 mm)
Lowered position	0.063 in (1.6 mm)
Idle mixture adjusting screw preset position	
1A-C and 3A-C	2-$\frac{1}{4}$ turns out
3A	2-$\frac{3}{4}$ turns out
Accelerating pump stroke	0.118 in (3.0 mm)
Choke valve fully closed angle from bore	20°
Unloader angle from horizontal plane	47°
Choke breaker angle from horizontal plane	
1st	39°
2nd (Fed 1A-C and 3A-C W/4-speed; Canada – all)	50°
2nd (all others)	55°
Choke opener angle from horizontal plane	77°
Throttle valve closed angle from bore	
Primary	7°
Secondary	20°
Throttle valve fully opened angle from bore	
Primary	89 to 91°
Secondary	75 to 76°
Secondary touch angle from bore	43 to 47°
Kick-up	
Secondary throttle valve to body clearance (Primary throttle valve fully opened)	0.0130 to 0.0177 in (0.33 to 0.45 mm)
Fast idle angle from bore	
1A-C and 3A-C	22°
3A	21°
Maximum carburetor base plate or manifold face warpage	0.0039 in (0.10 mm)

Torque specifications

	ft-lb	kg-m
Catalytic converter-to-exhaust pipe connecting bolt	26 to 32	(3.5 to 4.5)

1 General information

The fuel system consists of a rear mounted tank, combination metal and rubber fuel hoses, an engine-mounted mechanical pump and a two-stage, two-venturi carburetor.

The exhaust system is composed of a cast iron exhaust manifold feeding a double chamfered head pipe. The head pipe makes the transition into a single front exhaust pipe which feeds a catalytic converter. The catalytic converter leads into a combination muffler and tailpipe assembly.

The emissions control systems modify the functions of both the exhaust and fuel systems. There will be many cross-references throughout this Chapter to Sections in Chapter 6 because the emissions control systems are heavily interrelated to both the exhaust and particularly the carburetion system. This may seem like a difficult reference method at first glance, but careful adherence to the instructions will provide the necessary information without the clutter of unnecessary, non-applicable facts in this Chapter.

Extreme caution should be exercised when dealing with either the fuel or the exhaust system. Fuel is a primary element for combustion. Any spills, leaks or fumes can turn a normal maintenance session into a disaster. Be very careful! The exhaust system is also an area for exercising caution as it operates at very high temperatures, particularly with the use of emissions control systems. Serious burns can result from even momentary contact with any part of the exhaust system and the fire potential is ever present.

2 Fuel filter – replacement

See instructions in Chapter 1, Tune-up and Routine maintenance.

3 Air cleaner assembly – removal and installation

Refer to Chapter 1, Routine maintenance, for air cleaner removal and installation procedures.

4 Fuel pump – removal, testing and installation

Note: *If the required pressure gauge is available, hook it up to the pump outlet with a 'T' fitting and check the pump outlet pressure before removing it from the engine.*

1   Remove the air cleaner (see Chapter 1 for detailed procedure).

2   Exercise caution regarding flammable fuel and mark the location of the fuel hoses before performing the following step.

3   Remove the fuel pump line clamps and lines.

4   Remove the two bolts holding the fuel pump and heat shield to the cylinder head.

5   Remove the fuel pump and gasket.

6   Before performing the following checks on the removed fuel pump make certain that fuel has recently been run through the pump. A dry pump will not seal properly due to the nature of the internal check valve.

7   Refer to Fig. 4.1 and operate the pump lever by hand and note the amount of force required to move the arm. This same amount of force should be used in making the following checks.

8   Block the outlet pipe (on the side of the pump), and return line (on top of the pump body) and check for a rise in force necessary to move the arm. The arm should then move freely without the reaction force it had in Step 7. This checks the inlet valve.

9   Block the inlet pipe and the arm should lock. Be sure to apply the same amount of effort as used in Step 7. This checks the operation of the fuel pump outlet valve.

10 Block all three of the pipes and check to see if the operating arm locks. If the pump fails all three of the above tests, the sealing of the upper housing and the body is ineffective. If the pump fails only this test, the check diaphragm is defective.

11 Seal the vent hole and check the pump arm for lost motion. If the pump fails the above tests, replace it with a new one.

12 Installation is the reverse of removal. Use a new gasket when installing the fuel pump and check for oil leaks at the pump-to-cylinder head mating surface, and for fuel leaks at the pipe-to-hose connections.

5 Automatic choke – operation and inspection

1   For automatic choke operation, see Chapter 1.

2   For automatic choke inspection, see Chapter 6.

6 Automatic choke – dismantling and reassembly

The automatic choke is an integral part of the carburetor. The carburetor must be removed from the vehicle and partially disassembled to facilitate choke dismantling and reassembly. Therefore, this procedure is covered in Sections 9 to 11 in this Chapter.

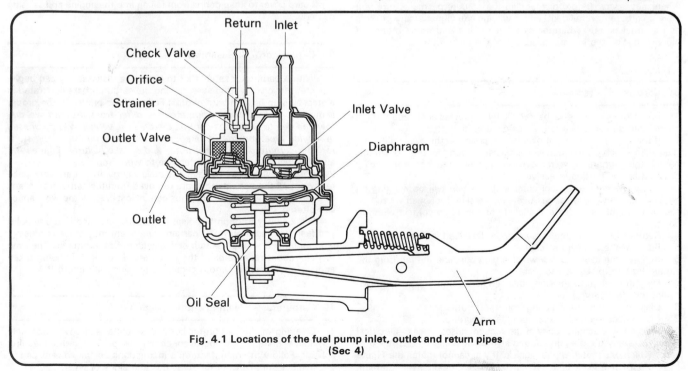

Fig. 4.1 Locations of the fuel pump inlet, outlet and return pipes
(Sec 4)

7 Carburetor – servicing

1 A thorough road test and check of carburetor adjustments should be done before any major carburetor service. Specifications for some adjustments are listed on the vehicle emission control information label found in the engine compartment.

2 Some performance complaints directed at the carburetor are actually a result of loose, misadjusted or malfunctioning engine or electrical components. Others develop when vacuum hoses leak, are disconnected or are incorrectly routed. The proper approach to analyzing carburetor problems should include a routine check of the following areas:

3 Inspect all vacuum hoses and valves for leaks and proper installation (see Chapter 6, *Emission control systems).*

4 Tighten the intake manifold nuts and carburetor mounting nuts evenly and securely.

5 Perform a cylinder compression test.

6 Clean or replace the spark plugs as necessary.

7 Test the resistance of the spark plug wires (refer to Chapter 5).

8 Inspect the ignition primary wires and check the vacuum advance operation. Replace any defective parts.

9 Check the ignition timing with the vacuum advance line disconnected and plugged.

10 Set the carburetor idle mixture as described in Chapter 1.

11 Check the fuel pump as described in Section 5.

12 Inspect the hot air intake system operation (refer to Chapter 6).

13 Remove the carburetor air filter element and blow out any dirt with compressed air. If the filter is extremely dirty, replace it with a new one.

14 Inspect the crankcase ventilation system (see Chapter 6).

15 Carburetor problems usually show up as flooding, hard starting, stalling, severe backfiring, poor acceleration and lack of response to idle mixture screw adjustments. A carburetor that is leaking fuel and/or covered with wet-looking deposits definitely needs attention.

16 Diagnosing carburetor problems may require that the engine be started and run with the air cleaner removed. If you decide this is necessary, follow the guidelines listed in Chapter 6 Section 2. While running the engine without the air cleaner it could possibly backfire so do not position portions of your body directly over the carburetor. A backfiring situation is likely to occur if the carburetor is malfunctioning, but removal of the air cleaner alone can lean the air-fuel mixture enough to produce an engine backfire.

17 Once it is determined that the carburetor is indeed at fault, it should be disassembled, cleaned and reassembled using new parts where necessary. Before dismantling the carburetor, make sure you have a carburetor rebuild kit, which will include all necessary gaskets and internal parts, carburetor cleaning solvent and some means of blowing out all the internal passages of the carburetor.

8 Carburetor – removal

1 If the carburetor is to be rebuilt by a professional repair shop, money can be saved if it is first removed at home.

2 If the carburetor is being overhauled, check on the availability of a rebuild kit which will contain all the necessary parts for the job. Do this before the carburetor is removed to prevent the car from being disabled as the parts are received.

3 Allow the engine to cool completely, as you will be working on areas which can cause serious burns to the skin if touched when hot. Also, fuel might be spilled and should not come into contact with hot parts.

4 Remove the air cleaner assembly as described in Chapter 1.

5 Remove the accelerator cable.

6 Remove the cable hold-down clamping nuts and the tab from the slotted hole in the carburetor cable guide.

7 On automatic transmission equipped cars, remove the kick-down cable from the throttle rod.

8 Disconnect the return spring from the throttle lever.

9 Disconnect the fuel hoses from the carburetor.

10 Before you disconnect any of the vacuum hoses, lines or electrical switches, study the diagrams found at the beginning of Chapter 6 to verify which one matches your vehicle. If you cannot match the Figure to your particular vehicle, or even if you can, it would be wise to mark

the locations of the hoses and related components with stringed tags, taped labels or any other effective identifying device. A polaroid picture is another method. One misplaced hose or misconnected switch can make the engine run poorly or sometimes not at all.

11 Disconnect vacuum hoses from the carburetor and any other related emissions control devices which will remain on the vehicle after the carburetor is removed.

12 Disconnect the two electrical wires leading to the carburetor control valves (photo).

8.12 The two electrical connectors leading to the carburetor control valves and switches must be disconnected before removing the carburetor

13 Remove the two retaining bolts (one at the rear and one at the top) for the emission control metal hose loom.

14 Remove the four carburetor hold-down nuts from the studs in the intake manifold.

15 Remove the carburetor.

16 Remove the carburetor base plate gasket.

17 Remove the carburetor heat shield.

18 Cover the holes in the intake manifold with clean rags or make a cardboard cover to keep debris from falling into the engine and causing damage.

9 Carburetor – disassembly

1 With a carburetor rebuild kit to hand, the disassembly can begin. The steps involved with disassembling the carburetor are illustrated in a step-by-step fashion with photos. Follow these photos in the proper sequence. **Note:** *Your carburetor may differ from the one we dismantled due to emissions control, the area the vehicle was purchased in, engine type and year differences. Make sure you follow the steps for your carburetor and make notes and/or take pictures. Figures 4.2 and 4.3 will also provide a reference to work from.*

2 It will be necessary to have a relatively large and clean workspace to lay out all the parts as they are removed from the carburetor. Many of the parts are very small and thus can be lost easily if the work space is cluttered.

3 Work slowly through the disassembly process, and if at any point you feel the reassembly of a certain component may prove confusing, stop and make a rough sketch or apply identification marks. The time to think about reassembling the carburetor is when it is being taken apart. Now follow the photo sequence starting with photo 9.4/1.

10 Carburetor – cleaning and inspection

1 Cleaning of the carburetor body, base plate, and cover assembly should be done in an approved chemical-type carburetor cleaning solvent. Follow the manufacturer's instructions on the solvent can.

2 Inspect the pivot pin for scratches and signs of wear.

For 3A-C

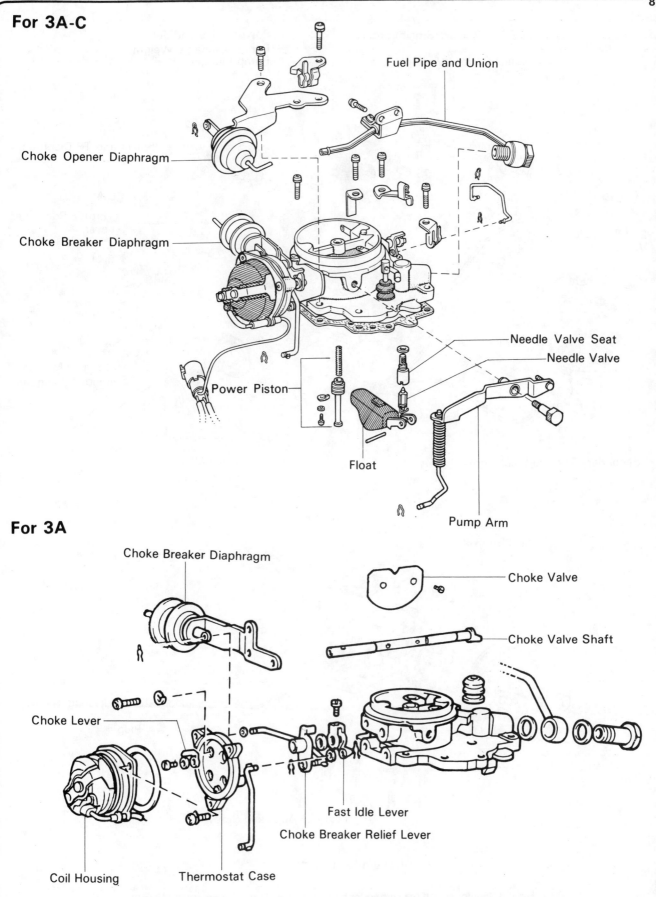

Fuel Pipe and Union

Choke Opener Diaphragm

Choke Breaker Diaphragm

Needle Valve Seat

Needle Valve

Power Piston

Float

Pump Arm

For 3A

Choke Breaker Diaphragm

Choke Valve

Choke Valve Shaft

Choke Lever

Fast Idle Lever

Choke Breaker Relief Lever

Coil Housing

Thermostat Case

Fig. 4.2 Components of the carburetor air horn and choke assembly – exploded view (Sec 9)

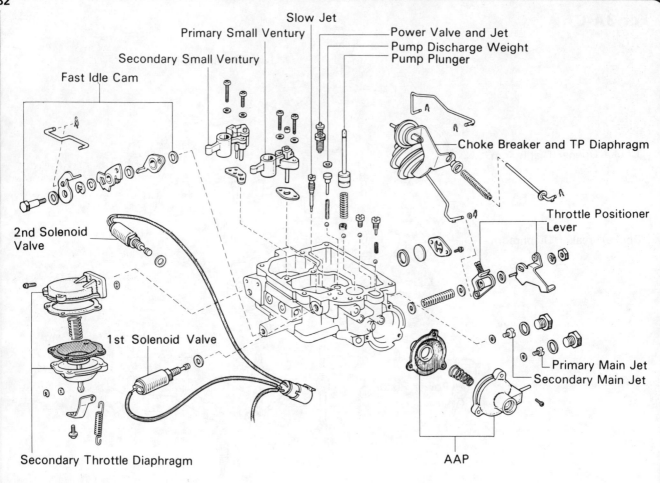

Fast Idle Cam

Secondary Small Ventury

Primary Small Ventury

Slow Jet

Power Valve and Jet

Pump Discharge Weight

Pump Plunger

Choke Breaker and TP Diaphragm

Throttle Positioner Lever

2nd Solenoid Valve

1st Solenoid Valve

Primary Main Jet

Secondary Main Jet

Secondary Throttle Diaphragm

AAP

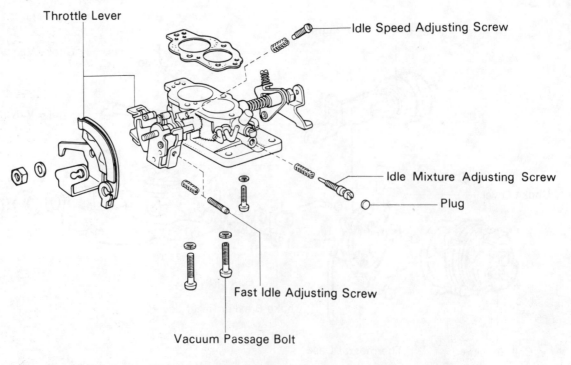

Throttle Lever

Idle Speed Adjusting Screw

Idle Mixture Adjusting Screw

Plug

Fast Idle Adjusting Screw

Vacuum Passage Bolt

Fig. 4.3 Components of the carburetor body and base plate – exploded view (Sec 9)

9.4/1 Remove the fuel inlet line bracket and clamp assembly

9.4/2 Disconnect the choke breaker link from the choke breaker diaphragm B

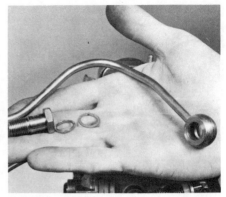

9.4/3 Remove the fuel inlet tube through bolt, the fuel inlet tube and the sealing washers (two)

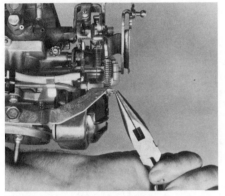

9.4/4 Disconnect the accelerator pump lever from the link

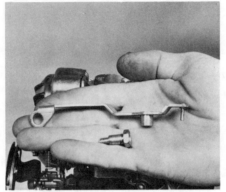

9.4/5 Remove the accelerator pump lever from the air horn by removing the pivot bolt

9.4/6 Release the electric wire harness from retainer clips (arrow)

9.4/7 Drill out the pop rivets (arrows) and remove the choke shield

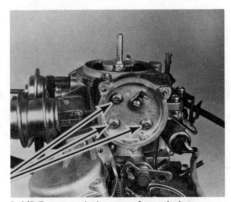

9.4/8 Remove choke cover from choke assy; remove 3 screws (arrows) retaining choke assy to air horn. Remove screw retaining choke shaft lever; remove choke plate

9.4/9 Disconnect the choke breaker diaphragm A vacuum hose (arrow) from the carburetor base

9.4/10 Remove the choke breaker linkage from the shaft, then remove the choke breaker diaphragm assembly A from the air horn

9.4/11 Disconnect the fast idle linkage from the choke shaft lever

9.4/12 Remove 8 air horn retainer screws (arrows); note brackets and retainer clamp locations. Lift air horn from carburetor body

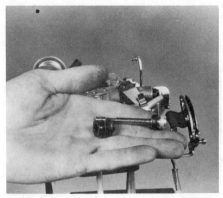
9.4/13 Remove the accelerator pump plunger assembly and seal from the air horn

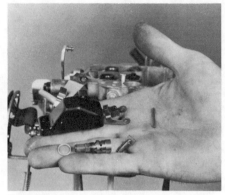
9.4/14 Remove the float, float pivot pin, float needle and float seat from the air horn

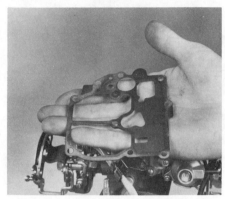
9.4/15 Remove the air horn gasket

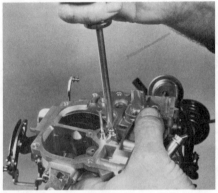
9.4/16 Carefully remove the power piston hold-down screw and the associated assembly (there's spring pressure behind the piston)

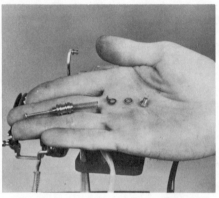
9.4/17 Components of the plunger assembly

9.4/18 Remove the first solenoid valve, which is located on the throttle linkage side of the carburetor body

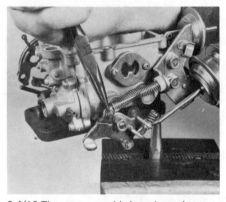
9.4/19 The next assembly is under spring tension so use caution as it could fly apart

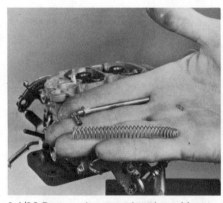
9.4/20 Remove the upper throttle positioner link assembly

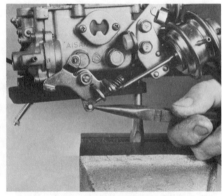
9.4/21 Remove the lower throttle positioner link

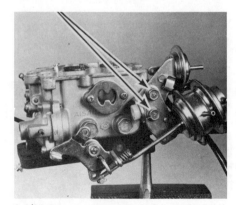
9.4/22 Remove the two bolts (arrows) securing the throttle positioners and the number two breaker diaphragm

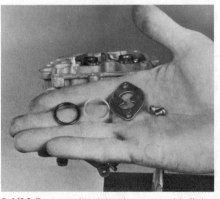
9.4/23 Remove the sight glass assembly (it is held in place with two screws)

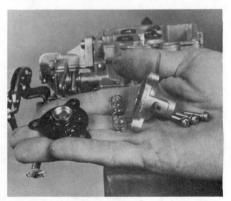
9.4/24 Remove the AAP assembly (it has three screws retaining it)

9.4/25 Disconnect and remove the secondary lock-out return spring

9.4/26 Disconnect and remove the secondary diaphragm link clip and washer

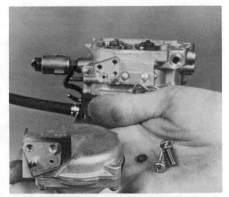

9.4/27 Remove secondary diaphragm assembly with gasket. Do not disassemble; rebuild parts are not included in kit

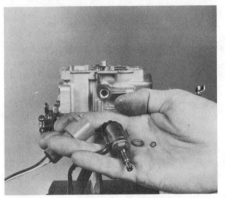

9.4/28 Remove the second solenoid valve, seal and O-ring

9.4/29 Remove the accelerator discharge plunger, spring and check ball

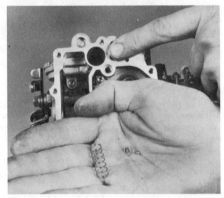

9.4/30 Remove the accelerator pump spring, discharge ball and retainer

9.4/31 Remove the slow jet

9.4/32 Remove the primary and secondary venturi assemblies complete with gaskets and hold-down screws

9.4/33 Remove the power valve and jet

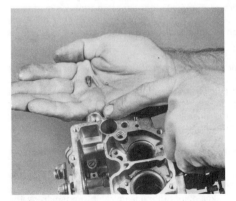

9.4/34 Remove the AAP output check ball, spring and cap

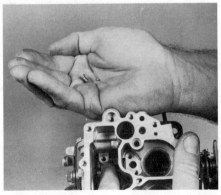

9.4/35 Remove the AAP inlet check ball and cap

9.4/36 Remove 4 baseplate-to-main body screws (one is used as jet/venturi); remove baseplate

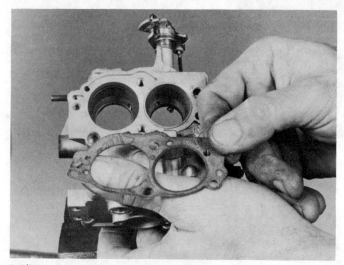

9.4/37 Remove the base plate-to-main body gasket

9.4/38 Remove the jet access plugs and seal rings, then remove the two jets and seal gaskets (make sure that you keep them separated so they may be re-installed in their correct position)

3   Inspect the float for broken areas on the lip and cracks in the body. Also inspect the pivot pin holes for excessive wear.
4   Inspect the spring for deformation or breakage.
5   Inspect the needle valve and plunger for damage or wear.
6   Inspect the strainer for breaks or rust.
7   Replace any of the above if they show signs of wear or damage.
8   Inspect the power piston and make sure that it moves smoothly throughout its travel.
9   Inspect the power valve for opening and closing action. It should be smooth and without any variation in travel.
10 Inspect the first fuel cut solenoid as outlined in Chapter 6.
11 Inspect the second fuel cut valve as outlined in Chapter 6.
12 Inspect the choke heater by referring to Chapter 6, Section 15.
13 Carefully depress the diaphragm plunger (photo).
14 With the plunger still held in the depressed position, seal the vacuum orifice with a finger and release the plunger. The plunger should not return to its extended position until the vacuum is released. If the diaphragm does move while the orifice is still sealed, a new diaphragm must be installed before the unit is attached to the carburetor.
15 Inspect the AAP diaphragm for tears, deformation or signs of leakage. If any of the above conditions exist, replace the AAP diaphragm with a new one.

11 Carburetor – reassembly

Note: *The reassembly process will be easier if the sequenced photos in the disassembly section are followed in reverse.*
1   Install the jets and sealing rings in their respective bores.
2   Install the jet plugs and sealing rings.
3   Using a new gasket, install the base plate to the carburetor main body. Make sure that the vacuum passage bolt is installed in the correct position.
4   Install the AAP inlet check ball and cap.
5   Install the AAP outlet check ball, spring and cap.
6   Install the power valve and jet assembly.
7   Install the primary and secondary venturi assemblies, making sure that the boss on the assemblies lines up with the alignment valve on the carburetor body. **Note:** *There is a gasket and two hold-down screws for each venturi assembly.*
8   Install the slow jet.
9   Install the accelerator pump output check ball and output check ball retainer clip. To accomplish this, push the output retainer clip half its length into a $\frac{6}{32}$ in deep socket or equivalent. Guide it into its bore using the socket and then use a small screwdriver through the center of the socket to push it the rest of the way into its seat.
10 Install the accelerator pump plunger return spring.
11 Install the accelerator pump discharge check ball, spring and weight into its bore.

12 Install a new O-ring onto the second solenoid plunger and lubricate it with oil. Using a new sealing washer, install the plunger into its bore.
13 Before installing the secondary throttle diaphragm, place a new sealing washer in its bore in the carburetor body. Install the secondary diaphragm onto the carburetor using the two screws. Connect the linkage at the bottom with the connecting clip. Note the washer used at this connection.
14 Install the secondary lock out lever return spring.
15 Install the AAP diaphragm, and spring. **Note:** *The diaphragm is installed with the brass seat facing outward.*
16 Install the float bowl sight glass assembly consisting of the O-ring, sight glass, retainer and two retaining screws.
17 Install the choke breaker and throttle positioner diaphragm assemblies.
18 Connect the throttle positioner linkage utilizing the washer and retaining clip.
19 Install the upper throttle positioner linkage to the throttle positioner lever. **Note:** *The small end of the spring faces the retainer end of the linkage.*
20 Install the power piston and power piston spring into its bore in the air horn using the retainer tab, screw and washer.
21 Install the seat assembly and gasket onto the air horn.
22 Install the needle into the seat assembly.
23 Install the float and pivot pin onto the air horn assembly.
24 Set the float level as shown in the accompanying photo. **Note:** *For float adjustment, the retainer clip should not be installed onto the needle.* For adjustment with the air horn still inverted, lift the float to its full extended position and use a feeler gauge to measure the clearance between the needle valve and the float lip (photo). After making the float adjustment, install the retaining clip onto the needle. Place the gasket in position and install the float and pivot pin.
25 Install the accelerator pump plunger seal into its boss on the air horn. Lubricate the accelerator pump plunger seal with light oil. Place the flat seal washer on top of the discharge pump and press it into its boss in the carburetor body.
26 Slide the accelerator pump plunger through the seal on the air horn and install the air horn onto the carburetor body. Ensure that the gasket is properly positioned before tightening down the screws. Loosely install two screws, one at each end of the air horn, to secure the air horn into position.
27 Install the choke rod linkage into the plunger of the secondary choke breaker. Sequentially tighten the remaining air horn-to-body bolts.
28 Press the accelerator pump plunger into position and make sure that it moves freely.
29 Install the fast idle cam linkage into the choke lever, utilizing the spring clip and washer.
30 Place the choke breaker diaphragm assembly into position on the air horn. Note that the lever must be installed on the throttle rod above the linkage.

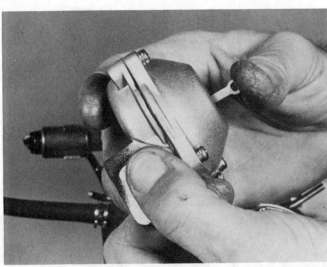

10.13 Depressing the diaphragm plunger and plugging the intake orifice to check diaphragm condition

11.24a Measuring the float in its highest position

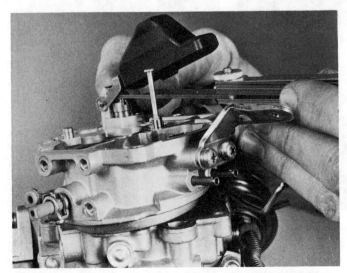

11.24b Measuring the clearance between the needle valve and the float lip

31 Install the choke housing utilizing the three hold-down screws which also secure the choke breaker assembly.

32 Install the choke rod lever utilizing the screw and washer.

33 Place the choke housing gasket into position, making sure that the notch in the gasket is situated at the ten o'clock position.

34 Place a new O-ring on the plunger of the first solenoid valve and lubricate it with oil.

35 Install a new seal washer and install the solenoid valve into its bore.

36 Line up the mark on the choke heater housing with the hole on the choke heater shield situated at the ten o'clock position. Install the choke heater housing in this position using new pop rivets.

37 Install the accelerator pump lever.

38 Connect the accelerator pump linkage to the accelerator pump lever.

39 Install the fuel inlet tube using the through bolt and two new seal rings.

12 Carburetor installation

1 Follow the removal sequence in reverse for installation. Always observe the following rules, whether a new, used or rebuilt carburetor is being installed.

2 Lay a straightedge across both the intake manifold flange face and the gasket surface of the carburetor base plate. Check for any warpage or unevenness by shining a light behind the carb or manifold with the straightedge held against the surface being checked. Any irregularities or warpage will show up as slivers of light. Use a feeler gauge to measure any areas with high amounts of light leakage. Any gap over the prescribed minimum listed in the Specification table at the front of this Chapter is cause for resurfacing or replacement.

3 Check the four hold-down studs for clean, straight threads. Run the carburetor hold-down nuts over the studs before installing the carburetor for a trial check of the thread match.

4 Clean both the carburetor base plate and the manifold face surface before installing a new gasket.

13 Carburetor – adjustments

1 Check that the primary throttle butterfly opens completely. If the throttle valve does not open completely, the tang must be bent as shown (photo).

2 Check the secondary throttle butterfly to see that it is 75° from the horizontal plane in its fully open position. This angle may be checked with the special service tool or a protractor and straightedge can suffice if needed (photo). If the opening is not correct, bend the stopper lever as shown (photo).

3 To check kick-up clearance, the special service tool or a feeler gauge may be inserted between the throttle butterfly and the main body as shown (photo). **Note:** *The primary throttle should be in its fully opened position for this check.*

4 Bend the stop tang if the kick up measurement is incorrect.

5 To check the secondary touch angle, open the primary throttle valve while at the same time ensuring that the first kick lever is just contacting the second kick lever. The standard angles should be 45° from the horizontal plane (photo). If this adjustment is not correct, adjust by bending the first kick lever as shown (photo).

6 To check the fast idle setting, set the throttle shaft lever to the first step of the fast idle cam. With the choke valve fully closed, check the primary throttle valve angle in the same manner as in the previous step. If the angle is not correct, adjust by turning the fast idle adjusting screw.

7 For the 3A engine only, the automatic choke may be adjusted by setting the coil housing scale mark so it is aligned with the center of the choke housing body. The choke should be fully closed when the atmospheric temperature reaches 86°F (30°C or lower). If the choke setting is too rich, correct it by turning the housing clockwise. If it is too lean, it can be corrected by turning counterclockwise.

8 To check the choke unloader, open the throttle valve completely and measure the choke valve angle (Refer to the Specifications at the beginning of this Chapter) (photo). If the unloader is incorrect, adjust by bending the fast idle lever as shown (photo).

9 For 1982 3AC engines, the choke opener may be checked by setting the fast idle cam while holding the throttle slightly open. Push

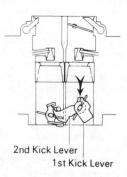

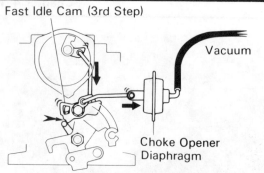

Fast Idle Cam (3rd Step)

Vacuum

Choke Opener
Diaphragm

2nd Kick Lever

1st Kick Lever

Fig. 4.4 First kick lever contacting the second kick lever to check the secondary touch angle (Sec 13)

Fig. 4.5 Checking the choke linkage and fast idle cam movement (vacuum application to the choke opener diaphragm initiates this action) (Sec 13)

13.1 Bend the tang on the primary throttle stop to adjust the primary throttle butterfly opening

13.2a Checking secondary throttle butterfly opening angle

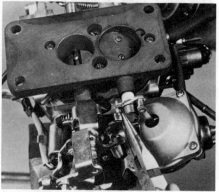

13.2b Bending the stop lever to adjust the secondary throttle butterfly opening angle

13.3 Checking the kick-up clearance with a feeler gauge

13.5a Measuring the secondary touch angle

13.5b Bending the first kick lever to adjust the secondary touch angle

13.8a Measuring the choke unloader with the primary throttle valve held open

13.8b Adjusting the choke unloader by bending the fast idle lever

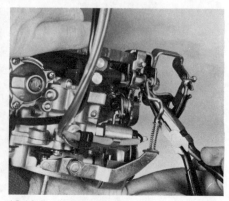

13.12 Bending the choke relief lever to adjust the choke valve angle

13.14 Checking the accelerator pump stroke

13.15 Bending the connecting link to adjust the accelerator pump stroke

the choke valve closed and hold it closed as the throttle valve is released. Apply vacuum to the choke opener diaphragm and check that the choke linkage moves while the fast idle cam releases to the third step (Fig. 4.5). If this does not occur correctly, adjust by bending the relief lever.

10 To check choke breaker diaphragm A, apply a vacuum to the center port of the breaker. Measure the choke valve angle at the top of the carburetor as shown in photo 13.82.

11 If the choke plate angle is incorrect on the 3A engine only, adjustment may be made by bending the tab underneath the choke housing cover.

12 Choke diaphragm B may be tested in the same manner as choke diaphragm A (3AC engine only). If this angle is incorrect, the adjustment may be made at the choke relief lever (photo).

13 For diaphragms that are adjustable, apply vacuum to choke breaker diaphragms A and B. Check the choke valve angle. If the angle is incorrect, adjust by turning the diaphragm adjusting screw.

14 To check the accelerator pump stroke, apply vacuum to both throttle positioner diaphragms. Loosen the idle speed adjusting screw with the choke valve fully open and set the primary throttle valve to the fully closed position. With the choke valve open, check the length of the stroke (photo).

15 If the stroke is not correct, adjust by bending the connecting link (photo).

16 To temporarily set the idle speed adjusting screw, apply a vacuum to the throttle positioner and choke opener diaphragms. Now set the fast idle cam to the third step. Turn in the idle speed adjusting screw until it just begins to touch the throttle lever. Check for smooth operation of the linkage.

14 Fuel lines and tank – general description

1 The fuel tank is of galvanized metal construction and is retained by two cross support assemblies under the rear of the vehicle.

2 Repairs to a fuel tank which requires welding or any application of heat are jobs for a professional. Fumes present inside the tank are easily ignited, causing the tank to explode. A professional welder will thoroughly purge the tank with water and then steam to remove all traces of explosive gas fumes.

3 If the tank has rusted inside, there is little hope that it can be re-used. The corrosion will continually be drawn into the fuel system, clogging the filter and eventually the carburetor components.

4 Metal fuel lines connect to rubber intermediate hoses at the tank, fuel pump and evaporative emissions canister. The metal lines are secured by clamps and looms throughout the length of the vehicle. See Chapter 6 for servicing information.

5 The fuel filler neck is connected to the body by screws which clamp it to the inlet shields. A rubber hose connects the filler neck to

the tank. Additional information on the placement and functions of the fuel, vapor and return lines throughout the vehicle is available in Chapter 6.

15 Fuel tank – removal and installation

Note: *Refer to Figures 4.6 and 4.7 when performing the procedure described in the following steps.*

1 *Before doing any work around the fuel tank, make sure that the ignition switch is off and remove the key from the ignition lock.* Block the front wheels to keep the vehicle from rolling, then raise the rear of the vehicle and set it on jack stands.

2 Remove the tank filler cap so pressure in the tank can escape.

3 Position a suitable container (large enough to hold the fuel that is in the tank) under the tank. Remove the drain plug and allow the fuel to drain into the container. *Be very careful when working around gasoline, it is highly explosive.* After the fuel has drained completely, reinstall the drain plug. Once again, exercise extreme caution as you are performing one of the most dangerous operations in working on your own vehicle.

4 Remove the cover found under the carpeting in the rear cargo area or under the trunk mat if your vehicle has a trunk. This cover is retained by screws. Once this cover is removed, access is gained to the fuel hoses and the fuel level sender.

5 Unplug the electrical wires from the fuel level sending unit.

6 Loosen the hose clamps on the main, return and vapor fuel hoses then pull the hoses off the trunk.

7 Remove the filler neck mud shield from the inside of the left rear wheel well. It is held in place with three bolts.

8 Loosen the hose clamps on the filler connecting hose (large) and the breather hose (small) where they attach to the tank. Pull the hoses off the tank. (Be careful not to damage them in the process).

9 Support the fuel tank, preferably with a portable jack and a block of wood. Remove the four mounting bolts and the two retaining straps. Lower the tank carefully and move it out from under the vehicle.

10 Check the tank interior for rust and corrosion. If the tank is not extremely corroded, it can be cleaned and reused. Special solvents made especially for cleaning fuel tanks are available. If you use one, be sure to follow the directions on the container. The inside of the tank is plated with zinc so be sure to use a cleaner that will not harm it in any way.

11 If the tank is severely corroded, replace it with a new one or a clean used one.

12 Look for evidence of leaks and cracks. If any are found, take the tank to a repair shop to have it fixed.

13 Inspect all fuel and breather hoses for cracks and deterioration. Check all hose clamps for damage and proper operation.

14 Installation of the tank is basically the reverse of removal. Be sure

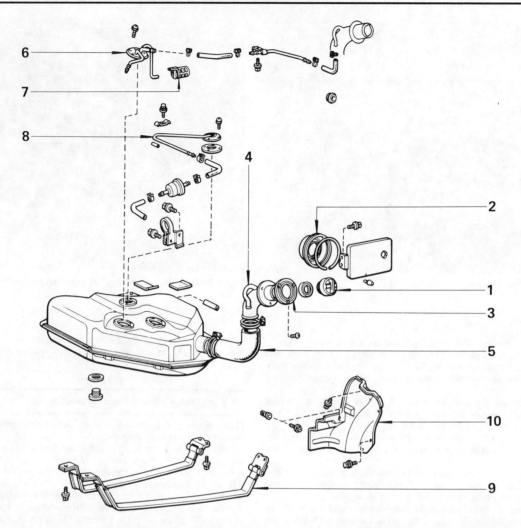

Fig. 4.6 Typical fuel tank components – exploded view (Sec 15)

1 *Fuel tank cap*	4 *Filler pipe*	7 *Suction tube filter*	9 *Fuel tank strap*
2 *Inlet shield*	5 *Inlet hose*	8 *Evaporative vent tube*	10 *Inlet pipe protector*
3 *Filler pipe shield*	6 *Vent tube*		

to double check all hoses for proper routing. Also, if you have not already done so, be sure to tighten the drain plug securely.
15 Fill the tank with fuel and check for leaks. After the engine has been run, make a second check for leaks, particularly at the hose fittings that were removed.

16 Exhaust system – general description

1   The exhaust system consists of four main pieces: the manifold, head or down pipe, the catalytic converter and the rear muffler-tailpipe combination.
2   The attending sub-components of the above main pieces are: system hangers, brackets, heat shields, gaskets and thermo-sensor, along with oxygen-sensor on three-way catalyst equipped vehicles.
3   Replacement procedure will be easiest if you replace one (or more) of the four main pieces rather than trying to segment the system (such as separating the rear tailpipe from the rear muffler). This would require the use of equipment which would only be found in a muffler shop or other well-equipped repair facility.
4   Causes for exhaust system failure vary from rust-out to external damage resulting from an encounter with a rock or other road hazard. Occasionally a leak will develop at a connecting joint and can be cured by tightening a bolt or replacing a gasket. Examine the system thoroughly, especially where age or rust has caused the damage. If a spot has rusted through, there is a good chance that the rest of the system is in equally poor condition.

5   Raise the vehicle and support it securely on jackstands as described in the preliminary material near the front of this manual. Determine exactly where your probem areas exist through visual and audio inspection. Check the system completely from its source at the engine all the way to the tip of the tailpipe. Use a metal tool and take a 'sounding' every six inches to determine the thickness of the metal. Sometimes a section of pipe will appear good but when tested in this way will be found to be rusted out from inside. **Note:** *If you must run the vehicle to find a defect, secure the aid of a helper and limit the running time to as short a period as possible. Carbon monoxide is a deadly gas and should never be confined in a contained area like a garage.*
6   After you have located the leaking or damaged component(s), procure all of the necessary parts. Don't forget all of the attending hardware like gaskets, bolts, nuts and hangers. It is always a good idea to replace the connecting hardware because the heat in a modern exhaust system causes the fasteners to be unusable after removal.

17 Exhaust manifold/pipes – removal and installation

1   This Section will cover the replacement of all of the components of the exhaust system. If you need to replace only certain individual parts of the system, follow the instructions for that part only.
2   Raise the vehicle and support it securely with jack stands. It is far easier to work on a vehicle with a cool exhaust system and the likelihood of burns is diminished.

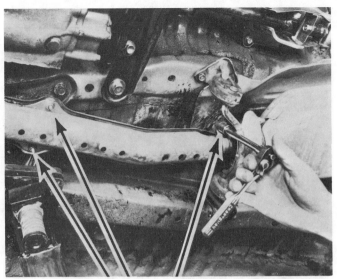

17.3 Location of the head pipe heat shield retaining bolts (arrows)

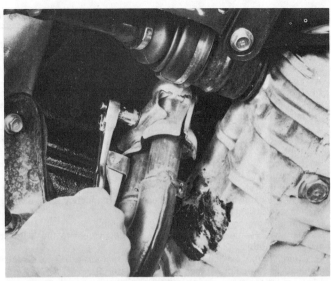

17.4 Removing the head pipe retainer plate and fastener

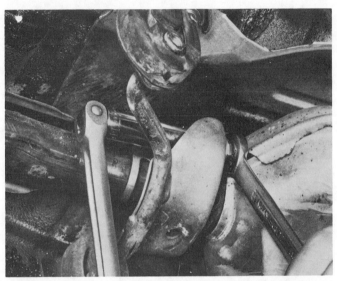

17.6 Removing the catalytic converter-to-head pipe retaining bolts

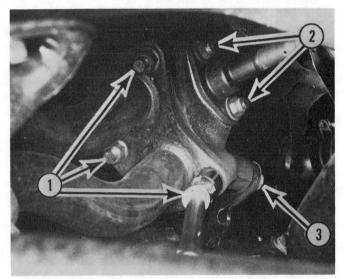

17.8 Location of the head pipe-to-manifold retainer bolts (1), the oxygen sensor retainer bolts (2) and the exhaust manifold support bracket bolt (3)

17.14 Location of the connecting bolts for the catalytic converter-to-rear tailpipe assembly (1) and the thermo sensor retaining bolts (2)

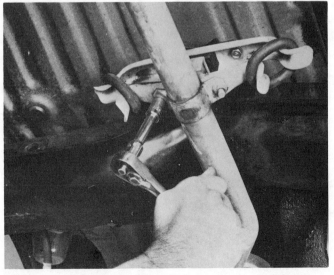

17.17 Bolts retaining the U-clamp which supports the rear tailpipe assembly

3   Lubricate all fasteners with a penetrating type of lubricant and allow it to saturate for a few minutes. Sometimes several applications are necessary, particularly on vehicles that have been exposed to snow and road salt.
4   Remove the air cleaner and carburetor (this Chapter) plus the intake manifold (Chapter 2). Remove the heat shield clamp bolts from the head pipe (photo). Remove the head pipe lower heat shield.
5   Remove the head pipe flange heat shield clamp bolts. Remove the two-piece upper head pipe heat shield along with the retainer plate (photo).
6   Support the catalytic converter with a jack and board or other similar set up.
7   Omit this step if the exhaust manifold only is being removed. Remove the catalytic converter to head pipe connecting bolts using a wrench and socket (photo).
8   Remove the converter front hanger assembly.
9   Remove the three nuts securing the down pipe to the exhaust manifold (photo).
10 Remove the oxygen sensor from the rear area of the exhaust manifold (if so equipped) (see photo from step 9).
11 Remove the exhaust manifold-to-engine block supporting bracket from the vehicle.
12 From under the hood of the vehicle, remove the bolts retaining the exhaust manifold to the cylinder head.
13 Remove the exhaust manifold from the top of the engine compartment.
14 Remove the down pipe from the bottom of the vehicle. If the down pipe is being removed without the exhaust manifold being removed, the following three steps for catalytic converter removal should be performed first.
15 Remove the thermo-sensor from the catalytic converter (if so equipped) (photo).
16 Remove the rear connecting bolts between the catalytic converter and the rear tailpipe assembly (see photo for step 15).
17 Lower the catalytic converter carefully and remove it from under the vehicle.

17.18 Rear tailpipe hanger mounting bolts

18 The tailpipe-muffler assembly may be removed by unbolting the U-clamp from the bracket located near the rear crossmember (photo).
19 Unbolt the rear tailpipe hanger located near the back bumper (photo).
20 Remove the rear tailpipe-muffler.
21 Installation is the reverse of removal.
22 When installing new rubber 'doughnut' type hangers, always unbolt the bracket, install the hangers and resecure the bracket. Although it is easier to stretch the hangers over the bracket, this tends to elongate the rubber, causing loss of tension and sometimes leading to premature failure.

Chapter 5 Engine electrical systems

Contents

Specifications

Spark plugs
Type .... Refer to Chapter 1, Routine maintenance
Gap .... Refer to Chapter 1, Routine maintenenace
Spark plug wire resistance .... 25 000 ohms or less

Distributor
Distributor part number
  1A-C and 3A-C engine 19100-15030
  1A-C and 3A-C (Canadian) engine 19100-15050
  3A engine 19100-14030
Distributor direction of rotation .... Counterclockwise

(crankshaft rpm)
Mechanical advance begins
  19100-15030 and 19100-15050 .... 1200 rpm
  19100-14030 .... 1000 rpm

(degrees at crankshaft rpm)
Maximum mechanical advance
  19100-15030 and 19100-15050 .... 13.6° at 6000 rpm
  19100-14030 .... 22.8° at 6000 rpm

	in/HG	mm/HG
Sub vacuum advance begins	7.17	182
Maximum sub vacuum advance	4° at 11.46	4° at 291
Vacuum advance begins		
19100-15030 and 19100-15050	2.36	60
19100-14030	3.94	100
Maximum vacuum advance		
19100-15030 and 19100-15050	13° at 12.20	13° at 310
19100-14030	7.5° at 7.87	7.5° at 200

Rubbing block gap (3A engine only) .... 0.0177 in (0.45 mm)
Dwell angle (3A engine only) .... 52°
Damping spring gap (3A engine only) .... 0.004 to 0.016 in (0.1 to 0.4 mm)
Air gap (1A-C and 3A-C engines only) .... 0.008 to 0.016 in (0.2 to 0.4 mm)
Signal generator resistance .... 130 to 190 ohms
Distributor shaft thrust clearance .... 0.004 to 0.024 in (0.1 to 0.6 mm)

Ignition coil
Primary coil resistance (1A-C and 3A-C) .... 0.4 to 0.5 ohms
Primary coil resistance (3A only) .... 1.3 to 1.7 ohms
Secondary coil resistance (1A-C and 3A-C) .... 8.5 to 11.5 ohms
Secondary coil resistance (3A only) .... 12000 to 16000 ohms
External resistor resistance (3A only) .... 1.3 to 1.5 ohms

Battery
Specific gravity reading at 68°F (20°C)
  Fully charged 1.260
  Half charged 1.160
  Discharged 1.060
Charging rates
  Slow charge .... 6 amps
  Fast charge .... 15 amps maximum

Alternator
Rated output .... 30, 40, or 50 amps at 5000 rpm
Regulating voltage (external regulator) .... 13.8 to 14.8 volts
Rated output (internal regulator) .... 55 amps at 5000 rpm
Regulating voltage (internal regulator) .... 14.0 to 14.5 volts
Charging output test (external regulator) .... 13.8 to 14.8 volts/less than 10 amps at idle to 2000 rpm
Charging output test (internal regulator) .... 13.8 to 14.8 volts/less than 10 amps at idle to 2000 rpm

Charging output test at 2000 rpm (under load) .... 30+ amps
Minimum exposed brush length (installed) .... 0.217 in (5.5 mm)
Standard exposed length (new) .... 0.492 in (12.5 mm)

Voltage regulator (external only)
Relay actuating voltage .... 4.5 to 5.8 volts

Starter motor
Rated voltage and output power
   Conventional .... 12 volts/0.8 kw
   Reduction .... 12 volts/1.0 kw

No-load characteristics	Conventional	Reduction
Current	Less than 50A at 11 volts	Less than 90A at 11.5 volts
Speed	5000+ rpm	3000+ rpm
Starter pinion gear-to-collar clearance	0.008 to 0.150 in (0.2 to 3.8 mm)	

1 General information and precautions

The engine electrical systems include the ignition, charging and starting components. They are considered separately from the rest of the electrical system because of their proximity and importance to the engine and its prime function in the car.

Exercise caution when working around any of these components for several reasons; they are easily damaged if tested, connected or stressed incorrectly.

respond directly to the engine types. 3-A engines use a breaker point type system along with a standard ignition coil and resistor. A relay, two fusible links and an ignition switch complete this system (Fig. 5.1). 1A-C and 3A-C engines use a transistorized igniter triggered by a signal generator which fires a high voltage coil. This type of system is relatively trouble-free, requires little maintenance and provides long spark plug life (Fig. 5.2).

Both types of ignition fire spark plugs of different types through a standard secondary ignition system: coil, coil high tension lead,

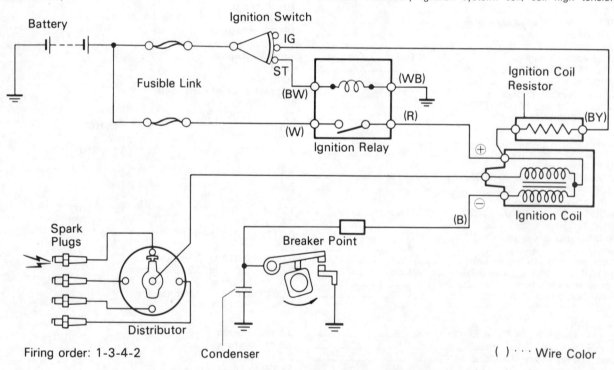

Firing order: 1-3-4-2

( ) · · · Wire Color

Fig. 5.1 3-A engine ignition system schematic (Sec 2)

The alternator is driven by an engine drive belt which could cause serious bodily harm if your fingers or hands become entangled in it while the engine is running. The starter and alternator are both sources of direct battery voltage which could arc or even cause a fire if overloaded or shorted.

Never leave the ignition switch on for longer than ten minutes with the engine not running. Do not disconnect the battery cable while the engine is running. Do not cross connect the battery cables from another source (such as another vehicle) when jump starting. Don't ground either of the ignition coil terminals, even momentarily. Hook up a testing tachometer to the negative terminal of the coil and make sure it is compatible with the type of ignition system on the vehicle.

2 Ignition system – description

Two types of ignition systems are used on Tercels. They cor-

distributor cap and four spark plug wires.

Both types of ignitions have diaphragm type vacuum advance units attached to their distributors. 3-A engines use a single vacuum diaphragm unit while 1A-C and 3A-C engines use dual diaphragm units. For more information on the controls used to activate these advance units, see Chapter 6. Both distributors have mechanical advance units utilizing centrifugal weights and governor springs internally mounted.

3 Ignition system – inspection and testing

Secondary ignition wires
1 Remove one wire from its spark plug and position on the distributor cap (see Chapter 1 if necessary).
2 Using a multi-meter set to measure resistance, measure the

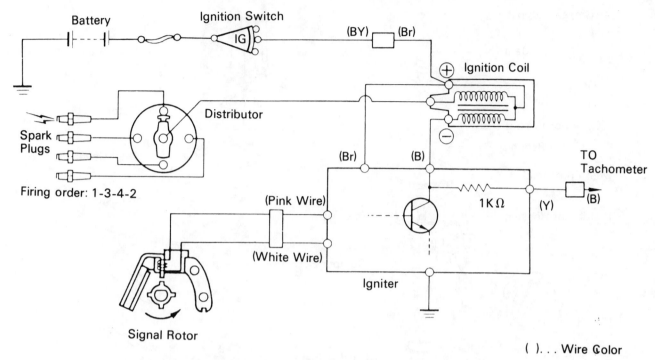

Fig. 5.2 1A-C and 3A-C engine ignition system schematic (Sec 2)

resistance value from the spark plug end to the distributor end of the wire. Check each wire, one at a time, so as not to mix them up. If resistance is high, replace the wires with new ones.

Ignition coil

Primary coil resistance

3   Disconnect the high-tension wire between the coil and the distributor.

4   With the coil cold, measure the resistance between the positive and negative terminals of the coil. Compare the results to the Specifications.

Secondary coil resistance

5   Measure the resistance between the positive terminal and the high-tension terminal of the coil.

Igniter (1A-C and 3A-C engines only)

6   Turn the ignition switch to ON for steps 7 thru 11.

7   To check power source line voltage, connect the positive lead to the positive side of the coil and the negative lead of the tester to ground. The meter should indicate approximately 12 volts.

8   To check the power transistor in the igniter, connect the positive test probe to the negative terminal of the coil and the negative test probe to ground.

9   Disconnect the wiring leading to the distributor. **Caution:** In the following step, do not apply voltage for more than five seconds or serious damage will result to the power transistor in the igniter.

10   Using a 1.5 volt dry-cell battery, connect the positive pole of the battery to the pink wire terminal, and the negative pole to the white wire terminal.

11   With the multi-meter set for voltage, connect the positive probe to the negative ignition coil terminal, and the negative test probe to ground. If the voltage reading on the meter is not 5 to 8 volts, replace the igniter with a new one.

12   Reconnect the distributor connector and turn the ignition switch off.

Breaker point ignition system (3A engine only)

13   Check the ignition coil external resistor condition by connecting the positive probe of the ohmmeter to one terminal of the external resistor and the negative probe to the other resistor terminal. Replace the resistor with a new one if the resistance is out of the specification range.

14   Turn the ignition switch to ON and set the meter to check voltage. Connect the positive probe of the meter to the black/yellow side of the resistor. Connect the negative probe to the body ground. If approximately 12 volts is not indicated, proceed to steps 16 thru 19 below. If the voltage is low, check the voltage throughout the system, starting at the battery and working progressively through the system.

15   Turn the ignition switch to Start and measure the voltage at the positive terminal of the coil. If 12 volts is not indicated, check the relay and wire harness.

16   Inspect the ignition relay by first removing the relay (which is located in the fuse/relay box under the hood). Connect the positive probe of the voltmeter to the number three terminal connector (Fig. 5.3). Connect the negative probe to the body ground. Battery voltage should be present.

17   Turn the ignition switch to Start and connect the positive voltmeter probe to the number one terminal connector and the negative probe to the body ground. The voltage should be the same as the reading in Step 16.

18   Use the ohmmeter to check resistance between terminal 2 of the connector and the body ground. There should be no resistance present. If there is resistance, the ground is bad to the connector.

19   Check the wiring between terminal 4 of the connector and the positive terminal of the coil. There should be no resistance. If there is, the wiring between the coil and the relay box is defective.

20   Reconnect the relay to its connector.

21   If steps 15 thru 17 don't check out, there is a problem in the wiring. If they meet the specifications, but there is no voltage to the resistor, the relay should be checked as described in Chapter 10.

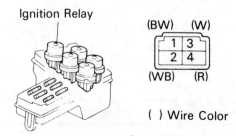

Fig. 5.3 Ignition relay terminal connector locations and coding (Sec 3)

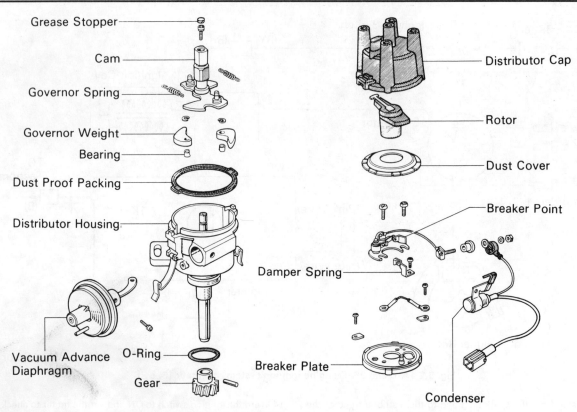

**Fig. 5.4 3-A engine distributor components – exploded view
(Sec 4)**

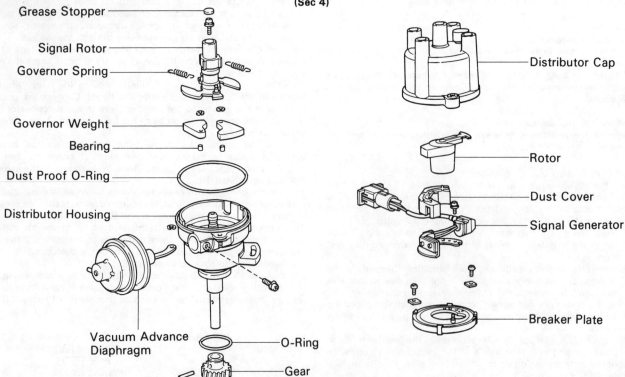

**Fig. 5.5 3A-C and 1A-C engine distributor components – exploded
view (Sec 4)**

4   Distributor – removal, inspection and installation

Removal
1   After carefully marking, remove the coil wire and four plug wires
from the distributor cap.

2   Remove the number one spark plug.
3   Manually rotate the engine to top-dead-center on the compression
stroke for number one piston (see Chapter 1 for instructions on this
procedure).
4   Carefully mark the vacuum hoses leading to the two advancer
diaphragms and one retard diaphragm of the distributor.

4.7 Mark the distributor body opposite the rotor before removing the distributor from the engine

5　Disconnect the vacuum hoses.
6　Disconnect the electrical wires to the distributor.
7　Use a small brush and paint or a scribe to mark the rotor position in relation to the body of the distributor (photo). Scribe a similar mark between the distributor body and the mating surface on the engine cylinder head.
8　Remove the adjusting bolt and clamp.
9　Remove the distributor. **Note:** *Do not rotate the engine with the distributor out.*

Inspection (3A engine)
10　To inspect vacuum advancers, see Chapter 6.
11　To check the mechanical advance operation, turn the rotor counter-clockwise while holding the drive gear stationary. The rotor should return smoothly to its original position.
12　Feel the rotor for excessive clearance.
13　Inspect the O-ring at the distributor base for cracks or damage.
14　Replace the O-ring if any damage or signs of leakage is evident.

Inspection (1A-C and 3A-C engines)
15　Check the air gap as described in Chapter 1.
16　To check the signal generator, use the multi-meter set for resistance. Connect the positive and negative test leads to the two connectors on the distributor (refer to the resistance specification at the front of this Chapter).
17　To remove the signal generator, gently pry the dust cover up.
18　Remove the two screws holding the signal generator in place.
19　Installation is the reverse of removal.
20　Measure the signal generator air gap as described in Chapter 1.

Installation
21　Make certain the number one piston is at top-dead-center on the compression stroke.
22　Align the drilled mark on the driven gear with the center of the number one spark plug terminal on the distributor cap. Insert the distributor into the engine with the adjusting flange centered over the hold-down hole. Make sure that the gear does not turn as the distributor is inserted.
23　Install the hold-down bolt. The marks previously made on the distributor housing and on the rotor and cylinder head should line up before the bolt is tightened.
24　Install the distributor cap.
25　Connect the wiring for the distributor.
26　Install the spark plug wires.
27　Install the vacuum hoses as previously marked.
28　Time the engine as described in Chapter 1.

5　Charging system – description

Two types of electrical charging systems are used. The type of regulator utilized is the most obvious difference between the two, but wiring circuitry and overload protection are also specific to each system.

The charging system with an external regulator uses three fusible links plus three regular fuses for overload protection. This system is readily identified by its external regulator and by the three-pole connector at the rear plate of the alternator (Fig. 5.6).

The internal regulator charging system has no external regulator and a two-pole rear plate connector. This system uses a single fusible link along with two regular fuses for overload protection. In addition, a charge light relay is integrated into this system's circuitry (Fig. 5.7).

Both systems mount the alternator on the left front of the engine and utilize a V-belt and pulley drive system. Maintenance of this drive belt tension along with battery terminal service are the two primary maintenance items in the system. Details are provided in Chapter 1.

6　Alternator – checking on car

1　The following steps require a multi-meter and some basic knowledge of its use as well as electrical basics. If you don't have these skills, it would be wise to have an authorized dealership or shop specializing in electrical systems diagnose your problem. You can save money by removing the alternator and replacing it yourself if it is bad, but often times an alternator is replaced when the problem with the electrical system has another cause. Spend your money and time wisely by testing the system accurately before beginning any repairs.
2　Check the battery, battery terminals and drive belt tension according to the instructions found in Chapter 1.
3　Check the engine, charge and turn signal fuses located in the combination fuse-relay box and the interior fuse box (Figs. 5.8 and 5.9).
4　Check the connections on the rear of the alternator and at the regulator (if so equipped).
5　Use caution during the following step because the engine must be running. Keep hands and tools away from the drive belts and pulleys. Perform this test with the engine at normal operating temperature. Allow the engine to run at normal idling speed and listen carefully to the alternator. It should make a smooth whirring sound if it makes any discernible noise at all. There should be no abnormal noises or excessive grinding sounds. If unusual noises exist, remove the alternator and check it internally for bad bearings and brushes or take it to an alternator rebuilding shop or dealership. Do not disassemble the unit if you do not have the knowledge and tools required for this process.
6　While the engine is running, see that the charge light is off. Turn the engine off and turn the ignition switch back to On but don't start the engine. The charge light should be on. If it isn't, check the charge light circuit and bulb.

Output test
7　Perform the following steps with the engine off. Make certain all connections are tight and making good contact. Damage to the charging system components, test equipment or the operator may result if the connections are improperly made.
8　Disconnect the wire from terminal B of the alternator and connect it to the negative terminal of an ammeter. Connect the positive lead of the ammeter to terminal B. Connect the positive lead of the voltmeter to terminal B. Connect the negative lead of the voltmeter to ground (Fig. 5.10).
9　Start the engine. Advance the engine speed from idle to 2000 rpm. Check the ammeter and voltmeter readings throughout the range.
10　If the readings do not follow the Specifications listed at the front of the Chapter, adjust the regulator if it is the external type. Replace the internal type regulator if the voltage reading is greater than the voltage specification.
11　If the voltage reading is lower than the specification (with an internal type regulator only), ground terminal F and check the voltage reading again. If it rises to above the specified reading, the internal regulator should be replaced. If the voltage reading is still less than the specification, the alternator itself should be checked for total output capability by a repair shop.
12　Check the charging circuit with a load by turning the headlights On (high beam) and set the heater fan switch to High. The ampere reading should be above the specification listed in the specifications at 2000 rpm. If it is slightly lower and the battery is fully charged, the charging system is probably all right. If the reading is an appreciable amount

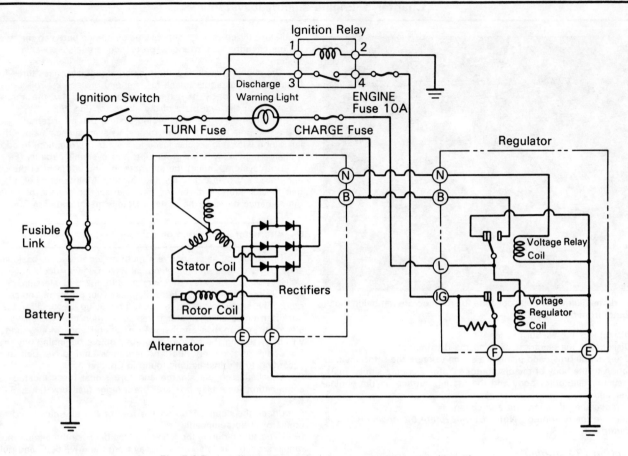

Fig. 5.6 Externally regulated charging system schematic (Sec 5)

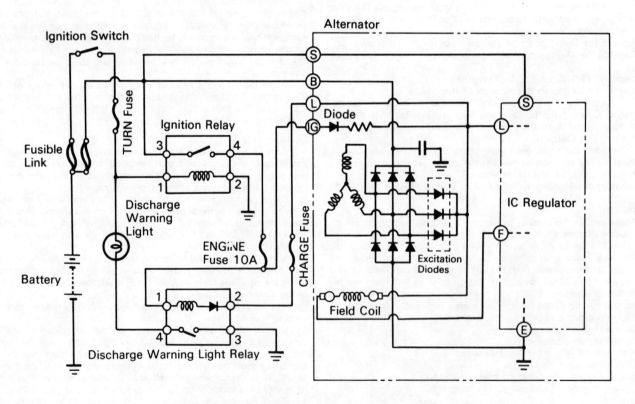

Fig. 5.7 Internally regulated charging system schematic (Sec 5)

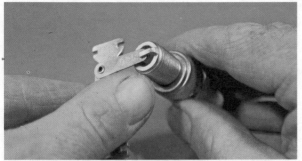

Measuring plug gap. A feeler gauge of the correct size (see ignition system specifications) should have a slight 'drag' when slid between the electrodes. Adjust gap if necessary

Adjusting plug gap. The plug gap is adjusted by bending the ground electrode inwards, or outwards, as necessary until the correct clearance is obtained. Note the use of the correct tool

Normal. Gray brown deposits, lightly coated core nose. Gap increasing by around 0.001 in (0.025 mm) per 1000 miles (1600 km). Plugs ideally suited to engine, and engine in good condition

Carbon fouling. Dry, black, sooty deposits. Will cause weak spark and eventually misfire. Fault: over-rich fuel mixture. Check: carburetor mixture settings, float level and jet sizes; choke operation and cleanliness of air filter. Plugs can be re-used after cleaning

Oil fouling. Wet, oily deposits. Will cause weak spark and eventually misfire. Fault: worn bores/piston rings or valve guides; sometimes occurs (temporarily) during running-in period. Plugs can be re-used after thorough cleaning

Overheating. Electrodes have glazed appearance, core nose very white – few deposits. Fault: plug overheating. Check: plug value, ignition timing, fuel octane rating (too low) and fuel mixture (too weak). Discard plugs and cure fault immediately.

Electrode damage. Electrodes burned away; core nose has burned, glazed appearance. Fault: pre-ignition. Check: as for 'Overheating' but may be more severe. Discard plugs and remedy fault before piston or valve damage occurs

Split core nose (may appear initially as a crack). Damage is self-evident, but cracks will only show after cleaning. Fault: pre-ignition or wrong gap-setting technique. Check: ignition timing, cooling system, fuel octane rating (too low) and fuel mixture (too weak). Discard plugs, rectify fault immediately

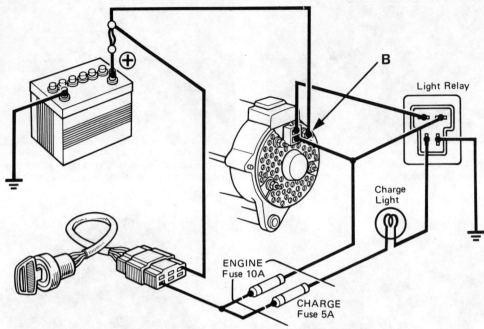

Fig. 5.8 Fuse, fusible link and relay locations for *internally* **regulated charging system (Sec 6)**

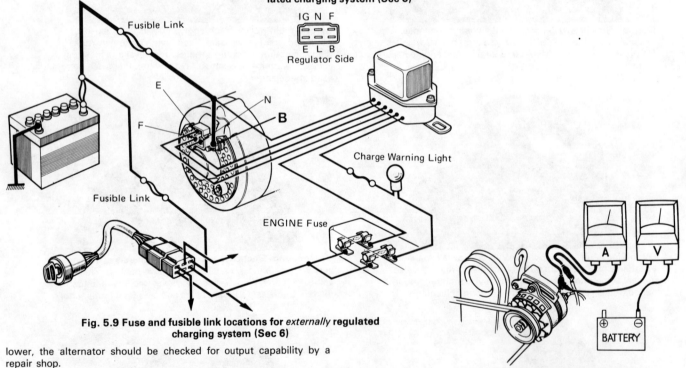

Fig. 5.9 Fuse and fusible link locations for *externally* **regulated charging system (Sec 6)**

Fig. 5.10 Test connections for on car charging system check (Sec 6)

lower, the alternator should be checked for output capability by a repair shop.

7 Alternator – removal and installation

1   Disconnect the negative cable from the battery. **Note:** *Make sure that you have either a wiring diagram or make a diagram for yourself to indicate the proper position of each wire in the following step.*

2   Disconnect the wires at the rear of the alternator (photo).

3   Remove the lower alternator swivel retaining bolt and nut.

4   Remove the adjustment bolt and nut. **Note:** *The belt guard is retained by the adjusting bolt and nut combination.*

5   Release the drivebelt, and remove the alternator by pulling it rearward to clear the adjustment bracket.

6   Installation is the reverse of removal. **Note:** *The alternator adjusting tab is threaded. When installing the alternator, make the belt adjustment, tighten the bolt and then install the locknut.*

8 Alternator – inspection and brush replacement

Note: *Refer to Figs. 5.11 and 5.12 during the following procedure.*

1   Remove the alternator as described in the previous Section.

2   Remove the three alternator through bolts.

3   Clamp the alternator pulley into a vise equipped with soft jaws. **Note:** *Be careful not to damage the alternator pulley.*

4   Remove the four nuts, two terminal insulators and the rear end cover.

5   Remove the rear end frame from the stator. Remove the rear end frame using two pry bars or screwdrivers. **Note:** *Be very careful not to*

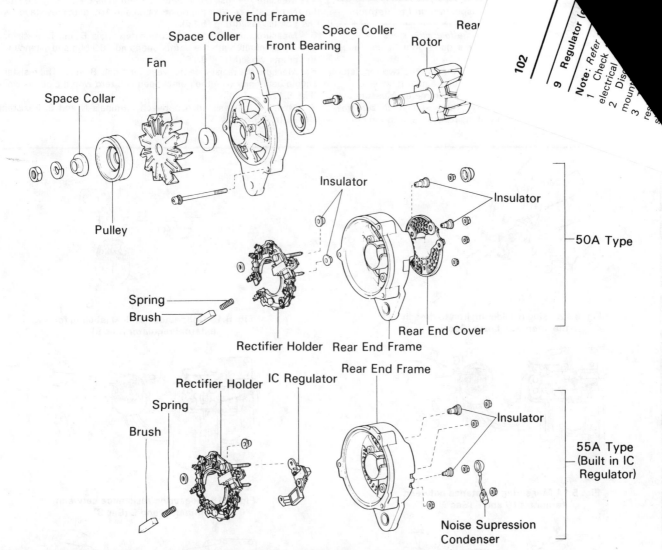

Fig. 5.11 Exploded view of the alternator components (Sec 8)

7.2 Remove the electrical connections (arrows) from the rear of the alternator only after marking each one to simplify installation

8.7 Measuring the alternator exposed brush length

8.12 A length of wire can be used to facilitate brush installation during alternator reassembly

damage any internal wiring or the external housings.

6 Remove the stator assembly.

7 Measure the exposed brush length (photo) and compare it to the specifications. If the brushes are worn beyond the specified limits, replace them with new ones as follows:

8 Unsolder the brushes at their connecting points.

9 Pull the brushes out of their respective slots in the brush holder.

10 Position the new brushes in the holder.

11 Re-solder the new brushes to the connecting points. Make sure that the exposed length of the brush meets the specification.

12 Reassembly is the reverse of disassembly. **Note:** *Take care that the housing is realigned in the same manner that it was when disassembled.* Using a small piece of wire, fashion a brush holder to fit through the slots provided in the retainer (photo). This will hold the brushes in the retracted position while installing the stator.

external type only) – inspection and adjustment

to Figs. 5.13 thru 5.19 for the following steps.
the regulator connections for a good tight fit and good
continuity.
connect the electrical connector and remove the two regulator
ing bolts. Remove the regulator and the regulator cover.
he following tests require the use of an ohmmeter. Measure the
istance between terminals IG and F. There should be zero re-
istance with the points open and 11 ohms resistance with the points
closed (Fig. 5.14).

4   Measure the resistance between terminals L and E. There should
be zero resistance with the points open and 100 ohms resistance with
the points closed (Fig. 5.15).
5   Measure the resistance between terminals B and E. Resistance
should be infinity with the points open and 100 ohms resistance with
the points closed (Fig. 5.16).
6   Measure the resistance between terminals B and L. The resistance
should be infinity with the points open and zero with the points closed
(Fig. 5.17).
7   Measure the resistance between terminals N and E. Resistance
should be 23 ohms.

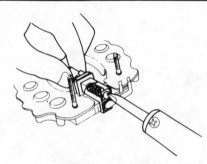

**Fig. 5.12 Using a soldering iron to detach
the alternator brush (Sec 8)**

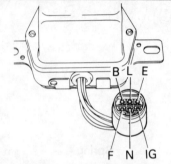

**Fig. 5.13 Connector terminal labeling for
external regulator (Sec 9)**

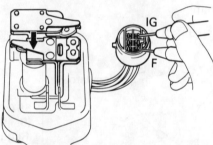

**Fig. 5.14 Measuring resistance between
terminals IG and F (Sec 9)**

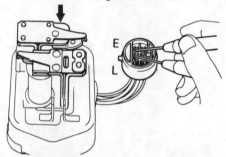

**Fig. 5.15 Measuring resistance between
terminals L and E (Sec 9)**

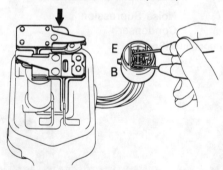

**Fig. 5.16 Measuring resistance between
terminals B and E (Sec 9)**

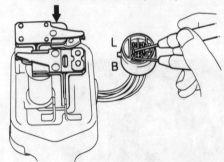

**Fig. 5.17 Measuring resistance between
terminals B and L (Sec 9)**

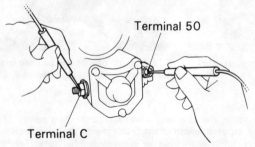

**Fig. 5.18 Checking for an open circuit in
the magnetic switch (solenoid) pull-in
coil (Sec 12)**

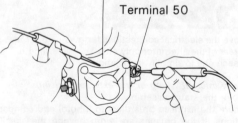

**Fig. 5.19 Checking for continuity in the
magnetic switch (solenoid) hold-in coil
(Sec 12)**

11.2 The starter electrical connections are accessible from under the vehicle

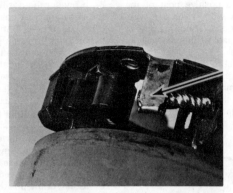

12.14 The brush leads (arrow) are soldered in place and must be removed with a soldering iron

12.16 Holding the spring with a screwdriver to facilitate brush installation

8   If the regulator fails any of the above checks, replace it with a new one.
9   Check point surfaces for excessive burning or damage. Replace the regulator with a new one if the points are bad.
10   If the regulator checks described above indicate that the regulator is in good condition, but the charging system output is not as specified, the regulator can be adjusted (a job that should be left to an automotive electrician). It is usually easier and may be cheaper to simply replace the regulator with a new one.

10 Starting system – description

Two types of starting systems are used. A conventional starter with direct drive, which is readily identified by its top mounted solenoid or magnetic switch, is one type. The second type of starter is a gear reduction type with bottom mounted magnetic switch. It is also identifiable by the side terminals on its bottom solenoid or magnetic switch.
Both starters are activated through the starter switch and a neutral safety switch is provided on automatic transmission equipped vehicles. Direct battery current is provided to the starter motor by the solenoid, which also engages the drive pinion into the engine flywheel.

11 Starter motor – removal and installation

1   Disconnect the negative battery cable from the battery.
2   Disconnect the leads from the underside of the starter. There is one clip connection and one terminal held by a nut and washer (photo).
3   Remove the two bolts retaining the starter to the bell housing.
4   Remove the starter.
5   Installation is the reverse of removal. **Note:** *There is a tab on the clip which connects to the starter that must be properly aligned.*

12 Starter motor (reduction type) – inspection and checking

1   Clamp the motor into a vise equipped with soft jaws.
2   Disconnect the wire lead from the magnetic switch.
3   Using an ohmmeter, perform the magnetic switch pull-in coil open circuit test. Connect the ohmmeter from terminal 50 to terminal C (Fig. 5.18). If there is no continuity, replace the magnetic switch with a new one.
4   Connect the ohmmeter to terminal 50 and to the switch body. If there is no continuity, replace the magnetic switch with a new one.

Starter disassembly
5   Disconnect the wire leading to the magnetic switch.
6   Remove the field frame end cover.
7   Remove the two screws that retain the end cover to the field frame.
8   Remove the end cover from the field frame.
9   Slide the armature out of the field frame.
10   Using a screwdriver, remove the spring tension from the brushes.
11   Remove the brushes from the brush holders.

Brush length measurement
12   Measure the brushes as shown (Fig. 5.20).
13   If the brushes are less than the minimum length, replace them with new ones.

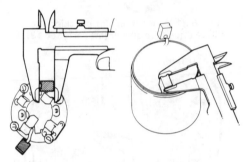

Fig. 5.20 Measuring the starter brush length (Sec 12)

Brush replacement
14   Using a soldering iron, detach the brushes from the pinch clamp (photo).
15   Install the new brushes and solder the leads in position.

Starter reassembly
16   Insert a screwdriver between the spring and the brush holder (photo). This will hold the spring back and allow the brush to be inserted into the brush holder. After the brush is inserted, release the spring by withdrawing the screwdriver. **Note:** *When installing the brush, insert it approximately half way or less (photo) to allow the assembly to be put over the armature before releasing the brush into its fully seated position.*
17   Insert the armature.
18   Position the brush holder.
19   Release the brushes into their fully seated position against the commutator.
20   Install the end cover. **Note:** *If difficulty is encountered when pushing the end cover over the brush holder, use a small awl or similar tool to line up the hole that the screw passes through. Be careful when performing this operation.*
21   Install the motor onto the reduction gear/magnetic switch assembly, making sure that the gear on the end of the motor meshes with the gear on the reduction unit.
22   Install the through-bolts and tighten them securely.
23   Reconnect the lead to the magnetic switch C terminal.

13 Starter solenoid (direct drive) – inspection and checking

1   The following tests are performed on the starter after it is removed from the vehicle. You will need an ammeter, a fully charged battery and three heavy gauge jumper wires.

2   Secure the starter in a vise. Connect the positive post of the battery to the positive ammeter connection with a jumper wire. Connect the negative post of the battery to the starter body. Connect the negative ammeter terminal to the 30 terminal of the starter (Fig. 5.21).

3   Connect a jumper wire from the 30 terminal to the 50 terminal of the starter (Fig. 5.22). The starter should spin at an even rpm and at an amperage less than the specification. The pinion gear should also be thrust forward (away from the motor) into the driving position as long as this connection is maintained. If the starter passes the above tests, it is functioning correctly.

4   Connect the positive post of the battery to the 50 terminal. Leave the negative post connected to the starter body. This will allow the drive pinion gear to move forward into the starting position. Push the pinion back towards the armature side and measure the clearance between the gear and the thrust face of the stop collar. Measure this clearance using a feeler gauge and make sure it falls within the specification.

14   Starter solenoid (direct drive starter) – testing

1   Remove the starter feed coil wire from the solenoid C terminal. Before performing any of the following tests, plan ahead carefully so that they do not take longer than five seconds. Leaving the solenoid connected to a power source for longer than that will burn it out.

2   Connect the positive terminal of the test battery to the 50 terminal of the solenoid. Connect the negative terminal to the solenoid body and to the C terminal (Fig. 5.23). The drive pinion gear should move out into the starting position. This tests the solenoid pull-in coil.

3   Leave the test leads connected the same way as in the above step but withdraw the ground lead connected to the C terminal (Fig. 5.24). The pinion should remain in the start position. If it doesn't, replace the solenoid with a new one.

4   Remove the ground from the solenoid body with the positive connection remaining as in steps 2 and 3 above (Fig. 5.25). The drive pinion should retract into its non-starting position immediately. This tests the plunger return.

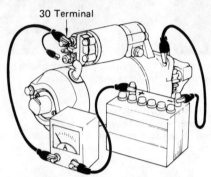

Fig. 5.21 Connections for checking the direct drive type starter (off car) (Sec 13)

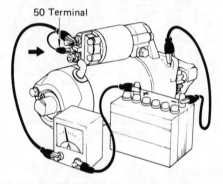

Fig. 5.22 Connecting a jumper wire (arrow) to activate the starter (Sec 13)

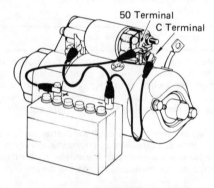

Fig. 5.23 Test connections for checking the starter solenoid pull-in coil (Sec 14)

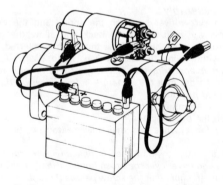

Fig. 5.24 Removing the ground lead (arrow) from the C terminal to check the solenoid (Sec 14)

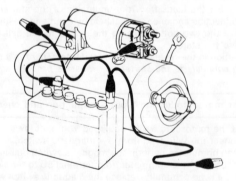

Fig. 5.25 Checking the plunger return by removing the ground lead (arrow) from the solenoid body (Sec 14)

Chapter 6 Emissions control systems

Contents

Specifications

General

Air pump drive belt tension (with Barroughs drive belt tension gauge)	New belt 125 ± 25 lb Used belt 80 ± 20 lb
Throttle positioner setting rpm w/EGR off	1400 rpm
Engine idle rpm (warm with cooling fan off, in Neutral)	550 rpm 4 speed manual 650 rpm 5 speed manual 800 rpm automatic

Torque specifications

EGR valve bolts	27 to 42 ft-lb (20 to 30 kg-m)

1 General information

1   The Toyota Tercel is equipped with several systems for controlling crankcase, evaporative and exhaust emissions. The major emission control systems are: *fuel evaporative; throttle positioner; crankcase emissions; spark control; exhaust gas recirculation; air suction; air injection; catalytic converter and a high altitude compensator.* In addition, the auxiliary emissions control systems are: *hot air intake; hot idle compensator; choke; auxiliary acceleration pump; deceleration fuel cut-off; and a heat control valve.* These systems are for the most part complex and sophisticated in relationship to current automotive emissions control technology. They are very effective in reducing automotive emissions of hydrocarbons, carbon monoxide, and oxides of nitrogen.

2   Abbreviations used in this Chapter:

AAP   Auxiliary acceleration pump
ABV   Air bypass valve
ACV   Air control valve
AI   Air injection
AS   Air suction
ASV   Air switching valve
BTDC   Before top dead center
BVSV   Bi-metal vacuum switching valve
CB   Choke breaker
EGR   Exhaust gas recirculation
EVAP   Evaporative emission control
HAC   High altitude compensation
HIC   Hot idle compensation
HAI   Hot air intake
MC   Mixture control
OC   Oxidation catalyst
PCV   Positive crankcase ventilation
SC   Spark control
S/W   Switch
TP   Throttle positioner
TVSV   Thermostatic vacuum switching valve
TWC   Three way catalyst
VCV   Vacuum control valve
VSV   Vacuum switching valve
VTV   Vacuum transmitting valve

2   General precautions

1   The following Sections will discuss each system individually, its use, its components, and a brief description of how it works. If you are attempting work on these components, you should have some mechanical background and knowledge. Read through each Section carefully to ascertain your level of comprehension. If you don't understand the theory and function of the system you are attempting to repair or troubleshoot, it would be best to leave this task for an authorized specialist or dealership.

2   The emissions control systems are designed as an integral part of the car and should not be modified or changed. In most cases it is illegal to do so and driveability, economy and hazard to the occupants can result from modifications or disablement.

3   Periodic maintenance is the most important preventative measure for problems in the emissions control systems. Follow the recommended intervals and services carefully and trouble-free service should result.

4   Emissions control systems should be checked only after the fuel, ignition and caburetion systems have been found to be fault-free. Poor engine performance is usually the result of a problem in one of these areas rather than in the emissions control systems.

5   Leaking vacuum hoses from a loose or cracked connection are a regular source of problems. Heat contributes to this situation by making rubber hoses brittle. Always check that hoses and connections are tight and correctly routed. Electrical connections are also prone to separation and corrosion. Check them carefully before investigating possible component failure.

6   When working on components or replacing vacuum hoses, identify hoses with a tag or tape. It is also best to work on only one hose at a time. Note that some check valves in-line with some hoses have a direction; if replaced in the wrong direction, a malfunction can result. When disconnecting vacuum hoses, pull from the ends rather than the middle and a twisting motion sometimes helps. Electrical connections should also be disconnected at the connector or terminal rather than by pulling on the wire. When checking for continuity at a terminal, be careful not to push the test light or meter lead in too far or damage may result to the connection.

7   Do not drop electrical relays or sensors as they are very fragile. For the same reason, do not use an impact type of wrench while removing or replacing these parts. When steam cleaning an engine, do not get these parts, as well as the distributor, coil, EGR vacuum modulator, or air pump, wet.

8   If adjustments need to be made to the engine while it is running but with the air cleaner removed, plug the air suction hose and the HIC hose to prevent exhaust gas leakage and rough idle.

9   On a vehicle equipped with either type of catalytic converter, use only unleaded gasoline and do not allow the engine to run with the fuel tank on or near empty. Also, when testing for compression or spark, perform the tests as rapidly as possible. Catalytic converters can become a fire hazard when they overheat from large amounts of unburned fuel passing through them so observe all safety precautions.

3   Positive crankcase ventilation system

1   Crankcase blow-by fumes are routed through the PCV valve to the intake manifold to be burned in the combustion chambers along with a fresh intake charge (Fig. 6.5). The PCV valve is basically a one-way valve and can be tested as such.

2   Remove it from the valve cover (instructions are found in Chapter 1) and attach a clean hose to the cylinder head side of the valve (big end).

3   Blow through the hose and see that air flows freely. Now attach a hose to the other side of the valve and blow through it. Very little, if any air should pass through it.

4   If the valve fails either one of these tests, replace it.

5   Inspect the hose, grommet and valve for any signs of cracks or leakage. Replace any deteriorated part.

4   Fuel evaporative emission control system

General description

1   The fuel evaporative emission control system (EVAP) removes evaporated fuel from the fuel tank and flow chamber, passes it through a charcoal canister and on to the intake manifold to be burned in the combustion process. This system uses two control valves, a thermostatic vacuum switching valve (TVSV), and a vacuum control valve (VCV).

2   The preliminary areas of inspection for the (EVAP) system are the fuel tank, fuel lines and all connections (see Chapter 1). At this time also look at the fuel filler cap. Remove it from the car, remove the four screws and retainer and check the gasket for damage or deformation. Also observe the safety valve to make sure it is operating and not stuck. Reinstall the safety valve, retainer, and screws.

System component checks

3   Inspection of the charcoal canister is an important part of servicing this system. See Chapter 1 for details on this process.

4   Locate the outer vent control valve in the system (Fig. 6.6). Disconnect the hoses from the valve. By using a small amount of air pressure (less than 10 PSI) check that the valve flows freely from one port to the other when the ignition switch is Off. Turn the ignition switch On and check that the valve does not flow any air. If the valve is inoperative, check the fuse and the wiring connections before replacing it with a new one.

5   To inspect the thermostatic vacuum switching valve (TVSV) it must be removed from the car. To do this, first drain the coolant from the cooling system and remove the TVSV. Cool the TVSV to below 45°F (7°C) by putting it in a pan of cold water. Check that the air flow from pipe J to pipes M and L is open (Fig. 6.7). Also check air flow from pipe K to pipe M. Next heat the TVSV to above 63°F but not more than 122°F (17 to 50°C). Now check that the air flows from pipe K through to pipes N and L. Also check that the air flows from pipe J to pipe M. Now heat the TVSV to above 154°F (68°C). Check that the air flows from pipe K to pipes M and L. Make sure there is no air flow from pipe J to any other pipe. Reinstall the TVSV into the car, fill the cooling system and be sure to bleed the cooling system after this process (Chapter 3). If any problem is found with the TVSV, replace it with a new one.

6   To inspect the vacuum control valve (VCV), a vacuum above 3.54 in Hg (90 mm Hg) must be applied to pipe S (Fig. 6.8). Air (10 PSI or less) pressure is blown into pipe T while blocking off pipes R and Y. Check that there is air flow coming out of pipes U, V, Z (and W in California cars only). Now release the vacuum at pipe S. While continuing to blow air into pipe T and closing pipes R and Y, air should not flow out of any of the other pipes. Also check the check valve, which is in-line from the advancer port of the carburetor, to see that it blows air from the orange side to the black side only. If any faults are found during the above tests, replace components as necessary.

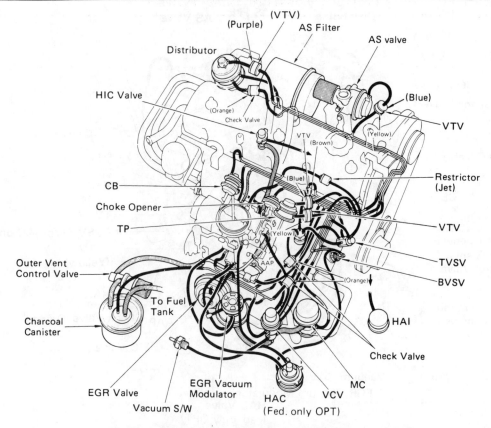

Fig. 6.1 Emission control systems component layout for 1980 and 1981 1A-C & 3A-C 49-state engines

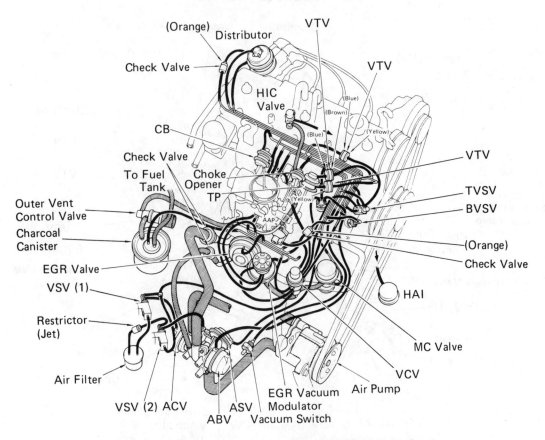

Fig. 6.2 Emission control components for 1980–1981 3A-C and 1A-C engines in California

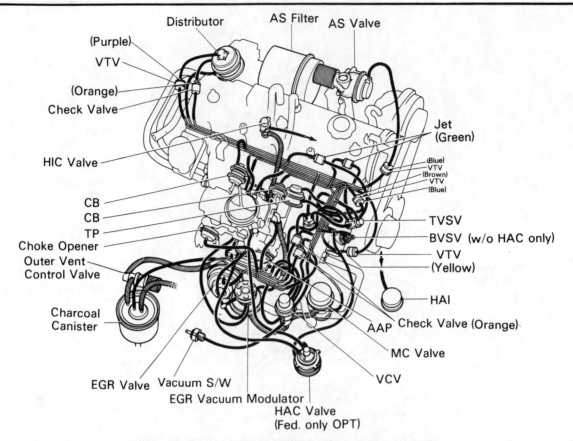

Fig. 6.3 Emission control systems component layout for 1982 3A-C 49-State engines

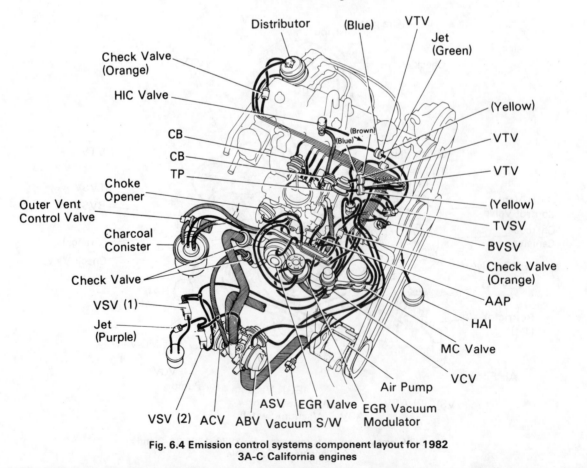

Fig. 6.4 Emission control systems component layout for 1982 3A-C California engines

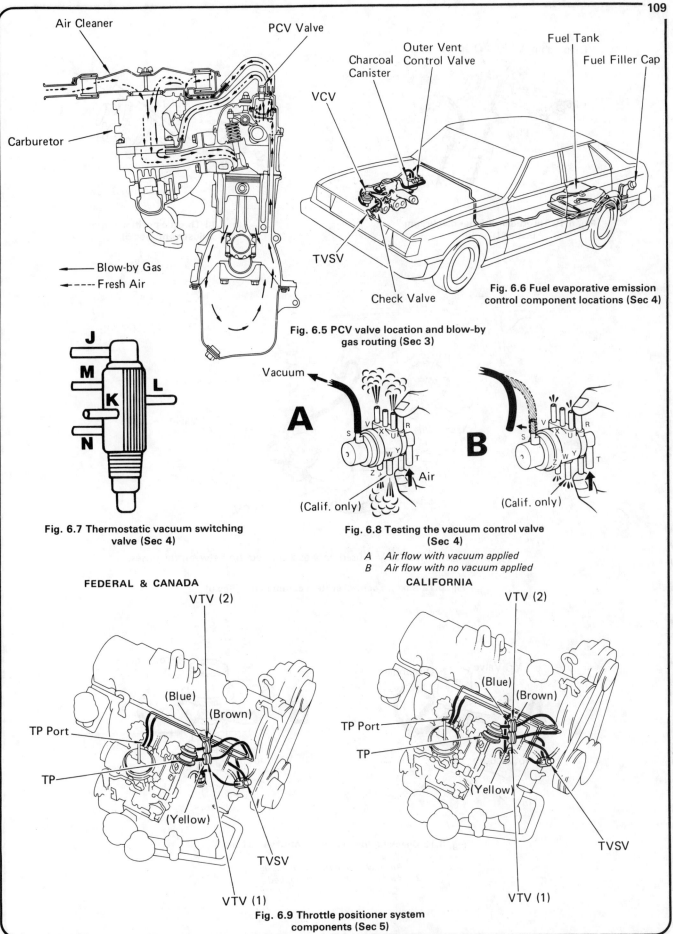

Air Cleaner

PCV Valve

Charcoal Canister

Outer Vent Control Valve

Fuel Tank

Fuel Filler Cap

VCV

Carburetor

TVSV

Check Valve

Fig. 6.6 Fuel evaporative emission control component locations (Sec 4)

→ Blow-by Gas
---→ Fresh Air

Fig. 6.5 PCV valve location and blow-by gas routing (Sec 3)

J

M

K

L

N

Fig. 6.7 Thermostatic vacuum switching valve (Sec 4)

Vacuum

A

(Calif. only)

Air

B

(Calif. only)

Fig. 6.8 Testing the vacuum control valve (Sec 4)

A   Air flow with vacuum applied
B   Air flow with no vacuum applied

FEDERAL & CANADA

VTV (2)

(Blue)

(Brown)

TP Port

TP

(Yellow)

TVSV

VTV (1)

CALIFORNIA

VTV (2)

(Blue)

(Brown)

TP Port

TP

(Yellow)

TVSV

VTV (1)

Fig. 6.9 Throttle positioner system components (Sec 5)

110

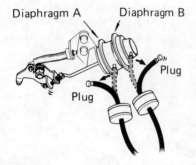

Fig. 6.10 Throttle positioner diaphragm testing (Sec 5)

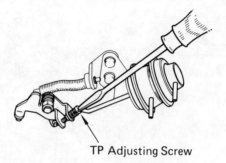

TP Adjusting Screw

Fig. 6.11 Throttle positioner rpm adjustment (Sec 5)

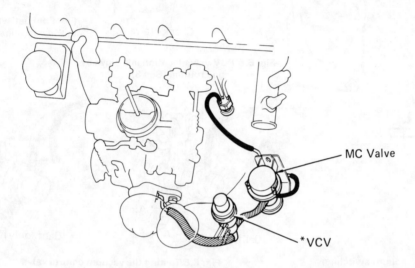

MC Valve

*VCV

*The VCV is used only as a connection between the hoses.

Fig. 6.12 Mixture control system components (Sec 6)

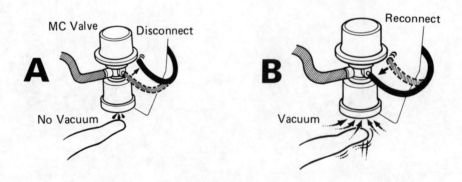

Fig. 6.13 Checking the mixture control valve (Sec 6)

A   Air flow with no vacuum applied
B   Air flow with vacuum applied

5 Throttle positioner system

General description

1 When decelerating, the throttle positioner system (TP) opens the carburetor slightly more than its normal idle position in order to make a more complete combustion of the fuel-air mixture. This system uses the throttle vacuum switching valve and two vacuum transmitting valves along with its actual diaphragm and linkage to the carburetor (Fig. 6.9).

System check and adjustment

2 First check the TVSV with the engine cold. The engine should be below 122°F (50°C). Start the engine and bring it to 3500 rpm or higher. Disconnect the vacuum hose from the TP diaphragm A (Fig. 6.10) and check that the linkage to the carburetor does not move.
3 Warm up the engine and make sure the idle speed is set to the proper specification.
4 Remove the vacuum hose to the EGR valve to disable it temporarily. Be sure to plug the vacuum hose.
5 Disconnect the vacuum hoses from both of the TP diaphragms, plugging these hoses as well. The TP system linkage should now be holding the car at a high rpm. Check Specifications at the front of this Chapter for the correct setting. Adjust the rpm to the proper specification if it is incorrect (Fig. 6.11). Be sure that the cooling fan is off while making this adjustment.
6 Reconnect the vacuum hose to the TP diaphragm B. The engine should return to idle speed within two to six seconds.
7 To check the operation of the vacuum transmitting valve (1) (Fig. 6.9) reconnect the vacuum hose to the TP diaphragm A.
8 Disconnect the vacuum hose between the TVSV and the vacuum transmitting valve (1) at the VTV (1) side and plug the hose.
9 Disconnect the vacuum hose from the TP diaphragm B and plug that vacuum hose. Increase the engine speed to 4500 rpm or above and make sure that the stopper lever is separated from the TP adjusting screw. Plug the VTV (1) pipe.
10 Release the accelerator and check that the engine speed drops to between 2500 and 3000 rpm.
11 Now remove the plug from the VTV (1) and check that the engine speed returns to the TP setting speed within three to ten seconds.
12 Now reconnect the vacuum hose to the TP diaphragm B and reconnect the other vacuum hose to the vacuum transmitting valve.
13 If no problem is found with this overall inspection, the system checks out properly.

System component checks

14 If a problem is found in the above systematic check out, the individual components can be checked in the following way.
15 The vacuum transmitting valve (1) can be checked by blowing air into each side. Air should flow freely between side B over to side A. Air should flow with difficulty from side A to side B. If a problem is found with this, replace the VTV.
16 The VTV (2) can be checked by blowing air from each side as in the previous inspection. Air should flow with difficulty from either side.
17 The diaphragms can be checked by opening the throttle valve to the point where the TP adjusting screw separates from the stopper. Apply vacuum to the diaphragm A and check to see that the linkage moves when the vacuum is applied. While still applying vacuum to diaphragm A, also apply vacuum to diaphragm B. The linkage should move in accordance with that vacuum application.
18 Replace components with new ones as necessary.

6 Mixture control system

General description

1 The mixture control system allows outside atmospheric air to enter the intake manifold on sudden deceleration. This helps to reduce hydrocarbon and CO emissions. The system is composed of the mixture control valve and uses the vacuum control valve simply as a connection between the hoses (Fig. 6.12).

MC valve check

2 To check the mixture control valve disconnect the vacuum hose and place your fingers over the air inlet (Fig. 6.13). A vacuum should not be present. Reconnect the vacuum hose and a vacuum should be felt momentarily. The engine may die or idle rough at this point but this is a normal situation.

7 Spark control system

General description

1 The spark control system (SC) controls the vacuum advance to the engine during different temperature phases of its operation. A small amount of advance is given to the engine during its cold running operation to improve driveability. Normal advance is given to the engine after it is warmed up thoroughly and in some cases the advance is pulled shut for improvement of hydrocarbon emissions. The major components of this system are the distributor with dual vacuum advance diaphragms, the thermostatic vacuum switching valve (TVSV), the bi-metal vacuum switching valve (BVSV), a vacuum control valve (VCV) abd on 49 State and Canada cars only, a vacuum transmitting valve (VTV) (Fig. 6.14). While these components are basic to this system, hose routing and locations may vary slightly between model years and optional equipment choices.

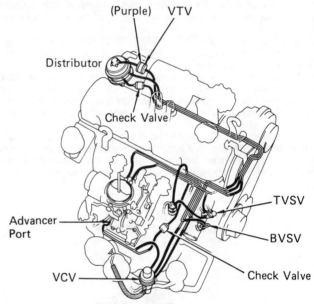

Fig. 6.14 Spark control system components and locations (Sec 7)

System checking

2 Two vacuum gauges will be necessary to check the system correctly. Since two diaphragms are present in the distributor, the gauges are used to show which diaphragm receives vacuum and at what time.
3 Connect a vacuum gauge to the distributor main diaphragm. This will be referred to in the future as vacuum gauge A.
4 Connect the second vacuum gauge to the BVSV port which does not lead to the distributor sub-diaphragm. Be sure to plug the removed hoses.
5 To check the engine it should be cold (below 122°F/5°C). Start the engine. Both vacuum gauges should indicate zero no matter what accelerator position is present.
6 Allow the engine to warm up to normal operating temperature.
7 Once the engine has reached its normal operating temperature, vacuum gauge B should indicate high vacuum no matter what throttle position is present. This checks the BVSV and the check valve.
8 To check the operation of the TVSV, VCV, and VTV on non-California vehicles, warm the engine and run at idle. Pinch the hose shut between the VTV and the vacuum hose.
9 Now advance the engine speed to 2500 rpm. At this point, release the pinched hose and vacuum gauge A should show a high vacuum for one to five seconds.
10 Allow the engine to return to idle speed and vacuum gauge A should returned to 0 smoothly.

11 For California cars only, the TVSV on a warm engine may be checked by blipping the throttle open and closed quickly. The vacuum gauge A should show quick changes corresponding to the accelerator opening and closing.

12 This concludes the checks requiring the use of two vacuum gauges. Disconnect both vacuum gauges and reconnect the hoses to their proper ports.

13 To check the operation of the advancer mechanism inside the distributor, shut off the engine and remove the distributor cap and rotor.

14 Apply vacuum using a vacuum source such as a hand pump, to both the advance diaphragms. The advance rod should move in accordance with the vacuum applied at either port. If no problem is found with this check, the distributor advancers are working correctly.

System component checks

15 The TVSV can be checked using the procedure in Section 4.

16 The vacuum control valve (VCV) can also be checked by using the procedure in Section 4.

17 To inspect the bi-metal vacuum switching valve it must be removed from the car. First drain the coolant from the radiator.

18 Submerge the BVSV in cool water to a temperature below 122°F (50°C). Blow air into the top pipe and check that the BVSV closes (no air exiting other port).

19 Now heat the water to above 147°F (64°C). Blow air into the pipe and the BVSV should open. If the BVSV fails either one of these tests replace it with a new one.

20 To inspect the vacuum transmitting valve (present on non-California cars only) blow air from side A to side B (Fig. 6.15). It should flow with resistance. Now blow air from side B to side A. It should also flow with resistance. If a malfunction is present in this test, replace VTV.

21 The check valve can also be tested with an air blowing technique similar to the VTV. Blow air into the orange pipe and it should flow freely out the black pipe. Blowing air into the black pipe should not emit from the orange pipe. Again, replace this check valve if it fails the test.

Fig. 6.15 Inspecting the vacuum transmitting valve (Sec 7)

---

8 Exhaust gas recirculation system

General description

1 The exhaust gases are recirculated through the exhaust gas recirculation valve and delivered to the intake manifold and ultimately to the combustion chamber to be burned. The burning of already processed gases lowers the combustion temperature which results in reduced NOx emissions.

2 There are two type of systems used. One system is for 49-State and Canadian vehicles. The other system is for California vehicles.

3 Both systems use an EGR valve, EGR vacuum modulator, the thermostatic vacuum switching valve, a check valve, and in the case of the California cars only, a vacuum control valve (Fig. 6.16).

System check

4 The first items to check in the EGR system are the filters which are located in the vacuum modulator (Fig. 6.17). Remove the cap for the filters (2) and check each filter for damage or contamination. Use only compressed air to clean the filters, a solvent will damage them and

render the system ineffective.

5 To check the EGR valve, a 3-way connector, a vacuum gauge, and some additional vacuum hose will be required. Using a 3-way connector, connect the vacuum gauge to the hose between the EGR valve and the vacuum pipe leading to it (Fig. 6.18). Start the engine and check that the engine runs at a normal idle.

6 When starting the engine with the coolant temperature below 122°F (5°C) increase the engine speed to 2500 rpm. The vacuum gauge should read 0. This checks the operation of TVSV.

7 Warm up the engine to a normal operating temperature. Increase the engine speed to 2500 rpm. The vacuum gauge should indicate a low vacuum. If the above is functioning, the TVSV, the EGR vacuum modulator, and the VCV (California only) are all functioning properly.

8 Now disconnect the vacuum hose from port R of the EGR vacuum modulator and connect port R directly to the intake manifold using an extra piece of vacuum hose (Fig. 6.19). Increase the engine speed to 2500 rpm, and the vacuum gauge should indicate a high vacuum. The engine is likely to stumble or mis-fire slightly when this test is performed.

9 Disconnect the vacuum hose from port S of the EGR modulator and plug the hose. With port R still receiving intake manifold vacuum the vacuum gauge should indicate a low vacuum.

10 If no problem is found in the above test, disconnect the vacuum gauge and reconnect the vacuum hose to their proper locations. If a problem is found, inspect each individual part to determine the cause.

System component checks

11 To check the TVSV and the VCVs (California only) see the checks performed in Section 4.

12 The check valve can be inspected by blowing air into one direction and then the other. Air should flow from the orange pipe to the black pipe, but it should not flow in the opposite direction from black to orange.

13 To check the EGR valve, visually check the valve for sticking and heavy carbon deposits. It is best to replace this valve if any of these conditions exist. Always use a new gasket when replacing the EGR valve.

14 Inspecting the EGR vacuum modulator requires disconnecting the vacuum hoses from ports P, Q and R of the EGR vacuum modulator.

15 Plug ports P and R with your fingers and blow air into port Q. Air should pass through to the filter side (Fig. 6.20). Start the engine and maintain the engine speed at 2500 rpm. Repeat the same conditions as the above test. There should now be a high resistance to air flow.

---

9 Air suction system

General description

1 This system is incorporated on all vehicles except those destined for California. Air which is drawn in past the fuel filter, is passed through the air suction valves and to the exhaust ports of the numbers three and four cylinders to complete the burning process. Both hydrocarbon and CO content is lessened in the exhaust system by this process.

System check

2 Visually inspect the hoses and tubes in the AS system for cracks, kinks, damage or poor connections (Fig. 6.21).

3 To check the air suction valve A (Fig. 6.22), the vacuum hose from air suction valve B must be removed and plugged. Start the engine and allow it to idle, checking for a bubbling noise in the area of the air cleaner with only the air cleaner lid removed.

4 To check air suction valve B, reconnect the vacuum hose disconnected in the previous step and note that with the engine still idling a bubbling noise should be heard at the AS valve inlet. If the valve follows these guidelines, this system is functioning properly. If a problem is noted, each part must be check individually.

System component checks

5 Remove the air filter and the air suction valve A from the air cleaner. Check and clean this air filter if it is dirty. If it is damaged, replace it.

6 Check that the valve is working properly by blowing through the AS valve pipe. There should be no passage of air when blowing hard and air will pass through when suction is applied to the pipe. If this

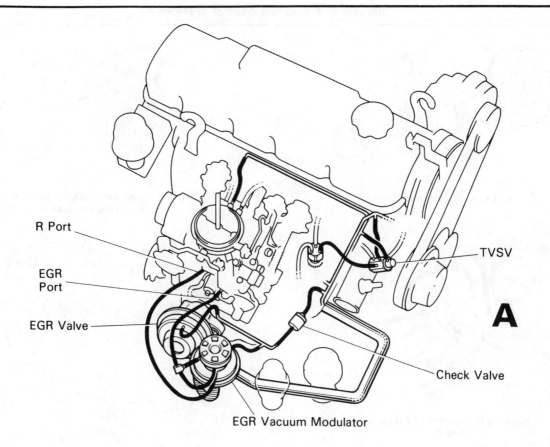

R Port

EGR
Port

EGR Valve

TVSV

Check Valve

EGR Vacuum Modulator

A

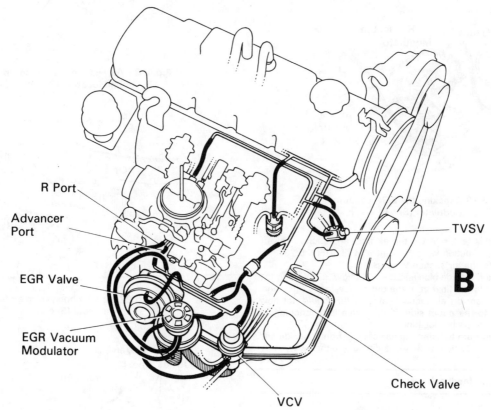

R Port

Advancer
Port

EGR Valve

EGR Vacuum
Modulator

TVSV

Check Valve

B

VCV

Fig. 6.16 Exhaust gas recirculation component location (Sec 8)

A   49-state system   *B   California system*

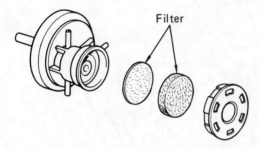

Fig. 6.17 EGR system filters (Sec 8)

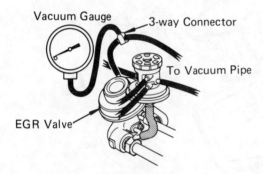

Fig. 6.18 Checking the EGR valve
(Sec 8)

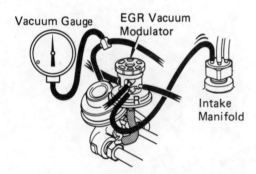

Fig. 6.19 Checking the EGR vacuum
modulator (Sec 8)

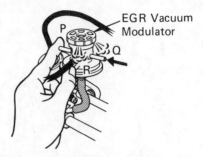

Fig. 6.20 Function checking the EGR
vacuum modulator (Sec 8)

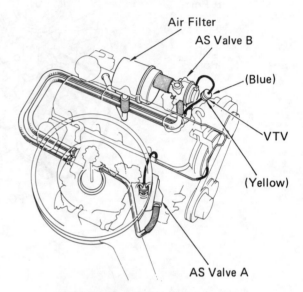

Fig. 6.21 Air suction system component
and location (Sec 9)

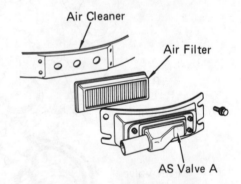

Fig. 6.22 Air suction system air filter
removal (Sec 9)

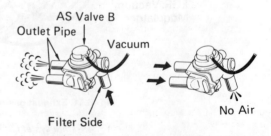

Fig. 6.23 Inspection of air suction valve
B (Sec 9)

component passes this test, reinstall the air filter and suction valve.
7   To inspect the air suction valve B, remove it first (Fig. 6.23).
8   Apply vacuum to the air suction valve B.
9   Blow air into the filter side pipe and it should flow out through the outlet pipes. Air should not flow from the outlet side to the filter side.
10   Release the vacuum on air suction valve B. Air should not flow from the filter side to the outlet side. If this valve is functioning as stated, reinstall it in its proper location.
11   To inspect the vacuum transmitting valve, blow from one side and then the other. Air should flow with some difficulty either way.

10 Air injection with feedback system

General description
1   This system, which comes on California vehicles only, uses an air pump to provide compressed air to three separate sub-systems.
2   The first sub-system ports this compressed air to the air cleaner. The second sub-system pumps air into the exhaust ports, while the third sub-system diverts air to the EGR valve pressure chamber.
3   A small computer is used to receive information from a sensor in the exhaust manifold. A thermo sensor feeds exhaust temperature

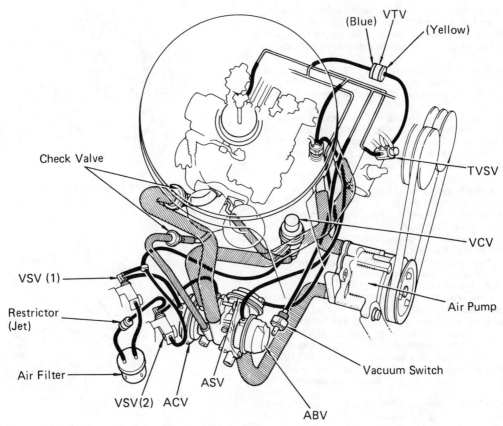

**Fig. 6.24 Air injection with feedback
system components and locations
(Sec 10)**

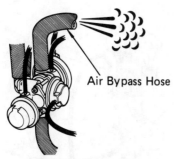

**Fig. 6.25 Checking the thermostatic
vacuum switching valve (Sec 10)**

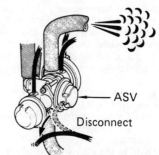

**Fig. 6.26 Checking the vacuum
transmitting valve (Sec 10)**

from a point at the exit of the three-way catalytic converter. The computer processes this information to balance the three sub-systems utilizing two vacuum switching valves (VSV's) which in turn operate an air control valve (ACV), an air bypass valve (ABV), and an air switching valve (ASV). A thermostatic vacuum switching valve (TVSV) also controls all the sub-systems by allowing them to operate only through certain temperature ranges. A vacuum transmitting valve (VTV) restricts vacuum between the TVSV and the ACV while a restrictor jet performs a similar function on the vacuum inlet source for VSV number 2. All of these components and sub-systems work together to provide the engine with the ideal (stoichiometric) air-fuel ratio throughout its many temperature and operating cycles. This also results in a minimum of tailpipe emissions of hydrocarbons, carbon-monoxide and oxides of nitrogen (Fig. 6.21).

System check

4   To check the TVSV with a cold engine, the coolant temperature should be below 46°F (7° C). The air by-pass hose should discharge air when the engine is started at this temperature (Fig. 6.25).
5   The TVSV, ASV, and ACV should be checked with a warm engine. The engine should be in the temperature range of 63° to 127°F (17°

to 53°C). Increase the engine speed to about 2000 rpm and check that air is not discharging from the air by-pass hose.
6   The ACV, VSV's, and the oxygen sensor to the VSV's should also be checked with the engine at normal operating temperature. Again increase the engine speed to 2000 rpm and check that air is discharging intermittently from the air by-pass hose. With the engine idling no air should emit from the air bypass hose.
7   To check the VTV, allow the engine to idle at normal operating temperature. Disconnect the vacuum hose from the ASV and check that air is discharging from the air by-pass hose (Fig. 6.26). Reconnect the vacuum hose to the ASV and air should stop discharging within 2 to 6 seconds.
8   To check the ABV, allow the engine to idle and disconnect the vacuum hose from the ABV. Air should not discharge from the air by-pass hose. Now reconnect the vacuum hose to the ABV and check that air emits momentarily from the air by-pass hose and then stops.
9   To check the vacuum switch to the VSV's, punch the vacuum hose to the vacuum switch at idle. Slowly increase the engine speed and check that the intermittent air stops discharging from the air by-pass hose above 1600 rpm. The engine should also misfire slightly above 2100 rpm with the deceleration fuel cut system on.

10 To check the TWC thermal sensor, it is necessary to first locate the service connection which is on the left fender apron near the ignition coil (Fig. 6.27). With the engine idling, connect a jumper wire between the TWC and E terminals as shown. Air should now discharge from the air by-pass hose.

11 To check the check valve leading to the EGR valve with the engine idling, disconnect the hose between the check valve and the EGR valve on the check valve side. Air should be discharging from the check valve.

12 If the above systems are found to be operating properly, the parts are functioning as they should. If a problem is noted at this time, each individual part will have to be inspected. Remember to reconnect all disconnected hoses and place all parts which have been rendered inoperative for testing, back in their working condition.

System component checks and adjustments

13 The air pump drive belt should be kept at the specification listed at the front of this Chapter. To adjust the belt, loosen the adjusting lever bolt and the pivot bolt (Fig. 6.28). Move the air pump in the direction of the belt tension and re-tighten the bolts. Do not attempt to move the air pump by prying on the by-pass housing as it can crack or break. Pry on the rear cover only when making this adjustment.

14 The air pump itself should first be checked for abnormal noise which is an indication of more extensive problems.

15 Because the air pump provides air to three different systems in the AI system, the output volume is critical. Initially, you should check the air pump for output pressure. If the output seems low or the related functions seem weak, the flow will have to be checked with a special tool (No. SST09258-14010) available through a Toyota dealership. This tool tests the output through a controlled orifice of 0.193 in diameter (4.9 mm) at an engine speed of 1800 rpm. You could also have the car tested for this function through the service department of the dealership.

16 Refer to Fig. 6.29 for the following ABV check. Disconnect the air hose from the check valve leading to the exhaust manifold and the air by-pass hose from the air cleaner. Disconnect the vacuum hoses from the ACV chamber B and the ASV. Compressed air should now come out of the air by-pass hose while idling.

17 Refer to Fig. 6.31 for the following ASV check. Release the vacuum from the ACV chamber B and ASV, and apply a vacuum directly to the ACV chamber A. Compressed air should now come out of the air by-pass hose at an idle. The pressure relief valve should open at a given pressure of 3.3 to 5.6 psi (0.23 to 0.39 kg-cm^2). This must be checked with the appropriate tool listed in the inspection of the air pump.

18 To inspect the check valve which leads to the exhaust manifold, remove the check valve from both the ACV and manifold side. Check that air flows from the ACV side to the manifold side. Air should not flow from the manifold side to the ACV side.

19 To inspect the check valve leading to the EGR valve, check that air flows from the ACV side to the EGR valve side. Air should now flow from the EGR valve side to the ACV side.

20 The VTV can be checked by blowing air from either direction. Air should flow with resistance from both sides.

21 Check the restrictor jet by blowing air into each side. The jet should allow little or no air flow.

22 The TVSV can be inspected using the procedure in Section 4.

23 The procedure for checking the VSVs requires the use of electrical jumper wires. Refer to Fig. 6.32 to illustrate. Connect jumper wires between the battery terminals and VSV terminals as shown, then blow into pipe E. Air should emit from pipe F. Now disconnect the battery from the switch and blow into pipe E. Air should now come out of pipe G. To check for a short circuit in the VSVs, use an ohmmeter to check that there is no continuity between the positive terminal and the body of the VSV.

24 To check the vacuum switch, an ohmmeter should be inserted between the body and the switch terminal. With the ignition off, there should be continuity. With the engine running there should be no continuity.

25 To inspect the thermo switch, drain the coolant from the radiator and remove the thermo switch from the intake manifold. Cool the thermo switch in water below 127°F (53°C). Use an ohmmeter to check that there is continuity between the terminal and body. Now heat the switch to above 149°F (65°C) and check that there is no continuity. Apply sealer to the threads and reinstall the switch if it checks out properly.

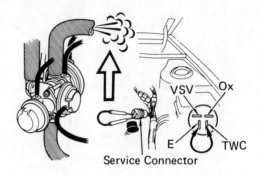

Fig. 6.27 Checking the thermo sensor (Sec 10)

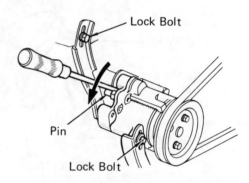

Fig. 6.28 Adjusting the air pump belt tension (Sec 10)

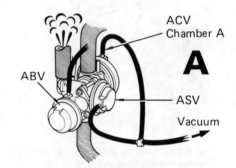

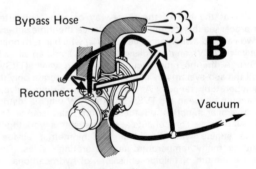

Fig. 6.29 Checking the ACV operation (Sec 10)

A   *Proper hose routing for check procedure*
B   *Momentary blast of air after ABV hose reconnection*

26 To check the thermo sensor, unplug the wiring connector for the thermo sensor under the driver's seat. Use an ohmmeter to measure the resistance between both terminals with the engine idling. The resistance should be 2 to 200 kilo-ohms. The ohmmeter should always be inserted from the rear side of the connector. Closely examine all of the related wiring for damage and tight connections.

27 To inspect the oxygen sensor, warm up the engine to the normal operating temperature. Connect a voltmeter to the service connector on the left fender apron near the ignition coil. The positive (+) testing probe should be connected to the OX terminal and the minus (-) testing probe to the E terminal. Raise the engine speed to 2500 rpms for about 90 seconds. Continue to run the engine at this speed and check that the needle of the voltmeter fluctuates eight times or more in 10 seconds within a 0 to 7 volt range. If this is the case, the oxygen sensor is functioning correctly. If a malfunction occurs, inspect the other parts, hose connections and wiring of the AI system. If no problem is found in this area, replace the oxygen sensor.

11 Catalyst

General description

1 Two types of catalysts are used to convert outgoing exhaust air from the engine into other chemicals. The oxidation catalyst in the 49 State and Canada versions, converts hydrocarbons and carbon monoxide to water and carbon dioxide. The 3-way catalyst used on the California system reduces hydrocarbons, carbon monoxide and oxides of nitrogen emissions to dinitrogen, carbon dioxide, and water. In addition, if the California catalyst is over-heated above 1445°F (785°C), the thermo sensor in the catalyst turns the air injection system off.

System checking

2 Visual inspection of either type of catalyst is the main form of checking it. Any type of dents, damage, loose connections, or cracks can affect the operation of the catalyst. In addition, the heat insulator which is situated between the car body and the catalyst, must be in place and covering the area intended in this design in order to function correctly. Serious damage can result to the car or the occupants if the heat insulator is not functioning correctly.

3 The 3-way catalyst should be shaken by inserting a block of wood against the bottom, especially if it is hot, and tapping the block lightly to check for any loose, rattling noises inside. This is a sign that the beads of catalyst material have come loose and replacement of the converter is necessary.

4 If the oxygen sensor needs replacement, it must be carefully fitted into its position on the catalytic converter. A new gasket should be used and the tightening torque should be 53 to 78 in-lbs (*not* ft-lbs) (0.6 to 0.9 Kg-meters).

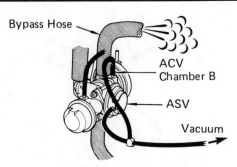

Fig. 6.30 Testing the operation of the ACV (Sec 10)

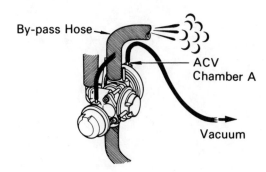

Fig. 6.31 The ASV during test procedures (Sec 10)

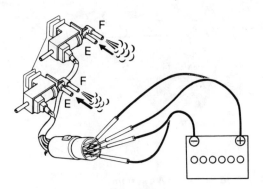

Fig. 6.32 Inspecting the vacuum switching valve (Sec 10)

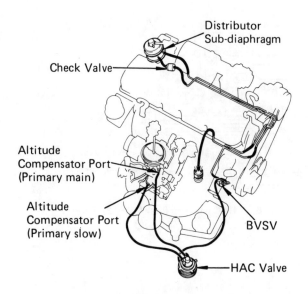

Fig. 6.33 High altitude compensation system components and locations (Sec 12)

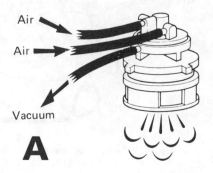 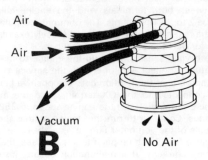

Fig. 6.34 Determining the position of the HAC valve (Sec 12)

A   HAC valve in high altitude position
B   HAC valve in low altitude position

Fig. 6.35 Checking the BVSV with a cold engine (Sec 12)

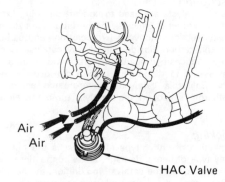

Fig. 6.36 Checking the carburetor function in the HAC valve (Sec 12)

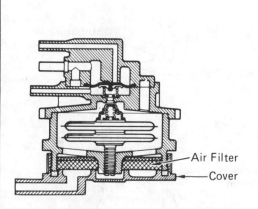

Fig. 6.37 HAC valve air filter (Sec 12)

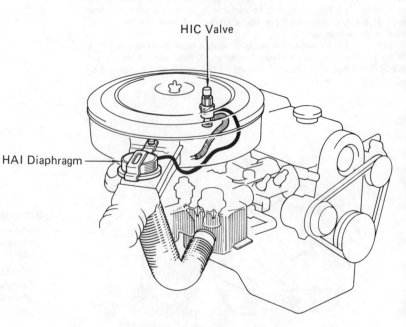

Fig. 6.38 Hot air intake system components and locations (Sec 13)

12 High altitude compensation system

General description

1   The high altitude compensation (HAC) system is an option of 49 State vehicles where the mean altitude of the area is above 3000 ft. If your vehicle is equipped with such a device, an underhood decal indicating this will be present. This system works to ensure that the proper air-fuel mixture supplied to the carburetor is present even at altitudes of 3930 ft (1198 meters) and above. It accomplishes this through two methods. Additional air is supplied to the primary high speed circuit of the carburetor and ignition timing is advanced for improved driveability. The main components of this system consist of carburetor altitude compensator ports (both primary main and primary slow), the high altitude compensation valve, the BVSV, and a check valve leading to the distributor sub-diaphragm (Fig. 6.33).

System checking

2   Before checking the HAC system, the position of the HAC valve must be determined. This can be done by blowing into any one of the three ports on top of the HAC valve while the engine is idling at normal operating temperature (Fig. 6.34). If the passage is open, the valve is in the high altitude position and if it is closed it is in the low altitude position.

High altitude

3   To check the BVSV with a cold engine, the coolant temperature should be below 122°F (50°C). Blow air into the lower port and check that the BVSV closes (Fig. 6.35). To check the BVSV with a hot engine, make sure that the engine is at its normal operating temperature. Blow air into the pipe again and check that the BVSV opens.
4   Check the ignition timing at idle by disconnecting the vacuum hose between the distributor sub-diaphragm and the check valve at the sub-diaphragm side and plug the hose in. Observe the ignition timing and make sure it is at the proper 5° BTDC setting. Reconnect the hose to the distributor sub-diaphragm and observe that the ignition timing now advances itself to about 13° BTDC.
5   Now the check valve can be examined by disconnecting the vacuum hose from the check valve at the black side and plugging the hose end. The ignition timing should remain stationary for more than one minute. Now stop the engine and reconnect the hose to the check valve.
6   To check the carburetor function in the HAC system disconnect the two hoses from the pipes on top of the HAC valve (Fig. 6.36). Blow air into each hose and check that air flows into the carburetor.

Low altitude

7   Check the BVSV with a cold engine that has a coolant temperature below 122°F (50°C). Blow air into a pipe and check that the BVSV closes. Now warm up the engine and allow it to idle at a normal operating temperature. Blow air into the pipe and check that the BVSV opens.
8   Check the ignition timing at idle by disconnecting the vacuum hose between the HAC valve and the BVSV at the HAC valve side and plug the hose end.
9   Disconnect the vacuum hose between the distributor sub-diaphragm and check valve at the sub-diaphragm side and plug the hose end.
10 The ignition timing should read 5° BTDC.
11 Reconnect the hose to the distributor sub-diaphragm and the ignition timing should now read about 13° BTDC.
12 Check the check valve by disconnecting the vacuum hose from the check valve on the black side and plugging the hose end. Check that the ignition timing remains stationary for more than one minute. Reconnect the hoses if this is correct.
13 If no problem is found in the above system checks, the system is working properly and no further testing is needed. If a problem is found, each individual part must be inspected to determine the problem.

System component checks

14 Check the BVSV by removing it from the car and submerging it into a suitable container of cool water. Maintain the temperature of the water to below 122°F (50°C). Blow air into the pipe and check that the BVSV closes. Now heat the water containing the BVSV to above

147°F (64°C). Blow air into the pipe and check that the BVSV opens. If no problem is found, reinstall the BVSV.
15 To inspect the check valve, blow air first from the white (orange in 1982) pipe to the black pipe and see that it flows freely. Now blow air from the black pipe to the white (orange) pipe and see that air does not flow through.
16 To inspect the distributor vacuum advancer, remove the distributor cap and rotor. Apply a vacuum from an outside source to the diaphragms and check that the vacuum advancer moves in relationship with the vacuum applied. If a problem is found, repair or replace the distributor vacuum advancer.
17 Inspect the HAC valve for cleanliness and corrosion. Clean the air filter in the HAC valve (Fig. 6.32) on a periodic basis using compressed air.

13 Hot air intake system

General description

1   The HAI system provides a hot air supply to the carburetor in cold weather to improve driveability and to prevent the carburetor from icing in very cold weather. It uses a HIC valve and a HAI diaphragm with a connecting vacuum hose (Fig. 6.38).

System checking

2   To check the air control valve operation, remove the air cleaner cover and cool the HIC valve by blowing cool air on it. Examine the air control valve and see that it is closed under this situation (allowing air through the flexible hot-air duct leading to the engine).
3   Now reinstall the air cleaner and warm up the engine to normal operating temperature. The air control valve should now open to allow cool air from the outside of the car to enter the air cleaner.
4   Visually check all the hoses and connections for cracks, leaks or damage.

14 Hot idle compensator system

General description

1   The HIC system allows air controlled by the HIC valve to enter the intake manifold in order to provide a proper air-fuel mixture (stoichiometric) during high temperatures at an idle. This system utilizes the HAI diaphragm, the HIC valve, and a connecting vacuum hose (Fig. 6.38).

System checking

2   To check the HIC valve, blow air from the HAI diaphragm side into the valve while closing the atmospheric port with a finger. Air should not flow from the carburetor side to the HAI diaphragm side. With the engine below 72°F (22°C), check that air does not flow from the HAI diaphragm side to the atmospheric port while closing the intake manifold side. Now heat the HIC valve to above 84°F (29°C) and check that air flows from the HAI diaphragm side to the atmospheric port while closing the intake manifold side. While performing this check, be sure to prevent water from getting inside the HIC valve as it will damage it.

15 Automatic choke system

General description

1   The automatic choke system temporarily supplies a rich mixture to the engine by closing the choke valve when the engine is cold. This system uses a choke valve at the inlet of the carburetor, a heater, and a bi-metal ceramic diaphragm to control the valve movement. Electrical power is supplied to the heater through a regulator and from the engine electrical system.

System checking

2   To inspect the automatic choke system, start the engine (cold). Remove the top of the air cleaner and observe that the choke valve is closed as the engine initially starts, and begins to open as the choke housing is warmed by the electrical flow.

3   To inspect the heating coil, unplug the wiring connector leading to it. Measure the resistance with an ohmmeter and it should be 19 to 24 ohms at 68°F (20°C).

16 Choke breaker system

General description
1   When the choke is operated, this system opens the choke valve slightly to prevent too rich a mixture, particularly when the car is driven immediately after being started in cold temperatures. It also helps to pull open the choke valve as the engine warms up (Figs. 6.39 and 6.40).

System component checks
2   Check the TVSV with a cold engine below 45° (7°C). Disconnect the vacuum hose from the choke breaker diaphragm A (Fig. 6.41) and check that the choke linkage does not move. Reconnect the vacuum hose to diaphragm A after this test is performed.
3   To check diaphragm B, disconnect the vacuum hose from the choke breaker at diaphragm B and see that the linkage moves. Reconnect the vacuum hose after this check has been made.
4   To check the TVSV, the restrictor (or VTV) and the diaphragm A with a warm engine, allow the engine to reach normal operating temperature. Remove the vacuum hose from diaphragm A and check that the choke linkage returns. Reconnect the vacuum hose to diaphragm A and check that the choke linkage moves within the specified time after reconnecting the hose. The time for 49-State and Canada cars is 5 to 15 seconds, while Calfornia cars will take 4 to 10 seconds.
5   To inspect the restrictor jet, blow air from each side. There should be stoppage in either direction.
6   To inspect the VTV (California cars only) blow air from each side and check that air flows with resistance.
7   To inspect the choke breaker diaphragms, check that the choke linkage moves in accordance with an applied vacuum. Remove the hose and apply an external source and observe the movement of the choke linkage.
8   On 1982 3-AC engines, a second choke breaker was added for increased driveability when cold. This CB is situated on an uncontrolled (straight from the intake manifold) vacuum line with the exception of an in-line jet. The jet restricts vacuum flow in either direction giving a dampening effect to the linkage motion (Fig. 6.40).
9   To check diaphragm C (1982 only), disconnect the vacuum hose from the diaphragm and see that the linkage moves. Then, reconnect the vacuum hose to the diaphragm and see that the linkage moves within 5 to 15 seconds. The check valve for this diaphragm is tested in the same manner as described in paragraph 5 above.

FEDERAL & CANADA

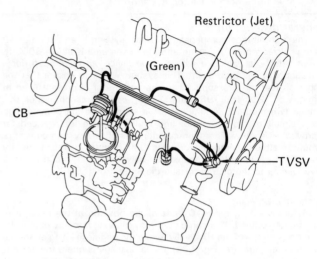

CALIFORNIA

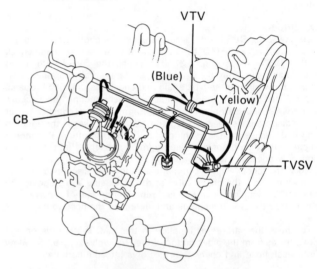

Fig. 6.39 1981 Choke breaker system components and locations (Sec 16)

FEDERAL & CANADA

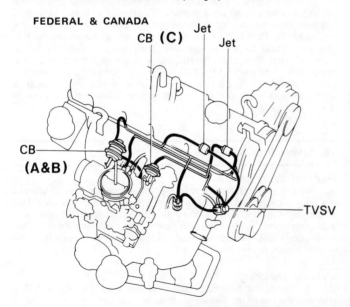

CALIFORNIA

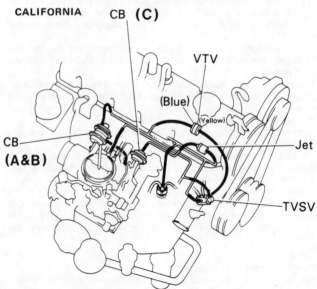

Fig. 6.40 1982 Choke breaker system components and locations (Sec 16)

17 Choke opener system

General description

1   The choke opener system forceably holds the choke valve open to prevent over-richness in the air-fuel mixture after the engine is warm but not at its fully operational temperature. This system also releases the fast idle to the third step on the cam, in order to lower the engine idle rpm during this phase. The system uses a choke opener, the TVSV, and several connecting lines and vacuum hoses (Fig. 6.43).

System checking

2   To inspect the choke opener system, first check the TVSV with the engine cold below 122°F (50°C). Disconnect the vacuum hose from the choke opener diaphragm and step down once on the accelerator pedal and release it. Now start the engine. Reconnect the vacuum hose and check that the choke linkage does not move.

3   Allow the engine to warm up to normal operating temperature and turn it off. You can now check the TVSV, diaphragm and linkage for correct operation.

4   Disconnect the vacuum hose from the choke opener diaphragm.

5   Set the fast idle cam to one of the higher idle speeds. While holding the throttle slightly open, push the choke valve closed and hold it closed as you release the throttle valve.

6   Start the engine, but do not change the accelerator position. Reconnect the vacuum hose and see that the choke linkage moves and the fast idle cam is released to the third step (Fig. 6.44).

7   To inspect the diaphragm, apply an external source of vacuum to its hose fitting after removing the vacuum hose leading to it. See that linkage movement accompanies applied vacuum.

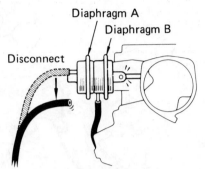

Fig. 6.41 Checking the TVSV with a cold engine (Sec 16)

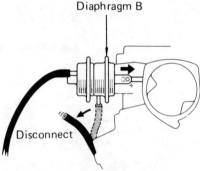

Fig. 6.42 Checking diaphragm B (Sec 16)

FEDERAL & CANADA

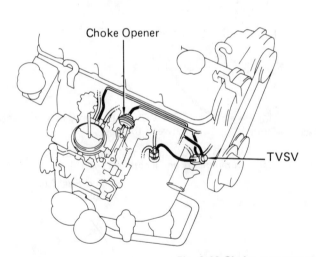

CALIFORNIA

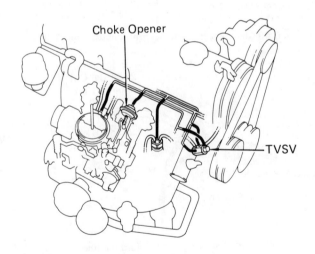

Fig. 6.43 Choke opener system components and locations (Sec 17)

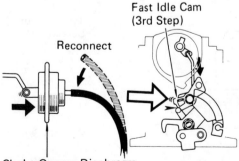

Fig. 6.44 Checking the choke opener diaphragm and fast idle cam (Sec 17)

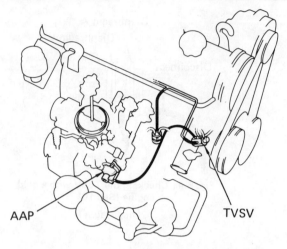

AAP   TVSV

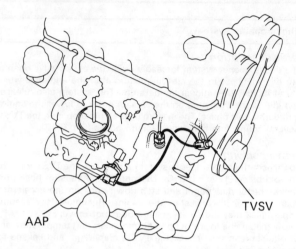

AAP   TVSV

Fig. 6.45 Auxiliary acceleration pump system components and
locations (Sec 18)

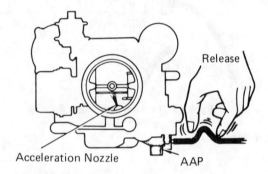

Release

Acceleration Nozzle   AAP

Fig. 6.46 Checking the AAP system function (Sec 18)

2nd Fuel Cut
Solenoid Valve

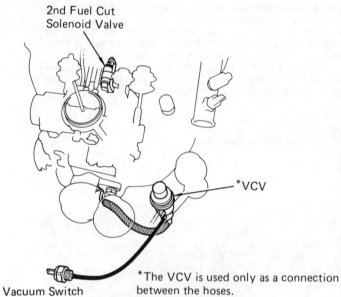

*VCV

Vacuum Switch

*The VCV is used only as a connection
between the hoses.

Fig. 6.47 Deceleration fuel cut system
components and locations (Sec 19)

2nd Fuel Cut
Solenoid Valve

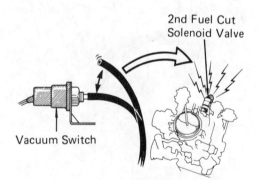

Vacuum Switch

Fig. 6.48 Checking the deceleration fuel
cut system (Sec 19)

Solenoid Valve

O-ring

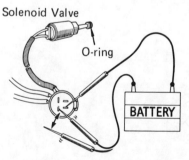

BATTERY

Fig. 6.49 Inspecting the 2nd fuel cut
solenoid valve (Sec 19)

2nd Fuel Cut
Solenoid Valve

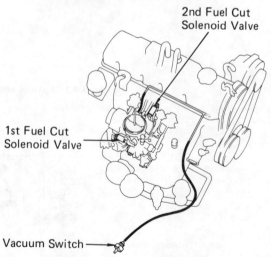

1st Fuel Cut
Solenoid Valve

Vacuum Switch

Fig. 6.50 Deceleration fuel cut system
(California) components and locations
(Sec 19)

18 Auxiliary acceleration pump system

General description

1   When the engine is cold, the main acceleration pump capacity is insufficient to provide good engine response. This is due to the very lean air-fuel mixture required by emissions controls regulations. The AAP system compensates for this by forcing a supplemental fuel squirt to the engine during the acceleration mode. This system uses the auxiliary acceleration pump along with the TVSV and accompanying vacuum hoses (Fig. 6.45).

System checking

2   To check the function of this system with a cold engine make sure that the coolant temperature is below 122°F (50°C).
3   Remove the air cleaner cover and start the engine.
4   Pinch the hose shut leading to the AAP diaphragm and turn the engine off.
5   Now release the hose and see that gasoline spurts from the auxiliary acceleration pump nozzle (Fig. 6.46).
6   Further check this system by allowing the engine to warm up to normal operating temperature and performing the same check. Fuel should *not* spurt out at this temperature.
7   To check the AAP diaphragm start the engine. Now disconnect the hose from the diaphragm and apply and release the vacuum directly to the AAP, while the engine is running, by repeatedly removing and applying the hose. The engine rpm should change as the vacuum is released.
8   The TVSV can be checked by following the procedure in Section 4.

19 Deceleration fuel cut system (49 State and Canada)

General description

1   The deceleration fuel cut system cuts off part of the fuel to the secondary slow circuit of the carburetor to prevent over-heating and after-burning in the exhaust system. This system uses a vacuum switch, the VCV as a hose connection, and the second fuel cut solenoid valve (Fig. 6.47).

System checking

2   Start the engine and disconnect the vacuum hose from the vacuum switch and plug the hose end (Fig. 6.48). You should feel a click as the second fuel cut solenoid valve closes when the vacuum hose is connected and disconnected alternatively.
3   To inspect the second fuel cut solenoid valve, remove it from the carburetor.
4   Connect two terminals to a 12-volt source as shown in Fig. 6.49. The solenoid valve should audibly click when the power source is connected.
5   Check the O-ring visibly for damage.
6   To inspect the vacuum switch, use an ohmmeter and check for continuity between the switch terminal and the switch body. Start the engine and note that there is no continuity between the switch terminal and body.

20 Deceleration fuel cut system (California)

General description

1   The deceleration fuel cut system cuts off part of the fuel to the slow circuit of the carburetor to prevent over-heating and after-firing in the exhaust system. This system uses a vacuum switch, a fuel cut solenoid valve, and a line and vacuum hose connecting the two (Fig. 6.50).

System checking

Caution: *Perform the following tests as quickly as possible to avoid over-heating of the catalyst.*
2   To check the operation of this system, a tachometer will be necessary. Start the engine and allow it to return to a smooth idle.
3   Pinch off the hose to the vacuum switch and gradually increase the engine speed to 2300 rpm. The engine should misfire slightly

between the 1900 to 2300 rpm range.
4   Release the pinched hose. Gradually increase the engine speed to 2300 rpm and the engine should operate normally through the previously mentioned cycle.
5   To check the engine idling portion, unplug the wiring connector to the solenoid valve. The engine should now idle roughly or die.
6   To check the operation of the second fuel cut system, disconnect the vacuum hose from the vacuum switch and plug the hose end. The second fuel cut solenoid valve should audibly click when the vacuum hose is connected and reconnected at idle.
7   To inspect the fuel cut solenoid valve, remove it from the engine. Connect two terminals to a 12-volt source as seen in Fig. 6.51. An audible click should emit from the solenoid valve when the battery is connected and disconnected. Visually check the O-ring for any sign of damage.
8   To inspect the vacuum switch, use an ohmmeter and check the continuity between the switch terminal and the body while the engine is running. There should be no continuity.

21 Heat control valve

General description

1   The heat control valve improves driveability of the car when cold by heating the intake manifold through the use of exhaust manifold gases. It also controls intake manifold temperature after the engine is warmed up. This system is incorporated within the junction between the intake and the exhaust manifold. It consists of a bi-metal spring and a heat control valve.

System checking

2   To inspect the system when the engine is cold, observe that the counter weight of the heat control valve is in the upper position as seen in Fig. 6.52. After the engine has warmed up, check that the counter weight of the heat control valve is in the lower position. Since there are no adjustments available to this valve, a malfunction could be caused by the mechanism seizing up or the spring may fail. If either of these cases occur, replace the entire valve. Occasionally a heat control valve that has frozen in one position, can be freed through the use of de-rusting type chemicals. This is generally only an emergency cure, and should not be used in lieu of replacing a defective control valve.

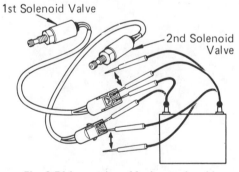

Fig. 6.51 Inspection of fuel cut solenoid valves (Sec 19)

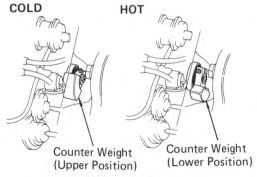

Fig. 6.52 Checking the position of the heat control valve (Sec 20)

22 Troubleshooting emissions systems

Before looking for any problems in the emissions control systems always check the vacuum lines for leaks or cracks. Any car over one year old is particularly susceptible to this problem. High under hood temperatures dictated by late model engine emission controls is a prime example, by causing vacuum hose deterioration. Also check vacuum hoses for proper routing. A problem may spring up after a tune-up, for example, due to two hoses being switched or misrouted. The best source of information for vacuum hose routing is the under-hood decal. There are also diagrams in the earlier Sections of this Chapter showing the hose routing for individual systems.

If vacuum hoses need to be replaced, always do so one at a time so as not to mix up the hoses or connections. Always use vacuum hoses of the correct size and quality equal to the original equipment.

Electrical connections on switches and valves in the emissions control systems are another source of potential problems. Always check that the wiring connections are complete and not corroded. If a component is found to be defective, always replace it with an original equipment unit. Most components are not re-buildable, therefore, a failure dictates new parts.

The following troubleshooting chart will include problems found within the emissions control systems only. Other causes may be involved in the same problems such as ignition, carburetion or fuel system. Be sure to determine that other areas are not causing your problem before turning to the emissions control systems.

Condition	Possible cause
Hard starting	HIC line leaks
	PCV leaks
	EGR leaks
	MC line leaks
Rough idle or stalls	HIC line leaks
	PCV line leaks
	EGR leaks
	MC line leaks
	HAC line leaks
	HAI system faulty
	EGR valve faulty
	Choke system faulty
Engine hesitates/poor acceleration	HIC line leaks
	PCV line leaks
	EGR line leaks
	HAC line leaks
	Choke system faulty
	HAI system always on (hot engine)
	EGR system always on (cold engine)
	AAP faulty (cold engine)
	HAC system faulty
Engine 'runs on' (continues to run) when ignition turned off	Fuel cut solenoid faulty
	Vacuum leaks in intake area
Backfiring (at deceleration only)	AI system faulty
	AS system faulty
	Deceleration fuel cut system always off
	MC system faulty
	TP system faulty
Backfiring (all the time)	Air induction system clogged
	Choke system faulty
	Choke valve open (cold engine)
	Vacuum leak in carburetor
Excessive oil consumption	PCV line clogged
Poor fuel economy	Air induction system clogged
	Choke system faulty
	Deceleration fuel cut system faulty
	EGR system always on

Chapter 7 Transaxle

Contents

Specifications

Manual transaxle
Fluid capacity .... 3.5 US qt (2.9 Imp qt 3.3 liters)

Gear thrust clearance (1st gear)
Standard .... 0.0059 to 0.0108 in (0.15 to 0.275 mm)
Limit .... 0.0118 in (0.30 mm)

Gear thrust clearance (2nd and 3rd gears)
Standard .... 0.0059 to 0.0098 in (0.15 to 0.25 mm)
Limit .... 0.0118 in (0.30 mm)

Gear thrust clearance (4th gear)
Standard .... 0.0008 to 0.0094 in (0.02 to 0.24 mm)
Limit .... 0.0118 in (0.30 mm)

Counter gear thrust clearance (5th gear)
Standard .... 0.0059 to 0.128 in (0.15 to 0.325 mm)
Limit .... 0.0157 in (0.40 mm)

Output shaft flange thickness limit .... 0.118 in (3.0 mm)

Synchronizer ring-to-gear clearance limit .... 0.024 in (0.6 mm)

Hub sleeve-to-shift fork clearance limit .... 0.039 in (1.0 mm)

1st gear oil clearance
Standard .... 0.0004 to 0.0024 in (0.009 to 0.062 mm)
Limit .... 0.0028 in (0.07 mm)

2nd and 3rd gear oil clearance
Standard .... 0.0024 to 0.0040 in (0.06 to 0.101 mm)
Limit .... 0.0043 in (0.11 mm)

Snap ring thicknesses
Input shaft .... 0.0945 to 0.0965 in (2.40 to 2.45 mm) or
0.0886 to 0.0906 in (2.25 to 2.30 mm)
Idler gear .... 0.0945 to 0.0965 in (2.40 to 2.45 mm) or
0.1004 to 0.1024 in (2.55 to 2.60 mm)
Counter gear .... 0.0709 to 0.0728 in (1.80 to 1.85 mm) or
0.0768 to 0.0787 in (1.95 to 2.00 mm)

Interlock pin hole measurement tool
No pins installed .... 4.72 in (120 mm)
3 interlock pins installed .... 3.15 in (80 mm)

Automatic transaxle
Fluid
Automatic transmission dry refill .... 4.8 US qt (4.0 Imp qt 4.5 liters)
Automatic transmission drain and refill .... 2.3 US qt (1.9 Imp qt 2.2 liters)

Neutral-to-Drive shift time lag .... Less than 1.2 seconds

Neutral-to-Reverse shift time lag .... Less than 1.5 seconds

Differential
Axle seal installation depth .... 0.331 to 0.354 in (8.4 to 9.0 mm)

Torque specifications

Manual transaxle	ft-lb	kg-m
Neutral safety switch bolt	3 to 5	(0.4 to 0.7)
Transaxle-to-engine retaining bolts	37 to 57	(5.0 to 8.0)
Engine rear mount-to-extension housing	55 to 79	(7.5 to 11.0)
Rear crossmember-to-body retaining bolts	26 to 36	(3.5 to 5.0)
Output shaft rear bearing retainer	8 to 11	(1.0 to 1.6)
Input shaft bearing retainer	15 to 21	(2.0 to 3.0)
Counter gear plate (4-speed only)	8 to 11	(1.0 to 1.6)
Locking ball plug	8 to 11	(1.0 to 1.6)
Extension housing-to-transmission case retaining bolts	15 to 21	(2.0 to 3.0)
Restrict pin plug	27 to 32	(3.7 to 4.5)
Transmission-to-transaxle retaining bolt	15 to 21	(2.0 to 3.0)

Automatic transaxle		
Transmission-to-transaxle retaining bolt	11 to 15	(1.5 to 2.2)
Extension housing retaining bolt	11 to 15	(1.5 to 2.2)
Flex plate-to-crankshaft retaining bolt	33 to 43	(4.5 to 6.0)
Torque converter-to-flex plate retaining bolt	11 to 15	(1.5 to 2.2)
Oil pan retaining bolt	4.4 to 6.5	(0.6 to 0.9)
Cooler pipe connecting nut	15 to 18	(2.0 to 2.5)
Differential cover retaining bolt	8 to 11	(1.0 to 1.6)

1 Transaxle – general information

The transaxle assembly consists of a transmission; automatic, 4-speed or 5-speed, and a differential. The power flow passes from the engine through a clutch (torque converter on automatic transmission equipped vehicles) into the transmission and back into the differential, which drives the front wheels through two independent axles. The differential case is situated directly below and to the side of the bell-housing (torque converter housing on automatic transmission) and both are part of the same integral casting. The transmission bolts to the rear of this housing and is situated the same as in a rear drive vehicle, although the power is transferred out of the lower front rather than the rear of the unit.

Major repair work on the differential requires many special tools and a high degree of expertise, and therefore should not be attempted by the home mechanic. Should major repairs be necessary, we recommend that they be performed by a dealer-authorized service department or a reputable repair shop.

The manual transmission may be removed separately from the differential assembly. The automatic transmission must be removed and installed as an integral unit with the differential and instructions for this procedure are listed under Section 7 *Transaxle (automatic) – removal and installation.*

2 Transaxle mount – description and inspection

1 The transaxle is bolted to the engine at the bellhousing (or torque converter housing on automatic transmission equipped vehicles) and supported in the middle of the vehicle by a crossmember and rubber mount.

2 Two engine stiffener plates tie the base of the engine block (on each side) to the differential housing, directly adjacent to the half-shaft outlets. These stiffener plates provide an extra measure of rigidity to the entire engine/drive train assembly.

3 The rear transaxle mount is designed in such a way that even with rubber deterioration, the transaxle will remain relatively secure in relationship to the vehicle. However, vibration and/or hard inaccurate shifting can result from a loose or worn mount.

4 Whenever the vehicle is raised for under-chassis work, or if problems are encountered with the transaxle system, check the transaxle mount for excessive play or deterioration. A small pry bar or large screwdriver is helpful in checking this mount. Always support the vehicle securely as it will be jostled in the following steps.

5 Push upward and pull downward on the transaxle case and observe the mount.

6 If the case can be pushed upward but cannot be pulled down, this is an indication that the rubber is worn and the mount is bottomed out.

7 If the rubber portion of the mount separates from the metal plate, this also means that the mount should be replaced with a new one.

8 Replace any mount in which the rubber exhibits hardening or cracking.

9 Check that all of the attaching nuts or bolts are tight.

10 Inspect the isolater mount for damage, wear and delamination from the metal collar.

11 Remove the shift lever housing rod adapter by removing the through bolt and nut (photo).

12 Withdraw the extension housing from the mount.

13 Installation is the reverse of removal. **Note**: *A silicon based lubricant* would be beneficial in the process of fitting the rubber mount over the housing.

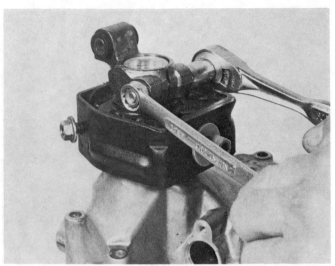

2.11 Removing the nut and bolt retaining the shift lever housing rod adapter

3 Transmission (manual) – removal and installation

Note: *The manual transmission can be removed separately from the vehicle with the bellhousing/differential case remaining. This is the easiest method to use when servicing the transmission assembly. If there is a problem with the differential or the clutch, the entire transaxle assembly will have to be removed as described in Section 4.*

1 Follow steps 1 through 10 in Section 4.
2 Remove the bolts attaching the transmission to the transaxle assembly.
3 **Caution**: *Support the transmission before performing the following steps.* Remove the bolts retaining the transmission rear crossmember.
4 Using a transmission jack or other similar device, gradually lower the rear of the transmission.
5 Pull the transmission straight back until it clears the coupler and the two guide pins.
6 Lower the transmission from the vehicle.
7 Installation is the reverse of removal. Install a new O-ring gasket on the input shaft hole of the bellhousing (photo). Be careful when installing the transmission to the adapter plate. Make sure the splines on the collar correctly meet the output shaft splines of the transmission and that the splines of the input shaft engage the clutch disc

3.7 Location of the bellhousing/input shaft O-ring

properly. Serious damage can occur to one or both units if this is not done.
8 Refill the transmission with the correct grade of lubricant and check the fluid level in the differential, as some loss may have occurred when the transmission was out of the vehicle.

4 Transaxle (manual) – removal and installation

1 Disconnect the air intake snorkel leading to the fresh air intake of the air cleaner. Drain the cooling system. Disconnect the upper radiator hose (at the engine).
2 Disconnect the negative battery cable from the battery.
3 Remove the distributor cap and secure it out of the way.
4 Raise the vehicle and support it securely.
5 Drain the oil from the transaxle assembly at all three drain points.
6 Remove the catalytic converter. Remove the exhaust header pipe and shields.
7 Disconnect the number one shift rod.
8 Remove the shift lever housing rod (photo).
9 Remove the ground strap.
10 Remove the speedometer cable from the transmission housing (photo).

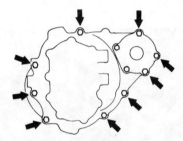

Fig. 7.1 Manual transmission-to-bellhousing assembly retaining bolt locations (Sec 3)

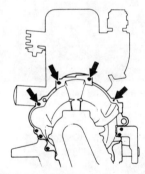

Fig. 7.2 Upper transaxle retaining bolt locations (Sec 4)

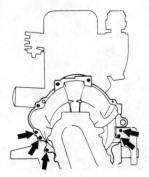

Fig. 7.3 Lower transaxle retaining bolt locations (Sec 4)

11 Disconnect the clutch cable (Chapter 8).
12 Disconnect the back-up light switch wire at the connector (photo).
13 Remove the left-hand stiffener plate, which is retained by two bolts at the bottom of the engine block and one bolt on the differential housing (photo).
14 Remove the right-hand stiffener plate, which is retained by two bolts at the bottom of the engine block and two bolts at the differential housing (photo). Notice the short bolts attach to the block while the longer bolt(s) belong in the differential housing.
15 Remove the left and right drive axles (Chapter 8).
16 Remove the four upper transaxle retaining bolts.
17 **Caution**: *Support the transaxle assembly before performing the following steps.* Remove the bolts retaining the transmission rear crossmember (photo).
18 Using a transmission jack or other similar device, gradually lower the rear of the transmission.
19 Remove the five lower transaxle retaining bolts (Fig. 7.3).
20 Slowly and carefully pull the transaxle assembly straight back until the input shaft clears the clutch splines.
21 Lower the transaxle assembly out of the vehicle.
22 Installation is the reverse of removal.
23 Before installing the transmission, make sure it is in a gear (4th will work fine) so that the input shaft may be rotated by turning an axle-shaft if necessary.

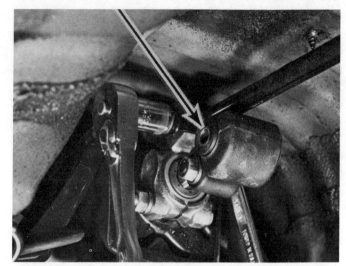

4.8 Removing the shift lever housing rod by using two wrenches. The number one shift rod has already been removed (arrow)

4.10 Removing the speedometer cable from the transmission

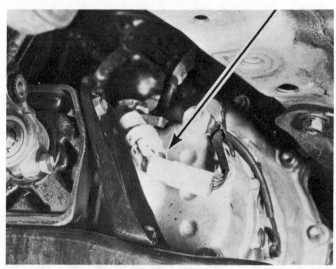

4.12 Disconnect the back-up light switch at the connector (arrow)

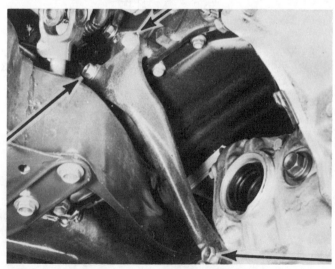

4.13 Left-hand stiffener plate and retaining bolts (arrows)

4.14 Right-hand stiffener plate and retaining bolts (arrows)

5 Transmission (manual) – overhaul

Disassembly

1 Clean the transmission as thoroughly as possible and prepare it for the following steps which will be performed on the bench.

2 Remove the two bolts and three nuts securing the transmission crossmember to the rear yoke. Remove the crossmember.

3 Remove the back-up light switch (photo).

4 Remove the reverse shift arm pivot (photo).

5 Remove the speedometer drive gear retainer assembly (photo).

6 Remove the two restrict bolts (photo).

7 Remove the remainder of the restrict pin assembly.

8 Remove the extension housing. Note the position of the ground strap and the wiring harness retainers.

9 Remove the speedometer gear retainer (photo), gear, and ball.

10 Remove the shift shaft lock-out levers. Start with the bottom one by driving out the roll pin (photo) and proceed upward to the middle and upper lock-out levers.

11 Remove the three shift shaft locking assemblies consisting of caps, springs and balls.

12 Remove the input shaft cover and gasket (photo).

13 Remove the input shaft.

14 Remove the rear countershaft bearing retainer ring.

15 Pull the case housing straight up and off the transmission assembly.

16 Remove the spring clip from the reverse shift arm (photo).

17 To remove the reverse shift fork, first put the transmission in 1st gear by moving the upper shift shaft to the rear position in the transmission (first gear position). Push the reverse gear towards the rear of the transmission and disengage the shift fork from the shift lever. The shift fork can now be removed. The shift fork fits only in one direction.

18 Drive the roll pin out of the 5th gear shift fork (photo).

Note: *The following step is for 5-speed transmissions only.*

19 Slide the lower or number three shift shaft to the rear and out of the transmission assembly (photo). Make sure that the inner locking pin is pulled out after removing the third shift shaft. It fits into a chamber directly above the shift shaft passage in the intermediate housing.

20 Drive the pin out of the reverse shift arm pivot. Remove the pivot from the number three shift shaft.

21 Withdraw the 5th gear shift fork from the synchronizer hub assembly.

Note: *The following step is for 5-speed transmissions only.*

22 Drive the roll pin out of the intermediate shift fork from the bottom (photo).

23 Withdraw the intermediate shift shaft (photo), being careful to retrieve the inner locking pin from the chamber in the intermediate housing.

24 The shift fork for 3rd and 4th gear can now be withdrawn from the synchronizer hub.

25 Drive the roll pin from the 1st and 2nd gear shift fork (photo).

26 Pull the first shift rod to the rear of the transmission while separating the 1st/2nd shift fork and the reverse shift fork. Remove the 1st/2nd shift fork and the reverse shift fork.

27 Remove the 5th gear retainer snap ring (photo).

Note: *The following four steps are for 5-speed transmissions only.*

28 Measure the 5th gear thrust clearance (see Specifications at the beginning of the Chapter) (photo).

29 Using a suitable puller, remove the 5th gear assembly from the shaft (photo). Notice the spacer located behind the 5th gear assembly.

30 Remove the locator ball from the shaft after removing the 5th gear assembly (photo).

31 Remove the reverse gear shaft bearing retainer ring (photo).

32 Remove the cluster shaft bearing retainer which is secured by four bolts (photo).

33 Remove the cluster shaft bearing retainer ring (photo).

34 Drive the output or cluster shaft bearing and assembly half-way out of its retainer.

35 Remove the idler gear and reverse gear assembly simultaneously while supporting the end of the cluster gear assembly (photo).

36 Drive the output or cluster gear assembly the rest of the way out of the intermediate plate.

37 Measure the thrust clearance of the 1st gear using a dial indicator (photo).

38 Remove the connecting sleeve using a suitable puller (photo).

39 Remove the snap ring (photo).

40 Using a suitable puller, remove 5th gear (photo).

41 Remove the bearing retainer snap-ring.

42 Remove the front cluster shaft bearing using a suitable puller.

43 Remove the spacer, using the puller.

44 Remove the thrust bearing.

45 Remove the snap-ring retaining 4th gear.

46 Remove the 4th gear. Note that the bearing halves will be loose at this point and should be retained if not in a vertical position (photos).

47 Remove the snap-ring.

48 Remove the spacer.

49 Remove the 4th gear synchronizer hub, synchronizer ring, alignment keys and springs.

50 Remove the snap-ring.

51 Remove the thrust bearing.

52 Remove the number two clutch hub, synchronizer ring and 3rd gear with a puller.

53 **Note:** At this point, move to the other end of the shaft. Remove the snap-ring (photo).

54 Remove the 1st gear assembly, which includes the bearing and spacer.

55 Remove the anti-rotation ball (photo).

56 Remove the hub, the synchronizer ring, the alignment keys and the springs.

57 Remove 2nd gear with a suitable puller.

Inspection

Idler gear and bearing – inspection and replacement

58 Inspect the idler gear and bearing for wear or damage. If the bearing is worn or damaged, replace it as described in the following steps.

59 Remove the retaining snap-ring.

60 Remove the idler gear bearing with 2 suitable pullers (photo).

61 Press the new bearing onto the shaft using a hydraulic press.

Note: *The groove in the bearing goes to the opposite side of the big gear on the shaft.*

62 Install a snap-ring that will provide the minimum of axial play on the shaft.

Reverse idler gear and shaft – inspection and replacement

63 Inspect the shaft, gear and inner gear bushing for wear and/or damage.

64 If either the gear or the shaft are excessively worn or damaged, replace them with new ones.

65 The gear is a slip fit over the shaft. Notice that the shift fork groove in the gear assembly faces the notch in the shaft.

Counter gear assembly – inspection and bearing replacement

66 Check the bearing, gears, bearing surfaces and shaft for wear or damage.

67 Replace the bearing as described below if it is excessively worn or damaged.

68 Remove the snap-ring.

69 Remove the bearing with a suitable puller (photo).

70 Press the bearing onto the shaft with a suitable hydraulic press.

71 Install a snap-ring that will provide the minimum clearance between the bearing and the snap-ring.

72 Press the counter gear center bearing out of the intermediate plate using a suitable drive tool.

73 Installation is the reverse of removal.

Input shaft assembly – inspection and replacement

74 Inspect the input shaft assembly for wear or damage.

75 Replace the bearing if it is worn or damaged as described in the following steps.

76 Remove the outer snap-ring (photo).

77 Remove the snap-ring from the outer bearing race.

78 Remove the input shaft bearing using a suitable puller (photo).

79 Inspect the input shaft and gear for wear or damage. Replace the input shaft if the gear or splines are worn or damaged.

80 Install the bearing onto the shaft with a hydraulic press. Note that the groove on the bearing goes toward the transmission end of the input shaft.

4.17 Removing the rear crossmember retaining bolts (arrows)

5.3 Removing the back-up light switch

5.4 Removing the reverse shift arm pivot

5.5 Removing the speedometer drive gear retainer assembly

5.6 Removing the two restrict bolts

5.9 Removing the speedometer gear retainer

5.10 Removing the shift shaft lock-out levers

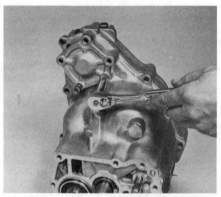

5.12 Removing the input shaft cover

5.16 Removing the spring clip from the reverse shift arm

5.18 Driving the roll pin out of the 5th gear shift fork

5.19 Sliding the number three shift shaft out of the transmission assembly

5.22 Driving the roll pin out of the intermediate shift fork

5.23 Withdrawing the intermediate shift shaft

5.25 Driving the roll pin from the 1st and 2nd gear shift fork

5.27 Removing the 5th gear retainer snap-ring

5.28 Measuring the 5th gear thrust clearance with a feeler gauge

5.29 Removing the 5th gear assembly from the shaft

5.30 Locator ball (arrow) for the 5th gear assembly

5.31 Remove the reverse gear shaft retaining ring

5.32 Removing the cluster shaft bearing retainer

5.33 Removing the cluster shaft bearing retainer ring

5.35 Removing the idler gear and reverse gear assemblies simultaneously

5.37 Measuring the 1st gear thrust clearance with a dial indicator

5.38 Using a puller to remove the connecting sleeve

5.39 Removing the 5th gear snap-ring

5.40 Using a puller to remove 5th gear

5.46a Removing 4th gear

5.46b 4th gear bearing halves (arrows)

5.53 Removing the snap-ring retaining 1st gear

5.55 Removing the 1st gear anti-rotation ball

5.60 Removing the idler gear bearing with a puller

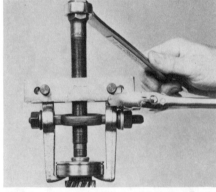

5.69 Removing the counter gear bearing with a puller

5.76 Removing the input shaft bearing retaining snap-ring

5.78 Removing the input shaft bearing with a puller

5.88 Driving the oil seal from the intermediate plate

5.89 Installing the new oil seal using a socket and extension

5.91 Removing the input shaft bearing lock clip

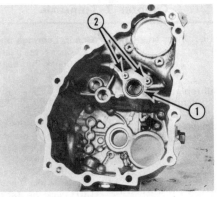

5.96 Inspect the idler gear rear bearing (1) and remove the oil receiver screws (2)

5.99 Pushing the bearing back into the case with a socket and extension

5.101 Remove the oil receiver bolts (arrows)

5.114 Removing the nut and washer from the taper pin on the shift rod adapter

5.115 Tapping the taper pin out with a soft-faced hammer

5.117 Removing the shift rod seal with pliers

5.118 Installing the shift rod seal with a socket and extension

5.123 Checking 2nd gear thrust clearance with a feeler gauge

5.127 Measuring synchronizer ring clearance with a feeler gauge

5.129 Checking the shift fork-to-clutch hub assembly groove clearance

5.130 Checking the oil clearance of 1st gear with a dial indicator

81 Install the outer race snap-ring. Select a correct inner snap-ring which will provide the minimum amount of axial play.
82 Install the inner snap-ring.

Intermediate plate – component inspection and replacement
83 Inspect the plate and bearings for wear and/or damage.
84 Check the counter gear bearing for wear.
85 Check the input shaft bearing for wear or damage.
86 Check the oil seals for evidence of damage and/or wear. Be particularly careful to note any signs of leakage.

Oil seal – replacement
87 Clamp and support the intermediate plate between two wooden blocks in a vise.
88 Using a suitable punch, drive the oil seal from the plate (photo).
89 Install the seal using a suitable drive tool. Note that the edge of the seal fits flush with the intermediate plate (photo). Coat the inner face of the seal with a general purpose lubricant.

Input shaft bearing – replacement
90 Remove the seal as described above.
91 Remove the bearing lock clip (photo).
92 Using a suitable drive tool, push the bearing out of the intermediate plate in the direction opposite the input shaft.
93 To install the bearing, press it into the intermediate plate with the grooved end of the bearing opposite the input shaft side (grooved end up).
94 Install the bearing retainer plate.

Transmission case – component inspection and replacement
95 Inspect the case visually for wear or damage.
96 Inspect the idler gear rear bearing (photo).

Replacement of idler gear bearing
97 Remove the oil receiver which is held in place by two screws.
98 Using an internal puller, remove the idler gear rear bearing.
99 Using a suitable drive tool, push the bearing back into the case (photo). Be certain the bearing face is flush with the surface of the case.
100 Install the oil receiver using two bolts.

Output shaft rear bearing – replacement
101 Remove the oil receiver which is held in place by two bolts (photo).
102 Remove the output shaft rear bearing.
103 Remove the outer snap-ring.
104 Install the outer snap-ring.
105 Install the bearing into the case using a suitable drive tool.
106 Install the oil retainer using the two bolts.

Extension housing – inspection and repair
107 Inspect the housing for wear or damage.
108 Check the radial and axial motion of the shift rod.
109 Check the shift lever for wear or damage. Pay particular attention to the wear surfaces.
110 Check the oil seal for wear, evidence of damage or leakage.
111 Inspect the restrict pins and springs for wear or damage. Note there are two different springs used.
112 Check the speedometer drive gear assembly for damage and/or wear.
113 Inspect the shift rod selector lugs for damage and/or wear.

Shift rod seal – replacement
114 Remove the nut and washer from the taper pin on the shift rod adapter (photo).
115 Tap the taper pin out with a soft-faced hammer (photo). Note that the taper pin has a flat on one side.
116 Remove the shifter rod.
117 Remove the seal with a suitable tool (photo).
118 Press the new seal into position with a suitable tool (photo).
119 Lubricate and install the shaft.
120 Install the shift shaft adapter.
121 Install the taper pin and washer mount combination. Note that the flat side of the taper pin fits the accompanying groove.

Gears, bearings and synchronizer assemblies – inspection
122 Check 1st gear thrust clearance with a dial indicator.
123 Check 2nd gear thrust clearance with a feeler gauge (photo).
124 Check 3rd gear thrust clearance with a feeler gauge as in the previous step.
125 Inspect 4th gear and bearing for damage or wear.
126 Inspect 5th gear for damage or wear.
127 Measure the synchronizer ring clearance (photo). All of the synchronizers are measured the same way.
128 Inspect the number one and two clutch hub assemblies for wear and/or damage.
129 Check the clearance between the groove in the hub sleeve and the shift forks (photo).
130 Check the 1st gear oil clearance (photo).
131 Check the fit of the synchronizer to the gear and make sure that it locks up firmly when pressure is applied.
132 Inspect the components of the synchronizer hub assembly for wear and/or damage.

Shift shafts and forks – inspection
133 Inspect the shaft for damage and/or wear.
134 Inspect the forks for wear and/or damage (photo). Be especially watchful for cracks or wear at the contact points.
135 Inspect the locking balls and springs for damage or wear.
136 Replace any components that are worn or damaged with new ones.

Reassembly
137 Build-up the synchronizer assembly following the steps below.
138 Install the tension rings into the hub.
139 Position the locking keys into their slot in the hub.
140 Install the slider ring onto the hub assembly.
141 Install the shifting key retainer into its recessed portion of the hub.
142 Install the snap ring into the hub. **Note:** *Make sure that the hub assembly is installed in the correct direction.*
143 Coat the center of the cluster shaft with a general purpose lithium-based grease.
144 Place the 2nd gear onto the shaft loosely. Place the number one clutch hub assembly onto the shaft loosely.
145 Loosely install an approved pusher onto the shaft over the number one clutch hub assembly.
146 Place the approved pusher onto the bed of the hydraulic press. Make sure that the shifting keys are lined up with the key slots in the synchronizer ring. Press the number one clutch hub into position.
147 Place the locking ball onto its recess on the shaft.
148 Lubricate the 1st gear bearing with the multi-purpose lithium-based grease. Assemble the 1st gear, 1st gear bearing and 1st gear bushing.
149 Place the 1st gear assembly onto the shaft, making sure that the locking ball aligns with the groove on the 1st gear bushing.
150 Ensure that the shifting keys are lined up with the T slots on the synchronizer ring. Select a snap-ring that will allow a minimum thrust clearance of the 1st gear assembly.
151 Install the snap-ring onto the shaft.
152 Check the thrust clearances of the 1st and 2nd gears to see if they meet the specification.
153 Loosely install 3rd gear onto the output end of the shaft.
154 Loosely install the number two clutch hub assembly onto the output end of the shaft.
155 Place the approved pusher onto the output end of the shaft.
156 Place the pusher onto the bed of the hydraulic press. Press the number two clutch hub assembly into position.
157 Lubricate the widest thrust bearing with the multi-purpose lithium-based grease. Install this bearing onto the shaft.
158 Lubricate the 4th gear bearing with multi-purpose lithium-based grease. Place the 4th gear bearing onto the shaft.
159 Place the 4th gear assembly onto the shaft. Ensure that the shifting keys are aligned with the key slots in the synchronizer rings.
160 Place the spacer onto the shaft.
161 Install the 4th gear snap-ring.
162 Lubricate the remaining thrust bearing with multi-purpose lithium-based grease. Place the thrust bearing on the bearing surface of the remaining spacer.
163 Using an approved pusher, press the remaining spacer onto the shaft.
164 Loosely install the output front bearing onto the shaft. Note that

the snap-ring groove goes toward the output end of the shaft.

165 Using an approved pusher, press the output bearing into position on the shaft.

166 Select a snap-ring that will reduce the clearance between the ring and the bearing inner race to a minimum, then install the snap-ring.

167 Check the thrust clearance of 3rd and 4th gears.

168 Loosely install 5th gear onto the shaft.

Note: *The following four steps are for 5-speed transmissions only.*

169 With an approved pusher, press 5th gear onto the shaft.

170 Select a snap-ring that will reduce the clearance between the gear and the ring to a minimum, then install the snap-ring.

171 Using an approved pusher, press the coupler onto the shaft. Note that the recess fits to the gear side of the shaft.

172 Intermesh the countershaft gears with the output shaft cluster gears.

173 Install both gear assemblies into their respective bearings. Note that the output shaft assembly bearing is installed halfway into the intermediate plate.

174 Align the notch in the reverse idler gear shaft with the idler gear (photo).

175 Install the reverse idler gear shaft and the idler gear bearing into the intermediate plate.

176 With a soft-faced hammer, sequentially push each shaft into its respective race a little at a time until all are in their fully installed positions.

177 Install the two retaining snap-rings for the idler gear bearing and the output shaft. Make sure that the snap-rings are seated snugly against the intermediate plate.

178 Install the output shaft bearing retainer. **Note:** *The retainer also fits into a slot on the reverse idler gear shaft.*

179 Tighten the four retainer bolts to the specified torque.

180 If equipped with a counter gear plate, align the plate protrusion with the shaft cut-out. Tighten the counter gear plate bolt to the specified torque. **Note:** *Ensure that the gears are properly meshed before tightening.*

181 Install the locking ball into the hole on the shaft.

182 Install the spacer, aligning the notch with the locking ball.

183 Lubricate the 5th gear bearing (use lithium-base all-purpose grease).

Note: *The following four steps are for 5-speed transmissions only.*

184 Install the 5th gear assembly onto the shaft.

185 Using a suitable push tool, press the number three clutch hub assembly into position.

186 Select a snap-ring which allows the clearance between the ring and the number three clutch hub to be held to a minimum, then install the snap-ring. Measure the 5th gear thrust clearance.

187 Install the reverse shift fork, 1st/2nd gear shift fork and shift shaft.

188 Insert the number three shift shaft, taking care to align the hole at the end with the bore in the intermediate case. Take a piece of wire and mark it at 4.72 in (120 mm) and 3.15 in (80 mm) (photo). Use the

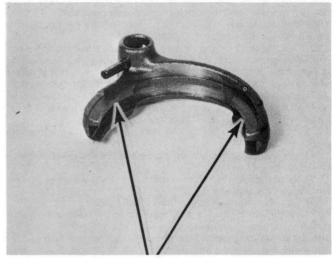

5.134 Check the shift forks for excessive wear at the contact points of the clutch sleeve (arrows)

5.174 Aligning the notch on the reverse idler gear shaft with the idler gear

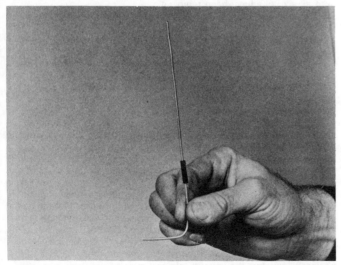

5.188 Piece of wire marked to use as an alignment tool and interlock pin gauge

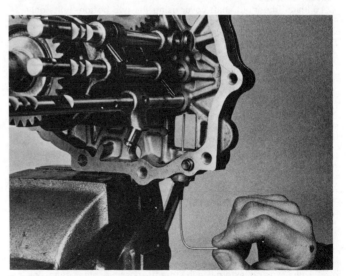

5.190 Using the wire to install the interlocking pins

tool to line up the hole in the number three shaft, the hole in the number two shaft and the notch on the number one shaft.
189 Using the above-mentioned tool, insert a large pin through the slotted hole into the number one shift shaft.
190 Insert the small locking pin through the hole into the number two shift shaft (photo). **Note:** *White lithium-based grease would be helpful to hold these pins in place.* It may be necessary to adjust slightly the alignment of the three shift shafts in order to fit the interlocking pins.
191 Install the last large interlock pin. The pins will be in their proper position if the tool remains at the shorter of the two marks.
192 Install the number three shift fork.
193 Put gasket sealant on the plug and install it in the intermediate plate.
194 Place all three shift shafts into the neutral position (all of the tangs on the shaft will line up).
195 Line up the pin holes with the shift fork holes and drive each taper pin through the shift shafts.
196 Install the reverse shift lever and locking clip.
197 Now drive in the final locating taper pin on the number three shift rod.
198 Secure a new gasket to the inside of the intermediate plate.
199 Install the transmission case.
200 Push the output shaft to the rear and install the snap-ring.
201 Insert the locking balls and springs into the bores.
202 Install the reverse arm lower pivot using a new sealing gasket. **Note:** *On the Z-50 transmission, when shifting the 5th gear reverse slider into position, be careful not to overrun the reverse position as the 5th gear synchronizing assembly will come apart.*
203 Install the number one shift shaft lockout lever (note its position).
204 Press in the tapered pin.
205 Follow the above procedure for the number two shift shaft lockout lever.
206 Repeat the above procedure for the number three shift shaft lockout lever.
207 Install the speedometer drive gear anti-rotation ball.
208 Install the speedometer drive gear making sure that the slot lines up with the lock ball. Install the speedometer drive gear snap ring.
209 Install a new gasket onto the transmission case. Be sure to use gasket sealant in this process.
210 Install the shift cover, making sure that the shifter arm engages the number one and two shift shaft lockout levers.
211 Secure the shifter housing with the proper bolts making sure that the ground cable and wiring loom clamps are located properly. Tighten the bolts to the proper torque.
212 Install the rear extension housing. Install the restrictor pin and spring assemblies making sure that the tighter coiled of the two springs goes in the left side of the transmission shift housing.
213 Tighten the restrictors to the specified torque.
214 Install the input shaft into the intermediate housing.
215 Install a new gasket on the input shaft cover using sealant on both gasket surfaces.
216 Install the input shaft cover using the two bottom bolts only.
217 Check the gear selector action by moving the shift lever while turning the input shaft. **Note:** *Make sure the input shaft is turning when changing gears.*
218 Install a new O-ring on the speedometer drive adapter. Lubricate this assembly with lithium-based grease.
219 Install the speedometer adapter into the transmission.
220 Install the speedometer retainer into its slot and install the retainer bolt. Tighten the retainer bolt to the specified torque.
221 Install a new sealing ring on the back-up switch. Install the back-up switch. Tighten the switch to the specified torque.
222 Install the rear mount. Tighten the bolts to the specified torque.
223 Fill the transmission with the correct type and amount of lubricant.

6 Transmission (automatic) – general description

The Tercel uses a 3-speed fully automatic transmission with a torque-multiplying converter linking it to the engine.
The transmission must be removed from the vehicle with the differential/torque converter housing.
There are no external adjustments possible other than linkage changes.
If any performance problems are noted, check the fluid for proper level and condition as described in Chapter 1.
Troubleshooting this automatic transmission requires pressure gauges and an experienced technician. If you are experiencing problems, and the fluid condition is acceptable, your best course of action is to have the problem diagnosed by a dealership or quality transmission shop familiar with this vehicle. The special tools required, along with the complexity of the unit make it too difficult for the average home mechanic to overhaul this transmission. You can remove it and re-install it after repairs are made to reduce some of the costs.

7 Transaxle (automatic) – removal and installation

Note: *Due to the complexity of the automatic transaxle and the special equipment needed to service it, an automatic transaxle overhaul is not practical for the home mechanic to perform. Considerable money can be saved however, by removing and installing the transaxle yourself. Read through this Section to become familiar with the procedure and the tools needed for the job. The car must be raised high enough so the transaxle can be lowered from the vehicle and slid out from underneath.*
1 Prior to removal of the transaxle, have the vehicle test driven and diagnosed by a qualified transmission specialist, so that he may determine the nature and cause of the problem.
2 Disconnect the negative battery cable from the battery.
3 Drain the coolant from the radiator and engine at the coolant drain points.
4 Disconnect the upper radiator hose from the engine side.
5 Disconnect the wiring leading to the neutral start switch. The two plastic connectors are located near the starter.
6 Remove the air cleaner assembly.
7 Remove the throttle link assembly at the transmission.
8 Remove the cooler pipe clamp located near the transmission throttle link connection.
9 Disconnect the cooler inlet pipe.
10 Remove the four upper transaxle-to-engine block retaining bolts.
11 Remove both driveshafts as described in Chapter 8.
12 Remove the front engine down-pipe assembly as described in Chapter 4.
13 Remove the right-hand stiffener plate.
14 Disconnect the transmission shift linkage at the control lever junction located near the center of the vehicle.
15 Disconnect the speedometer cable at the transmission.
16 Remove the front engine undercover.
17 Remove the three bolts retaining the front torque converter access cover plate.
18 Turn the engine crankshaft until one of the six torque converter retaining bolts is exposed.
19 Remove this retaining bolt.
20 Rotate the crankshaft until the next bolt is exposed and continue until all six bolts have been removed.
21 Remove the four lower torque converter cover-to-engine block retaining bolts.
22 Disconnect and remove the rear ground cable.
23 Support the transmission with a transmission jack.
24 With the jack supporting the transmission, pull the transaxle assembly back away from the engine until the torque converter has separated itself completely from the drive plate and rear crankshaft hub.
25 Lower the transaxle assembly to the ground.
26 Upon installation apply molybdenum disulphide grease to the center hub of the torque converter and to the pilot hole in the torque converter drive plate.
27 Install a guide pin onto one of the torque converter mounting holes. The guide pin can be made by using a bolt exactly like one of the retaining bolts with the head removed.
28 Raise the transmission assembly to its approximate even position with the back of the engine and slowly move it forward. Pilot the guide pin to enter one of the six holes in the torque converter flex plate and align the torque converter and transmission. Push the transaxle assembly straight forward until it meets the engine block.
29 After the torque converter housing is mated to the rear face of the engine block, start the lower retaining bolts.
30 Temporarily install two of the six torque converter retaining bolts directly across from each other and remove the guide pin.

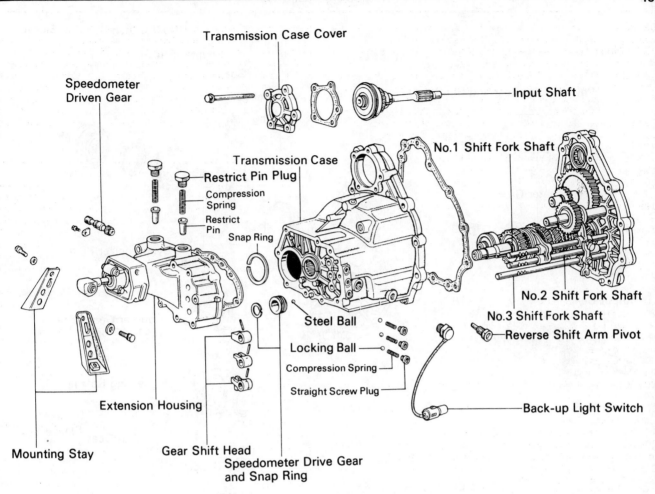

Transmission Case Cover

Speedometer Driven Gear

Input Shaft

Transmission Case

No.1 Shift Fork Shaft

Restrict Pin Plug

Compression Spring

Restrict Pin

Snap Ring

No.2 Shift Fork Shaft

No.3 Shift Fork Shaft

Reverse Shift Arm Pivot

Steel Ball

Locking Ball

Compression Spring

Straight Screw Plug

Back-up Light Switch

Extension Housing

Mounting Stay

Gear Shift Head

Speedometer Drive Gear and Snap Ring

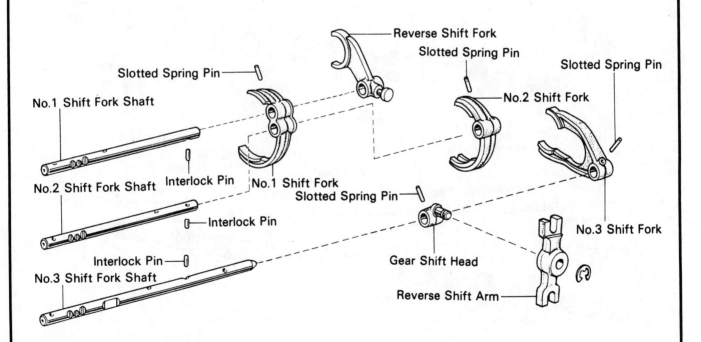

Reverse Shift Fork

Slotted Spring Pin

Slotted Spring Pin

Slotted Spring Pin

No.1 Shift Fork Shaft

No.2 Shift Fork

No.2 Shift Fork Shaft

Interlock Pin

No.1 Shift Fork

Slotted Spring Pin

Interlock Pin

No.3 Shift Fork

Interlock Pin

Gear Shift Head

No.3 Shift Fork Shaft

Reverse Shift Arm

Fig. 7.4 Manual transmission case, shifter mechanisms and major component exploded view (Sec 5)

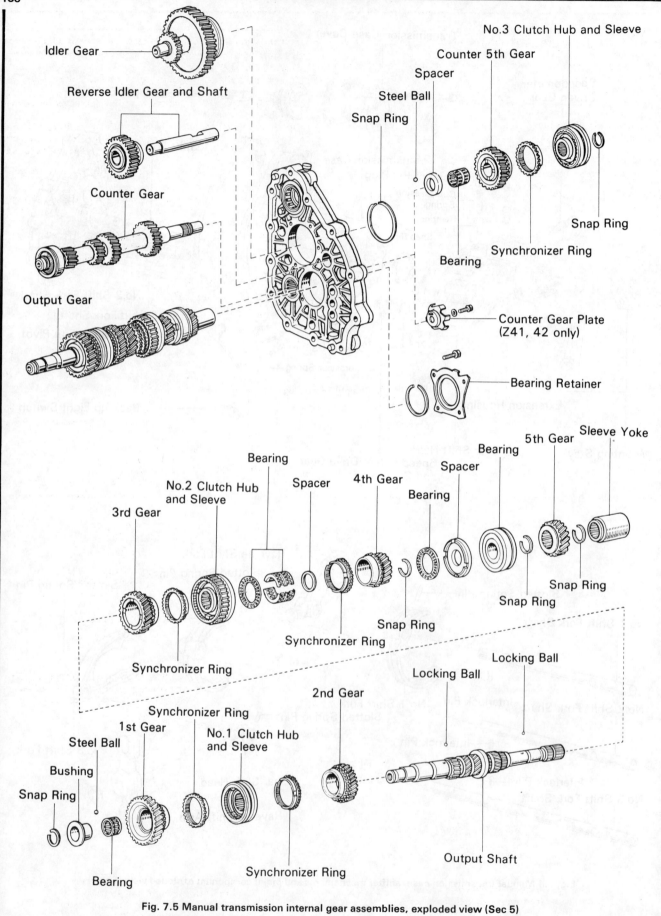

Idler Gear

Reverse Idler Gear and Shaft

Counter Gear

Output Gear

No.3 Clutch Hub and Sleeve

Counter 5th Gear

Spacer

Steel Ball

Snap Ring

Snap Ring

Bearing

Synchronizer Ring

Counter Gear Plate
(Z41, 42 only)

Bearing Retainer

Bearing

Spacer

Bearing

5th Gear

Sleeve Yoke

4th Gear

No.2 Clutch Hub
and Sleeve

3rd Gear

Bearing

Spacer

Snap Ring

Snap Ring

Snap Ring

Synchronizer Ring

Synchronizer Ring

Synchronizer Ring

Locking Ball

Locking Ball

2nd Gear

1st Gear

Synchronizer Ring

No.1 Clutch Hub
and Sleeve

Steel Ball

Bushing

Snap Ring

Bearing

Synchronizer Ring

Output Shaft

Fig. 7.5 Manual transmission internal gear assemblies, exploded view (Sec 5)

31 Tighten the four transaxle retaining bolts.
32 Raise the rear of the transaxle assembly and install the rear support member.
33 Install the remaining four torque converter-to-flex plate retaining bolts by turning the crankshaft as in disassembly Step 20.
34 Tighten the bolts evenly to their final torque.
35 Install the torque converter access cover.
36 Install the ground cable.
37 Connect the cooler outlet pipe.
38 Install the engine undercover.
39 Install the engine stiffener plates.
40 Install the exhaust pipe as described in Chapter 4.
41 Connect the speedometer cable to the transmission.
42 Connect the rear ground cable to the rear of the transmission.
43 Connect the shift linkage into its slot on the shift lever. Align the shift lever and the control lever at the Neutral position and tighten the bolt.
44 Install both driveshafts.
45 Install the four upper transaxle-to-engine block retaining bolts and tighten them to the specified torque.
46 Connect the cooler inlet pipe using two flare nut wrenches.
47 Install the cooler pipe clamp to the transmission housing.
48 Connect the throttle link.
49 Connect the wiring for the Neutral start and back-up light switches.
50 Connect the upper radiator hose.
51 Fill the radiator with coolant.
52 Install the air cleaner assembly.
53 Connect the negative battery cable.
54 Fill the transmission with transmission fluid as described in Chapter 1.
55 Fill the differential with the correct lubricant as described in Chapter 1.
56 Have the front end alignment checked at an authorized service garage equipped to do so.
57 Adjust the linkages (Sec 8).
58 Perform an on-road performance check and stop to check for transmission and/or differential oil leakage after the first few miles of test.

8 Transmission (automatic) – linkage and switch adjustments

Kick-down adjustment

1 To adjust the throttle link (kick-down cable), first remove the air cleaner.
2 Check the throttle lever and the throttle link bracket for warpage or deflection.
3 Open the carburetor throttle lever completely and make sure the carburetor butterflies are fully open. If the carburetor won't open all the way, adjust the accelerator cable to allow the butterflies to reach their maximum travel.
4 Have a helper hold the throttle open with the pedal.
5 Raise the vehicle and support it securely on jackstands.
6 Check the throttle lever indicator (under the vehicle) for alignment with the mark on the transmission case. If the mark doesn't line up, loosen the turnbuckle locknut and adjust the linkage length by turning the turnbuckle. Be sure to tighten the locknut after the adjustment is made.
7 Reinstall the air cleaner.

Shift linkage adjustment

8 The shift linkage is adjusted by placing the shift lever in the Neutral position.
9 Loosen the nut on the connecting rod (under the vehicle) next to tthe transmission housing until the transmission linkage will move independent of the shift lever linkage.
10 Push the transmission control lever all the way forward, then move it back three notches. This will place the transmission in Neutral. Be sure to count carefully and make sure the transmission is shifted exactly on the detent. Double check that the shift lever is still in the Neutral position.
11 Have a helper push the shift lever towards the Reverse position lightly. Don't override the detent but push the lever enough to take the play out of the linkage.
12 Tighten the connecting rod nut.

Neutral start switch adjustment

13 If the engine won't start in Neutral or Park, of if it will start in any

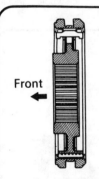

Fig. 7.6 Synchronizer assembly details and installation direction (Sec 5)

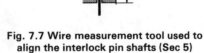

Fig. 7.7 Wire measurement tool used to align the interlock pin shafts (Sec 5)

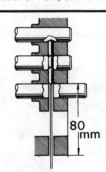

Fig. 7.8 Wire measurement tool used to determine proper installation of the interlocking pins (Sec 5)

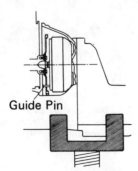

Fig. 7.9 Guide pin started into torque converter for transmission installation (Sec 7)

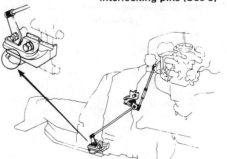

Fig. 7.10 Aligning the throttle lever indicator with the mark on the transmission case while the accelerator is held fully open (Sec 8)

of the other positions, an adjustment is required. Also, if the back-up lights work in either the wrong shift position or if they don't work and the wiring and bulbs are all right, the switch needs to be checked.

14 Loosen the neutral safety switch bolt.

15 Set the shift lever in the Neutral position.

16 Align the shaft groove with the neutral base line on the transmission case.

17 Hold the switch in this position and tighten the bolt.

18 If the switch still does not operate properly, disconnect the two wiring connectors and check for continuity with an ohmmeter as follows (refer to Fig. 7.12).

19 With the shift lever in the Park or Neutral position, there should be continuity between terminals B and N.

20 In the Reverse shifter position, there should be continuity between terminals RB and RL.

21 If the switch fails either one of these tests, replace it with a new one.

22 To remove the neutral safety switch, remove the bolt and nut retaining it to the transmission case and shaft.

23 Slide the switch off the shaft.

24 Slide the new switch onto the shaft with the grommet facing the groove toward the shift body.

25 Install the washer and nut onto the shaft. Align the switch as described in Step 16 above.

26 Install the bolt retaining the switch to the transmission case. Tighten the bolt and nut.

9 Differential assembly – removal (manual transmission removed)

1 Disconnect the bottom link of the engine shock absorber.

2 Disconnect the tension spring for the clutch release sector (underneath the dash) from the clutch pedal.

3 Disconnect the cable end from the clutch release lever.

4 Remove the drive axles as described in Chapter 8.

5 Remove the left and right-hand stiffener plates.

6 Remove the starter as described in Chapter 5.

7 Remove the six bellhousing-to-engine retaining bolts.

8 Remove the 10 mm bolt facing the rear of the vehicle on the passenger side which retains the dust plate to the transmission.

9 Withdraw the bellhousing/differential assembly by pulling it to the rear and down out of the vehicle. **Note:** *Two alignment dowels, at the 11 and 4 o'clock positions looking from the rear toward the front of the vehicle, must be cleared before the assembly can be removed.*

10 Differential

General information

The differential assembly is incorporated within the transaxle housing. Since special equipment and techniques are required to overhaul and repair the differential, no procedures are included for the home mechanic. The tools and knowledge required are more than some repair shops are equipped to handle. If you suspect differential problems because of excessive noise or lash in the drive train, take your vehicle to a dealership or shop specializing in this type of work. If differential problems are confirmed, you will either have to have the unit repaired by the dealership or repair shop or, you could replace it with another complete unit from a salvage yard or rebuilder.

Axle oil seals – inspection

1 Inspect the axle seals by first raising the vehicle and supporting it securely. Visually check the area immediately surrounding the axle shaft couplers where they emerge from the differential. If evidence of oil leakage is present, the axle seal will have to be replaced with a new one. Be sure to check both the left and the right axle seals.

Axle oil seal replacement

2 Remove the axle shaft as described in Chapter 8.

3 Remove the oil seal with Service tool number 09308-00010 or a screwdriver. Be careful when prying the old seal out with a screwdriver not to damage the case around the seal seat.

4 Clean the seal seat and make sure it is free from burrs or defects.

5 Press the new seal in with Service tool number 09223-46011 or a socket of a slightly larger diameter than the outer diameter of the seal. Install the seal to the correct depth below the lip of the differential housing.

6 Coat the inner lip of the seal with molybdenum disulphide grease. Install the axle shafts by referring to Chapter 8.

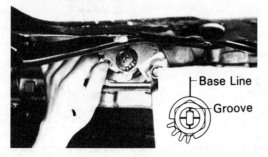

Fig. 7.11 Aligning the shaft groove with the neutral base line on the transmission case (Sec 8)

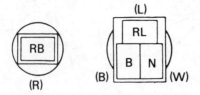

( ) . . .Wire Color

Fig. 7.12 Terminal and wire color coding for neutral safety switch testing (Sec 8)

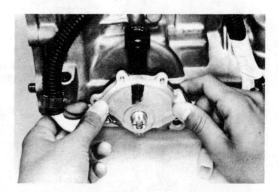

Fig. 7.13 Sliding the neutral safety switch off the automatic transmission shift shaft (Sec 8)

Chapter 8 Clutch and drive axles

Contents

Specifications

Clutch
Clutch pedal height (from floor panel)	6.65 in (169 mm)
Clutch pedal freeplay	0.79 to 1.38 in (20 to 35 mm)
Clutch disc rivet head depth limit	0.012 in (0.3 mm)
Clutch disc runout limit	0.031 in (0.8 mm)
Clutch diaphragm spring alignment limit	0.020 in (0.5 mm)
Clutch diaphragm spring finger wear limit	0.024 in (0.6 mm)

Drive axles
Driveshaft length (left side)	27.09 in (688 mm)
Driveshaft length (right side)	23.07 in (586 mm)
Distance between the left and right drive shaft	7.626 in (193.7 mm)
Outboard driveshaft joint grease capacity	0.5 lb (245 grams)
Inboard driveshaft joint grease capacity	0.31 lb (140 grams)

Torque specifications
	ft-lb	kg-m
Front hub-to-axle retaining nut	73 to 108	(10.0 to 15.0)
Flywheel-to-crankshaft retaining bolts	55 to 61	(7.5 to 8.5)
Clutch cover-to-flywheel retaining bolts	11 to 15	(1.5 to 2.2)
Clutch release fork-to-fork lever retaining bolts	44 to 57	(6.0 to 8.0)
Clutch pedal shaft retaining nut	22 to 32	(3.0 to 4.5)

1 Clutch – general information

1 The clutch is located between the engine and the transaxle and its main components are the flywheel, clutch disc, the pressure plate assembly and the release bearing. Other components which make up the clutch system are the clutch pedal, self-adjusting mechanism, clutch cable, clutch release lever and the clutch release fork assembly.

2 The clutch disc is mounted on the transaxle's input shaft. The clutch disc is sandwiched between the flywheel and the pressure plate and has a splined hub which engages and turns the input shaft. When engaged, the pressure plate is held against the clutch disc by the spring pressure of its metal fingers, and the clutch disc, in turn, is held against the engine's flywheel. The spinning of the engine is thus transmitted from the flywheel to the clutch disc and into the input shaft.

3 When the clutch pedal is depressed it pulls on the clutch cable which, in turn, pulls on the release lever at the transaxle. The other end

of the release lever, located inside the clutch housing, is fork-shaped. This fork engages the clutch release bearing and forces the bearing against the pressure plate assembly's release fingers. When the fingers receive pressure from the release bearing they withdraw the mating surface of the pressure plate from the clutch disc which disengages the clutch assembly from the engine's flywheel.

4 The self-adjusting mechanism is mounted to the clutch pedal assembly. This mechanism controls the tension on the clutch cable, pulling it the proper amount when the clutch pedal is depressed and maintaining a constant light pressure on the cable when the pedal is released. This mechanism also automatically adjusts for any stretching the clutch cable may do over a period of time.

5 Because access to the clutch components is difficult, any time either the engine or the transaxle is removed, the clutch components should be carefully inspected and, if necessary, replaced. Since the clutch disc is the highest wear item, it should be replaced as a matter of course if there is any question as to its quality.

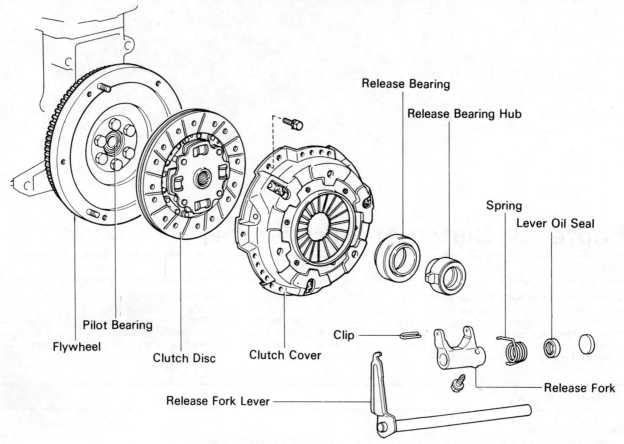

Fig. 8.1 Clutch assembly components – exploded view (Sec 3)

2 Clutch – inspection

1 The following check can be made to see if the clutch is releasing fully when the clutch pedal is applied. With the engine running and the brake held on, hold the clutch pedal approximately $\frac{1}{2}$ in from the floor mat. Now shift between 1st and reverse gears several times. If the shift is smooth, without any noticeable vehicle movement either forward or backward, the clutch is releasing fully, if the shift is not smooth, then the clutch linkage should be inspected and corrected.

2 Road test the car to check clutch operation. Watch for smooth engagement when accelerating from a stop. The clutch should also release cleanly as the vehicle is shifted. Notice if there is any shuddering or vibration at the friction or take-up point as the vehicle begins to move from a stop.

3 Accelerate the vehicle in high gear, on an upgrade if possible, and listen for engine over-speeding. The tachometer on SR-5 models will also give a good indication of a slipping clutch. If the engine rpms on the tachometer rise but the vehicle speed registered on the speed-ometer does not, the clutch is slipping.

4 Clutch slippage is usually due to an excessively worn clutch disc or a weak pressure plate spring. Oil on the clutch disc can also cause similar problems.

5 If any of the above problems are apparent, have the vehicle road checked by an experienced mechanic. Since repair of the clutch assembly is a lengthy, costly procedure, a second opinion would be worthwhile.

6 No other outside visual method is provided to inspect the clutch mechanism. Any confirmed problems willl dictate either engine or transmission removal for further physical inspection.

3 Clutch assembly – inspection and replacement

1 Because of the clutch's location between the engine and transaxle the clutch cannot be worked on without removing either the engine or transaxle. If repairs which would require removal of the engine are not needed, the quickest way to gain access to the clutch is by removing the transaxle, as described in Chapter 7.

2 With the transaxle removed, mark the relationship of the pressure plate assembly to the flywheel for installation purposes.

3 Before removing the pressure plate assembly from the flywheel, check that none of the metal fingers on the pressure plate are distorted or bent. If any damage is evident the pressure plate will need to be replaced.

4 In a diagonal pattern to keep from distorting the pressure plate, loosen the attaching bolts a little at a time until the spring pressure is relieved.

5 While supporting the pressure plate assembly, remove the bolts. Then remove the pressure plate and clutch disc.

6 From the inside of the transaxle, remove the clutch release bearing, which is retained by two 'U' shaped spring clips.

7 Clean the pressure plate, flywheel mating surfaces and the bearing retainer outer surfaces of any oil and grease.

8 Examine the pressure plate surface where it contacts the clutch disc. This surface should be smooth, with no scoring, gouging or warping. Check the pressure plate cover and fingers for damage. If any fault is found with the pressure plate assembly it must be replaced as an entire unit.

9 Inspect the clutch disc for lining wear. Check for loose or broken rivets or springs. Inspect the rivet head depth with a caliper (Fig. 8.2).

10 Inspect the surface of the flywheel for rivet grooves, burnt areas or scoring. If the damage is slight, the flywheel can be removed and reconditioned using a lathe. If the damage is deep, the flywheel should be replaced. Check that the ring gear teeth are not broken, cracked or seriously burned. Refer to Section 4 for the flywheel removal process.

11 Check that the release fork has not been cracked or bent. Slowly turn the front face of the release bearing, making sure it turns freely and without any noise. The release bearing is pre-lubricated and should not be washed in gasoline or any other solvent. Whenever a new clutch is installed a new release bearing should automatically be used.

12 If any traces of oil are detected on the clutch components the source should be found and eliminated. If oil is coming from the center of the flywheel, this indicates a failure of the rear oil seal (Chapter 2).

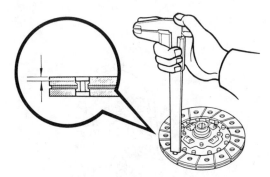

Fig. 8.2 Inspecting clutch disc rivet head depth with a caliper (Sec 3)

Oil at the rear of the clutch assembly may indicate the need to replace the transaxle input shaft (Chapter 7).

13 To install, noting the alignment marks made during the removal procedure, hold the clutch disc and pressure plate together against the flywheel and insert a centering tool through the center of them. Since the transaxle input shaft must pass through the center of these components, they must be properly aligned to ease the installation of the transaxle. The clutch disc must be installed with the damper springs offset toward the transaxle. The flywheel side is sometimes identified as such by stamped letters in the disc or hub.

14 Install the mounting bolts and tighten them in sets and in a diagonal cross-pattern until they are torqued to specs.

15 Lubricate both the outer groove and inner recess of the release bearing and reinstall it and the release fork into the transaxle.

16 Install the transaxle.

---

4 Flywheel and pilot bearing – inspection and replacement

1 Remove the clutch as described in Section 3. Examine the flywheel for scoring, wear patterns, glazing or heat marks. If any question exists about the flywheel condition, it should be resurfaced by an automotive machine shop equipped to do so.

2 Check the flywheel for runout with a dial indicator. A warped flywheel can cause accelerated clutch wear as well as poor clutch operation.

3 The flywheel ring gear should be carefully examined for any damage to the teeth. If any damage is found, the flywheel should be replaced with a new one.

4 For flywheel replacement see Chapter 2, Section 17.

5 The pilot bearing can be checked by turning it by hand. If the bearing sticks, has excessive rotational resistance or turns roughly, replace it with a new one. This bearing is permanently lubricated, so no additional grease is necessary.

6 See Chapter 2, Section 22 for the pilot bearing replacement procedure.

---

5 Clutch pedal assembly – removal and installation

Caution: *When removing springs as directed in the following steps, be careful as they are all under tension and can cause bodily injury.*

1 Remove the pedal return spring.

2 Remove the sector tensioning spring.

3 Remove the mounting nut from the left side of the pedal support shaft.

4 Exert pressure on the clutch pedal in a clockwise direction and pull out the pedal shaft.

5 Disconnect the release cable end from the release sector and remove the clutch pedal.

6 Remove the collar and bushings.

7 Using a screwdriver, remove the E-ring and washer from the shaft.

8 Take off the pawl spring and remove the pawl.

9 Remove the lever return spring.

10 Remove the snap-ring with the correct type of pliers, and the spacer behind it.

11 Remove the release sector.

12 Remove the release lever and bushings.

13 Coat the release lever bushing with multi-purpose grease.

14 Install the bushing on the release lever.

15 Coat the small release lever bushing with multi-purpose grease and install it into the proper hole on the release lever.

16 Install the release lever and bushing combination in the clutch pedal.

17 Coat the release sector with multi-purpose grease.

18 Fit the release sector onto the clutch pedal assembly.

19 Install the spacer and fit the snap-ring over the spacer to retain the release sector.

20 Coat the pawl with multi-purpose grease.

21 Install the pawl and spring over the shaft on the pedal assembly.

22 Install the washer. Install the E-ring over the assembly to retain it.

23 Install the lever return spring. Make sure that the release sector moves smoothly.

24 Coat the pedal shaft bushings with multi-purpose grease. Insert the bushings onto the pedal shaft assembly.

25 Install the collar onto the pedal shaft assembly.

26 Connect the release cable end to the release sector.

27 Install the clutch pedal into its proper position.

28 Insert the pedal shaft through the bracket and pedal assembly.

29 Install the nut and lockwasher onto the pedal shaft and tighten it to the specified torque.

30 Install the sector tension spring.

31 Install the pedal return spring.

32 Check and adjust the clutch pedal as described in Chapter 1.

---

6 Clutch release assembly – removal and installation

Note: *The engine or transmission must be removed to gain access to the clutch release mechanism as it is contained in the bell housing.*

1 Remove the throwout bearing assembly retained by the two U-clips.

2 Remove the release fork retainer bolt (photo).

3 Withdraw the clutch pivot release fork lever. Be careful not to let the spring fly out as it is under tension.

4 Inspect the clutch throwout bearing, throwout bearing retainer clips, release fork lever, release fork and release fork return spring for wear and/or damage. Also inspect the throwout flange for wear and/or damage.

5 Inspect the release lever seal for damage or signs of leakage (photo). Replace the seal if there is any question of condition.

6 Check the release bearing and make sure that it has smooth motion when turned. Replace the bearing with a new one if any problem is found.

7 Using an approved pusher tool remove the release bearing from the release bearing hub.

8 Use the same tool to install the new bearing on the hub.

9 Installation of the release assembly is the reverse of removal.

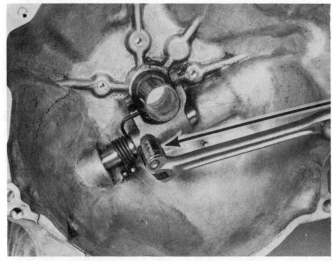

6.2 Release fork retainer bolt shown being removed with a socket

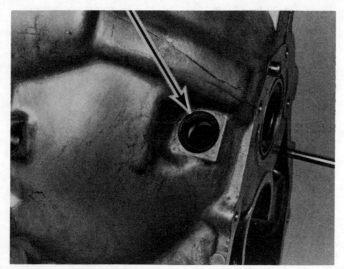

6.5 Location of release lever seal

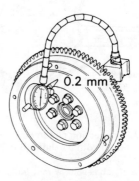

0.2 mm

Fig. 8.3 Inspecting flywheel runout with
a dial indicator (Sec 4)

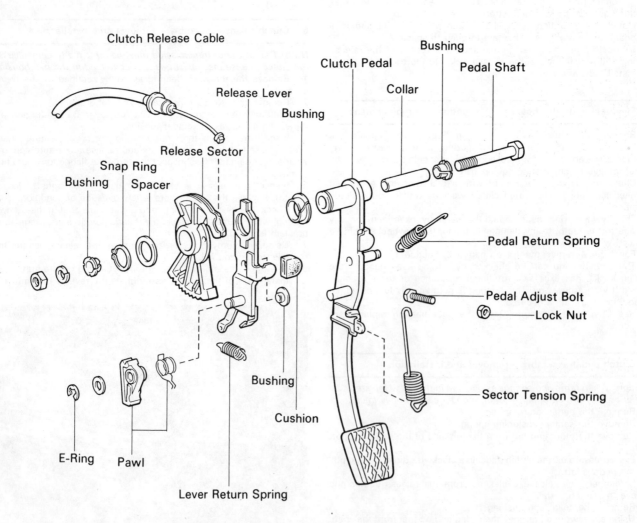

Clutch Release Cable

Release Lever

Bushing

Clutch Pedal

Bushing

Collar

Pedal Shaft

Release Sector

Snap Ring

Spacer

Bushing

Bushing

Pedal Return Spring

Pedal Adjust Bolt

Lock Nut

Sector Tension Spring

Cushion

Bushing

E-Ring

Pawl

Lever Return Spring

Fig. 8.4 Clutch pedal assembly components – exploded view
(Sec 5)

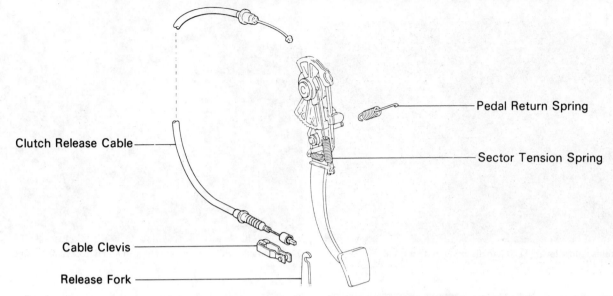

Clutch Release Cable

Pedal Return Spring

Sector Tension Spring

Cable Clevis

Release Fork

Fig. 8.5 Clutch release cable components and locations (Sec 7)

7 Clutch release cable – removal and installation

1   Disconnect the sector tension spring from the pedal and the top of the link.
2   Disconnect the clutch release cable end from the release fork lever (photo).
3   Turn the release sector toward the front (in a counterclockwise direction when you look from the driver's side of the vehicle) and disconnect the clutch release cable end from the release sector.
4   Remove the clutch release cable from its hole in the firewall, pulling it through to the engine side.
5   Remove the cable clevis from the release cable where it connects to the release fork lever next to the bellhousing.
6   Install the cable clevis to the clutch release cable.
7   Feed the cable through the firewall and make sure that it is not kinked or binding along its length.
8   Turn the release sector in a clockwise direction as viewed from the left side of the vehicle and connect the cable end to the groove in the release sector.
9   Connect the release cable end to the release fork lever.
10   Connect the pedal tension spring.
11   Check the pedal free play as described in Chapter 1.
12   Depress the pedal several times. This will actuate the self-adjusting mechanism on the release sector and pawl.
13   Check the release sector and see that there are at least six notches remaining on it.
14   If there are less than six notches remaining, the clutch disc may need replacing.

8 Drive-axles – general information

The Tercel uses two driveaxles which run directly from the transaxle to the front hub assemblies. The drive-axles use a tripod joint on their inside (transaxle) side to connect the shafts to a splined male coupler. The outer end of the drive-axles use a constant velocity joint to drive another splined male coupler and this joint is not replaceable. If the outer joint fails, the entire shaft must be replaced with a new one.

Rubber boots are used on both the inner and outer joints to contain the grease that the joints run in. These boots also serve to keep dirt and moisture from entering the bearings of the joints. The boots are very susceptible to damage from rocks and road hazards so they should be checked periodically. A small tear in a boot, although seemingly insignificant, can let the grease leak out of an axle joint and cause failure. Be careful when working around these rubber boots as a slipped tool could also damage one. Anytime you are working on or near these boots, it would be smart to wrap them with a shop towel to protect them from potential damage.

If a drive-axle is damaged or bent, it must be replaced with a new one. Under no circumstances should any attempt be made to heat or bend a drive-axle.

9 Drive-axle – removal and installation

Removal
1   Remove the cap and the cotter pin from the wheel or wheels from which the drive-axle is to be removed.
2   Have a helper hold the brake pedal down and remove the bearing locknut.
3   Remove the brake caliper assembly as described in Chapter 9.
4   Disconnect the stabilizer bar end at the lower suspension arm (Chapter 11).
5   Disconnect the strut bar from the lower suspension arm (Chapter 11).
6   Remove the bolts that retain the steering knuckle to the bottom of the shock absorber/strut assembly. If the steering knuckle will not slide off the bottom of the shock/strut assembly it may need to be spread open slightly (Chapter 11).
7   Pull the front axle hub from the driveshaft spline with service tool 09950-20014 or an equivalent wheel puller.
8   Separate the shock absorber from the steering knuckle and pull the driveshaft out of the back of the axle hub (photo).
9   Remove the stiffener plate if the left-side axle is being removed.
10   Use special tool No. 09648-16010 or an equivalent (photo) to remove the axle from the differential assembly.
11   After pulling out the shaft, insert special tool No. 09563-16010 or an equivalent to retain the grease within the differential assembly.

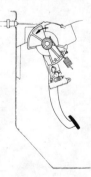

**Fig. 8.6 Turning the release sector
toward the front for cable disconnection
(Sec 7)**

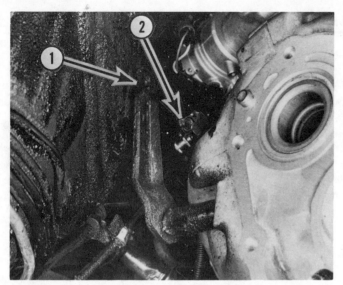

7.2 The release fork lever (1) shown disconnected from the release cable (2)

9.8 Drive-axle with the suspension arm and hub assembly removed

9.10 Two screwdrivers being used to remove drive-axle from the differential

10.4 Removing the snap-ring from the inboard joint boot

10.8 Tripod joint retaining snap-ring

10.9 Removing the tripod joint with a soft-faced punch

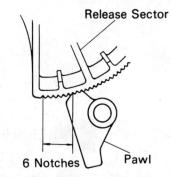

Fig. 8.7 Checking the release sector for remaining adjustment notches (Sec 7)

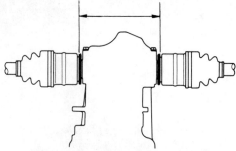

Fig. 8.9 Checking the distance between the left and right driveshafts (Sec 9)

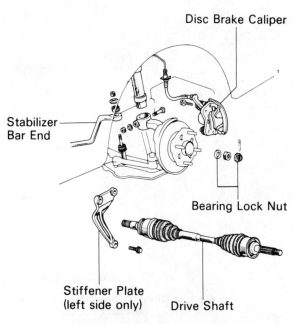

Fig. 8.8 Drive-axle assembly component locations (Sec 8)

Installation

12 Coat the inner lip of the driveshaft seal with molybdenum disulfide grease.

13 Install the driveshaft by using tool No. 09648-16010 or an equivalent.

14 Install the outer splines of the drive-axle to the axle hub.

15 Install the steering knuckle to the shock absorber making sure that the stop position on the shock absorber is aligned with the slot on the steering knuckle.

16 Tighten the steering knuckle bolt to the prescribed torque. Be careful not to damage the drive-axle boot during this process.

17 Connect the stabilizer bar end to the lower suspension arm.

18 Install the strut bar to the lower suspension arm.

19 Install the brake caliper assembly to the axle hub.

20 Install the bearing locknut while depressing the brake pedal and tighten it to the specified torque.

21 Install the cotter pin and adjusting nut cap.

22 Install the left-hand stiffener plate if it has been removed.

23 Check the boots on the drive-axle for alignment, damage and stretch.

24 Measure the assembled length of the driveshaft just installed and make sure that the distance is within Specifications.

25 Check the length between the right and the left driveshaft after installation and make sure it is the prescribed length.

26 Have the front end aligned by an alignment shop or dealer service department.

10 Drive-axle – disassembly and inspection

1 Check the boots of both the inboard shaft for any cracks, tears or signs of leakage.

2 Check the outboard joint to see that there is no play.

3 Check the inboard joint and see that it slides smoothly in the thrust direction. Make sure that the radial play of the inboard joint is minimal. This check, for the inboard joint, should be made both with the boot on and after it has been removed.

Disassembly

4 Remove the snap-ring from the inboard joint boot (photo).

5 Place match marks on the inboard joint shaft and yoke. Do not punch in the alignment marks but use some form of dye or paint.

6 Slide the inboard joint away from the drive yoke and remove it.

7 Place match marks on the body of the tripod joint and the driveshaft.

8 Remove the snap-ring with the correct tool (photo).

9 Tap uniformly around the outside of the tripod joint to remove it from the driveshaft (photo). Do not tap on the rollers.

10 The inboard joint boot may now be removed.

11 Remove the clamps from the outboard joint boot.

12 Remove the outboard joint boot. **Note:** *Do not attempt to remove the outboard joint at it is not a serviceable assembly.*

11 Drive-axle – reassembly

1 Install the boot to the outboard joint.

2 Use new boot clamps and install them on the driveshaft so that they are pointed in the same direction as the driveshaft normally turns.

3 Place the inboard shaft boot onto the driveshaft.

4 Assemble the tripod joint onto the driveshaft by placing the beveled side of the tripod body onto the axle. Make sure that the match marks on the body and axle are aligned.

5 Make sure that the inboard joint and the outboard joint axes correspond.

6 Use a brass drive bar or equivalent and tap the tripod onto the driveshaft.

7 Use a new snap-ring and install it onto the driveshaft.

8 Pack the inboard joint shaft with the prescribed type and amount of grease. Make sure you use only grease specially provided in the axle boot replacement kit.

9 Pack the inboard joint of the driveshaft with the special grease supplied in the boot kit.

10 Align the match marks of the drive yoke and shaft and install the inboard shaft to the drive yoke.

11 Install the boot onto the inboard driveshaft. Make sure that the boot fits in the groove on the driveshaft.

12 Install a new clamp on the inboard joint side into the recess provided by this groove.

13 Make sure that the boot is not stretched or compressed. Measure the driveshaft length and see that it fits the specification. Notice that the left and right driveshafts are different lengths.

14 Install a new snap-ring on the inboard joint.

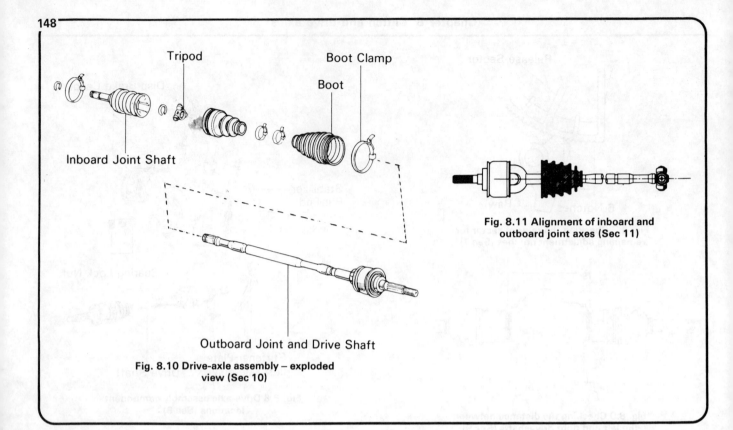

Tripod

Boot Clamp

Boot

Inboard Joint Shaft

Outboard Joint and Drive Shaft

Fig. 8.10 Drive-axle assembly – exploded view (Sec 10)

Fig. 8.11 Alignment of inboard and outboard joint axes (Sec 11)

Chapter 9 Braking system

Contents

Specifications

Brake pedal
Height from floor	6.437 to 6.476 in (163.5 to 164.5 mm)
Free play	0.157 to 0.276 in (4.0 to 7.0 mm)
Distance from floor @ 110.2 lb (50 kg)	More than 2.36 in (60 mm)

Front brakes
Disc thickness	0.394 in (10.0 mm)
Disc thickness limit	0.354 in (9.0 mm)
Disc pad thickness limit	0.039 in (1.0 mm)
Disc rotor runout limit	0.0059 in (0.15 mm)

Rear brakes
Drum inside diameter	7.087 in (180.0 mm)
Drum inside diameter limit	7.126 in (181.0 mm)
Lining thickness limit	0.039 in (1.0 mm)
Shoe and parking brake shoe lever clearance	0.000 to 0.0138 in (0.000 to 0.35 mm)
Shoe clearance	0.024 in (0.6 mm)

Parking brake lever travel @ 33 lb (15 kg)
2 to 5 clicks

Vacuum booster push rod-to-piston clearance
No vacuum	0.0236 to 0.0256 in (0.60 to 0.65 mm)
Idling vacuum	0.004 to 0.020 in (0.1 to 0.5 mm)

Torque specifications
	ft-lb	(m-kg)
Brake pedal shaft bolt	22 to 32	(3.0 to 4.5)
Master cylinder piston stopper bolt	6 to 10	(0.8 to 1.5)
Master cylinder oulet check valve torque	26 to 39	(3.5 to 5.5)
Front disc brake line-to-union	10 to 13	(1.3 to 1.8)
Disc brake caliper-to-torque plate	11 to 15	(1.5 to 2.2)
Flexible brake hose-to-brake cylinder	15 to 19	(2.0 to 2.7)
Torque plate-to-steering knuckle	33 to 39	(4.5 to 5.5)
Union-to-brake cylinder retainer nut	20 to 25	(2.7 to 3.5)

1 General description

The Toyota Tercel is equipped with sliding caliper-type disc brakes at the front and expanding drum brakes at the rear. Pedal pressure is assisted by a vacuum-powered servo unit.

The system is a dual line type with a double-chambered master cylinder and resulting separate hydraulic systems for the front and rear wheels. In the event of a brake line or seal failure, half of the braking system remains operative. The hand brake is a mechanical-cable type operating the rear brakes.

2 Disc brake pads – inspection

Refer to Chapter 1 for disc brake checking procedure.

3 Disc brake pads – replacement

Removal and inspection

1   Raise the front of the car and remove the front wheels as described in Chapter 1. Block the rear tires and set the parking brake to keep the vehicle from rolling. Disassemble only one side at a time because it is possible to push the opposite piston out of the caliper if both sides are done simultaneously. The opposite side will also serve as a guide if difficulties are encountered during reassembly.
2   Remove the two caliper slide bushings (bolts) using two wrenches (photo). It is very important to hold the bushing with the inside wrench as damage could result from allowing it to twist. **Note:** *Refer to Fig. 9.1 for components and their locations related to the following steps.*
3   Pull the caliper assembly straight back and suspend it from the suspension, being careful not to stretch or kink the brake hose (photo). Do not disconnect the brake hose.
4   Remove the inner brake pad by pulling straight back. It may be necessary to jiggle the pad sideways slightly to initially dislodge it. Do not use pliers or other hard-surfaced tools as they will damage the brake pad material.
5   Remove the outer brake pad together with the anti-squeal shim. Keep it separate from the inner pad if it is to be reused.
6   Remove the anti-rattle springs, support plate, inner anti-squeal shim and the guide plates. Inspect all of these parts for damage and make sure that the springs have not become weakened with age. Replace any parts in doubtful condition with new ones.
7   Measure the brake pads (check to see if they are worn evenly and have enough material to warrant reinstalling them) (photo). Measure the brake disc and check the surface for any cracks or deep scratches (photo). Measure the runout using a dial indicator (photo). If the runout exceeds the limit, check to make sure the wheel bearings are tight before replacing the disc. If the wheel bearings are found to be loose, they should be repacked and re-shimmed at this time. Refer to Chapter 11 for this procedure. If the pads are to be re-used, sand the surface lightly with a fine grade of sandpaper to clean and deglaze the material.

Installation

8   Install the anti-rattle springs, pad guide plates and pad support plate onto the pad retaining bracket (Fig. 9.2).
9   Attach the anti-squeal shim to the outer pad. Push the outer pad and shim assembly into the retaining bracket while depressing the anti-rattle spring.
10 Remove a small amount of brake fluid from the master cylinder using a syringe or siphon. **Note:** *Be careful when working with brake fluid. It is very corrosive and can damage your skin and the vehicle's paint.*
11 Push the piston back into the caliper using a hammer handle or other similar soft tool. Be careful not to damage the seal or bore while pushing on the piston.
12 Install the inner anti-squeal shim onto the piston.
13 Install the slide bushing, dust boots and collar onto the caliper assembly.
14 Install the inner brake pad while depressing the anti-rattle spring. Make sure the pads are both seated properly and all of the springs and plates are in their proper positions. **Caution:** *Before performing the next step, make sure the piston is still fully retracted into its bore.*
15 Install the caliper assembly onto the pads and bracket making sure

3.2 Removing the front disc brake caliper assembly bolts

3.3 Suspend the caliper assembly with a wire

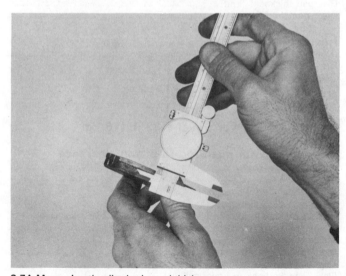
3.7A Measuring the disc brake pad thickness

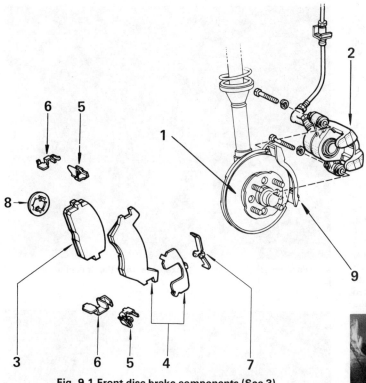

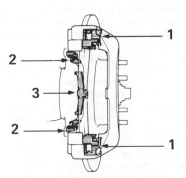

Fig. 9.2 Proper positioning of:
(Sec 3)

1   Anti-rattle springs   3   Pad support plate
2   Pad guide plates

Fig. 9.1 Front disc brake components (Sec 3)

1   Disc
2   Caliper assembly
3   Inner pad
4   Outer pad and anti-squeal shim
5   Anti-rattle springs
6   Pad guide plates
7   Pad support plate
8   Inner anti-squeal shim
9   Brake pad retaining bracket

that the dust boots on the bushing assembly are positioned properly and not wedged at an angle. This assembly will go together smoothly if all of the parts are properly positioned. Don't force anything into place.

16 Hold the bushings with a wrench and insert the mounting bolts. Start the mounting bolts into the threads by hand. Be very careful not to allow the bushings to turn, as they will bind and cause erratic or poor front brake performance. Hold the bushings with a wrench and tighten the bolts to the correct torque setting.

17 Perform the same steps to the other side. **Caution:** *Before driving the car, pump the brake pedal several times until a solid pedal is attained. Make sure that the brakes are working smoothly and make several slow speed stops before taking the vehicle into a traffic situation.*

---

4   Disc brake caliper assembly – removal and inspection

1   The front disc brake caliper assembly can be removed without disturbing the brake pads and related hardware. If the pads are to be replaced at the same time the caliper assembly is replaced or overhauled, follow the steps in the previous Section for brake pad removal before going on to the following procedures.

2   Remove all of the brake fluid from the brake master cylinder reservoir with a syringe or similar suction device. Be careful not to spill any of this fluid because it will corrode any surface.

3   Disconnect the brake line from the flexible brake hose at the junction located near the base of the spring tower (photo). Anchor the flex hose solidly with one wrench while turning the fitting with a flare nut wrench. These fittings are usually tight and the nuts damage easily, so apply some penetrating oil if possible but be careful not to allow it to get in or on the brake hoses. A catch can should be used to pick up the remainder of the brake fluid left in the lines as the connection is opened.

4   Pull the spring clip retainer from the junction, which will allow one end of the flex hose to come loose from the car. Pliers or a small pair

3.7B Measuring the disc thickness

3.7C Checking the disc for runout with a dial indicator

of vise-grips usually work well for this task (photo).

5   Use a can to catch any fluid remaining in the hose as you disconnect the flexible brake hose from the brake union located on the caliper assembly. Remove the angled brake union, noting the sealing rings located on either end. Omit the following two steps if you have already removed the brake pads.

6   Remove the two caliper mounting bolts using two wrenches (photo 3.2). It is very important to hold the bushing with the inside wrench while performing this operation.

7   Remove the brake caliper assembly by pulling straight back.

8   The brake caliper assembly should now be separate from the car and can be taken to a workbench for further disassembly and inspection. Remove the inner anti-squeal shim.

9   Remove the slide bushing, dust boots and collar from the piston assembly. Inspect them for corrosion or damage.

10   Remove the cylinder set ring and boot (photo).

11   Remove the piston from the caliper, taking care not to damage the bore surface in any way. There are a number of different ways to do this. Air pressure can be applied at the hose junction to blow the piston from its bore. Use low pressure and extreme caution with this method. The piston assembly can be tapped with a block of soft wood taking care not to damage the housing. You may hook the piston assembly back up to the car and use the pedal pressure to move the piston out of its bore (this method is messy and caution should be exercised to keep brake fluid from spraying on anything, particularly painted surfaces or brake pads). Lastly, a special tool is available that grips the inner surface of the brake piston and allows it to be pulled out with a twisting motion (photo).

12   Remove the piston seal using a wooden or plastic dowel, being careful not to damage the internal bore area as the smallest scratch could be cause for replacement.

13   Clean the brake piston and bore. Brake fluid may be used for this task or specially formulated brake cleaner which is available in aerosol cans. Ordinary rubbing alcohol can also be used if necessary, but under no circumstances should you use a penetrating-type cleaner that leaves an oily residue.

14   Inspect the piston bore and piston for rust, corrosion, roughness, scratches or other irregularities. Light surface rust or dirt can be cleaned out of the piston bore with emery cloth but corrosion or build-up on the piston will necessitate replacement. Inspect the rubber seals and replace them if any damage is found. Rubber seals get hard after use and it is always wise to replace them with new ones. Brake pistons work under high pressure and the surfaces of all the components must be near perfect. When in doubt, replace a part.

---

5   Disc brake caliper assembly – overhaul and installation

1   Always replace the piston seal and cylinder boot when overhauling the disc brake caliper. Lubricate all rubber parts with a suitable rubber brake part lubricant. Clean the packing grease off any new parts (it is used as a preservative and not as an assembly lube).

2   Apply lube to the piston seal and seat it into the piston bore. Make sure it is even and fits uniformly into its groove. Apply lube to the piston and push it into its bore.

3   Apply rubber lubricant to the new boot and place it into the bore (photo).

4   Install the cylinder boot retainer ring. Make sure it is seated uniformly in its proper groove.

5   Install the collar and rubber dust boots on the bushing assembly. Push the bushing bolt through this combination using assembly lube.

6   Insert the caliper assembly over the brake pad retaining bracket making sure that all of the brake pad hardware and the rubber bushing collars do not bind or fall out of place. Exercise care and caution in this step to prevent binding of the caliper assembly or misalignment of the brake pads.

7   Start the bushing bolts by hand and hold the bushing with a wrench during final tightening with a wrench or socket. Tighten the bushing bolts to the specified torque in the front of this Chapter.

8   Install the brake fitting union on the caliper using new gasket rings (photo). Make sure this part is very clean because any contamination of the brake fluid could result in diminished brake performance or even brake failure.

9   Connect the flexible brake hose to the brake fitting union using a new gasket. Again, make sure the hose is very clean inside.

4.3 Disconnecting the flexible brake hose from the brake line at the junction

4.4 Removing the spring clip retainer from the coupling

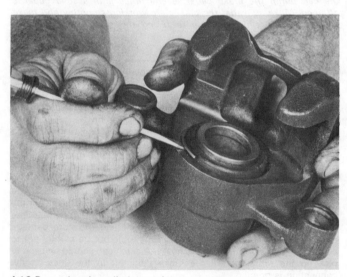
4.10 Removing the cylinder set ring

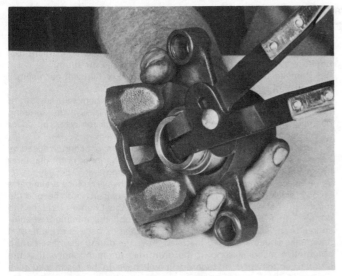

4.11 Removing the piston from the cylinder

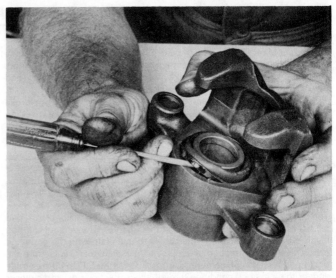

5.3 Installing cylinder boot (note the direction the lip faces)

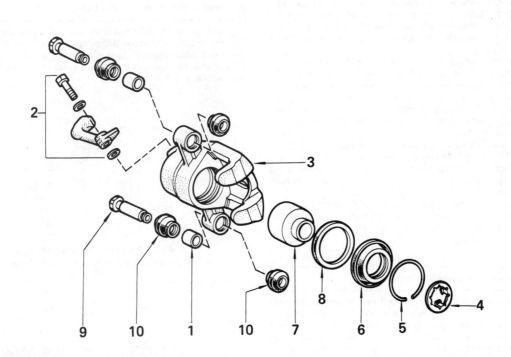

Fig. 9.3 Front disc brake caliper assembly components (Sec 4)

1	Collar	4	Inner anti-squeal shim	6	Cylinder boot	9	Caliper slide bushing (bolt)
2	Union assembly			7	Piston		
3	Cylinder	5	Cylinder boot set ring	8	Piston seal	10	Dust boots

10 Connect the brake hose to the body bracket using a new spring clip if the old one has lost its tension or is bent. Connect the brake line fitting to the brake hose being careful to start the threads first by hand. Always anchor the flexible brake hose with a second wrench and tighten the fitting with an appropriate size flare nut wrench.

11 After completing the same operation on both of the front brake assemblies, bleed the entire system as described in the brake bleeding section found at the end of this Chapter.

6   Disc brake rotor – inspection

1   The disc brake rotor may be inspected in one of two ways. The first method involves removing the brake caliper assembly and brake pads. You will find instructions for this method in the disc brake pad replacement section found earlier in this Chapter. The second method involves removing the entire disc brake torque plate with the pads and piston assembly intact. If a preliminary inspection reveals that the brake pads need replacement, use the first method. If the brake pads appear to be in good condition through the inspection port and a closer examination of the brake disc is needed, then follow the procedure listed below.

2   Raise the front of the vehicle and support it according to the instructions found in the front of the book. Remove the front wheels.

3   Remove the two retaining bolts for the brake assembly torque plate. Do not confuse these with the two brake caliper retaining bolts. The torque plate bolts are located closer to the axle center line and axle boots (photo).

4   Remove the entire torque plate assembly by pulling straight back from the rotor until the brake pads clear. Suspend the torque plate and be careful not to kink or stretch the flexible brake hose. Don't allow the assembly to hang from the brake hose and do not disconnect the brake hose.

5   Measure the disc thickness. Inspect the disc surface for any signs of scoring, cracking, heat checks or hot spots, and grooves caused by foreign material or excessively worn brake pads. If any grooves or scored spots in the disc fall below the minimum thickness, the disc will have to be replaced. If the scoring or grooves are within the minimum thickness, then the rotor will have to be removed and taken to an automotive machine shop to have the surface reground.

6   Measure the disc runout with a dial indicator (photo 3.7). If the runout (or wobble) is beyond the specification listed at the front of this Chapter, determine that the front wheel bearings are not causing this situation through looseness or wear. Grasp the disc firmly with both hands and use a rocking motion to check the wheel bearings. If they are loose, refer to the wheel bearing section of Chapter 11. If the wheel bearings are tight but the disc has more than the allowable runout, the disc will have to be removed and sent to an automotive machine shop for resurfacing.

7   Disc brake rotor – removal and installation

The disc brake rotor on the front of the Tercel is removable only after dismantling the entire front hub assembly. Because this procedure is very involved and requires some special equipment not normally found in the home workshop, we recommend that you read the entire procedure through thoroughly before undertaking it. If you feel that you can handle this job, prepare to use an automotive machine shop or dealership for the pressing of the hub. Refer to Chapter 11 for the procedure under wheel bearings to replace or repair the brake discs.

8   Rear brake drum – removal and inspection

1   Jack up the rear of the car and place it on jack stands after loosening the lug nuts. Make sure the car is supported solidly and remove the wheels.

2   Remove in order the grease cap, cotter pin, castellated nut, spindle nut, washer and outer bearing. Pull the drum off the spindle. If the drum will not come off, the shoes may have worn a ridge into the drum and they will have to be adjusted inward to release the drum.

3   To adjust the shoes inward, pry off the rubber inspection hole cover on the rear of the backing plate. Use a screwdriver to hold the

self-adjuster lever up from the star-wheel adjuster. With an upward movement, turn the star-wheel adjuster using a brake adjustment tool until the shoes have retracted enough to release the drum.

4   Remove the inner oil seal and bearing. Pry the seal out using a removal tool or a screwdriver and hammer handle.

5   Wash the bearings in clean solvent and dry them with a cloth or rag. Do not blow them dry with compressed air as a dry spinning bearing will gall the races. Inspect the bearings for wear, pitted or galled surfaces, or cracked rollers or retainers.

6   Inspect the brake drum for cracks, heat spots, or scoring caused by excessively worn rear brake shoes. Measure the inner drum diameter in several places using the proper inside micrometer.

7   Replace the rear drums with new ones (always replace brake parts on both sides to maintain braking equality) if they are worn beyond the minimum specification found at the front of this Chapter. Replace the drums if they are cracked or grooved beyond the minimum specification. If any scoring, deep scratching or heat damage is evident, or if new brake shoes are being installed, have the drums resurfaced at an automotive machine shop. If the drum measurement shows that the drum is egg-shaped or tapered, it will have to be resurfaced (see Chapter 1 for the exact measuring procedure).

Note: *If the drum is grooved but the brake linings are only slightly worn, the drum should not be resurfaced but only polished with fine emery cloth. Turning the drum and smoothing the lining surface would necessitate the removal of too much metal and lining material. If left as it is, the grooves and ridges match, giving satisfactory braking performance.*

9   Rear brake shoe – inspection

Measure the brake shoe lining thickness with a rule or micrometer (photo). Replace the shoes if they are less than the minimum thickness given in the Specifications listed in the front of this Chapter. The shoes should also be replaced if they are cracked, glazed (shiny surface) or wet with brake fluid or grease.

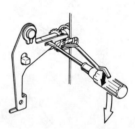

Fig. 9.4 Loosen the star wheel while holding the self-adjuster out of the way (Sec 8)

Fig. 9.5 Removing the inner oil seal using a screwdriver and hammer handle (Sec 8)

10 Rear brake shoe – removal, installation and adjustment

1   Remove the wheel and brake drum as described earlier in this Chapter.

2   Remove the U-shaped return spring by compressing it inward and pulling out with both hands.

3   Push the brake shoe retaining clip in and twist until the slot lines up with the tang on the end of the retaining nail. Note there is one retaining clip per shoe (photo).

4   Disconnect the parking brake cable from the rear shoe by pulling the spring forward and unhooking the cable from its hook (photo). If the shoes are to be replaced with new ones, the horseshoe clip must be spread out to remove the parking brake lever from the rear shoe (photo).

5   Pull the shoes off the backing plate and separate them by unhooking the lower shoe retracting spring (photo). The adjusting mechanism will also come free. Be sure to note the turning direction and location of the self-adjuster mechanism pieces.

6   Be careful of the brake dust coating the entire brake assembly and do not breathe this dust as it is very harmful to the body. Clean all of the brake hardware so it may be inspected to determine any need for replacement.

7   Inspect the wheel cylinders for leakage by pulling the boot away from the cylinder and visually checking for the presence of any brake fluid (photo). If any fluid is present or if it is leaking into the brake shoe area, go on to the next Section. If the wheel cylinders are dry and in good operating condition, the brakes may be replaced or reinstalled.

8   Installation is the reverse of removal. Lubricate the brake shoe contact points with a brake lube designed specifically for this purpose. Use grease sparingly and take care not to get it on the brake shoe lining material (photo). Use a new horseshoe clip if the old one is deformed. Make sure the brake lining material is clean. Use a special cleaner for this purpose if any oil or grease has contacted the friction surface.

9   Measure the clearance between the rear brake shoe (notice the lining on the rear brake shoe goes all the way to the top) and the parking brake lever. If the clearance is less than the minimum figure given at the front of this Chapter, a shim or shims (maximum of 2)

Fig. 9.6 Measuring the rear brake drum inner diameter (Sec 8)

must be inserted to maintain the minimum clearance (Fig. 9.8). Tighten the C-clip onto the brake shoe and move the lever back and forth in its travel to make sure it moves smoothly without binding.

10 Install the bottom shoe retracting spring (notice that it is longer than the spring used to retract the parking brake mechanism). Install the parking brake adjusting mechanism and make sure it is seated properly in the slots of both brake shoes.

11 Install the brake shoe assembly onto the backing plate and install the shoe hold-down spring and nail.

12 Retract the screw on the adjuster mechanism (if new shoes are installed) until the diameter of the shoes is smaller than the drum diameter. Adjust this shoe diameter so that it, when added to the shoe clearance specification, equals the drum diameter. This will ensure that the brakes are set at the proper initial adjustment for the automatic adjustment mechanism to work properly after the brakes are put into service.

13 Install the U-shaped return spring and install the brake drum and wheel bearings as described in Chapter 11.

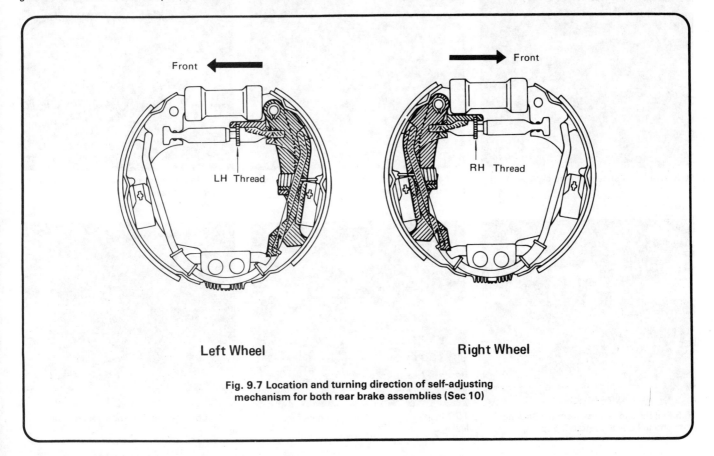

Left Wheel   **Right Wheel**

Fig. 9.7 Location and turning direction of self-adjusting mechanism for both rear brake assemblies (Sec 10)

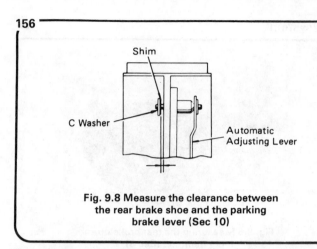

Fig. 9.8 Measure the clearance between the rear brake shoe and the parking brake lever (Sec 10)

Fig. 9.9 Measuring the rear brake shoe overall diameter (Sec 10)

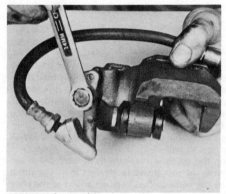

5.8 Installing the brake union on the caliper

6.3 Removing the torque plate mounting bolts (arrows)

9.1 Measuring rear brake shoe lining thickness

10.3 Rear brake shoe retaining clips (arrows)

10.4A Disconnecting the parking brake cable from the rear shoe

10.4B Removing the horseshoe clip from the parking brake lever

10.5 Pull the shoes away from the backing plate and unhook the retracting spring

10.7 Inspecting the wheel cylinders for leakage

10.8 Lubricate the rear shoe contact points (arrows)

11 Rear brake wheel cylinders – removal and inspection

1   Remove the rear brake shoes as described in the previous Section of this Chapter.
2   Remove the rear brake line fitting at the back of the backing plate (photo). Use a can to catch and contain the brake fluid as you uncouple the fitting from the cylinder. Use a flare nut wrench to prevent damage to the flare nut.
3   Remove the two bolts holding the wheel cylinder to the backing plate on the rear of the plate (photo).
4   Plug the brake line or leave the catch can in place as gravity and cylinder pressure will continue to push brake fluid out.
5   Remove the protective cap from the bleeder screw. Remove the bleeder screw from the wheel cylinder. Do not use an open end or adjustable wrench for this operation (photo).
6   Remove the dust caps from both ends of the wheel cylinder. **Note:** *The inner piston may pop out when the dust caps are removed. It would be best to work away from the car and any surface which brake fluid can harm.*
7   Remove the internal pistons and spring from the wheel cylinder. Clean the cylinder bore with brake fluid or a commercial brake cleaner.
8   Inspect the cylinder bore for rust, abrasions, cracks, or corrosion. Check the cylinder bore for excessive wear. Replace the cylinder with a new one if any of these conditions exist.

12 Rear brake wheel cylinders – overhaul and installation

1   Always use new piston cups and dust boots when overhauling the brake cylinders. Clean any packing grease off these rubber parts before installation. This grease is a preservative and not designed as an assembly lube.
2   Coat the new piston cups with a brake assembly lube or brake fluid. Make sure the cups are installed with the wide side of the cup turned toward the center of the wheel cylinder. Insert the cups into the new or cleaned cylinder with the spring positioned between them. Insert the pistons into the cylinder with the tang facing outward to mate up with the corresponding tab on the brake shoes. Install the dust covers with assembly lube but not with brake fluid.
3   Install the bleeder valve finger tight.
4   Install the wheel cylinder onto the backing plate using the two

bolts and washers. Tighten the bolts to the specified torque found in the front of this Chapter.
5   Install the brake line into the back of the wheel cylinder. Do not tighten the fitting with a wrench until you are sure the threads are started by hand correctly. The brake line should be clean and the plug (if one was installed) removed prior to assembly.
6   Bleed the brake system as described later in this Chapter before attempting to drive the vehicle. The entire brake system must be assembled before any application or bleeding of the brakes is attempted.

13 Parking brake system – removal and installation

1   The parking brake system consists of a handle assembly located in the middle of the interior of the vehicle. A lever attached to the bottom of the handle assembly operates an equalizer rod, which in turn pulls two cables. The cables run to each rear brake and hold the vehicle stationary by expanding the rear shoes in the brake drums. Adjustment for cable stretch is accomplished by a threaded nut at the equalizer bar and is accessible from under the vehicle. The parking brake system also is used to activate the automatic brake adjusters on the rear brake shoes. Each time the parking brake is activated, it adjusts the rear adjuster one notch until all of the slack is taken up in the brake system.
2   It is not necessary to remove the entire parking brake system to replace an individual part such as a parking brake cable. Determine the part in need of replacement through visual inspection before dismantling the entire system. A helper is beneficial in this process to operate the system while you observe its operation from under the vehicle.
3   Jack up the vehicle and support it on jackstands. Remove the adjuster nut from the lever under the center of the vehicle (photo). When unthreading this nut, it will probably be helpful to spray the exposed pull rod threads with a rust penetrant.
4   Remove the console cover after withdrawing the three Phillips head screws holding it to the floor brackets (some vehicles are not so equipped). Remove the flexible hand brake cover by pulling it up and off the handle. Pull the handle all the way up. Remove the pin and clip holding the pin to the bottom of the handle.
5   Remove the four bolts holding the handle assembly to the bottom of the vehicle. Make sure the equalizer bar is free of the pull rod under the vehicle. Withdraw the handle assembly by pulling forward and upward from the interior.

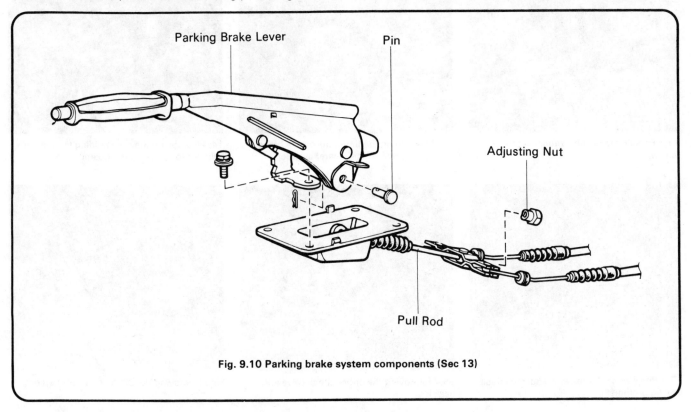

Fig. 9.10 Parking brake system components (Sec 13)

11.2 Removing the brake line fitting from the back of the wheel cylinder (note the flare nut wrench being used)

11.3 Two bolts (arrows) retain the wheel cylinder to the brake backing plate

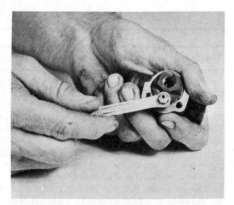

11.5 Removing the bleeder screw from the wheel cylinder

13.3 Removing the adjuster nut from the brake rod

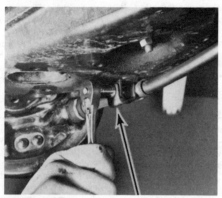

13.6 Removing the parking brake cable clamps

13.7 Disconnecting the parking brake cables from the equalizer bracket

13:8 Parking brake cable retaining prongs (arrow)

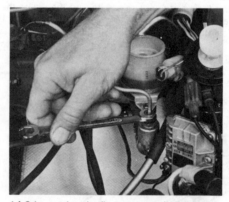

14.3 Loosening the flare nuts on the brake lines connected to the master cylinder

14.4 Removing the nuts holding the master cylinder to the vacuum booster

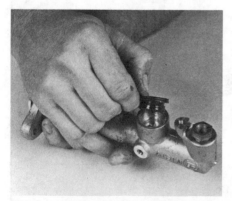

15.3 Removing the master cylinder reservoir sealing grommets

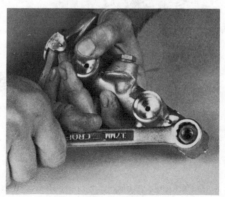

15.4 Removing the outlet check valve and gasket

15.5 Removing the piston retainer snap ring

6   The remainder of the parking brake system is removed from under the vehicle. Locate the parking brake cables. They originate at the equalizer bracket, run through the crossmember, and ultimately end up at each rear brake backing plate. Remove the three cable clamps located along the route of each cable. They are attached with small bolts (photo).

7   Disconnect the parking brake cables from the equalizer by turning the cables until they line up with the slots in the equalizer bracket. The cables will then slide out (photo).

8   To remove the cables from the brake shoes and backing plates, first remove the drum and brake shoes as described in this Chapter. Squeeze the prongs on the brake cable, where it goes through the backing plate on the brake shoe side, until the cable slips past the hole in the backing plate. A pair of pliers or vise-grips will work for this task (photo).

9   Installation is the reverse of removal. Before installing the brake cables, thoroughly lubricate them with a good quality cable lube or penetrating oil if necessary. Check the cable for signs of stretching or fraying. Put a small amount of light grease on the handle ratchet assembly.

10   Adjust the parking brake as described in Chapter 1.

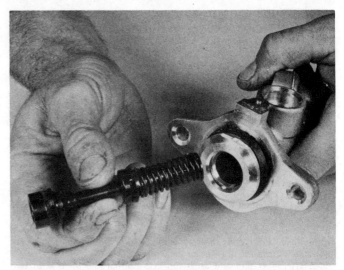

15.6 Removing the primary piston and spring assembly

14   Master cylinder – removal and installation

Caution: *Brake fluid is corrosive. Be careful not to get it on painted surfaces as it will remove paint. If it should accidently splash onto such a surface, wipe it off immediately and sponge off the area.*

1   Locate the brake master cylinder. It is attached to the brake booster chamber which is mounted on the firewall on the engine side directly in front of the steering wheel.

2   Remove the cap from the master cylinder. Remove the fluid from the master cylinder reservoir using a syringe or similar suction tool.

3   Use a flare nut wrench to loosen the flare nuts on the brake lines connected to the master cylinder (photo).

4   Remove the nuts holding the master cylinder to the vacuum booster chamber (photo).

5   Remove the lines from the master cylinder using a can to catch any fluid left in the bottom of the cylinder reservoir or in the lines.

6   Remove the master cylinder by pulling out and lifting it out of the engine bay.

7   Installation is the reverse of removal. Always hand start the flare nuts into the master cylinder before turning them with a wrench. Tighten the fittings with a flare nut wrench only.

8   The brake system must be filled and bled as described in Section 19 of this Chapter. Make sure the brake pedal height and rear brake shoe clearance is within the Specifications listed at the front of this Chapter before bleeding the system.

15   Master cylinder – inspection and overhaul

1   Use a soft rod (such as a wooden dowel) to push the piston to the bottom of the bore. While holding the piston in this bottomed position, remove the piston stopper bolt and washer.

2   Remove the two Phillips head screws holding the reservoir to the main body of the master cylinder. Remove the plastic master cylinder reservoir.

3   Remove the two brake reservoir sealing grommets (photo).

4   Remove the outlet check valve and gasket. It may be necessary to hold the master cylinder in a vise with soft jaws for this operation (photo).

5   Remove the snap-ring from the end of the master cylinder bore. Note that this requires special pliers with jaws intended for this specific purpose (photo).

6   Remove the primary piston and spring assembly. Note the direction and order of parts as you remove them from the master cylinder bore (photo).

7   Remove the secondary piston spring assembly (photo).

8   Carefully clean the master cylinder piston bore using a special cleaner or brake fluid if necessary. **Note** *Do not use any petroleum-based cleaners.* Inspect the piston bore for rust, scale, cracks or other defects. If it is scored, pitted or rusted, a light hone may be used to clean it. If any major honing is required, replace the cylinder with a new one.

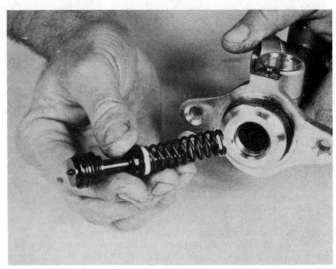

15.7 Removing the secondary piston and spring assembly

9   Check the primary and secondary piston return springs for loss of tension and damage. If they are defective, the entire piston assembly must be replaced. It is a good practice, and highly recommended, that the piston assemblies be replaced whenever the master cylinder needs any type of repair work done on it.

10   Assembly is the reverse of disassembly. Coat all of the parts with an approved brake assembly lube or brake fluid before installation.

11   Always replace the copper washers under the check valves and tighten the check valves to the specified torque.

12   Due to the construction of the master cylinder and reservoir, a gap may exist between the hold-down screw and the reservoir. This is normal. Do not insert a washer or any other type of spacer when installing the reservoir.

16   Vacuum power booster – inspection, removal and installation

1   Make sure the brake system is in good condition before performing the following checks on the vacuum booster. The master cylinder, in particular, must be functioning correctly because a defective master cylinder will often give similar symptoms to vacuum booster problems. If the vacuum booster appears to be defective, check the vacuum source to the unit while the engine is running. When the vacuum line is disconnected, there should be a strong, continuous vacuum present

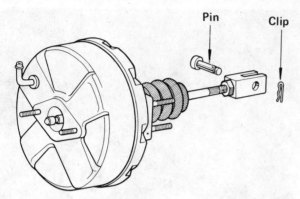

Fig. 9.11 Remove the clip and pin from the brake fork to detach the booster (Sec 16)

at the hose. If not, check the hose, manifold and engine condition for probable causes for the lack of vacuum.

2   Start the engine and let it run at a normal idle for one to two minutes. Shut the engine off and pump the brake pedal several times. If the pedal sinks close to the floor on the first application, and then gradually comes up after the second or third applications, the booster is operating correctly. If there is no change in pedal height on the second and successive applications, the booster is defective.

3   With the engine still stopped, pump the pedal with the same pressure. The brake pedal height should not vary.

4   Start the engine with the pedal depressed. The pedal should sink slightly when the engine starts. If the pedal height doesn't change, the booster is defective.

5   With the engine running, step on the brake pedal and hold it. Turn the engine off. Keep holding the pedal down for 30 seconds. The pedal height should not change. If it does change, the booster is defective.

6   Vacuum brake booster units should not be disassembled. They require special tools not normally found in most automotive repair stations or shops. They are fairly complex and because of their critical relationship to brake performance it is best to replace a defective booster unit with a new or rebuilt one.

7   To remove the vacuum booster, first remove the brake master cylinder as described elsewhere in this Chapter.

8   Remove the hose leading from the engine to the vacuum booster by first sliding back the spring clamp. Be careful not to damage the rubber hose when removing it from the booster fitting.

9   Remove the spring clip and push rod pin connecting the booster to the brake pedal. This is accessible from the interior in front of the driver's seat.

10 Remove the two nuts and washers holding the brake booster to the firewall. You will probably need a light to see these as they are up under the dash area.

11 Slide the vacuum booster straight out from the firewall until the studs clear the holes and pull the booster from the engine compartment area.

12 Installation is the reverse of removal.

13 If a master cylinder and/or vacuum booster unit are overhauled or replaced, the clearance between the master cylinder piston and the pushrod in the vacuum booster must be measured. Using a depth micrometer or vernier calipers, measure the distance from the seat (recessed area) in the master cylinder to the master cylinder mounting flange. Next, measure the distance from the end of the vacuum booster pushrod to the mounting face of the booster (including gasket) where the master cylinder mounting flange seats. Subtract the two measurements to get the clearance. If the clearance is more or less than specified, turn the adjusting screw on the end of the power booster pushrod until the clearance is within the specified limit.

14 A second method to measure the pushrod-to-piston clearance is to install the master cylinder to the vacuum booster with a small piece of modeling clay placed on the end of the pushrod. Make sure the gasket is in place when making this trial fit. Remove the master cylinder and measure the resulting impression left in the clay. Again, adjust as needed to meet the specification. This method may require several trial-and-error fits to reach the proper clearance.

15 After the final installation of the master cylinder and lines, the brake pedal height, brake pedal free play, and system bleed must be done before attempting to drive the car.

17 Brake lines and hoses – inspection and replacement

1   About every six months the flexible hoses which connect the steel brake line with the rear brakes and front calipers should be inspected for cracks, chafing of the outer cover, leaks, blisters, and other damage. These are important and vulnerable parts of the brake system and inspection should be complete. A light and mirror will prove helpful for a thorough check. If a hose exhibits any of the above conditions, replace it with a new one.

2   Replacement steel and flexible brake lines are commonly available from dealer parts departments and auto parts stores. Do not, under any circumstrances, use anything other than genuine steel or approved flexible brake hoses as replacement items.

3   When installing the brake line, leave at least 19 mm (0.75 in) clearance between the line and any moving or vibrating parts.

4   When removing any brake line or hose flare-nut fitting, always use the proper flare-nut wrenches when loosening and tightening the connection (photo).

5   At the junction where a brake line meets a bracket supporting it and its connection, remove the spring clip with a pliers or vise-grip after loosening the connection (photo).

6   Steel brake lines are usually retained along their span with clips. Always remove these clips completely before removing any fixed brake line. Always replace these same clips when replacing a metal brake line as they provide support and keep the lines from vibrating which will fatigue and eventually break the line.

17.4 Disconnecting a brake line from a brake hose using flare nut wrenches

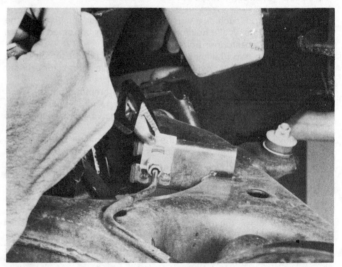

17.5 Remove the spring clip when changing a brake line secured to a bracket

18 Brake fluid replacement

1   Brake fluid absorbs moisture from air and excessive moisture content can diminish braking efficiency. Brake fluid deteriorates over a period of time and can pick up contaminants through leaks and corrosion. For these reasons, it is a good idea to flush the entire brake hydraulic system every 2 years or 25 000 miles and refill it with new fluid.

2   **Caution** *Brake fluid is highly corrosive so care must be taken when handling any containers to prevent damage to paint and other surfaces.* Begin the system flush by draining the master cylinder reservoir with a syringe or other suction device. Remove the reservoir as described in the master cylinder overhaul section in this Chapter. Clean the reservoir with a brake cleaning fluid or alcohol.

3   Open each bleeder screw (located at the four wheels) starting with the farthest (right rear) from the master cylinder. Pump the pedal until all of the fluid comes out, then close the bleeder valve and move on to the next closest until all four cylinders are empty.

4   Replace the master cylinder reservoir and refill it with *new* brake fluid (be sure to use the correct type of brake fluid).

5   Follow the instructions in the system bleeding section taking careful note to continue the process until only clean fluid with no air bubbles comes out of each bleeder screw.

19 Bleeding the brake hydraulic system

1   If the brake system has air in it, operation of the brake pedal will be spongy and imprecise. Air can enter the brake system whenever any part of the system is dismantled or if the fluid level in the master cylinder reservoir runs low. Air can also leak into the system through a fault too slight to allow fluid to leak out. In this case, it indicates that a general overhaul of the brake system is required.

2   To bleed the brakes, you will need an assistant to pump the brake pedal, a supply of new brake fluid, an empty glass jar, a plastic or vinyl tube which will fit over the bleeder nipple, and a wrench for the bleeder screw.

3   There are five locations at which the brake system is bled; the master cylinder; the front brake caliper assemblies; and the rear brake wheel cylinders.

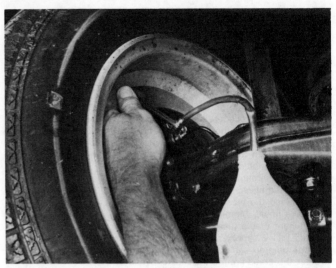

19.7 To bleed the brakes, loosen the bleeder valve on wheel cylinder or caliper with line submerged in plastic bottle of brake fluid

4   Check the fluid level at the master cylinder reservoir. Add fluid, if necessary, to bring the level up to the full mark. Use only the recommended brake fluid, and do not mix different types. Never use fluid from a container that has been standing uncapped. You will have to check the fluid level in the master cylinder reservoir often during the bleeding procedure. If the level drops too far, air will enter the system through the master cylinder.

5   Raise the vehicle and set it securely on jack stands.

6   Remove the bleeder screw cap from the wheel cylinder or caliper assembly that is being bled. If more than one wheel must be bled, start with the one farthest from the master cylinder.

7   Attach one end of the clear plastic or vinyl tube to the bleeder screw nipple and place the other end in the glass or plastic jar submerged in a small amount of clean brake fluid (photo).

8   Loosen the bleeder screw slightly, then tighten it to the point

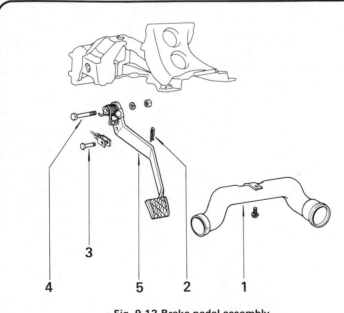

Fig. 9.12 Brake pedal assembly components (Sec 20)

1   Left air duct   4   Bolt
2   Spring clip   5   Brake pedal
3   Pin

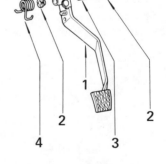

Fig. 9.13 Brake pedal pivot assembly components (Sec 20)

1   Brake pedal   3   Collar
2   Bushing   4   Pedal return spring

where it is snug yet easily loosened.

9   Have the assistant pump the brake pedal several times and hold it in the fully depressed position.

10 With pressure on the brake pedal, open the bleeder screw approximately one-half turn. As the brake fluid is flowing through the tube and into the jar, tighten the bleeder screw. Again, pump the brake pedal, hold it in the fully depressed position, and loosen the bleeder screw momentarily. Do not allow the brake pedal to be released with the bleeder screw in the open position.

11 Repeat the procedure until no air bubbles are visible in the brake fluid flowing through the tube. Be sure to check the brake fluid level in the master cylinder reservoir while performing the bleeding operation.

12 Fully tighten the bleeder screw, remove the plastic or vinyl tube and install the bleeder screw cap.

13 Follow the same procedure to bleed the other wheel cylinder or caliper assemblies.

14 To bleed the master cylinder, have the assistant pump and hold the brake pedal. Momentarily loosen the brake line fittings, one at a time, where they attach to the master cylinder. Any air in the master cylinder will escape when the fittings are loosened. Brake fluid will damage painted surfaces, so use paper towels or rags to cover and protect the areas around the master cylinder.

15 Check the brake fluid level in the master cylinder to make sure it is adequate, then test drive the vehicle and check for proper brake operation.

20 Brake pedal – removal and installation

1   Remove the screw holding the left side air duct under the dash and remove the air duct.

2   Remove the spring clip and the pin holding the brake booster fork to the pedal.

3   Disconnect the stoplight switch at the plastic connector. Pull it apart at the junction rather than with the wires.

4   Unscrew the pedal mounting bolt from the nut. The bolt is on the left side of the support bracket and the nut and washer are on the right.

5   The pedal assembly will now pull down and out of the mounting bracket.

6   Dismantle the remaining spring, bushings (1 per side) and collar. Inspect all pieces for wear or damage. Replace any worn parts with new ones.

7   Installation is the reverse of removal. Coat the bushings, collar, spring and pedal pin with a light grease before installation. Tighten the pedal mounting bolt to the correct torque.

Chapter 10 Electrical system

Contents

Specifications

Light bulbs

	Bulb No.	Wattage
Front turn signal lights	1157	27/8
Front parking and side marker lights		
1980	194	3.8
1981	194	5
Rear side marker lights	194	3.8
Rear turn signal lights	1156	27
Stop and tail lights	1157	27/8
Back-up lights	1156	27
License plate lights	89	7.5
Interior dome light	12V-10cp	10
Luggage compartment light	12V-3cp	5

Fuses

	Amperage rating
Headlights (1 fuse per side)	10
Engine	5
Turn	10
Stop	10
Tail light	15
Heater/Air Conditioner	20
Dome	5
Charge	5
Hazard/Horn	15
Engine charging system (1980)	20
Engine charging system (1981)	10
Wiper	20
Cigar lighter/clock	10
Radio	5

Torque specifications

Steering column-to-instrument panel retaining bolts	22 to 32 ft-lb (3.0 to 4.5 k-gm)

1 General information

1   This Chapter covers the repair and service procedures for the various lighting and electrical components not associated with the engine, as well as general information on troubleshooting the vehicle's various electrical circuits. Information on the battery, alternator, distributor and starter motor can be found in Chapter 5. Additional procedures involving body lighting can be found in Chapter 12.

2   The electrical system is of the 12-volt, negative ground type with power supplied by a lead/acid-type battery which is charged by the alternator.

3   Electrical components located in the dashboard do not use ground wires or straps, but rather use grounding provisions which are integrated in the printed circuit mounted behind the instrument cluster.

4   It should be noted that whenever portions of the electrical system are worked on, the negative battery cable should be disconnected to prevent electrical shorts and/or fires.

2 Electrical troubleshooting – general information

1   The basic tools needed for electrical troubleshooting include a circuit tester or voltmeter (a 12-volt bulb with a set of test leads can also be used), a continuity tester (which includes a bulb, battery and set of test leads) and a jumper wire, preferably with a circuit breaker incorporated, which can be used to bypass electrical components.

2   Voltage checks should be performed if a circuit is not functioning properly. Connect one lead of a circuit tester to either the negative battery terminal or a known good ground. Connect the other lead to a connector in the circuit being tested, preferably nearest to the battery or fuse. If the bulb of the tester goes on voltage is reaching that point, which means the part of the circuit between that connector and the battery is problem-free. Continue checking along the circuit in the same fashion. When you reach a point where no voltage is present, the problem lies between there and the last good test point. Most of the time the problem is due to a loose connection. Keep in mind that some circuits only receive voltage when the ignition key is in the 'Accessory' or 'Run' position.

3   A method of finding shorts in a circuit is to remove the fuse and connect a test light or voltmeter in its place to the fuse terminals. There should be no load in the circuit. Move the wiring harness from side to side while watching the test light. If the bulb goes on, there is a short to ground somewhere in that area, probably where insulation has rubbed off a wire. The same test can be performed on other components of the circuit, including the switch.

4   A ground check should be done to see if a component is grounded properly. Disconnect the battery and connect one lead of a self-powered test light such as a continuity tester to a known good ground. Connect the other lead to the wire or ground connection being tested. If the bulb goes on, the ground is good. If the bulb does not go on, the ground is not good.

5   A continuity check is performed to see if a circuit, section of circuit or individual component is passing electricity through it properly. Disconnect the battery, and connect one lead of a self-powered test light such as a continuity tester to one end of the circuit being tested and the other lead to the other end of the circuit. If the bulb goes on, there is continuity, which means the circuit is passing electricity through it properly. Switches can be checked in the same way.

6   If several components or circuits fail at one time, chances are the fault lies in the fuse or ground connection, as several circuits often are routed through the same fuse and ground connections.

7   Prior to any electrical troubleshooting, always visually check the condition of the wires and connections of the problem circuit. Often a connection is loose or corroded, and this simple check is all that's needed to pinpoint the problem.

3 Fuses – general information

1   The electrical circuits of the vehicle are protected by a combination of fuses, relays, and fusible links.

2   The fuse box is located underneath the dash on the left side of the vehicle. Access to the fuses is achieved by simply removing the cover of the box.

3   An additional combination fuse and relay block is located under the hood on the left side inner fenderwell near the spring tower. See Section 4 for more information on relays.

4   Each of the fuses is designed to protect a specific circuit, as is identified on the fuse box.

5   If an electrical component has failed, your first check should be the fuse. A fuse which has 'blown' can be readily identified by inspecting the element inside the glass tube. If this metal element is broken the fuse is inoperable and should be replaced with a new one.

6   When removing and installing fuses, it is important that metal objects are not used to pry the fuse in or out of the holder. Plastic fuse pullers are available for this purpose.

7   It is also important that the correct fuse be installed. The different electrical circuits need varying amounts of protection, indicated by the amperage rating on the fuse. A fuse with too low a rating will blow prematurely, while a fuse with too high a rating may not blow soon enough to avoid serious damage.

8   At no time should the fuse be bypassed by using metal or foil. Serious damage to the electrical system could result.

9   If the replacement fuse immediately fails, do not replace it with another until the cause of the problem is isolated and corrected. In most cases this will be a short circuit in the wiring system caused by a broken or deteriorated wire.

4 Relays – general information

1   The purpose of the electrical relays is to transfer the high current load required by the ignition system or choke; lights; heater blower; rear window defogger; wipers; charge light; and the A/C system. A low amperage switch is used to activate the relay which in turn provides the high amperage current needed by the above-listed accessories and systems. The relay thus eliminates the necessity of carrying a high amperage current from the source (battery and charging system) to the dash and back to the electrical unit.

2   The relays are located in the underhood combination fuse/relay box or under the driver's kick panel of the passenger compartment.

5 Fusible links – general information and replacement

1   In addition to the fuses, the wiring system incorporates fusible links for overload protection. These links are used in circuits with heavy current draw which are not normally fused, such as the ignition switch, cooling fan, and A/C cooling fan (if so equipped).

2   Although the fusible links appear to be physically of a heavier gauge than the wire they are protecting, they actually are of a smaller gauge. The heavy insulation around the fusible link causes this appearance. The locations of the fusible links are; between the battery and the ignition switch, between the battery and the ignition relay, between the ignition relay and the cooling fan, and between the alternator feed line and the A/C cooling fan when so equipped.

3   A melted (blown) fusible link can be detected by a swelling or discoloration of the insulation. If the fusible link is suspected, but does not appear discolored or swelled, check it for continuity. If no continuity exists, the fusible link is bad.

4   Replace the link with one of the same exact rating only after the cause of failure has been found and corrected. If a fusible link has melted, a current of 100 amps or more has been flowing through the circuit, so it is very important to locate and correct the fault before replacing the link. Check very carefully for a dead short in the wiring.

5   To replace a fusible link, follow the procedure listed below:

   a)   *Disconnect the negative battery cable.*
   b)   *Disconnect the fusible link from the source.*
   c)   *Cut the damaged fusible link out of the wiring system. Do this just behind the connector.*
   d)   *Strip the insulation from the circuit wiring approximately ½-inch.*
   e)   *Position the connector on the new fusible link and crimp it into place in the wiring circuit.*
   f)   *Use resin core solder at each end of the new link to obtain a good solder joint.*
   g)   *Wrap the soldered joints with electrical tape. No exposed wiring should show.*
   h)   *Connect the fusible link at the source and reconnect the negative battery cable. Test the circuit for proper operation.*

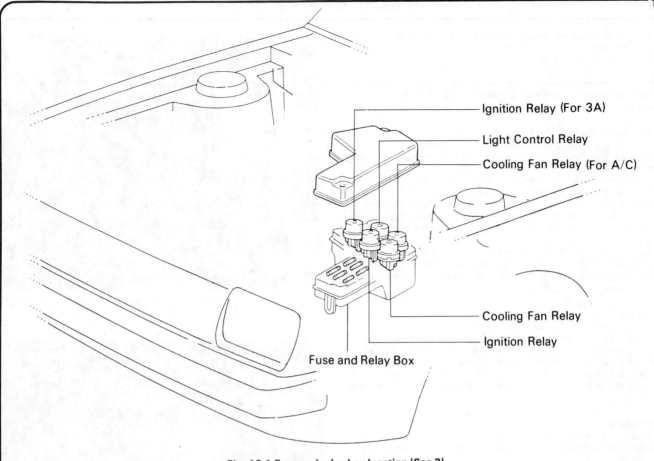

Ignition Relay (For 3A)

Light Control Relay

Cooling Fan Relay (For A/C)

Cooling Fan Relay

Ignition Relay

Fuse and Relay Box

Fig. 10.1 Fuse and relay box location (Sec 3)

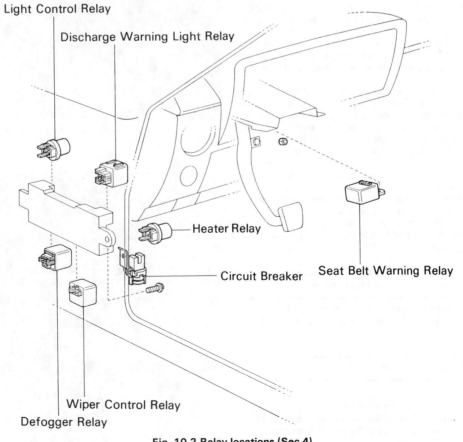

Light Control Relay

Discharge Warning Light Relay

Heater Relay

Circuit Breaker

Seat Belt Warning Relay

Wiper Control Relay

Defogger Relay

Fig. 10.2 Relay locations (Sec 4)

i)   As an added precaution, never cover the fusible link with vinyl
     electrical tape. If the link is covered, the fact that it has blown
     may go unnoticed.

6   Ignition switch – removal, inspection and installation

Removal
1   Disconnect the negative battery cable.
2   Remove the lower steering column switch cover.
3   Remove the three steering column bracket retaining bolts and
alignment wedge (photo).
4   Lower the steering column and remove the upper switch cover.
5   Turn the ignition key to the Accessory position.
6   Fashion a tool from a small diameter wire or a large paper clip to
use as a switch retaining pin release. Push in the retaining pin release
(photo) with the tool you have just made and withdraw the lock
cylinder.
7   Remove the ignition switch mounting screw. Pull the switch out
and disconnect it from the wiring connector. Remove the screw
retaining the wiring loom to the switch body and the screw retaining
the key warning unit (photos).

Inspection
8   Remove the steering column lower switch cover.
9   Disconnect the ignition switch at the wiring connector (photo).
10 Using the accompanying illustration, identify the terminals according to the chart and test them for continuity as the chart indicates. This
will require an ohmmeter or a self-powered test lamp. If the switch
fails the continuity test, in any position, it will need to be replaced with
a new one.

Installation
11 Connect the switch to the connector.
12 Install the switch into its recessed housing, making sure it is lined
up properly.
13 Install the ignition switch mounting screw.
14 Install the lock cylinder into the ignition switch housing. Notice
that the tang on the back of the lock cylinder fits the slot on the back
of the ignition switch (photo).
15 Install the upper switch cover.
16 Center the steering column shaft in the bracket by using special
service tool No. 09612-10070 or by making an alignment shim as
follows.
17 To make an alignment shim, use light cardboard or heavy paper
like the type used for gasket material. Cut a long narrow strip of this
material and wrap it around the steering column post until it fills the
recess designed for the steering column. Insert the wedge and the
three fasteners securing the steering column to the under dash.
18 Lightly tighten the three fasteners until the steering column is
retained.
19 Withdraw the roll of alignment paper (or the alignment tool) at this
time.
20 Finally torque the three retaining bolts for the steering column.
21 Install the steering column lower switch cover.
22 Install the negative battery cable to the battery.
23 Test the ignition switch in all positions to see that it is functioning
correctly.

7   Neutral safety switch – removal and installation

The Neutral safety switch found on vehicles equipped with an
automatic transmission can be removed, adjusted and replaced as
described in Chapter 7.

8   Light bulbs – replacement

Headlights
1   Remove the trim bezel from the headlight area.
2   Remove the four headlight retaining ring mounting screws (photo).
3   Pull the headlamp assembly away from the vehicle and unplug the
connector at the rear.
4   Installation is the reverse of removal. Make sure that the connec-

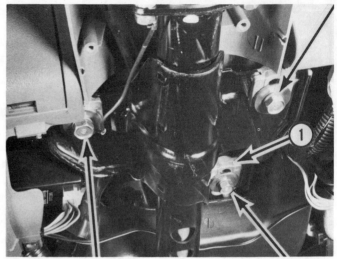
6.3 Steering column retaining bolts (arrows) and alignment wedge (1)
locations

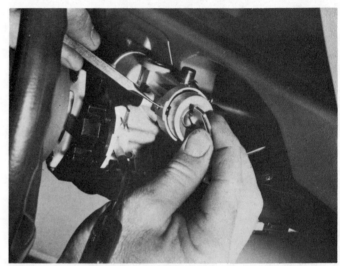
6.6 Removing the lock cylinder with a tool inserted in the retaining pin
release

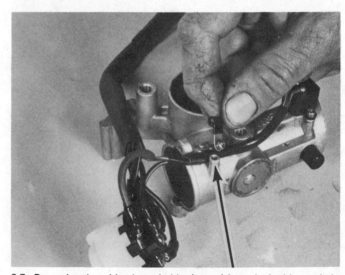
6.7a Removing the wiring loom holder (arrow) from the ignition switch
body

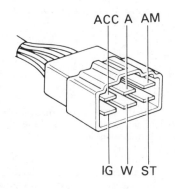

Terminal (Wire color) ⟍ Switch position	AM (BR)	ACC (LR)	IG (BY)	ST (BW)	W (GW)	A (B)
Lock					●	●
ACC	●	●			●	●
On	●	●	●			
Start	●		●	●		

Fig. 10.3 Ignition switch terminals and test positions (Sec 6)

6.7b Removing the key warning unit (arrow) from the switch body

6.11 Aligning the lock cylinder tang (1) with the ignition switch groove (2)

8.2 Headlight retaining ring screw locations (arrows)

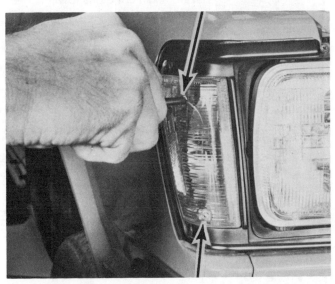

8.14 Removing the front side marker lens screws

tor is correctly attached at the rear of the new headlight unit. Test the headlight in both the low and high beam positions before assembling the final attaching hardware.

Combination lights
5   The rear combination lights consist of the rear turn signals, tail or running lights, brake lights and back-up lights. To replace the combination lights on two and four door vehicles, remove the bulb access cover with a screwdriver.
6   Turn the bulb socket and remove it from the lamp assembly.
7   Remove the bulb from the bulb socket by turning counterclockwise while pushing in slightly.
8   Installation is the reverse of removal.
9   To replace a combination bulb on three door vehicles, remove the access cover with a screwdriver or similar tool.
10 The bulb socket and light bulb are removed in the same manner as in steps 6 and 7 for two and four door vehicles.

Front turn signals
11 The front turn signals, located beneath the front bumper, must have the lens removed for access.
12 Push the bulb into its socket and turn it counterclockwise for removal.
13 Installation is the reverse of removal.

Side marker lights
14 Remove the lens retaining screws and remove the lens (photo).
15 Pull the small bulb from its socket.
16 Installation is the reverse of removal.
17 To replace the rear side marker bulbs, access is gained through the trunk or rear cargo area depending on the model of the vehicle.
18 The bulb socket is twisted in a counterclockwise manner and pulled from the housing.
19 Pull the lamp from the socket assembly.
20 Installation is the reverse of removal.

License plate light
21 On two and four door vehicles, remove the lamp assembly mounting nuts.
22 Remove the lamp assembly from the outside of the vehicle.
23 The lens retaining screws can now be removed.
24 Remove the lens from the housing.
25 Push the bulb in slightly and turn counterclockwise for removal.
26 Installation is the reverse of removal.
27 On three door vehicles, the rear inner cargo area cover must be removed to gain access to the lamp assembly mounting nuts. See

Chapter 12 for instructions on this procedure. Once the panel is removed, the license plate lamp is removed as in two and four door vehicles.

Interior light
28 Pry the lens from the housing.
29 Remove the bulb from the two clips.
30 Installation is the reverse of removal.

Luggage compartment light (three door models only)
31 Remove the lens retaining screws and remove the lens.
32 Pry the bulb from the two mounting clips.
33 Installation is the reverse of removal.

---

9   Combination switch – inspection, removal, disassembly, reassembly and installation

Note: *Refer to Fig. 10.4 for combination switch components and locations.*

Inspection
Note: *All terminals are shown from the component side of the connector.*
1   After unplugging the switch connector (photo), inspect the light control switch and the headlight dimmer switch by checking for battery voltage at terminals T, H and HF of the connector.
2   Check for continuity between terminals EL and ED and the body ground.
3   Inspect the switch continuity at the wire terminals in the positions shown in the accompanying illustration.
4   Do the same for the headlight dimmer switch.
5   To inspect the hazard or turn signal switch, check for battery voltage at terminal B2.
6   Turn the ignition switch to On. Now check for battery voltage at terminal B.
7   Check for continuity between terminals TL and TR and the body ground.
8   Check for switch continuity in the following positions at the various terminals as shown in the accompanying illustration.
9   To inspect the wiper switch, turn the ignition switch to On and check for battery voltage at terminals B and EW.
10 Check for continuity between terminal EW and ground.
11 Check the switch continuity according to the position and terminal as shown in the accompanying illustration. Notice that two different test charts are provided, depending on the type of wiper system your vehicle is equipped with.

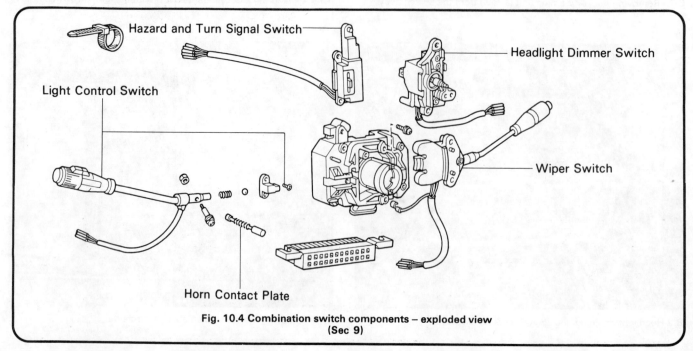

Fig. 10.4 Combination switch components – exploded view
(Sec 9)

Light Control Switch

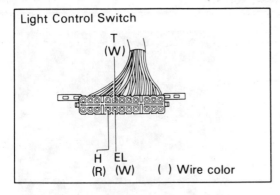

T
(W)

H   EL
(R) (W)   ( ) Wire color

Headlight Dimmer Switch

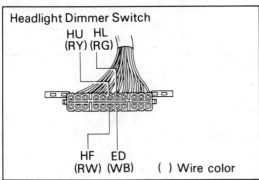

HU   HL
(RY) (RG)

HF   ED
(RW) (WB)   ( ) Wire color

Light Control Switch

Terminal (Wire color) / Switch position	T (B)	H (R)	EL (W)
Off			
Tail	●		●
Head	●	●	●

Headlight Dimmer Switch

Terminal (Wire color) / Switch position	ED (WB)	HU (RY)	HL (RG)	HF (RW)
Headlight F	●	●		●
Headlight L	●		●	
Headlight U	●	●		

Fig. 10.5 Light switch terminals and test positions (Sec 9)

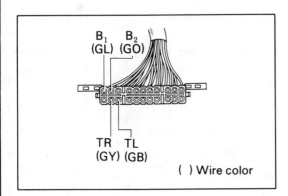

B₁   B₂
(GL) (GO)

TR   TL
(GY) (GB)   ( ) Wire color

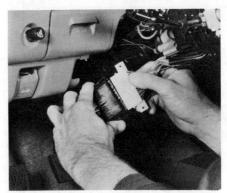

9.1 Disconnecting the combination switch wiring connector

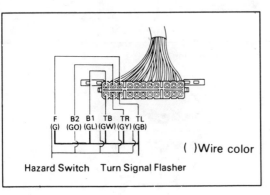

F   B2   B1   TB   TR   TL
(G) (GO) (GL) (GW) (GY) (GB)

( )Wire color

Hazard Switch   Turn Signal Flasher

Terminal (Wire color) / Switch position		TL (GB)	TB (GW)	TR (GY)	B₁ (GL)	F (G)	B₂ (GO)
Turn signal	R		●	●	●	●	
	N				●	●	
	L	●	●		●	●	
Hazard	ON	●	●	●		●	●

Fig. 10.6 Hazard and turn signal switch terminals and test positions (Sec 9)

Removal and installation

12　Due to the skill level required to dismantle the combination switch, often times it is replaced as an entire unit. If however, you wish to save some money, follow the steps listed below to replace only the segment of the combination switch (turn signal, wiper/washer or light) which needs replacement.

13　Remove the steering wheel as described in Chapter 11.

14　Remove the lower switch cover.

15　Remove the lower dash finish panel.

16　Remove the two steering column retaining bolts on the passenger side (including the shim). Loosen the driver's side steering column retaining bolt but don't remove it.

17　Remove the upper switch cover.

18　Remove the combination switch retaining screws (photo).

19　Unplug the wiring connector for the combination switch.

20　Pull the combination switch off the steering shaft.

21　Installation is the reverse of removal. Be sure to tighten the steering column retaining bolts to the proper torque.

9.18 Combination switch retaining screw locations (arrows)

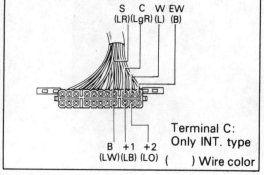

(d)　Inspect the switch continuity.

[MIST type]

Switch position \ Terminal (Wire color)	B (LW)	+1 (LB)	+2 (LO)	S (LR)	W (L)	EW (B)
Mist	●	●				
Off		●		●		
Lo	●	●				
Hi	●		●			
Washer					●	●

[INT. type]

Switch position on \ Terminal (Wire color)	B (LW)	+1 (LB)	+2 (LO)	S (LR)	C (LgR)	W (L)	EW (B)
Off		●		●			
Int.		●		●	●		●
Lo	●	●					
Hi	●		●				
Washer						●	●

Fig. 10.7 Washer and wiper switch terminals and test positions (Sec 9)

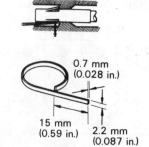

0.7 mm (0.028 in.)

15 mm (0.59 in.)　2.2 mm (0.087 in.)

Fig. 10.8 Tool used to bend the lugs in the wiring connector during removal (Sec 9)

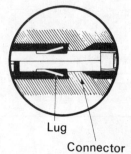

Lug

Connector

Fig. 10.9 Pushing the wiring in slightly to clear the retainer lugs (Sec 9)

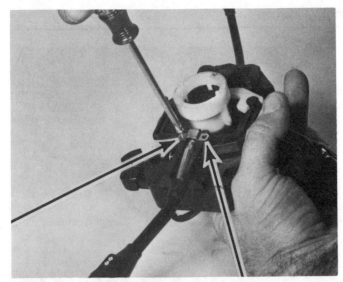

9.22 Screws (arrows) retaining the light control switch

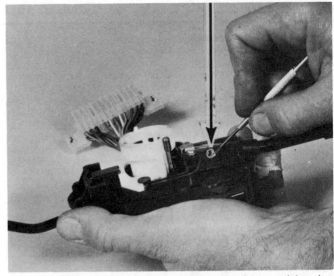

9.23a C—clip being removed from the light switch lever retaining pin

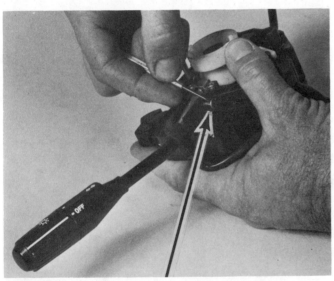

9.23b Removing the light switch lever retaining pin (arrow)

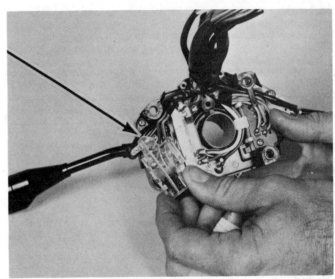

9.24 Removing the insulating cover (arrow) that shields the headlight dimmer switch

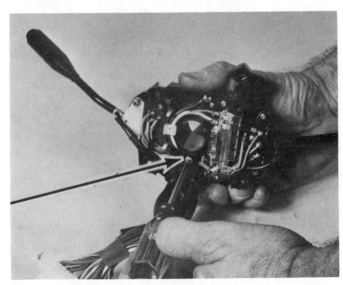

9.26 Removing the wire loom retaining screw and clamp

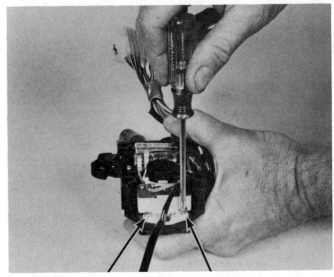

9.30 Removing the screws retaining the wiper switch

Disassembly and reassembly

22 Remove the screws retaining the light control switch (photo).
23 Remove the C-clip and pin for the light control switch (photos).
24 Remove the insulating cover that shields the headlight dimmer switch (photo).
25 Remove the screws retaining the headlight dimmer switch. Remove the headlight dimmer switch.
26 Remove the screw retaining the wire looms (photo).
27 Withdraw the prongs for the individual switches from the bulk wiring connector by fashioning a tool as shown in the accompanying illustration. Push the wiring and the prong into the connector slightly to clear the lugs. Use the tool you have just made to bend the lugs so that the prong and wire may be withdrawn from the connector.
28 Remove the screw retaining the hazard and turn signal switch. Remove the hazard and turn signal switch.
29 Remove the prongs from the bulk connector for the hazard and turn signal switch as described in step 2.
30 Remove the screws for the wiper and washer switch (photo). Remove the wiper and washer control switch.
31 Withdraw the prongs from the bulk connector as described above.
32 Installation of all of the above switches, except for the light control switch, is the reverse of removal. Make sure the lugs on the individual wiring prongs are bent out slightly so they will retain the prong when pushed into the connector.
33 To replace the light control switch, first insert the handle into the switch with the pin and clip.
34 Lay the bracket into place with the ball in its bottom slot.
35 Slide the ball into the handle end and snap the clip over the top of the switch for screw installation.
36 Install the screw for the light switch.

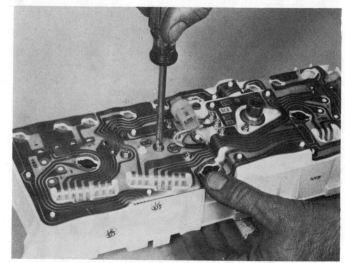

10.8 Removing the printed circuit retaining screws

10 Instrument cluster/printed circuit – removal and installation

Instrument cluster

1 Disconnect the negative battery cable from the battery.
2 Remove the upper dashboard housing covering the cluster (Chapter 12).
3 Reach behind the cluster and disconnect the speedometer cable and the cluster wiring harness.
4 Remove the cluster retaining screws.
5 Remove the cluster.
6 Installation is the reverse of removal. Make sure that the speedometer cable engages the speedometer correctly. Make sure that the wiring connector is put together and the retaining clips are snapped.

Printed circuit

7 Remove all light bulbs from the back of the instrument cluster.
8 Remove the retaining screws for the printed circuit (photo).
9 Remove the nuts retaining the gauges to the instrument cluster housing (photo).
10 Gently pry the printed circuit away from the plastic tabs on the housing in each position until it is fully removed (photo).
11 Install the printed circuit over the plastic mounting tabs in each position, being careful not to break or tear the thin copper strands.
12 The remaining steps are the reverse of removal.

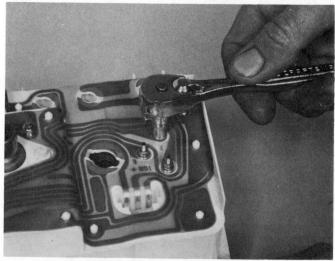

10.9 Removing the nuts retaining the gauges to the instrument cluster

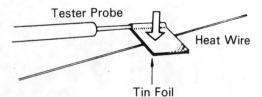

Fig. 10.10 Winding a piece of foil around the test probe for better continuity and protection of the defogger wire (Sec 11)

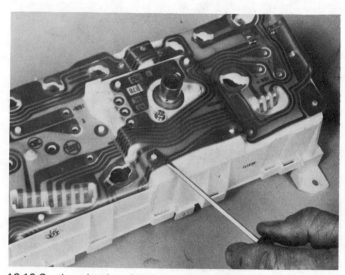

10.10 Gently prying the printed circuit from the instrument cluster housing

11 Rear window defogger – inspection

1   Visually inspect the entire circuit of the rear window defogger for broken wires. If this condition exists, special repair techniques will have to be applied by a glass or electrical specialist.

2   Inspect the voltage at the center of each wire with the defogger switch On. Use a voltmeter for this step. Wind a piece of aluminum foil around the tip of the negative probe for this process. If there are ten bolts present at the wire, there is a wire broken between the center of the wire and the positive end of the wire.

3   If there is no voltage, the wire is broken between the center of the wire and the ground.

4   To check for the wire break, use a voltmeter and place the positive lead on the defogger positive terminal.

5   Place the negative lead with the aluminum foil against the defogger wire at the positive terminal and move the lead toward the negative side.

6   The point where the voltmeter changes from zero to several volts, is the place where the wire is broken.

7   If the wire is not broken, the voltmeter will indicate 12 volts at the positive end of the heat wire and gradually decrease to zero as the meter probe is moved to the negative side.

8   The rear window defogger system also has a resettable circuit breaker located under the left hand kick panel. Remove the circuit breaker and insert a needle into the reset hole. Check for continuity between both terminals of the circuit breaker. If there is still no continuity after resetting, the circuit breaker must be replaced with a new one.

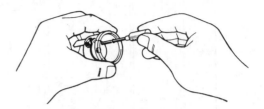

Fig. 10.11 Resetting the rear window de-fogger circuit breaker (Sec 11)

12 Radio – removal and installation

1   Remove the knobs from the radio controls.

2   Remove the face plate from the radio.

3   Remove the two retaining screws holding the radio in place.

4   Pull the radio forward, then disconnect the antenna and the wiring connectors at the rear.

5   Remove the radio from the dashboard.

6   Replacement is the reverse of removal.

Wiring diagrams commence overleaf

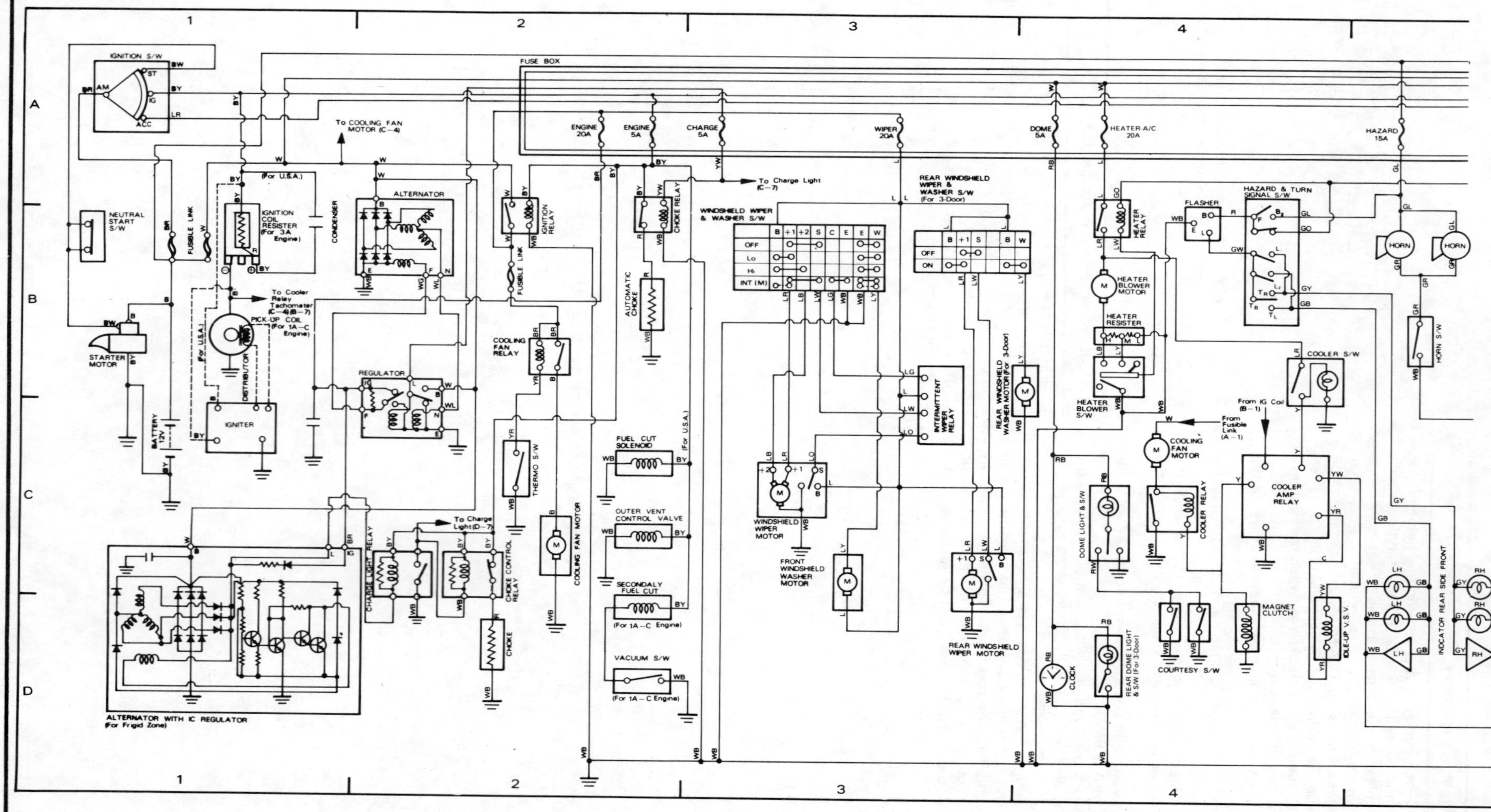

CONTINUED NEXT PAGE

HAZARD 15A

HORN S/W

HORN

HAZARD & TURN SIGNAL S/W

FLASHER

HEATER A/C 20A

HEATER RELAY

HEATER BLOWER MOTOR

HEATER RESISTER

HEATER BLOWER S/W

COOLER S/W

From IG Coil (B-1)

From Fusible Link (A-1)

COOLER AMP RELAY

COOLING FAN MOTOR

COOLER RELAY

MAGNET CLUTCH

IDLE-UP V.S.V

INDICATOR REAR SIDE FRONT

COURTESY S/W

REAR DOME LIGHT & S/W (For 3-Door)

DOME LIGHT & S/W

CLOCK

DOME 5A

REAR WINDSHIELD WIPER & WASHER S/W (For 3-Door)

REAR WINDSHIELD WASHER MOTOR (For 3-Door)

INTERMITTENT WIPER RELAY

REAR WINDSHIELD WIPER MOTOR

WIPER 20A

WINDSHIELD WIPER & WASHER S/W

FRONT WINDSHIELD WASHER MOTOR

WINDSHIELD WIPER MOTOR

To Charge Light (C-7)

CHARGE 5A

ENGINE 5A

ENGINE 20A

CHOKE RELAY

AUTOMATIC CHOKE

FUEL CUT SOLENOID

OUTER VENT CONTROL VALVE

SECONDARY FUEL CUT (For 1A-C Engine)

VACUUM S/W (For 1A-C Engine)

(For USA)

FUSE BOX

IGNITION RELAY

FUSIBLE LINK

COOLING FAN RELAY

COOLING FAN MOTOR

THERMO S/W

CHOKE CONTROL RELAY

CHOKE

To Charge Light (C-7)

To Cooling Fan Motor (C-4)

ALTERNATOR

CONDENSER

REGULATOR

CHARGE LIGHT RELAY

ALTERNATOR WITH IC REGULATOR (For Frigid Zone)

IGNITION S/W

NEUTRAL START S/W

FUSIBLE LINK

BATTERY 12V

STARTER MOTOR

IGNITION COIL RESISTER (For 3A Engine)

DISTRIBUTOR

IGNITER

PICK-UP COIL (For 1A-C Engine)

Tachometer To Cooler Relay (C-4B-7)

(For USA)

Fig. 10.12 1980 Wiring diagram

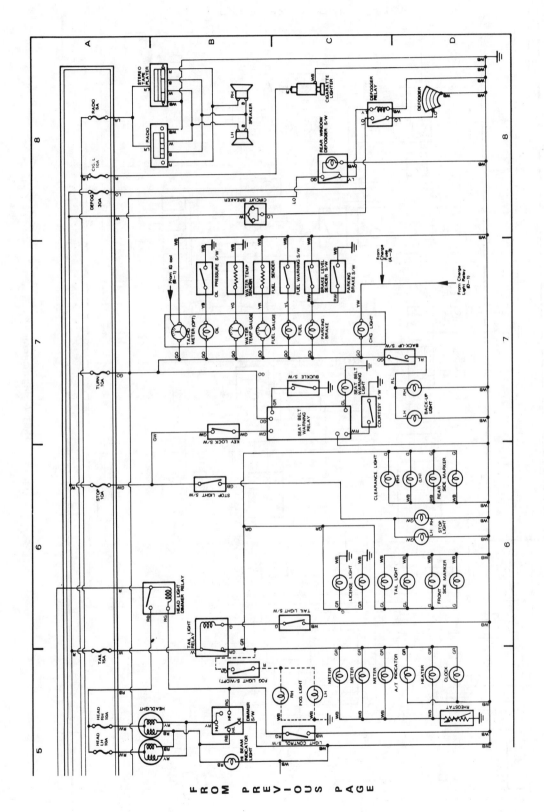

Fig. 10.13 1980 Wiring diagram (continued)

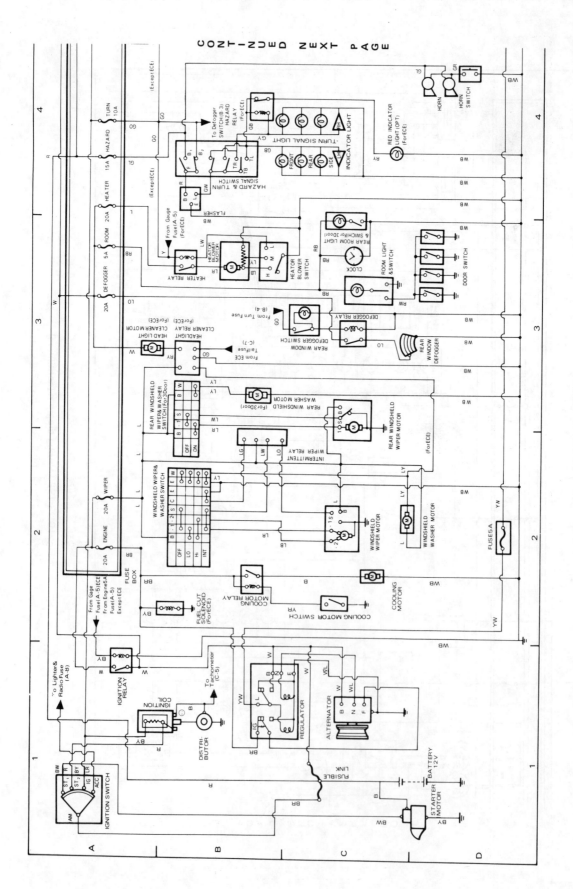

Fig. 10.14 1981 Wiring diagram

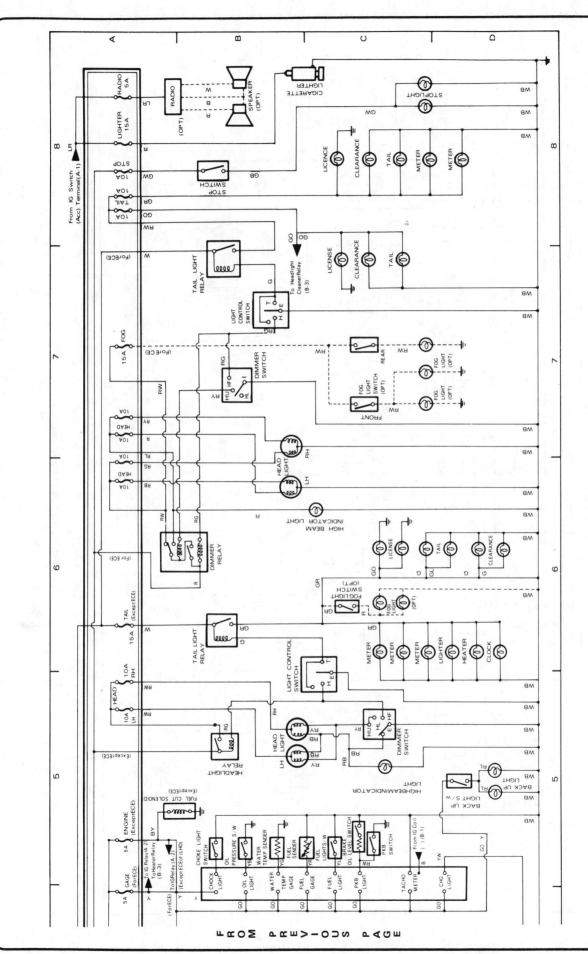

Fig. 10.15 1981 Wiring diagram (continued)

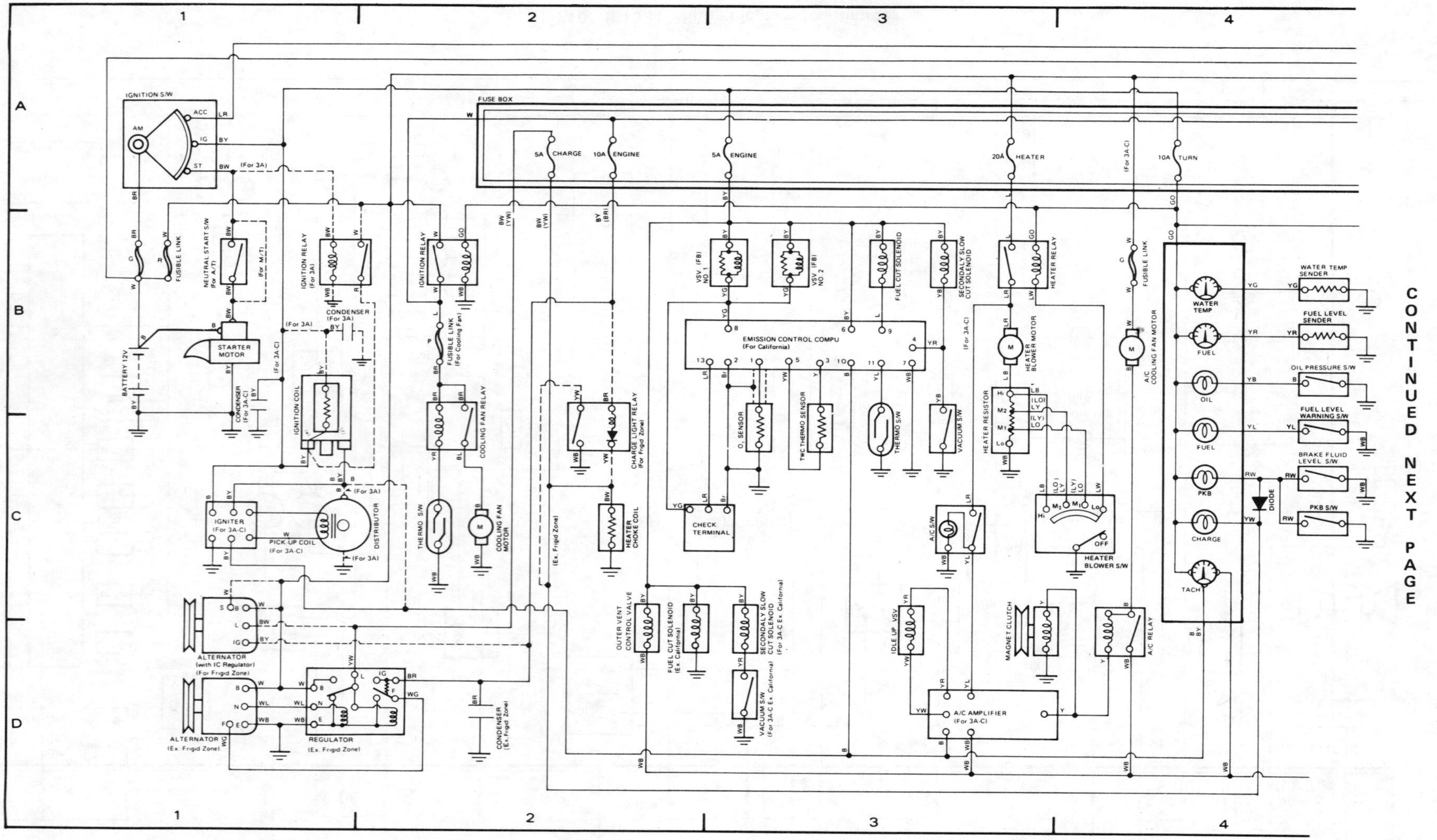

CONTINUED NEXT PAGE

Fig. 10.16 1982 Wiring diagram

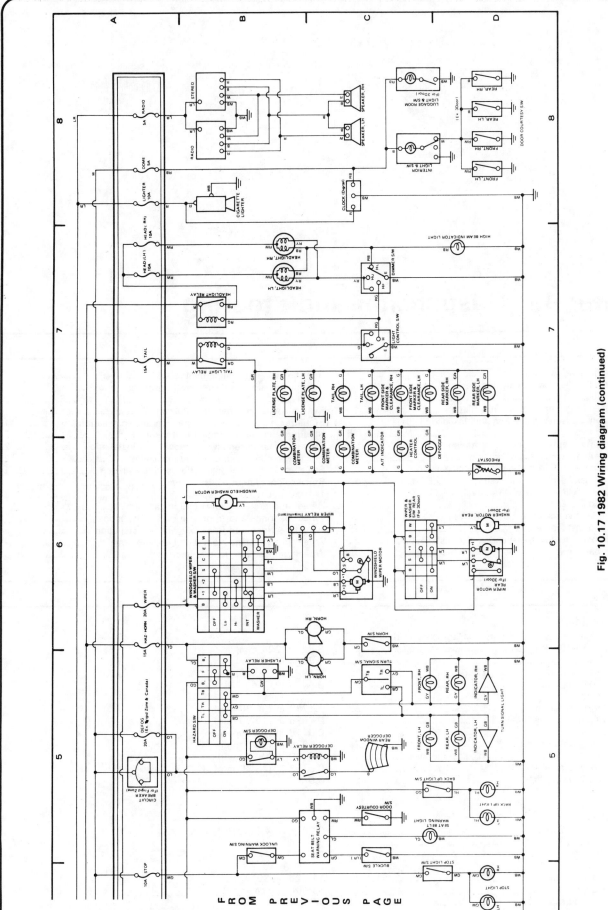

Fig. 10.17 1982 Wiring diagram (continued)

Chapter 11 Suspension and steering

Contents

Specifications

Front suspension

Front vehicle height at suspension arm bushing center with:
  155-13 or 6.15-13 4PR tires .... 8.82 in (224 mm)
  145 SR-13 tires .... 8.50 in (216 mm)
  155 SR-12 tires .... 8.19 in (208 mm)
  165/70 SR-13 tires .... 8.54 in (217 mm)
Front shock absorber
  Piston outer diameter limit .... 1.1732 in (29.80 mm)
  Piston rod outer diameter limit .... 0.7835 in (19.90 mm)
  Piston rod runout limit .... 0.0118 in (0.30 mm)
  Cylinder inner diameter limit .... 1.1929 in (30.3 mm)
  Cylinder runout limit .... 0.0039 in (0.10 mm)
  Rod guide inner diameter limit .... 0.9193 in (23.35 mm)
Front balljoint vertical play limit .... 0.0 in

Steering

Front wheel alignment
  Toe-in .... 0.08 ± 0.04 in (2 ± 1 mm)
  Camber .... 30' ± 30'
  Left-to-right error .... 30'
  Caster .... 2° 10' ± 30'
  King pin inclination .... 11° 20' ± 30'
  Steering angle inside .... 33° (reference value)
  Steering angle outside .... 34 to 36°
  Side slip .... less than 0.118 in /3.3 ft
                                                    (less than 3.0 mm/m)

Front wheel bearing preload spacer sizes
No. 1 .... 0.3161 in (8.03 mm)
No. 2 .... 0.3177 in (8.07 mm)
No. 3 .... 0.3193 in (8.11 mm)
No. 4 .... 0.3209 in (8.15 mm)
No. 5 .... 0.3224 in (8.19 mm)
No. 6 .... 0.3240 in (8.23 mm)
No. 7 .... 0.3256 in (8.27 mm)
No. 8 .... 0.3272 in (8.31 mm)
No. 9 .... 0.3287 in (8.35 mm)
No. 10 .... 0.3303 in (8.39 mm)
No. 11 .... 0.3319 in (8.43 mm)
No. 12 .... 0.3335 in (8.47 mm)
No. 13 .... 0.3350 in (8.51 mm)
No. 14 .... 0.3366 in (8.55 mm)
No. 15 .... 0.3382 in (8.59 mm)
No. 16 .... 0.3398 in (8.63 mm)
No. 17 .... 0.3413 in (8.67 mm)
No. 18 .... 0.3429 in (8.71 mm)
No. 19 .... 0.3445 in (8.75 mm)
No. 20 .... 0.3461 in (8.79 mm)
Steering wheel freeplay .... 0 to 1.18 in (0 to 30 mm)
Steering rack runout limit .... 0.0059 in (0.15 mm)
Steering pinion bearing preload .... 1.3 to 2.2 in-lb (1.5 to 2.5 kg-cm)
Steering rack guide spring cap installation
  1st step (tightening torque) .... 18 ft-lb (2.5 kg-m)
  2nd step (loosen cap) .... 25 to 30°
Total turning preload .... 8.7 to 11.3 in-lb (10 to 13 kg-cm) maximum
                                                                                       43 in-lb (5 kg-cm) minimum
Steering rack stroke .... 4.88 in (124 mm)

Rear suspension
Rear vehicle height at suspension arm bushing center with:
  155-13 or 6.15-13 4PR tires .... 10.47 in (266 mm)
  145 SR-13 tires .... 10.16 in (258 mm)
  155 SR-12 tires .... 9.84 in (250 mm)
  165/70 SR-13 tires .... 10.20 in (259 mm)
Rear wheel alignment
  Toe-in .... 0 ± 0.04 in (0 ± 1 mm)
  Camber .... 0 ± 30'
  Side slip .... less than 0.118 in/3.3 ft (less than 3.0 mm/m)

Torque specifications

	ft-lb	(kg-m)
Shock absorber piston rod-to-front suspension support	29 to 39	(4.0 to 5.5)
MacPherson strut upper support assembly-to-body	15 to 21	(2.0 to 3.0)
Shock absorber ring nut (with special service tool)	66 to 97	(9.0 to 13.5)
Shock absorber ring nut (without special service tool)	73 to 108	(10.0 to 15.0)
Lower suspension arm-to-strut bar retaining bolts	29 to 39	(4.0 to 5.5)
Steering knuckle-to-balljoint retaining bolt	40 to 52	(5.5 to 7.2)
Lower suspension arm-to-crossmember retaining bolt	51 to 65	(7.0 to 9.0)
Strut bar-to-strut bar bracket	55 to 79	(7.5 to 11.0)
Stabilizer bar-to-lower suspension arm retaining bolt	11 to 15	(1.4 to 2.2)
Stabilizer arm bracket-to-body retaining bolt	22 to 32	(3.0 to 4.5)
Front crossmember-to-frame retaining bolt	30 to 39	(4.1 to 5.5)
Tie rod end-to-knuckle arm retaining nut	37 to 50	(5.0 to 7.0)
Wheel bearing locknut	73 to 108	(10.0 to 15.0)
Engine front mount-to-crossmember retaining nut	26 to 39	(3.5 to 5.5)
Steering gear assembly-to-crossmember retaining bolts	22 to 32	(3.0 to 4.5)
Tie rod end clamp bolt	11 to 14	(1.5 to 2.0)
Steering knuckle stopper locknut	19 to 32	(2.5 to 4.5)
Rear shock absorber-to-body retaining nut	14 to 22	(1.9 to 3.1)
Rear shock absorber-to-rear suspension arm retaining bolt	11 to 15	(1.5 to 2.2)
Rear stabilizer bar-to-suspension arm retaining nut	11 to 15	(1.4 to 2.2)
Rear stabilizer bar bracket-to-suspension crossmember retaining bolt	11 to 15	(1.5 to 2.2)
Rear brake backing plate assembly-to-suspension arm retaining bolt ..	22 to 32	(3.0 to 4.5)
Rear suspension arm-to-rear crossmember pivot retaining bolt	73 to 97	(10.0 to 13.5)
Rear crossmember-to-body retaining bolts	58 to 72	(8.0 to 10.0)
Steering column tube-to-instrument panel retaining nuts	22 to 32	(3.0 to 4.5)
Steering wheel-to-steering shaft retaining nut	22 to 28	(3.0 to 4.0)
Intermediate shaft-to-steering assembly and steering shaft clamp bolt	22 to 28	(3.0 to 4.0)
Tie rod-to-steering rack end	11 to 14	(1.5 to 2.0)

1 General information

The Tercel has four wheel independent suspension for good handling and ride qualities. All four corners of the vehicle are suspended by coil springs and damped by shock absorbers. The front shock absorbers are incorporated in MacPherson strut assemblies. MacPherson struts are a lightweight, economical, space-saving suspension system especially useful in a vehicle of the Tercel's type.

Steering is accomplished through a rack and pinion system with tie rods connected to the front spindle assemblies. Body roll is controlled front and rear through the use of anti-sway bars. Removable crossmembers bolted to the body shell provide the framework on which the suspension components are supported.

2 Suspension system – inspection

1 The suspension components should normally last a long time, except in cases where damage has occured due to an accident. The suspension parts, however, should be checked from time to time for signs of wear which will result in a loss of precision handling and riding comfort.

2 Check that the suspension components have not sagged due to wear. Do this by parking the vehicle on a level surface and visually checking that it sits level. Compare with the photographs to see whether it has markedly sagged. This will normally occur only after many miles and will usually appear more on the driver's side of the vehicle. Measurements for correct ride height are listed in the Specifications.

3 Put the vehicle in gear and take off the handbrake. Grip the steering wheel at the top with both hands and rock it back and forth. Listen for any squeaks or metallic noises. Feel for free play. If any of these conditions is found, have an assistant do the rocking while the source of the trouble is located.

4 Check the shock absorbers, as these are the parts of the suspension system likely to wear out first. If there is any evidence of fluid leakage, they will definitely need replacing. Bounce the vehicle up and down vigorously. It should feel stiff, and well damped by the shock absorbers. As soon as the bouncing is stopped the vehicle should return to its normal position without excessive up and down movement. Do not replace the shock absorbers as single units, but rather in pairs unless a failure has occured at low mileage.

5 Check all rubber bushings for signs of deterioration and cracking. If necessary, replace the rubber portions of the suspension arm.

3 Wheels and tires – general information

Since wheels and tires form the initial and basic rolling element of the automobile, they should be cared for in a diligent manner. Tires are especially susceptible to road hazards and damage and should be looked after at regular intervals to ensure trouble-free, safe driving (see

Chapter 1). Rotation is also an important part of tire maintenance and should be carried out faithfully every 7500 miles (12 000 kilometers).

The tires will have tread wear indicators on them, which will indicate when the tires are worn beyond their useful life. Replace tires when the shallowest tread on the tire wears to 0.06 in (1.6 mm) or less. When replacing tires, use the exact same size and type as the original tyre. Also see that the load capacity equals or exceeds the specification of the original tire.

The tire tread wear pattern can give a good indication of problems in the maintenance or adjustment of suspension and front end components. The accompanying illustration gives some common examples of tire wear patterns and their usual causes. If a tire exhibits a wear pattern caused by incorrect alignment, refer to Section 5 or Section 22.

Do not, under any circumstances, use any other size or type of tire than the original or many factors such as speedometer calibration, ride height and ground clearance will be affected. Never mix radial, belted or conventional tires on the same vehicle. This will cause a very dangerous driving situation and should be avoided at all cost. If the vehicle is to be changed from conventional tires to radial-type or the reverse, always replace the entire set of tires.

If a tire is damaged beyond repair due to a cut or road hazard, it should be replaced. If it is the only one of the set that needs replacement, always mount it at the position on the vehicle that has the tire with the least amount of wear showing.

Wheels that are damaged or heavily corroded should be replaced. Never straighten, weld or heat a wheel that has been damaged. Don't repair a tubeless tyre with a tube if the wheel is the source of leakage, as the wheel is unsafe.

When replacing a wheel on the Tercel, make sure it is the exact replacement for this vehicle. Some wheels will fit the bolt stud mounting pattern, but the off-set and brake caliper clearance will be incorrect for this vehicle.

If the vehicle is equipped with aluminium wheels, the torque of the retaining bolts is especially important. Wheels of this type should also be checked for wheel torque more frequently than a normal steel wheel.

The Tercel is equipped with 13-inch tires and wheels except in some instances where 12-inch tires and wheels are used. Always use the correct tire in relation to rim size when replacing either or both. Also, make sure that the tire load range, speed capabilities and tread type are compatible with the vehicle.

Note: *Front wheel drive vehicles are especially susceptible to differences (drive wheel diameters and tread type) in the front tire types. Never, under any circumstances, replace a front tire with an odd or different type from the rest of the vehicle, as it will be unsafe and steer improperly.*

4 Wheel and tire – removal and installation

1 With the vehicle on a level surface, the parking brake on and the transmission in gear (manual transaxles should be in 'Reverse';

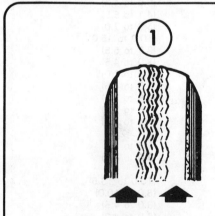

Fig. 11.1 Common tire wear patterns (Sec 3)

1 *Wear at outer edges –   2 Wear at center – tire   3 Wear at one side –*
   tire underinflated   *overinflated*   *incorrect wheel alignment*

automatic transaxles should be in 'Park') remove the hub trim ring and loosen, but do not remove, the wheel lug nuts.

2   Using a jack positioned in the proper location, raise the vehicle just enough so that the tire clears the ground.

3   Remove the lug nuts.

4   Remove the wheel and tire.

5   If a flat tire is being replaced, ensure that there's adequate ground clearance for the new inflated tire, then mount the wheel and tire on the wheel studs.

6   Apply a light coat of spray lubricant or light oil to the wheel stud threads and install the lug nuts snugly with the cone-shaped end facing the wheel.

7   Lower the vehicle until the tire contacts the ground and the wheel studs are centered in their wheel holes.

8   Tighten the lug nuts evenly and in a cross-pattern to the specified torque.

9   Lower the vehicle completely and remove the jack.

10 Replace the hub trim ring.

5   Front end alignment

1   A front end alignment refers to the adjustments made to the front wheels so that they are in proper angular relationship to the suspension system and to the ground. Front wheels that are out of proper alignment will lack steering control and cause excessive tire wear. The only easily made adjustments on Tercels are the toe-in and the caster.

2   Getting the proper front wheel alignment is a very tedious, exacting process and one which is complicated and usually costly. Special equipment is necessary to perform the job properly and the technician operating the equipment usually has special training and experience. It is, therefore, best to have front end alignments done by a professional.

3   We will, however, give you a basic idea of what is involved in front end alignment so you can better understand the process and deal intelligently with shops that handle this work.

4   Toe-in is the turning in of the front wheels when the vehicle is in the straight-ahead position. The purpose of a toe-in specification is to ensure parallel rolling of the front wheels. In a vehicle with zero toe-in, the distance between the front edges of the wheels will be exactly the same as the distance between the rear edges of the wheels. The actual amount of toe-in is normally only a fraction of an inch. The Tercels have a toe-in specification listed at the front of this Chapter.

5   The toe-in is set so that the front wheels are pointed slightly towards each other at the front while the vehicle is standing still. This way when the vehicle is rolling forward the tires will tend to run parallel due to small compression factors within the suspension system.

6   Toe-in adjustment is controlled by the outer tie rod's position in relationship to the rack and pinion of the vehicle. Incorrect toe-in can cause tires to wear incorrectly by making them scrub or run slightly side-ways in relationship to the road surface.

7   Caster is the angle or inclination of the front wheel as viewed from the side of the vehicle. Caster is set so that the axis running through the suspension components at the front of the vehicle is canted slightly backwards at the top. This helps the wheels to return and run in a straight line after being turned. The caster is controlled by the strut bracket length, which is adjusted at the large nuts at the mounting point on the crossmember. Again, this is a job for experts and should not be attempted by the home mechanic.

8   Other factors of alignment such as camber, the angle that the front tire runs when viewed from the front in a top-to-bottom line, and kingpin inclination, which is a measurement of the suspension component axis, are adjustable through the use of heavy machines that actually bend certain parts of the vehicle's sub-frame. These adjustments sometimes have to be made if the vehicle has been involved in an accident or has hit a road hazard of an extreme nature. This type of work will require a frame shop and will often be part of a body shop type of arrangement. If the adjustments are out far enough that the frame needs to be bent to correct it, make sure that all of the components are in good condition and seek out the best possible shop to do this work due to its very critical nature.

6   Front suspension system – general information

Because the Tercel is a front wheel drive vehicle, the front suspension and hub assembly have a task of propelling the vehicle as well as steering and suspending it. This makes the front suspension system somewhat complex. If the suspension system is damaged in an accident or by road hazard, have it looked at by an expert at a dealership or repair facility. Due to the critical relationship of all of the components, one overlooked part could cause an ill handling, possibly unsafe vehicle.

Similar advice pertains to loose or worn front suspension components. Even if you are able to do the work yourself, seek an expert's advice on what components should be replaced.

Always have the front end re-aligned after any components are replaced.

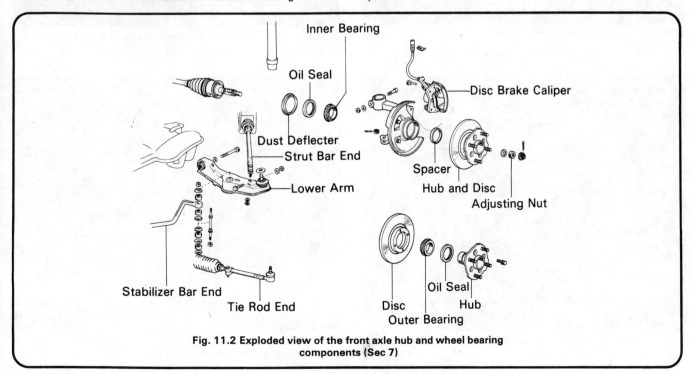

Fig. 11.2 Exploded view of the front axle hub and wheel bearing components (Sec 7)

7   Wheel bearings and front axle hub – removal

Note: *Refer to Fig. 11.2 for front axle and wheel bearing assembly components.*

1   Raise the front of the vehicle and support it securely.
2   Remove the adjusting nut cap and cotter pin from the front axle hub.
3   Have an assistant hold the brake pedal down to lock the wheel assembly, then loosen the wheel bearing locknut.
4   Remove the two bolts retaining the brake caliper and pad assembly to the axle hub (Chapter 9). Remove the brake caliper assembly and suspend it out of the way. Be careful not to kink or damage the brake hose.
5   Disconnect the stabilizer bar end at the lower suspension arm.
6   Remove the nut retaining the strut bar to the lower suspension arm. Disconnect the strut bar end.
7   Disconnect the tie-rod end by first removing the cotter pin and then unscrewing the nut from the tie-rod end. Remove the tie rod end with a tool as shown in the accompanying photo.
8   Use a jack to raise the lower suspension arm and relieve the tension from the front suspension spring.
9   Remove the bolt retaining the lower suspension arm to the crossmember (photo).
10 Disconnect the lower suspension arm from the crossmember.

11 Remove the bearing retaining nut and washer.
12 Remove the bolt holding the clamp of the axle hub assembly to the base of the shock absorber.
13 Remove the axle hub from the driveshaft with a suitable puller (photo).
14 Separate the shock absorber and steering knuckle assembly and remove the axle hub. Be careful not to damage the boot.
15 Remove the bolt retaining the axle hub to the lower suspension arm (photo).
16 Remove the axle hub from the lower arm.
17 Remove the dust seal from the back of the front axle assembly (photo).

Note: *Steps 18 through 24 will require the use of special tools and presses not normally found in the home workshop. If you are not so equipped, it would be best to take the hub assembly to an automotive machine shop parts house equipped with the pullers and press necessary to do the work.*

18 Remove the axle hub from the steering knuckle using a puller.
19 Remove the inner bearing and spacer.
20 Separate the hub and disc after placing match marks on each one for assembly purposes. Remove the four bolts retaining the hub to the disc.
21 Start the wheel bearing race (outer) off the hub using a chisel and hammer. The bearing race needs to be moved away from the hub in order to provide clearance for a puller jaw to be inserted behind it. Be

7.7 Removing the tie-rod end with a puller

7.9 Removing the bolt and nut retaining the lower suspension arm to the crossmember

7.13 Removing the axle hub from the driveshaft with a puller

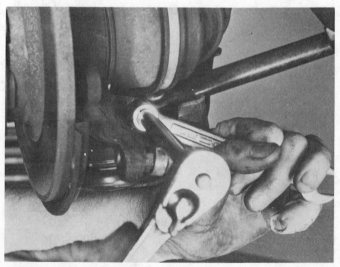

7.15 Removing the bolt and nut retaining the axle hub assembly to the lower suspension arm

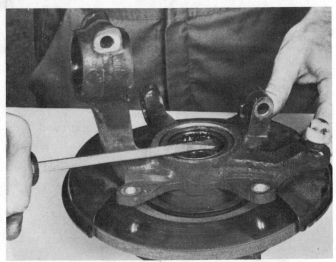

7.17 Removing the dust seal from the front axle assembly

careful not to damage the bearing as you use the chisel to move it off the hub.
22 Using a suitable puller, pull the bearing race off the hub. Be careful to maintain the bearings in good condition and mark them for location (inner and outer) for reassembly purposes.
23 Remove any minor scratches or galling from the hub surface with an oil stone.
24 Using a hammer and punch, drive out the outer wheel bearing race.

8 Wheel bearings and front axle hub – inspection

1 Inspect the hub for damage or wear.
2 Inspect the steering knuckle for any damage or wear. Pay particular attention to the bearing race area.
3 Check the brake disc (see Chapter 9).
4 Check the inner bearing and race for damage or wear.
5 Check the outer bearing for damage and/or wear.

9 Wheel bearings and front axle hub – installation

1 Replace the outer wheel bearing outer race with a new one.
2 Push the new outer race into place with a suitable tool designed for this application.
3 Assemble the inner bearing to the special service tool and insert a spacer between the inner and outer wheel bearings.
4 Apply a light coat of oil to all the wheel bearings and assemble the bearing, spacer and outer bearing as shown in the acompanying illustration.

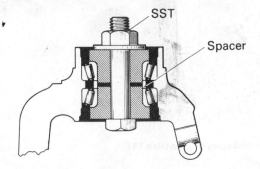

Fig. 11.3 Bearing, spacer and service
tool assembled together (Sec 9)

5 Tighten the nut on the special service tool to the specified torque.
6 Turn the bearings a couple of revolutions in both directions to help seat them into position.
7 Use a small torque wrench and measure the turning pre-load or effort and see that it meets the specification.
8 If the pre-load is not correct, select and install a new spacer and re-do Steps 3 thru 7. The turning torque will change three to four in-lb with each graduation of spacer size.
9 Align the match marks and install the hub on the brake disc assembly.
10 Tighten the four retaining bolts to the specified torque.
11 Pack the bearings with wheel bearing grease (preferably use a pressure bearing lubricator).
12 Install the outer bearing onto the outer race.
13 Using a suitable tool, drive the oil seal into the hub.
14 Pack the hub with wheel bearing grease between the bearings and the seals (some grease should be applied to the seal lips as well).
15 Assemble the spacer selected, and insert the inner wheel bearing into its race.
16 Press the steering knuckle into the hub with the suitable implement and a high-pressure hydraulic press.
17 Turn the steering knuckle with the bearings installed and the press set at the correct pressure. Turn it each direction a couple of times to seat the bearings.
18 Measure the frictional force required to turn the knuckle and see that it meets the specification.
19 If the pre-load does not meet the specification, the spacer will have to be changed. To change the spacer, remove the unit from the press and re-do steps 15 thru 18.
20 Once the pre-load is correct, install the oil seal under the steering knuckle.
21 Install the dust shield onto the steering knuckle.
22 Apply molybdenum disulfide grease to the oil seal lip.
23 Install the axle hub assembly to the lower arm. Tighten the lower arm bolt to the proper torque.
24 Install the axle hub onto the axleshaft and connect the hub assembly to the bottom of the shock absorber.
25 Install the lower strut bar to the lower arm and loosely install the nut.
26 Install the lower suspension arm to the crossmember. It will be necessary to jack the arm up slightly to take the load created by the suspension spring off the assembly. Jack the assembly up slowly until the lower suspension arm mounting bolt will slide into place. Install the mounting bolt and tighten the nut.
27 Install the stabilizer bar end to the lower arm. Tighten the stabilizer bar nut to the proper torque.
28 Install the tie-rod end to the axle hub assembly. Tighten the tie-rod end retaining nut to the proper torque.
29 Install the brake caliper to the axle hub assembly and tighten the bolt to the proper torque.
30 Install the wheel axle locknut. Tighten the wheel locknut to the proper torque, then install the cotter pin and cap.
31 Tighten the mounting bolts for the lower suspension arm and strut arm to the proper torque.
32 Tighten the nut retaining the strut bar to the lower suspension arm.
33 Check to see that the boots on the driveshaft have not been damaged in any way.

10 Front shock absorber – removal and installation

Note: Refer to Fig. 11.4 for components and locations.
1 Raise the front of the vehicle and support it securely.
2 Remove the wheel.
3 Remove the disc brake caliper (Chapter 9).
4 Disconnect the stabilizer bar at the lower suspension arm.
5 Disconnect the steering knuckle from the lower portion of the shock absorber (photo). Tap the steering knuckle downward to separate it from the lower end of the shock absorber. Be careful not to damage the driveaxle boot.
6 Remove the three bolts holding the top of the shock absorber to the top of the strut housing underneath the hood (photo). Do not remove the large center nut on top of the shock absorber.
7 Lower the shock absorber assembly away from the body.
8 Install the shock absorber to the body.

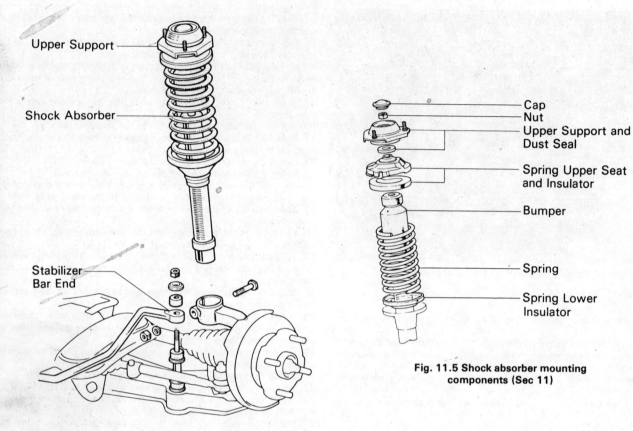

Upper Support

Shock Absorber

Stabilizer Bar End

Fig. 11.4 Components of the front shock absorber and strut assembly (Sec 10)

Cap
Nut
Upper Support and Dust Seal
Spring Upper Seat and Insulator
Bumper
Spring
Spring Lower Insulator

Fig. 11.5 Shock absorber mounting components (Sec 11)

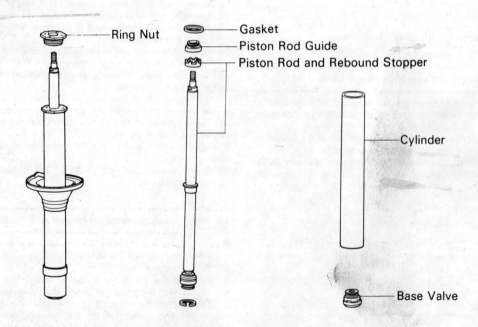

Ring Nut

Gasket
Piston Rod Guide
Piston Rod and Rebound Stopper

Cylinder

Base Valve

Fig. 11.6 Front shock absorber cartridge and components (Sec 11)

10.5 Disconnecting the steering arm from the bottom of the shock absorber

10.6 Three bolts retain the top of the shock absorber to the body

9   Install the three nuts holding the shock absorber and tighten the nuts to the proper torque.
10 Connect the axle hub to the lower section of the shock abosrber. A jack underneath the lower A-arm will help facilitate this operation. Notice that the stopper fits into the slot provided on the axle hub assembly.
11 Insert the bolt from the rear side, attach the nut and tighten the nut to the proper torque specification.
12 Connect the stabilizer bar to the lower suspension arm. Tighten the nut to the proper torque.
13 Connect the brake caliper to the axle hub. Tighten the bolts to the proper torque.
14 Have the front end alignment checked and adjusted if necessary.

11 Front shock absorber – disassembly, inspection and reassembly

1   Remove the shock absorber as described in the previous Section.
2   Mount the shock absorber in a vise, using the special tool or soft-jaws. Make sure that you do not damage or bend the body of the shock absorber.
3   Compress the coil spring using the special tool required (photo).
Caution: *Care should be exercised in this step as the coil spring is under a great deal of compression pressure and can cause serious injury if the tool slips.*
4   Remove the nut from the top of the shock absorber mount (photo).
5   Remove the suspension support, the spring seat, the spring and the dust cover.
6   Inspect the shock absorber shaft for leakage, damage or deformation.
7   Grasp the top of the shock absorber piston rod and pull it up and down at an even speed. The resistance or tension should remain the same throughout the entire stroke.
8   Abruptly move the piston rod up and down 0.20 to 0.39 inches (5 to 10 mm) and check to see if there is a change in the tension. There should be a difference.
9   Have the bearing knuckle area checked for cracks (magnafluxed) by an automotive machine shop.
10 If the shock absorber fails any of the above tests it should be replaced with a new one. Due to the critical nature of the operation, rebuilding of a shock absorber unit (cartridge) will not be covered. Removal from the housing, however, is easily accomplished. Be sure to dismantle the shock absorber in a clean place as the slightest bit of dust or dirt on the piston surface can cause fluid leakage and failure.
11 Remove the ring nut using the special tool designed for the job.
12 The piston rod assembly can now be pulled out of the cylinder.
13 Reassembly is the reverse of disassembly.

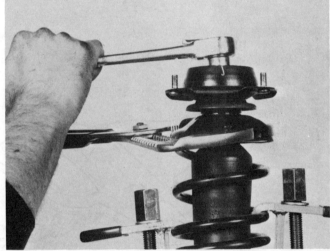

11.3 Compressing the spring for front shock absorber removal

11.4 Removing the nut from the top of the shock absorber mount

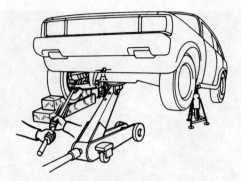

Fig. 11.7 Checking the balljoints for vertical play (Sec 12)

12 Lower front suspension arm and balljoint – inspection, removal and installation

Note: Refer to Fig. 11.7 for steps 1 to 7.

Inspection

1   Jack up the front of the vehicle and place wooden blocks of 7.09 to 7.87 in (180 to 200 mm) thickness under one front tire.
2   Lower the jack until there is about half a load on the front coil springs. Be sure to support the vehicle under the frame with jack stands for safety.
3   Make sure the wheels are turned in the straight-ahead position and block them securely.
4   Move the lower arm up and down with a pry bar or crowbar and check that the balljoint has no play (there should be no vertical play). If there is vertical play, the balljoint needs replacement.

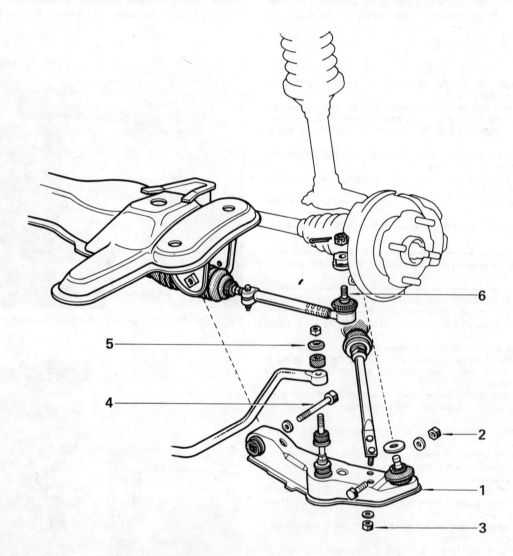

Fig. 11.8 Components of the lower front suspension arm assembly

1	Lower arm	3	Strut bar end	5	Stabilizer bar end
2	Nut	4	Bolt	6	Tie-rod end

Removal and installation

Note: *Refer to Fig. 11.8 for the following procedure.*
5 Raise the vehicle and support it securely.
6 Disconnect the tie-rod end from the axle hub assembly.
7 Remove the two nuts holding the strut bar to the lower suspension arm.
8 Remove the nut holding the stabilizer bar to the lower suspension arm.
9 Place a jack under the lower arm. Loosen the nut on the bolt holding the arm to the crossmember and remove the bolt and nut as the jack is raised to the point where the bolt will come out freely.
10 Remove the bolt holding the lower arm to the axle hub.
11 Remove the lower arm.
12 Inspect the lower arm for bending, cracks or excessive looseness at the balljoint. Inspect the lower arm bushing for deterioration or damage.
13 If any of the above conditions exist, the lower suspension arm must be replaced with a new one. The balljoint is not serviced as a separate unit from the lower arm and the lower arm bushing is too difficult to replace without the use of special tools by the home mechanic.
14 Installation is the reverse of removal. **Note:** *When starting the lower pivot bolt for the suspension arm installation, be sure to jack the lower arm up to the point that there is no binding as the pivot bolt is inserted.* A dowel pin or punch will help line up the lower arm to the mounting bracket (photo). Once the arm is inserted and the nut is installed on the thread, the jack may be released from the lower suspension arm and the nut and bolt may be torqued.

12.14 Lining up the lower arm pivot with a tool

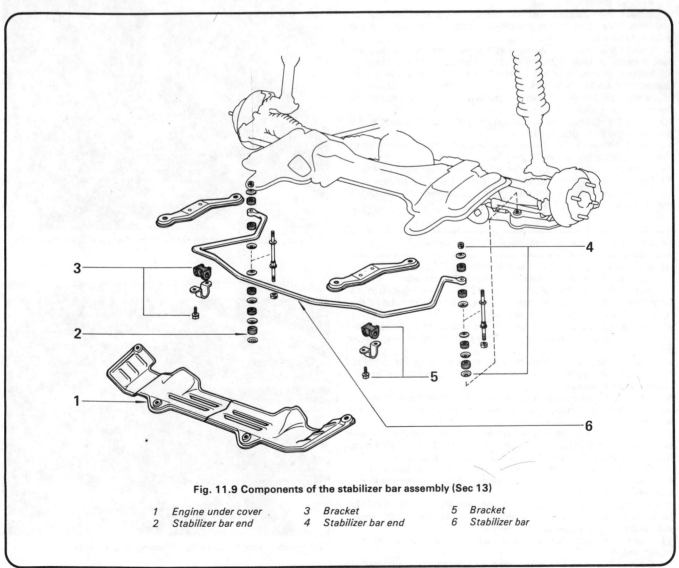

Fig. 11.9 Components of the stabilizer bar assembly (Sec 13)

1 Engine under cover	3 Bracket	5 Bracket
2 Stabilizer bar end	4 Stabilizer bar end	6 Stabilizer bar

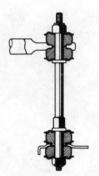

**Fig. 11.10 Assembly order of the
stabilizer bar link components (Sec 13)**

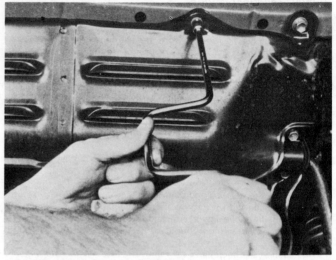

13.2 Removing the front splash shield

13 Stabilizer bar – removal, inspection and installation

Note: *Refer to Fig. 11.9 and Fig. 11.10 during the following
procedure.*
1   Raise and support the front of the vehicle securely.
2   Remove the splash shield undercover (photo).
3   Disconnect one side of the stabilizer bar end where it is bolted to
the lower suspension arm (photo).
4   Remove the stabilizer bar bracket on the same side (photo).
5   Repeat the above two steps on the other side of the vehicle.
6   Remove the stabilizer bar.
7   Inspect the stabilizer bar for damage from road hazards or
accidents. Make sure that it is not bent, cracked or corroded to the
point of breakage.
8   Inspect the stabilizer bushings at the front brackets. If they are
split, missing, or broken, they should be replaced with new ones.
9   Inspect the stabilizer bar bushings at the suspension arm end.
Notice there are four bushings, two at the bottom and two at the top
of the stabilizer bar link. If they are cracked, broken or worn, replace
them with new ones.
10   Install the stabilizer bar in position and place both brackets at the
front with the nuts attached loosely.
11   Install the washers, rubber spacers, rubber bushings and spacer as
shown in the accompanying illustration.
12   Connect the nuts on both sides to the lower suspension arms.
13   Tighten the stabilizer bar brackets to the prescribed torque.
14   Tighten the stabilizer bar ends to the suspension arm using the
prescribed torque.

13.3 Disconnecting the stabilizer bar from the lower suspension arm

14 Strut bar – removal, inspection and installation

Note: *Refer to Fig. 11.11 during the following procedure.*
1   Raise the front of the vehicle and support it securely.
2   Remove the nut at the end of the strut bar where it is bolted to the
crossmember bracket (photo). Be careful not to move the staked nut
on the inside of the crossmember bracket.
3   Disconnect the bolts retaining the strut bar to the lower suspension arm (photo). Remove the strut bar from the lower suspension
arm.
4   Remove the strut bar from the hole in the crossmember bracket.
5   Remove the bushings and washers for the strut bar at the
crossmember bracket.
6   If the vehicle alignment is correct do not perform the next step. If
you are installing a new strut bar, be sure to make the following
adjustment.
7   Check that the distance between the far end of the staked nut and
the center of the first (or closest bolt hole) is 13.008 in or 330.4 mm.
If it is not, adjust the staked nut to make this distance correct.
8   Check the strut bar to see that it is straight and undamaged.
9   Check the bushings at the crossmember end to make sure they are
not worn, split or damaged.
10   Assemble the plate washer and one of the cone-shaped rubber
bushings to the staked nut end of the strut rods. Notice that the cone-
shaped bushing faces away from the nut.
11   Insert the strut bar into the hole in the bracket at the
crossmember.
12   Connect the strut bar at the other end to the lower suspension

13.4 Removing the stabilizer bar retaining bracket bolts

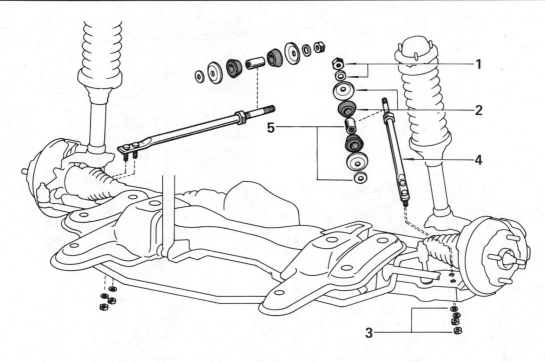

Fig. 11.11 Components of the strut bar assembly (Sec 14)

1 Nut	3 Bar end	5 Collar cushion and
2 Retainer and cushion	4 Bar	retainer

14.2 Removing the nut retaining the strut bar to the crossmember

arm. It may be necessary to raise the suspension arm slightly with a jack to get the strut bar to align properly.
13 Insert the spacer, the other cone-shaped bushing (the rubber bushings should face each other), the washer, the lockwasher and the nut.
14 Tighten the nuts on the strut bar retaining bolts at the lower suspension arm to the proper torque.
15 Tighten the nut retaining the strut bar to the crossmember bracket to the proper torque.
16 Lower the vehicle, install the wheel and have the front end alignment checked.

15 Front suspension crossmember — removal, inspection and installation

Note: *Refer to Fig. 11.12 for components related to the front crossmember assembly.*
1   Raise and support the frame of the vehicle securely.
2   Remove the stabilizer bar as described in Section 13.
3   Remove the steering link assembly as described in Section 25.
4   Remove both lower suspension arms from the crossmember (Section 12).
5   Remove the engine shock absorber from the right front side where it connects to the bracket on the crossmember (photo).
6   Support the engine with a jack or other suitable device.
7   Remove the nut from the bottom of each of the two front motor mounts.
8   Remove the six bolts retaining the crossmember and the lower arm brackets to the body.
9   Remove the crossmember and lower arm bracket.
10 Inspect the crossmember for damage. If any damage has occurred to this crossmember, replace it with a new one. This crossmember is an essential main suspension component of the automobile and should not be bent, heated or welded if it is damaged in any way.
11 Connect the lower suspension arm bracket to the crossmember.
12 Install the crossmember and bracket assembly to the frame with the six bolts. Tighten the bolts to the proper torque.
13 Install the engine mounting nuts to the engine mounts.
14 Lower the jack supporting the engine.
15 Install the engine shock absorber to the bracket on the crossmember with the bolt and nut combination. Tighten the nut to the proper torque.
16 Install both lower arms to the crossmember.
17 Install the steering link assembly to the crossmember.
18 Install the stabilizer bar to the crossmember.
19 Tighten the lower suspension arm bolt, and all other bolts related to the reassembly process, to the specified torque.
20 Check the rubber boots on the driveshafts for damage.
21 Lower the vehicle, install the wheels and have the front end realigned.

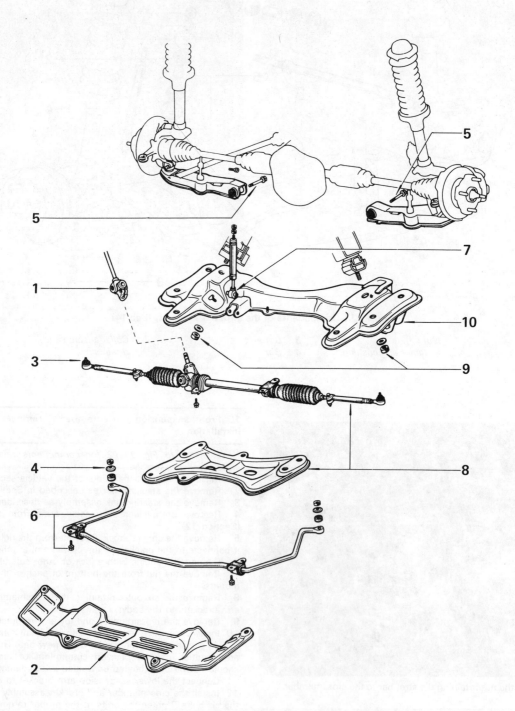

Fig. 11.12 Components related to the front crossmember assembly (Sec 15)

1	Steering intermediate shaft	4	Stabilizer bar end
2	Engine under cover	5	Lower arm bolt
3	Tie-rod end	6	Stabilizer bar

7	Engine shock absorber lower connection	9	Engine mount retaining nut
8	Cover and steering link	10	Crossmember

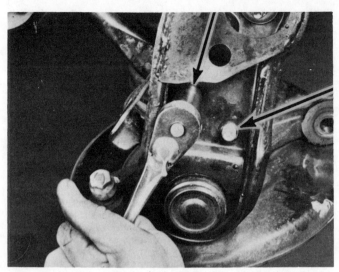

14.3 Removing the strut bar-to-lower suspension arm retaining bolts (arrows)

15.5 Removing the engine shock absorber retaining bolt from the crossmember

16 Rear suspension – general information

The rear suspension on the Tercel is of the independent type. Due to the design characteristics of this type of rear suspension, alignment of the rear wheel is a necessary part of maintenance, just as it is on the front suspension of all vehicles. Before aligning the rear suspension, make sure that all off the components such as the arms, bushings, springs, bearings, hub assembly and sway bar are in good condition and not worn or loose. Also check the tire condition, ride height and the driveability in general. Sometimes when a vehicle is thought to have front-end alignment problems, the rear-end alignment is adversely affecting the driveability and handling characteristics.

All the precautions for checking and replacing the rear suspension components are the same as for the front suspension components described in Section 2.

17 Rear axle hub and wheel bearing – removal, inspection and installation

Note: *Refer to Fig. 11.13 for components of the rear axle hub assembly.*
1 Raise the rear of the vehicle and support it securely.
2 Remove the axle hub and brake drum assembly as described in Chapter 1, Section 25.
3 Remove the inner wheel bearing and oil seal as described in Chapter 1, Section 25.
4 Clean the spindle and inspect it for any cracks, flaws or galling. It would be a good idea to use a magnetic flaw detector (such as Magnafluxing).
5 Inspect the wheel bearings and re-pack them as described in Chapter 1, Section 25, if they are to be re-used.

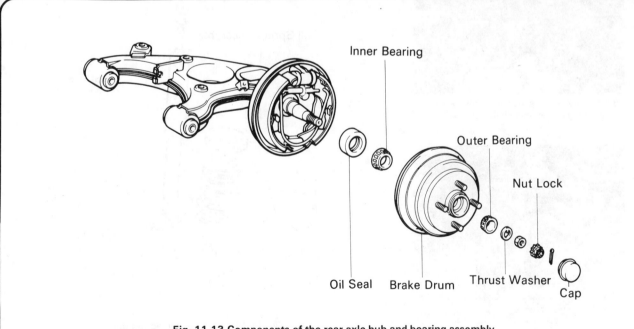

Inner Bearing

Outer Bearing

Nut Lock

Oil Seal   Brake Drum   Thrust Washer   Cap

**Fig. 11.13 Components of the rear axle hub and bearing assembly
(Sec 17)**

6   If the wheel bearings are to be replaced with new ones, the races will need to be replaced in the hub assembly. This is a job usually requiring a machine shop due to the special tools necessary to remove the race from the hub assembly. If you need to have this done, take the hub to an auto parts store or approved repair facility equipped to perform this operation.

7   Installation procedures are the same as described in Chapter 1, Section 25. Be sure to follow this procedure carefully as it is different from many other wheel bearing installation procedures. Always use a new cotter pin and install the cap and wheel after the bearings have been replaced and the hub and drum assemblies installed.

18 Rear coil spring and shock absorber – removal, inspection and installation

1   Raise the rear of the vehicle and support the body securely.
2   Remove the stabilizer bar end from the rear suspension arm.
3   Support the suspension arm with a jack and raise it slightly to take the rebound pressure off the shock absorber.
4   Remove the bolt holding the shock absorber to the suspension arm.
5   Disconnect the shock absorber from the suspension arm (photo).
6   If the shock absorber is being replaced with a new one, remove the trim cap, nut, washer and bushing holding the shock absorber to the body from the inside of the rear of the vehicle. **Caution:** *Lower the rear suspension arm gradually to relieve the pressure from the coil spring. Do this slowly and carefully as the coil spring is under pressure and could fly out and cause bodily injury.*
7   Lower the suspension arm sufficiently to remove the coil spring and the rubber upper coil spring seat.

8   Inspect the coil spring for damage, corrosion or other defects. If the vehicle ride height is incorrect, the coil spring has sagged and will need to be replaced with a new one (always replace the rear springs as a set).
9   Inspect the shock absorber for leakage, corrosion or damage. Replace the shock absorber with a new one if any of these conditions exist. Replace the shock absorber if the vehicle does not pass the shock absorber bounce test described in Section 2 of this Chapter.
10   Place the upper spring seat on top of the coil spring. Notice that the coil spring is directional and has a flat on the top for the upper spring seat to fit over. The bottom of the coil spring is not flat and has a coil end which also has a seat provided for it in the lower suspension arm.
11   Install the coil spring onto the vehicle with the tip of the coil spring at the end of the hollow channel provided in the lower suspension arm. Make sure that the upper spring seat is seated properly also.
12   Gradually raise the lower suspension arm with a jack, making sure that the spring does not bind, become unseated or slide away from its proper position. **Caution:** *Use care and work slowly as the coil spring will be under pressure and could fly out and cause bodily injury.*
13   Raise the suspension arm to a height sufficient to allow the shock absorber assembly to be installed (or only the lower mount installed if it has been left in the vehicle). Install the shock absorber lower mount bolts. Make sure that the angle of the lower shock absorber mount is tilted slightly forward to match the angle of the lower suspension arm (photo).
14   Install the upper shock absorber body mount with the bushings, washers and nut in the proper order.
15   Tighten the shock absorber lower mount retaining bolt to the proper torque.
16   Tighten the shock absorber upper mount retaining nut to the proper torque.
17   Fasten the stabilizer bar end to the lower suspension arm.

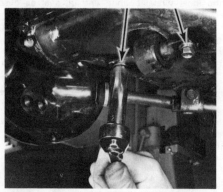

18.5 Removing the shock absorber-to-rear suspension arm retaining bolts (arrows)

18.13 Shock absorber installed in its correct angled position

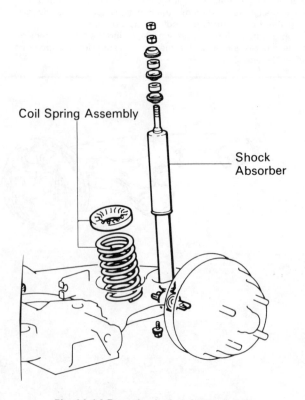

Coil Spring Assembly

Shock Absorber

Fig. 11.14 Rear shock absorber and coil spring (Sec 18)

19 Rear stabilizer bar – removal, inspection and installation

Note: *Refer to Fig. 11.15 for components of the rear stabilizer bar assembly.*

1 Raise the rear of the vehicle and support it securely.
2 Remove the bolts retaining the rear stabilizer bar bushing bracket to the crossmember at the center of the crossmember. Remove the bolts for the matching bracket on the other side.
3 Remove the stabilizer bar, bushing, nut and assembly from the lower suspension arm (photo).
4 Remove the stabilizer bar from the vehicle.
5 Inspect the stabilizer bar for cracks, bends and other damage.
6 Replace the stabilizer bar with a new one if any of these conditions are present. Under no circumstances should the stabilizer bar be welded, heated or bent in any attempt at repair.
7 Inspect the stabilizer bar bushings both at the mount and at the suspension arm end. If any of these rubber bushings are cracked, broken or missing, replace them with new ones.
8 Put the stabilizer bar into position and loosely install the stabilizer bar bushing brackets to the crossmember.
9 Install the stabilizer bar ends to the stabilizer bar connecting link assembly at the suspension arms. Loosely install the nuts retaining the stabilizer bar ends.
10 Tighten the stabilizer bar bracket bolts to the proper torque.
11 Tighten the stabilizer bar end retaining nuts to the proper torque.

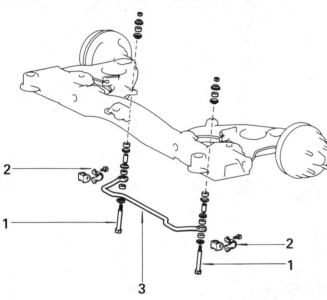

Fig. 11.15 Components of the rear stabilizer assembly (Sec 19)

  1   Stabilizer bar end bolt   3   Stabilizer bar
  2   Stabilizer bar bracket
       and bushing

20 Rear suspension arm – removal, inspection and installation

Note: *Refer to Fig. 11.16 for components related to the rear suspension arm.*

1 Raise the rear of the vehicle and support the body securely.
2 Remove the rear axle hub and brake drum as described in Section 17.
3 Remove the rear shock absorber and coil spring as described in Section 18.
4 Disconnect the rear sway bar mount at the lower suspension arm and pivot it out of the way.
5 Disconnect the brake tube at the junction near the pivot point of the lower suspension arm.
6 Disconnect the parking brake cables from the crossmember at the adjustment point near the center of the vehicle.
7 Disconnect the clamps retaining the parking brake cable along its length from the rear wheel assembly to the adjuster point (photo).
8 Remove the brake assembly with the backing plate and spindle by removing the four retaining bolts holding it to the rear suspension arm.
9 Carefully mark the rear suspension cam plates' positions (photo) so that alignment is not affected.
10 Remove the bolts retaining the suspension aligning cam and the suspension arm from the center bracket (photo).
11 Remove the other bolt retaining the suspension arm to the outer side of the rear crossmember bracket (photo).
12 Remove the rear suspension arm.
13 Inspect the suspension arm for damage. If any damage is present, replace the rear suspension arm with a new one. Under no circumstances should the rear suspension arm be welded or any attempts at repair or bending made to it.
14 Check the bushings for any wear, cracking or damage. If the bushings need replacement, they will need to be replaced at an automotive machine shop or repair facility equipped with a hydraulic press. The bushings are removed by cutting the flange area off with a chisel and driving them out with a hydraulic press. The press is also used to install the new bushings. If you need this done, take the entire lower suspension arm assembly to a shop where the procedure can be performed.
15 Install the suspension arm retaining bolts to the outer bracket on the crossmember.
16 Install the suspension arm retaining bolts to the inner bracket, making sure that the cam set for the alignment is positioned as it was when marked during the removal process.
17 Install the rear brake assembly and spindle to the rear suspension arm and tighten the four bolts to the proper torque.
18 Connect the brake hose and tube at the rear suspension arm.
19 Install the rear shock absorber and coil spring.
20 Tighten the rear suspension retaining bolts to the proper torque.
21 Install the rear sway bar ends to the rear sway bar connecting links.
22 Tighten the retaining nuts to the proper torque.
23 Install the wheel and lower the vehicle.
24 Bounce the vehicle on the springs several times and re-check the suspension arm torque setting.
25 Bleed the brake system (Chapter 9).
26 Have the rear wheels aligned.

19.3 Removing the stabilizer bar from the lower suspension arm

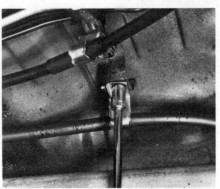

20.7 Disconnecting a clamp holding the parking brake cable to the body

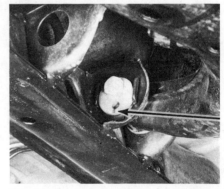

20.9 Marking the rear suspension arm cam plates for alignment purposes (Note that there is a cam plate at each arm pivot point)

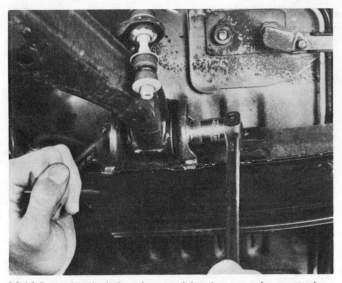

20.10 Removing the bolt and nut retaining the suspension arm to the center pivot bracket

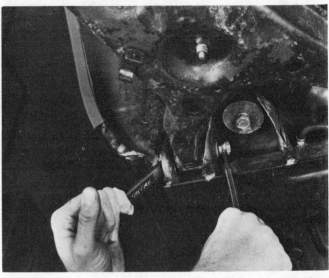

20.11 Removing the bolt and nut retaining the suspension arm to the outer side of the rear crossmember pivot bracket

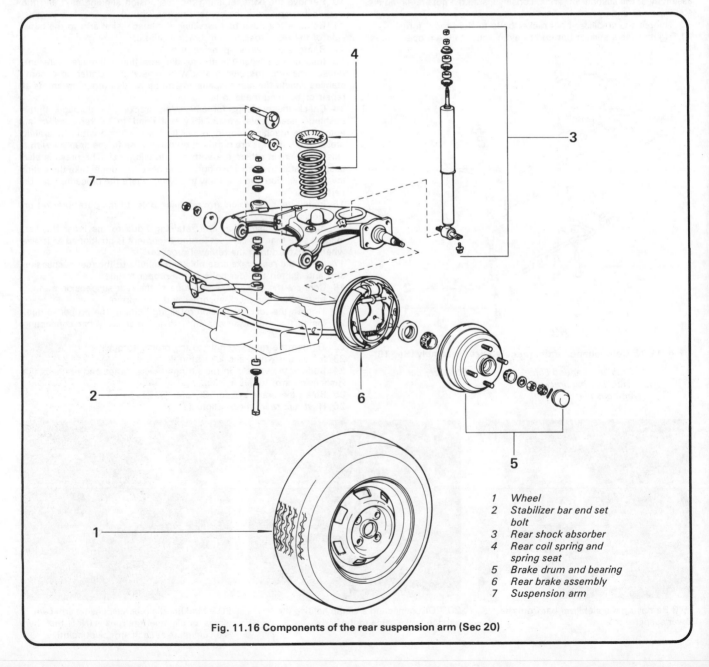

1 Wheel
2 Stabilizer bar end set bolt
3 Rear shock absorber
4 Rear coil spring and spring seat
5 Brake drum and bearing
6 Rear brake assembly
7 Suspension arm

Fig. 11.16 Components of the rear suspension arm (Sec 20)

21 Rear crossmember – removal, inspection and installation

1 Raise the rear of the vehicle and support it securely.
2 Remove the rear exhaust pipe/muffler unit (Chapter 4).
3 Remove the rear stabilizer bar (Section 19).
4 Remove the rear shock absorber and coil spring assemblies (Section 18).
5 Remove the rear suspension arms (Section 20). The parking brake cables can be moved out of the way at this point but take care not to kink the cables while doing so.
6 Remove the body-to-crossmember strap retaining bolts (two per side) (photo).
7 Support the rear crossmember with a jack or other similar tool and remove the four retaining bolts. Lower the crossmember away from the vehicle.
8 Inspect the large rubber insulator cushions (or bushings) for cracks or deterioration. Replace the cushions with new ones if either of these conditions exist.
9 Inspect the rear crossmember for bending or damage. If either of these conditions exist, replace the rear crossmember with a new one. Under no circumstances should the crossmember be heated or any attempt made to bend it if it has been damaged. Due to its role as a main foundation structure for the rear suspension it must be in perfect condition or all components attached to it will be out of alignment.
10 If the rubber insulator cushions are being replaced, tap the old ones out with a soft-faced hammer. Make sure the notches on the new insulator cushions face in the front and rear directions and tap them in from the under side of the crossmember with a soft-faced hammer. Be careful not to strike the rubber part of the cushion.
11 Installation of the remaining components is the reverse of removal. Tighten all components to the proper torque.
12 Align the rear suspension.

22 Rear suspension – alignment

1 Refer to the general precautions about alignment in Section 5 of this Chapter (the alignment must be done by a properly equipped shop).
2 Before having the rear suspension aligned, check the rear wheel bearings for looseness and the rear wheels for excessive run-out.
3 Check that the tires are in good condition and inflated properly.
4 The camber and toe-in are the two adjustments possible on the rear suspension. Make sure that the shop you take the vehicle to for alignment is properly equipped to make rear suspension adjustments.

23 Steering wheel – removal and installation

1 Remove the screws retaining the steering wheel pad from the rear of the steering wheel. Remove the steering wheel pad.
2 Remove the negative battery cable from the battery.
3 Hold the wheel securely and remove the steering wheel retaining nut from the steering shaft (photo).
4 Mark the steering wheel in relationship to the steering shaft with paint. **Note**: *Do not use a punch for this operation.*
5 Install a suitable steering wheel puller to the steering wheel and remove the steering wheel from the steering shaft (photo).
6 Install the steering wheel over the steering shaft making sure the match marks line up.
7 Install the steering wheel retaining nut and tighten it to the proper torque.
8 Install the steering wheel pad and the screws.

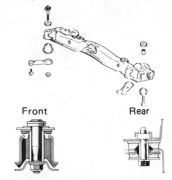

Front   Rear

Fig. 11.17 Location and cross-section of rear crossmember mounts and bushings (Sec 21)

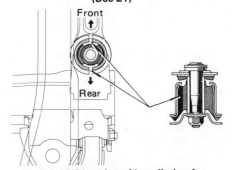

Fig. 11.18 Direction of installation for rear crossmember bushings (Sec 21)

21.6 Removing the bolts from the crossmember-to-body strap

23.3 Removing the steering wheel retaining nut

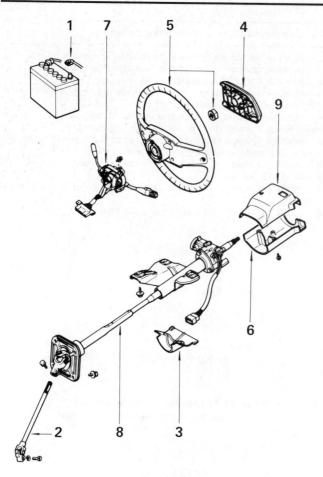

**Fig. 11.19 Steering column components
(Sec 24)**

1	Negative battery terminal	5	Steering wheel
2	Intermediate shaft	6	Column lower cover
3	Steering column garnish	7	Turn signal switch
4	Steering wheel pad	8	Steering column
		9	Column upper cover

24 Steering column – removal and installation

Note: *Refer to Fig. 11.19 during the following procedure.*
1   Remove the negative battery cable from the battery.
2   Remove the steering wheel as described in Section 23.
3   Remove the steering intermediate shaft by removing the clamp bolts from the top of the steering mainshaft and the bottom, where it connects to the rack steering assembly (photo).
4   Raise the intermediate shaft off the steering rack housing side and then remove it from the main steering column. The clamps may need to be spread apart slightly for the shaft to slide off the splines of the column and steering rack housing.
5   Remove the upper and lower steering column switch covers.
6   Remove the combination switch (Chapter 10).
7   Remove the three steering column support bolts from the lower underdash bracket.
8   Remove the column hole cover bolts retaining the cover and lower steering mainshaft assembly to the firewall.
9   Remove the steering column from the interior side of the passenger compartment.
10 Installation is the reverse of removal.
11 Make sure that all switches are connected before reconnecting the battery cable.
12 Make sure that the lower steering column bracket is aligned as described in Chapter 10.

23.5 Removing the steering wheel with a puller

24.3 Steering intermediate shaft clamp bolt (arrow)

25 Steering gear assembly – removal and installation

Note: *Refer to Fig. 11.20 for components related to the steering gear assembly.*
1   Raise and support the front of the vehicle in a secure manner.
2   Remove the front tires.
3   Remove the steering column intermediate shaft (Section 24).
4   Remove the cotter pins and nuts from the connecting links of the tie-rods at the left and right suspension knuckle arms.
5   Remove the left and right tie-rod ends from the suspension arms.
6   Remove the six bolts retaining the suspension arm braces to the crossmember (photo). Remove the two lower crossmember cover shield bolts.
7   Remove the steering gear assembly retaining bolts from the lower suspension crossmember (photos). Be careful not to damage the boots.
8   Remove the steering gear housing assembly.
9   Installation is the reverse of removal. When installing the steering gear assembly, be especially careful not to damage the boots on both the steering gear housing assembly and on the driveaxle ends.
10 Be sure to tighten all mounting bolts and nuts to the proper torque.

25.6 Six bolts retain the suspension arm bracket braces to the crossmember

25.7a Removing the steering gear assembly right side retaining bolts (arrows)

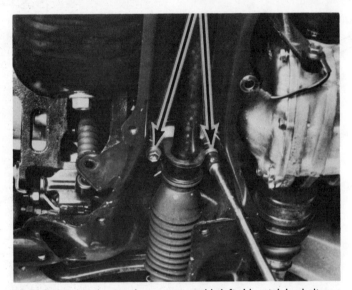

25.7b Removing the steering gear assembly left side retaining bolts (arrows)

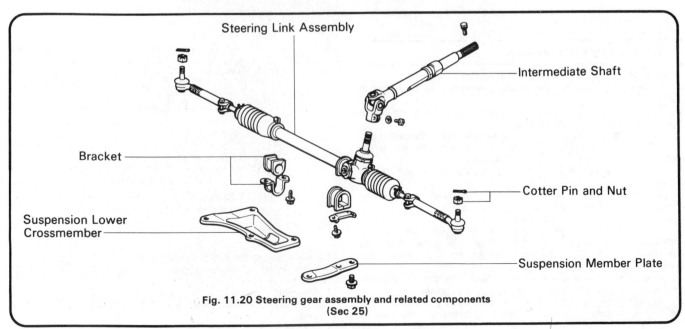

Steering Link Assembly

Intermediate Shaft

Bracket

Cotter Pin and Nut

Suspension Lower Crossmember

Suspension Member Plate

Fig. 11.20 Steering gear assembly and related components (Sec 25)

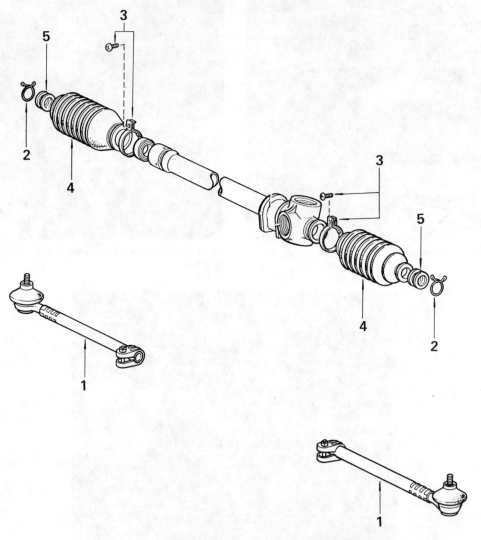

Fig. 11.21 Tie-rod rubber boot and related components (Sec 26)

1 Tie-rod end	3 Clamp	5 Rack end dust seal
2 Clip	4 Rack boot	

26 Tie-rod rubber boot – replacement

Note: *Refer to Fig. 11.21 during the following procedure.*

1   Remove the steering gear housing assembly as described in Section 25.

2   Place the steering gear housing assembly in a vise, being careful not to crush the aluminum housing.

3   Clamp onto the area shown in the accompanying illustration and wrap a piece of cloth around the tube. Do not tighten the vise to the point where it will bend the tube out of shape.

4   Mark the tie-rod ends for re-installation purposes and correct alignment.

5   Loosen the clamp for the tie-rod end and unthread the tie-rod end from the steering assembly shaft.

6   Do the same for the other side.

7   Remove the tie-rod end boots by removing the clamp on the outside and using a blunt tool to pull the boots from their channel in the steering shaft. Mark the right and left boots accordingly for replacement.

8   Installation is the reverse of removal. Make sure that the tube hole on the steering gear housing is not clogged with grease.

9   Assemble the rack boots to the housing and make sure that the left and right boots are positioned correctly. Notice that the tapered

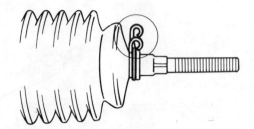

Fig. 11.22 Proper installation of steering rod boot clamps (Sec 26)

edge goes toward the steering housing side.

10   When installing the boots, make sure that they are in a straight line and not twisted in any way.

11   Assemble the steering tie-rod boot clamps as shown in the accompanying illustration. Make sure that the clamp ends are facing outward.

Chapter 12 Bodywork

Contents

1 General information

The Tercel comes in 2-, 3- and 4-door versions. The body is a single, unitized shell with bolt on front fenders and doors.

This Chapter provides information on replacement and adjustment procedures for doors, glass, hood and deck lid. Interior components as well as trim pieces are also covered. Some procedures will apply to only certain models. Light duty bodywork information is also provided so that you may repair minor dents, dings and scratches.

If your vehicle has suffered major collision damage, you will have to consult a body shop equipped to handle such work. Special equipment and techniques are required to repair damage of this nature on vehicles of the Tercel's construction type. Driveability and safety factors can only be retained if a vehicle with major collision damage is repaired according to the factory recommended procedures.

2 Maintenance – body and frame

1   The condition of your vehicle's body is very important, as it is on this that the secondhand value will mainly depend. It is much more difficult to repair a neglected or damaged body than it is to repair mechanical components. The hidden areas of the body, such as the fender wells, the frame, and the engine compartment, are equally important, although obviously not requiring as frequent attention as the rest of the body.
2   Once a year, or every 12 000 miles, it is a good idea to have the underside of the body and the frame steam cleaned. All traces of dirt and oil will be removed and the underside can then be inspected carefully for rust, damaged brake lines, frayed electrical wiring, damaged cables, and other problems.
3   At the same time, clean the engine and the engine compartment using either a steam cleaner or a water soluble degreaser.
4   The fender wells should be given particular attention, as undercoating can peel away and stones and dirt thrown up by the tires can cause the paint to chip and flake, allowing rust to set in. If rust is found, clean down to the bare metal and apply an anti-rust paint.
5   The body should be washed once a week (or when dirty). Thoroughly wet the vehicle to soften the dirt, then wash it down with a soft sponge and plenty of clean soapy water. If the surplus dirt is not washed off very carefully, it will in time wear down the paint.
6   Spots of tar or asphalt coating thrown from the road surfaces are best removed with a cloth soaked in solvent.
7   Once every six months, give the body and chrome trim a thorough wax job. If a chrome cleaner is used to remove rust on any of the vehicle's plated parts, remember that the cleaner also removes part of the chrome so use it sparingly.

3 Maintenance – upholstery and carpets

1   Every three months, remove the carpets or mats and thoroughly clean the interior of the vehicle (more frequently if necessary). Vacuum the upholstery and carpets to remove loose dirt and dust.
2   If the upholstery is soiled, apply an upholstery cleaner with a damp sponge and wipe it with a clean, dry cloth.

4   Body repair – minor damage

See color photo sequence on pages 204 and 205.

Repair of minor scratches

If the scratch is very superficial, and does not penetrate to the metal of the bodywork, repair is very simple. Lightly rub the area of the scratch with a fine rubbing compound to remove loose paint from the scratch and to clear the surrounding paint of wax buildup. Rinse the area with clean water.

Apply touch-up paint to the scratch using a small brush. Continue to apply thin layers of paint until the surface of the paint in the scratch is level with the surrounding paint. Allow the new paint at least two weeks to harden, then blend it into the surrounding paint by rubbing with a very fine rubbing compound. Finally, apply a coat of wax to the scratch area.

Where the scratch has penetrated the paint and exposed the metal of the body, causing the metal to rust, a different repair technique is required. Remove any loose rust from the bottom of the scratch with a pocket knife, then apply rust inhibiting paint to prevent the formation of rust in the future. Using a rubber or nylon applicator, coat the scratched area with glaze type filler. If required, this filler can be mixed with thinner to provide a very thin paste which is ideal for filling narrow scratches. Before the glaze filler in the scratch hardens, wrap a piece of smooth cotton cloth around the top of a finger. Dip the cloth in thinner and then quickly wipe it along the surface of the scratch. This will ensure that the surface of the filler is slightly hollowed. The scratch can now be painted over as described earlier in this Section.

Repair of dents

When denting of the vehicle's bodywork has taken place, the first task is to pull the dent out until the affected area nearly attains its original shape. There is little point in trying to restore the original shape completely as the metal in the damaged area will have stretched on impact and cannot be reshaped fully to its original contours. It is better to bring the level of the dent up to a point which is about $\frac{1}{8}$ in below the level of the surrounding metal. In cases where the dent is very shallow, it is not worth trying to pull it out at all.

If the underside of the dent is accessible, it can be hammered out gently from behind using a mallet with a wooden or plastic head. Whilst doing this, hold a suitable block of wood firmly against the metal to absorb the hammer blows and thus prevent a large area of the metal from being stretched out.

If the dent is in a section of the body which has double layers, or some other factor making it inaccessible from behind, a different technique is in order. Drill several small holes through the metal inside the damaged area, particularly in the deeper sections. Screw long self-tapping screws into the holes just enough for them to get a good grip in the metal. Now the dent can be pulled out by pulling on the protruding head of the screws with a pair of locking pliers.

The next stage of the repair is the removal of the paint from the damaged area and from an inch or so of the surrounding 'sound' metal. This is accomplished most easily by using a wire brush or sanding disc in a drill motor, although it can be done just as effectively by hand with sandpaper. To complete the preparation for filling, score the surface of the bare metal with a screwdriver or the tang of a file (or drill small holes in the affected area). This will provide a really good 'key' for the filler material. To complete the repair, see the Section on filling and painting.

Repair of rust holes or gashes

Remove all paint from the affected area and from an inch or so of the surrounding 'sound' metal using a sanding disc or wire brush mounted in a drill motor. If these are not available a few sheets of sandpaper will do the job just as effectively. With the paint removed you will be able to determine the severity of the corrosion and therefore decide whether to replace the whole panel if possible, or to repair the affected area. New body panels are not as expensive as most people think and it is often quicker and more satisfactory to install a new panel than to attempt to repair large areas of rust.

Remove all trim pieces from the affected area (except those which will act as a guide to the original shape of the damaged body ie. headlamp shells etc). Then, using metal snips or a hacksaw blade, remove all loose metal and any other metal that is badly affected by rust. Hammer the edges of the hole inwards to create a slight depression for the filler material.

Wire brush the affected area to remove the powdery rust from the surface of the metal. If the back of the rusted area is accessible, treat it with rust-inhibiting paint.

Before filling can be done it will be necessary to block the hole in some way. This can be accomplished with sheet metal riveted or screwed into place, or by stuffing the hole with wire mesh.

Once the hole is blocked off the affected area can be filled and painted (see the following section on filling and painting).

Filling and painting

Many types of body fillers are available, but generally speaking body repair kits which contain filler paste and a tube of resin hardener are best for this type of repair work. A wide, flexible plastic or nylon applicator will be necessary for imparting a smooth and contoured finish to the surface of the filler material.

Mix up a small amount of filler on a clean piece of wood or cardboard (use the hardener sparingly). Follow the maker's instructions on the package, otherwise the filler will set incorrectly.

Using the applicator, apply the filler paste to the prepared area. Draw the applicator across the surface of the filler to achieve the desired contour and to level the filler surface. As soon as a contour that approximates the correct one is achieved, stop working the paste. If you continue, the paste will begin to stick to the applicator. Continue to add thin layers of filler paste at 20-minute intervals until the level of the filler is just proud of the surrounding metal.

Once the filler has hardened, excess can be removed using a body file. From then on, progressively finer grades of sandpaper should be used, starting with a 180-grit paper and finishing with 600-grit wet-or-dry paper. Always wrap the sandpaper around a flat rubber or wooden block, otherwise the surface of the filler will not be completely flat. During the sanding of the filler surface the wet-or-dry paper should be periodically rinsed in water. This will ensure that a very smooth finish is produced in the final stage.

At this point, the repair area should be surrounded by a ring of bare metal, which in turn should be encircled by the finely feathered edge of the good paint. Rinse the repair area with clean water until all of the dust produced by the sand operation has gone.

Spray the entire area with a light coat of primer. This will reveal any imperfections in the surface of the filler. Repair these imperfections with fresh filler paste or glaze filler and once more smooth the surface with sandpaper. Repeat this spray-and-repair procedure until you are satisfied that the surface of the filler and the feathered edge of the paintwork are perfect. Rinse the area with clean water and allow to dry fully.

The repair area is now ready for painting. Paint spraying must be carried out in a warm, dry, windless and dustfree atmosphere. These conditions can be created if you have access to a large indoor working area, but if you are forced to work in the open, you will have to pick your day very carefully. If you are working indoors, dousing the floor in the work area with water will help to settle the dust which would otherwise be in the air. If the repair area is confined to one body panel, mask off the surrounding panels. This will help to minimise the effects of a slight mis-match in paint color. Trim pieces such as chrome strips, door handles, etc., will also need to be masked off or removed. Use masking tape and several thicknesses of newspaper for the masking operations.

Before spraying, shake the paint can thoroughly, then spray a test area until the technique is mastered. Cover the repair area with a thick coat of primer. The thickness should be built up using several thin layers of primer rather than one thick one. Using 600-grit wet-or-dry sandpaper, rub down the surface of the primer until it is very smooth. While doing this, the work area should be thoroughly rinsed with water, and the wet-or-dry sandpaper periodically rinsed as well. Allow the primer to dry before spraying additional coats.

Spray on the top coat, again building up the thickness by using several thin layers of paint. Begin spraying in the center of the repair area and then, using a circular motion, work out until the whole repair area and about two inches of the surrounding original paint is covered. Remove all masking material 10 to 15 minutes after spraying on the final coat of paint. Allow the new paint at least two weeks to harden, then using a very fine rubbing compound, blend the edges of the new paint into the existing paint. Finally, apply a coat of wax.

5 Body and frame repairs – major damage

1   Major damage must be repaired by an auto body/frame repair shop with the necessary welding and hydraulic straightening equipment.
2   If the damage has been serious, it is vital that the frame be checked for correct alignment, as the handling of the vehicle will be affected. Other problems, such as excessive tire wear and wear in the transmission and steering may also occur.

6 Maintenance – hinges and locks

Once every 3000 miles, or every three months, the door and hood hinges and locks should be given a few drops of light oil or lock lubricant. The door striker plates can be given a thin coat of grease to reduce wear and ensure free movement.

7 Door trim panel – removal and installation

1   Remove the window regulator handle with a special spring clip tool (photo) (a thin cloth can be rotated in the lip behind the handle to pop the spring loose).
2   Remove the two screws retaining the arm rest (photo).
3   Remove the screw holding the door handle trim plate to the panel.
4   Remove the door handle trim plate.
5   Use a wide-blade, soft-tipped implement such as a screwdriver or putty knife covered with tape to pry the inner door panel away from the door and pop the retaining clips loose.
6   When the door panel is completely loose from the door, lift it slightly to release it from the lip of the window molding and remove it from the car.
7   Before installing the door panel make sure that the trim clips are all in good condition. If they are broken or bent, insert new clips into the door panel before attempting to install the panel.
8   Make sure that the service hole cover is covering the inner portion of the door completely and has not fallen away in any spots before installing the inner door panel. Make sure that the inside edge of the service hole cover is situated in the slit at the bottom of the opening. Make sure that the inside edge of the service hole cover is not covering any of the holes for the door trim clips.
9   Check that the link holder is not interfering with the application of the inner door panel. Notice the cushioning pads under the lock and latch links (photo).
10 Install the door clip weatherstrip over the lip of the window molding with the window rolled down all the way.
11 Push the door panel into place on the door making sure that all the clips line up with all the retaining holes.
12 Gradually work your way around the outer edge of the door and push the clips into each individual hole.
13 Install the door inside handle trim plate.
14 Install the arm rest.
15 Install the window regulator handle, spring and inner washer.

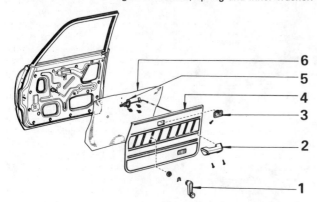

Fig. 12.1 Door trim panel components (Sec 7)

1   Window regulator handle
2   Arm rest
3   Door inside handle trim plate
4   Door trim
5   Door inside handle
6   Service hole cover

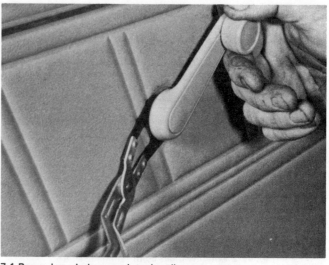

7.1 Removing window regulator handle

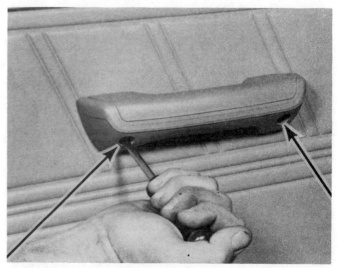

7.2 Removing the screws retaining the arm rest

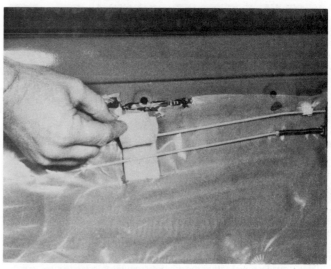

7.9 Pads located under lock and latch links

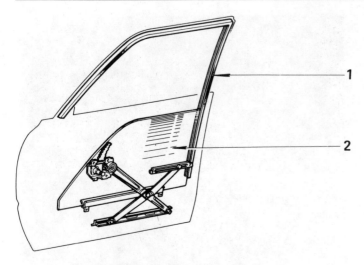

Fig. 12.2 Window glass components (Sec 8)

1   *Inner weatherstrip*
2   *Glass and channel assembly*

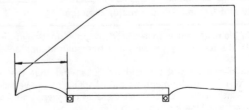

226 mm (8.90 in.) ... 2-door, 3-door
242.7 mm (9.555 in.) .. 4-door

**Fig. 12.3 Correct adjustment of window
glass in glass channel (Sec 8)**

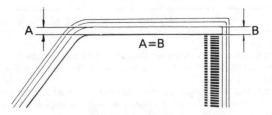

**Fig. 12.4 Make measurements A and B equal for proper door glass
alignment (Sec 8)**

8   Door window glass – removal, installation and adjustment

1   Remove the inner door trim panel as described in Section 7.
2   Lower the window glass to the bottom position.
3   Disconnect the door glass from the window regulator by removing the two connecting bolts.
4   Pull the inner weatherstrip out of the groove around the frame of the door.
5   Turn the glass at a 45° angle and pull it upward and out through the window channel and out of the door.
6   Remove the glass from the door channel using a screwdriver or other similar tool.
7   Apply soapy water solution to the inner part of the weatherstrip channel.
8   Tap the glass into the channel using a soft-faced hammer. Be sure to position the glass in the channel with the distance between the front of the glass and the front of the channel set to the specification (Fig. 12.3). Notice that the specification for 2-door and 3-door cars is different from the specification for 4-door cars.
9   Turn the glass at a 45° angle downward at the front and insert it into the door channel from the top. Straighten the glass out inside the door and position it in the channels.

10 Loosely install the door glass assembly to the window regulator with the two bolts.
11 Install the inner weatherstrip trim panel.
12 Roll the window up to an almost closed position.
13 Adjust the door glass so that the measurements at A and B (Fig. 12.4) are equal. Tighten the bolts to the window equalizer.
14 Complete the window installation by installing the service hole cover with new adhesive.
15 Install the door trim panel by referring to Section 7.

9   Door glass regulator – removal, adjustment and installation

1   Remove the door trim panel as described in Section 7.
2   Remove the door inside handle as described in Section 11.
3   Remove the service hole cover, being careful not to tear it so it may be re-used.

9.5 Five bolts (arrows) retain the window regulator to the door

9.6 Removing the regulator through the bottom access hole

4   Remove the door window glass as described in Section 8.
5   Remove the five bolts retaining the window regulator to the inside of the door (photo).
6   Remove the window regulator from the door through the bottom access hole (photo).
7   Inspect the window regulator for damage or breakage.
8   Check the gears for wear or damage.
9   Check the springs for breakage or loss of tension.
10 Check that there is lubrication on all regulator sliding mechanism surfaces.
11 Install the window regulator through the access hole in the bottom of the door.
12 Installation is the reverse of removal. Make sure that you adjust the door glass as described in Section 8.
13 Make sure that you re-seal the inner door glass service hole cover with new adhesive before installing the inner door panel.

10 Door latch assembly – removal and installation

1   Remove the inner door trim panel as described in Section 7.
2   Remove the door window glass and regulator as described in Section 9.
3   Disconnect the door outside locking control link (photo). Disconnect the door outside opening control link.
4   For 2- and 3-door cars only, remove the mounting bolt of the door inside locking link.
5   For 2- and 3-door cars only, remove the door rear-lower frame and mounting bolt.
6   Remove the door lock and latch assembly mounting screws (photo).
7   Installation of the latch assembly is the reverse of removal.

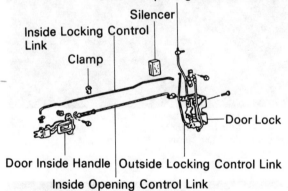

Fig. 12.5 Two-door and 3-door latch assembly components (Sec 10)

11 Interior door handle – removal and installation

1   Remove the interior door panel as described in Section 7.
2   Remove the door lock side link from the inner door handle.
3   Unscrew the inner door handle from the mounting surface (it is retained by three bolts) (photo).
4   Remove the inner door handle.
5   Looosely install the door handle to the door panel, making sure that the inner trim is covering the area directly behind it.
6   Install the door opening control link to the door handle.
7   To adjust the operating clearance, move the handle forward to the point where it begins to meet resistance from the door opening control link.
8   Move it back 0.02 to 0.04 in (0.5 to 1.0 mm) and tighten the three retaining bolts.
9   Install the interior door panel.

12 Door exterior handle – removal and installation

1   Remove the door trim panel as described in Section 7.

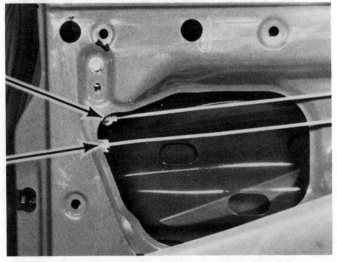

10.3 Removing the door opening link and the door locking link (arrows)

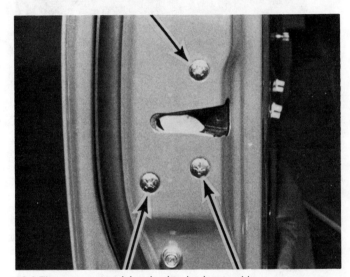

10.6 Three screws retaining the door latch assembly

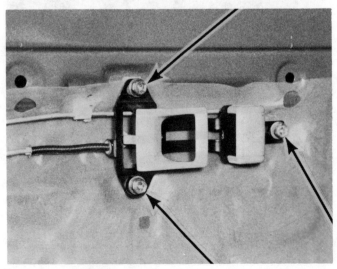

11.3 Inner door handle retaining bolts

This photo sequence illustrates the repair of a dent and damaged paintwork. The procedure for the repair of a hole is similar. Refer to the text for more complete instructions

After removing any adjacent body trim, hammer the dent out. The damaged area should then be made slightly concave

Use coarse sandpaper or a sanding disc on a drill motor to remove all paint from the damaged area. Feather the sanded area into the edges of the surrounding paint, using progressively finer grades of sandpaper

The damaged area should be treated with rust remover prior to application of the body filler. In the case of a rust hole, all rusted sheet metal should be cut away

Carefully follow manufacturer's instructions when mixing the body filler so as to have the longest possible working time during application. Rust holes should be covered with fiberglass screen held in place with dabs of body filler prior to repair

Apply the filler with a flexible applicator in thin layers at 20 minute intervals. Use an applicator such as a wood spatula for confined areas. The filler should protrude slightly above the surrounding area

Shape the filler with a surform-type plane. Then, use water and progressively finer grades of sandpaper and a sanding block to wet-sand the area until it is smooth. Feather the edges of the repair area into the surrounding paint.

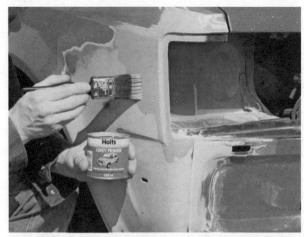

Use spray or brush applied primer to cover the entire repair area so that slight imperfections in the surface will be filled in. Prime at least one inch into the area surrounding the repair. Be careful of over-spray when using spray-type primer

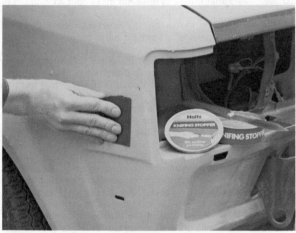

Wet-sand the primer with fine (approximately 400 grade) sandpaper until the area is smooth to the touch and blended into the surrounding paint. Use filler paste on minor imperfections

After the filler paste has dried, use rubbing compound to ensure that the surface of the primer is smooth. Prior to painting, the surface should be wiped down with a tack rag or lint-free cloth soaked in lacquer thinner

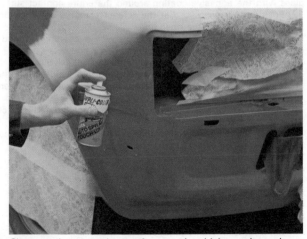

Choose a dry, warm, breeze-free area in which to paint and make sure that adjacent areas are protected from over-spray. Shake the spray paint can thoroughly and apply the top coat to the repair area, building it up by applying several coats, working from the center

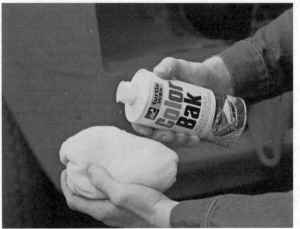

After allowing at least two weeks for the paint to harden, use fine rubbing compound to blend the area into the original paint. Wax can now be applied

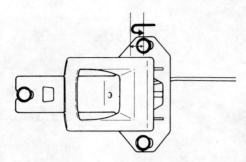

Fig. 12.6 Adjust the interior door handle operating clearance (Sec 11)

2   Roll the door window glass all the way to the top.
3   Disconnect the outside opening control link from the door handle assembly.
4   From the inside, remove the bolts retaining the door handle to the outside door sheet metal.
5   Remove the door handle from the outside of the vehicle. Notice the pad under the door handle assembly.
6   Position the door handle on the vehicle.
7   Insert the bolts and tighten the door handle to the outside sheet metal of the door.
8   With the control link adjuster pin removed from the hole in the handle assembly, turn the adjuster so that the pin is 0.028 to 0.039 in (0.5 to 1.0 mm) below the hole. Make sure that the control link is in its rest position.
9   Raise the control link and insert the pin in the hole.
10   Install the interior door service hole cover using new adhesive.
11   Install the interior door trim panel as described in Section 7.

13 Door cylinder lock – removal and installation

1   Remove the interior door handle (Section 7).
2   Roll the door window glass to the top of its travel.
3   Disconnect the door lock control link from the lock assembly.
4   Withdraw the clip retaining the door lock cylinder assembly to the outside door sheet metal.
5   Withdraw the door lock from the outside of the door.
6   Installation is the reverse of removal. Make sure that new adhesive is installed around the inner door service cover hole before installing the inner door trim panel.

14 Windshield glass – removal and installation

Note: *The windshield glass installation process is very critical due to the possibility of breaking an expensive windshield, as well as the steps needed to make a proper weather-tight seal. If you are installing a windshield glass for the first time, it might be wise to seek the help of someone who is experienced in this type of work. It is possible to install the windshield glass successfully, however, glass shops are usually able to perform the job at a quick and relatively inexpensive rate. Use care when installing the windshield not to damage the bodywork and to ensure a clean job around interior components.*

Removal

1   Remove the rear view mirror.
2   Remove the windshield pillar inner trim panels.
3   Remove the roof headliner trim.
4   Remove the wiper arms.
5   Remove the cowl ventilator panel.
6   Remove the radio antenna.
7   Remove the windshield corner moldings by using a flat bladed tool to pry them out of the groove. Be sure not to damage the bodywork or the moldings when performing this job.
8   Apply adhesive tape around the outer body opening of the window to protect the bodywork.
9   Remove the windshield outside molding by prying up with a wide-bladed, flat tool. Raise the molding clip and molding with this tool to detach them from the windshield gasket (Fig. 12.8).

10   Push a piece of piano wire attached to two boards through the channel between the gasket and the body molding. **Note:** *Be careful during the following steps not to damage the interior, exterior or glass.*
11   Pull the piano wire with the two pieces of board using a helper where necessary to reach around the center parts of the windshield.
12   Remove the glass from the car after the molding has been separated all the way around by the piano wire method.
13   Check the T-stud on the windshield mounting to make sure it is not damaged. If it is damaged, remove the old one and drill a new 0.12 in (3 mm) diameter hole into the body (Fig. 12.10). Then attach a new clip with a self-tapping sheet metal screw.
14   Remove any of the windshield gasket left on the body.
15   The urethane pad on the body lip can be left in place.
16   Clean the contact surface with a piece of cloth soaked in alcohol.
17   Make sure that the urethane gum sticking to the glass is removed if you are installing a used piece of glass. Clean the glass with alcohol.

Installation

18   Place the glass into the window opening and position it so that the lip of the glass is the same distance from the edge of the opening all the way around.
19   Check that the rubber spacers at the bottom of the glass support the glass adequately. If they don't, replace them with new ones.
20   Make sure that the glass does not make contact with the retaining clips.
21   Make reference marks on the masking tape around the body molding and the glass for alignment purposes.
22   Remove the glass.
23   Clean the contact surface of the glass with alcohol or a similar solvent in a strip 1½ in wide around the entire rim.
24   Apply double-stick tape at a point 0.28 in (7 mm) from the glass rim.
25   Stick the new gasket to the double-edge tape and install it all the way around the perimeter of the glass. Cut V-wedges into the corner so that the gasket fits around the edges.
26   Coat the surface of the body with the special primer M (available from Mazda dealers).
27   Let the primer coating dry for approximately ten minutes. Make sure that the glass installation is completed within two hours of applying the primer. Be careful that the contact surface is coated evenly, but not excessively around the entire area.
28   Coat the contact surface of the glass with primer G.
29   Clean any excess off with a clean cloth. Make sure that the glass is installed within 70 minutes of application of primer G.
30   Mix the adhesive coating within five minutes of the time you plan to use it.
31   Use an adhesive application cartridge with a 0.20 in (5 mm) hole cut in the nose of it. Load the gun with the adhesive coating. Coat the glass with the adhesive coating around the entire contact surface.
32   Position the glass so that the reference marks are lined up and push it carefully into the opening.
33   Apply adhesive to the outer edge of the opening. Immediately remove any excess that gets on the glass or bodywork.
34   Clamp the glass down securely until the adhesive is set.
35   After the adhesive has hardened, perform a leak test around the entire opening. If there are any leaks, seal them with a commercially available auto glass sealer.
36   Install the windshield outside upper side molding and joint covers using a sealer to prevent rust.
37   Attach the corner moldings to the remaining windshield moldings.
38   Install the windshield corner molding.
39   Install the radio antenna.
40   Install the cowl ventilator panel.
41   Install the wiper arms.
42   Install the roof headlining trim.
43   Install the windshield pillar inner panel.
44   Install the rear-view mirror.

15 Rear window glass – removal and installation

Note: *This procedure does not apply to 3-door vehicles.*

Removal

1   Remove the rear seat cushion.

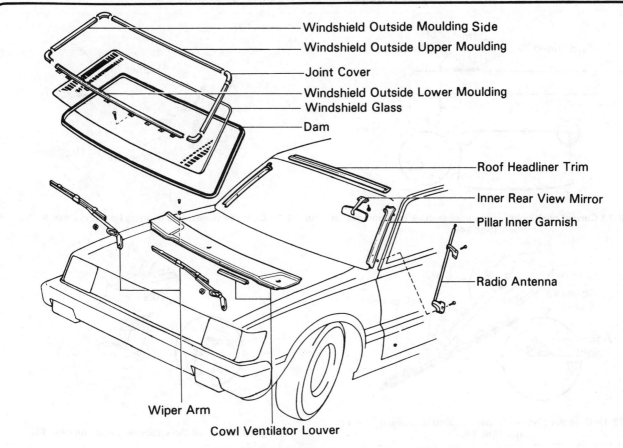

Windshield Outside Moulding Side
Windshield Outside Upper Moulding
Joint Cover
Windshield Outside Lower Moulding
Windshield Glass
Dam

Roof Headliner Trim
Inner Rear View Mirror
Pillar Inner Garnish

Radio Antenna

Wiper Arm
Cowl Ventilator Louver

Fig. 12.7 Windshield and related components (Sec 14)

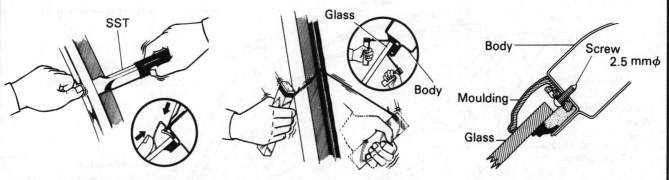

SST

Glass
Body

Body
Screw
2.5 mmφ
Moulding
Glass

Fig. 12.8 Raise the molding clips and molding before windshield removal (Sec 14)

Fig. 12.9 Use piano wire and two boards to cut the windshield from the opening (Sec 14)

Fig. 12.10 Replace the T-stud on the windshield mounting (Sec 14)

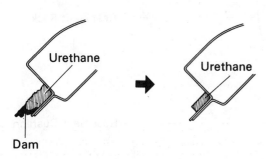

Urethane

Urethane

Dam

Fig. 12.11 Leave the urethane pad in place after stripping the gasket (dam) (Sec 14)

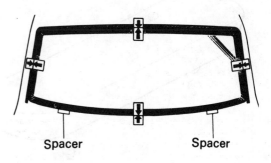

Spacer

Spacer

Fig. 12.12 Correct positioning of the windshield (Sec 14)

210

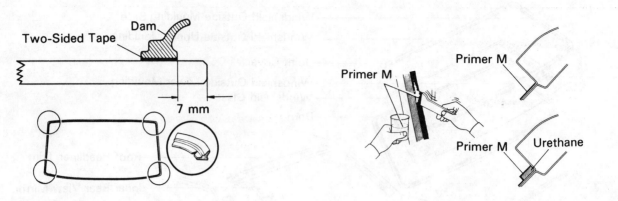

Fig. 12.13 Correct positioning of the double-stick tape and gasket (dam) (Sec 14)

Fig. 12.14 Coat the windshield opening lip with primer M (Sec 14)

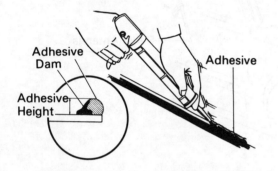

Fig. 12.15 Coat the glass with special adhesive using a caulking gun (Sec 14)

Fig. 12.16 Install the windshield molding (Sec 14)

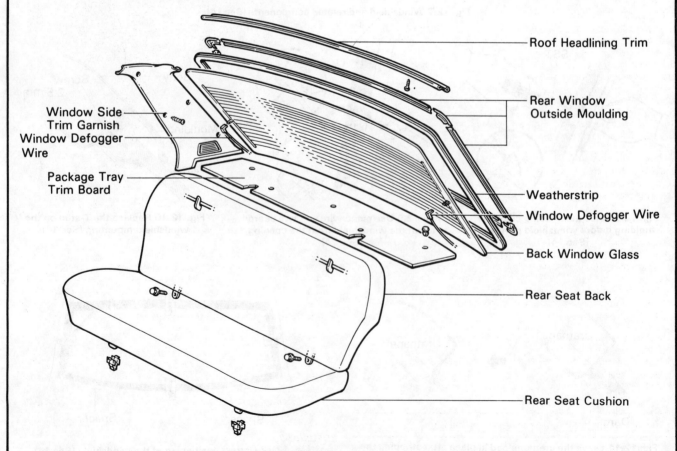

Roof Headlining Trim

Rear Window Outside Moulding

Window Side Trim Garnish

Window Defogger Wire

Package Tray Trim Board

Weatherstrip

Window Defogger Wire

Back Window Glass

Rear Seat Back

Rear Seat Cushion

Fig. 12.17 Rear window glass and related components (Sec 15)

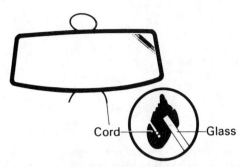

Fig. 12.18 Install a cord into the weatherstrip groove for rear window installation (Sec 15)

2   Remove the rear seat back (it is retained by two screws).
3   Remove the side trim panel (it is retained by four screws).
4   Remove the roof headlining trim.
5   Remove the rear package tray.
6   Disconnect the rear window defogger wires at the window.
7   Apply adhesive tape to the edge of the body directly around the window opening to protect the body during the window removal and installation procedures.
8   Remove the rear window outside corner molding with a screwdriver, being careful not to scratch the body.
9   Using a flat, wide-bladed screwdriver or similar tool, remove the remaining molding around the perimeter of the glass.
10 Use a similar flat-bladed tool to loosen the weatherstrip from the body. Be very careful not to damage the bodywork or paint.
11 Pry up the weatherstrip lip, working from the inside of the body to the outside of the body. Use a prying tool and work slowly along the lip. Be careful not to damage the bodywork on either side and work only a little at a time.

Installation

12 Clean the edge of the body and make sure that the lip has no adhesive left from the previous window installation. Wipe off any adhesive with plain rubbing alcohol.
13 Install the weatherstrip on the glass. If the weatherstrip is hardened, replace it or it will leak.
14 Install a small diameter nylon clothes line or similar flexible string along the weatherstrip groove as shown in Fig. 12.18.
15 Apply a soapy water solution to the contact face of the weatherstrip lip and to the body flange of the window.
16 Place the window over the opening in the body with the middle of the lower part of the molding positioned over the lip of the body flange.
17 Pull the string which you have previously installed along the inside lip slowly while a helper pushes the window into its seat on the flange.
18 Tap the glass carefully from the outside to make sure that it seats itself into the opening. Use caution when tapping the glass to avoid breakage.
19 Apply a line of masking tape around the glass directly next to the weatherstrip to protect the glass from the adhesive.
20 Apply the proper adhesive between the weatherstrip and the glass and between the weatherstrip and the body.
21 When the adhesive is dry, remove the masking tape from the glass.
22 Apply the soapy water solution to the weatherstrip groove.
23 Push the molding into place while using a flat-bladed tool to raise the lip of the weatherstripping.
24 Install the corner molding pieces in the same manner.
25 Connect the rear window defogger wires.
26 Install the package tray.
27 Install the roof headlining trim.
28 Install the side panel.
29 Install the rear seat cushion and back.

16 Seats and seat belts – removal and installation

Seat removal
1   The front seats are removed by first positioning them in their forward-most position. This will reveal the two rear track retaining bolts.

2   Remove the two rear track retaining bolts (photo).
3   Slide the front seats to the rear position.
4   Withdraw the two forward seat track retaining bolts.
5   Remove the seat.
6   The back seat is removed by prying the seat back bottom up from the retaining clips on the floor.
7   Pull the seat back bottom up and out of the car.

Rear seat back removal (fixed seat)
8   Remove the screws retaining the rear seat back cover.
9   Remove the seat back.

Rear seat back removal (hinged pull-down seats)
10 Remove the bolts retaining the inner hinge assembly to the floor of the car.
11 Remove the bolts retaining the outer hinge assembly to the seat.
12 Remove the rear seat back.

Seat belt removal
13 Remove the cover from the lower seat belt attaching point.
14 Remove the bolt retaining the lower seat belt.
15 Remove the bolt retaining the upper seat belt.
16 Remove the seat belt.

Installation
17 Installation of all components is the reverse of removal. Take care to tighten the seat belt retaining bolts to the proper torque, as they are a safety item and could be hazardous if loose during a collision. Make sure that the seats are securely bolted down as they are also safety related.

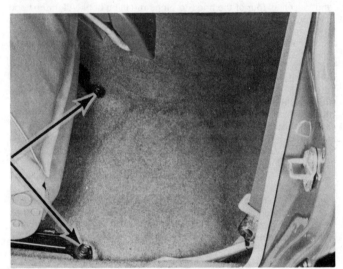

16.2 Two front seat rear track retaining bolts

17 Hood – removal, installation and adjustment

Note: The removal and installation procedures require two people. Do not attempt to remove or install the hood with only one person, as injury to the person as well as damage to the car can result.

Removal
1   Position one person on each side of the hood in the open position.
2   Scribe a mark around the hood hinges where they are positioned against the flat of the bottom of the hood. This will aid in positioning and adjustment when the hood is reinstalled.
4   Remove the four bolts retaining the hood to the hood hinges.
5   Lift the hood off the car.

Installation
6   Installation is the reverse of removal.
7   Make sure the hood is aligned with the previously scribed marks. If a new hood is being installed, follow the adjustment procedure below.

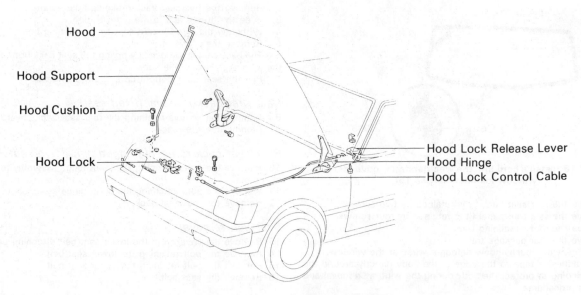

Fig. 12.19 Hood and related components (Sec 17)

Adjustment

8   To adjust the hood, make sure it is installed in the proper position and loosen all four of the hood-to-hinge retaining bolts. Align the hood and make sure that the gap along all edges is equal. Tighten the bolts once the hood is positioned properly. To adjust the front edge of the hood, raise or lower the rubber bumpers on the cowling so that the hood closes in the proper position.

9   Adjust the hood latch if the hood is pulled to one side or the other when closed. If the front of the hood is too loose (play between the latched position and the position the hood can be pulled up to in the front), adjust the latch to hold the hood down tightly. Readjustment of the rubber bumpers may also be necessary to achieve the right fit at the front of the hood.

18   Grille – removal and installation

1   The grille is retained by special snap clips positioned around its perimeter. If you look directly in at the clip you will see that it has two protruding prongs. To release the grille from its installed position on the car, insert a screwdriver or other flat tool between each protruding prong and spread it out (photo). This will release the grille from the retaining clips.

2   To install the grille, make sure all of the clips are installed and in good condition. If they are not, replace the clips with new ones.

3   Push the grille onto each individual clip making sure that it snaps into position.

19   Front bumper – removal and installation

1   Unplug the turn signal lights from their plugs located underneath the bumper.

2   Remove the front bumper assembly retaining bolts from the top and front of the lower frame horn (photos). Remove the bolts on both sides of the car.

3   Pull the bumper straight out from the car.

4   Disassemble the front bumper from the front bumper reinforcement by removing the retaining screws from the lower and side retainer brackets.

5   Unbolt the front bumper from the front bumper reinforcement bracket.

6   The front bumper pad is removed by withdrawing the upper retaining bolts.

7   Installation is the reverse of removal. Be sure to tighten all bolts to the proper torque. Make sure that the lights are plugged back in and check them for proper operation.

18.1 Removing the grille retaining clip by spreading it with a screwdriver

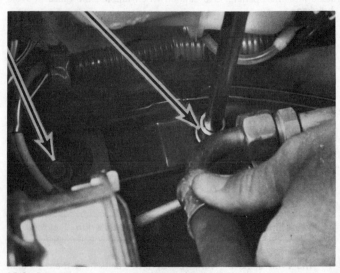

19.2a Removing the two bolts (arrows) holding the front bumper assembly to the top of the frame horn

19.2b Removing the bolts holding the front bumper assembly to the front of the frame horn

20.1 Removing the three bolts retaining the rear bumper bracket assemblies (arrows)

20 Rear bumper – removal and installation

1 From beneath the car remove the three bolts on each side (photo) retaining the combination bumper bracket and towing hook assemblies.
2 Withdraw the rear bumper straight back from the car.
3 Remove the bolts retaining the lower bumper retainers to the bumper.
4 Remove the rear bumper from the rear bumper reinforcement bracket.
5 Installation is the reverse of removal.

21 Side doors and latches – adjustment

1 Door adjustment is accomplished by first loosening the hinge bolts at the point they attach to the body. Fit the door to the opening carefully and see that the gap around the edges is equal.
2 It may be necessary to have a helper or jack or some other sort of support device to maintain the alignment while re-tightening the bolts.
3 Close the door carefully against the latch and see that it fits the opening correctly and the latch does not force the door up or down. If the latch causes the door to move as it engages the door, the latch will also need adjustment.

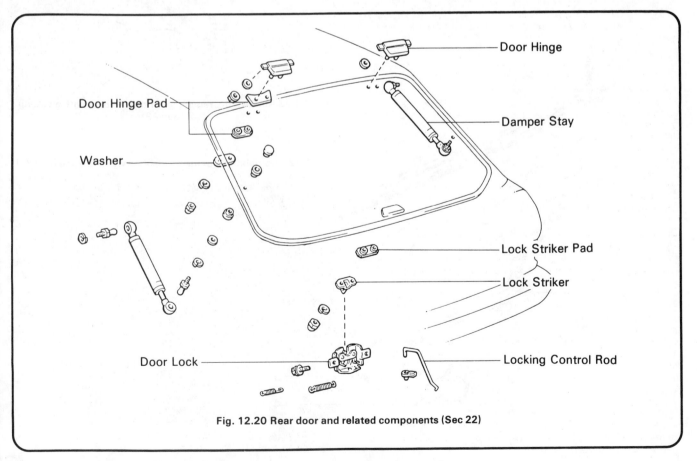

Fig. 12.20 Rear door and related components (Sec 22)

4   Loosen the door latch retaining screws. Adjust the latch up, down or to the side to attain the correct closing feel. It may be necessary to make several trial and error fits before this alignment is correct. Take your time and fit the door properly and it will close and latch easily with a minimum of effort.
5   Retighten the door latch screws when the adjustment is completed.

22 Rear door (3-door models) – removal, installation and adjustment

Removal
1   Remove the bolts retaining the back door hinge to the glass.
2   Remove the back door piston from the door assembly.
3   Remove the back door.

Installation
4   Installation is the reverse of removal. Adjust the door before adjusting the door striker.

Adjustment
5   With the door hinge installation nuts loose on the body side, make sure that the gaps at points A, B, C and D are equal (Fig. 12.21).
6   Adjust the back door striker so that the door closes properly and does not move in any direction as the striker engages the latch.
7   Make sure that the door opening pistons support the door securely and do not put any side force on the door in the open position. If the pistons are not equal in strength, they will force the door out of alignment and should be replaced with new ones. **Caution:** *The pistons should not be disassembled as they contain gas under high pressure.*

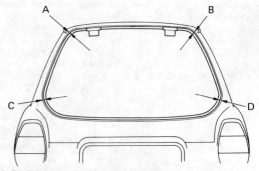

Fig. 12.21 Position the glass so that the gaps at A, B, C and D are equal (Sec 22)

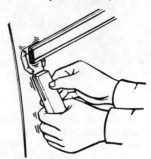

Fig. 12.22 Prying up the molding at the edge to begin removing the molding (Sec 23)

Fig. 12.23 Remove the remainder of the molding with a cutting tool (Sec 23)

Fig. 12.24 Components of the windshield wiper linkage (Sec 24)

1   Wiper arm and blade   3   Spring
2   Wiper link   4   Wiper motor

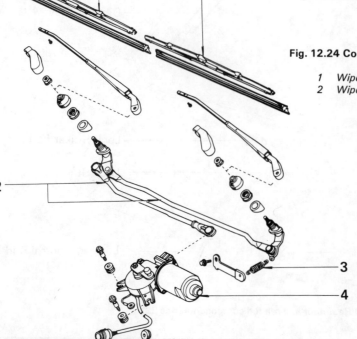

23 Body side molding – removal and installation

Note: *Make certain that the body side moldings on your vehicle are the originals from the factory. These are retained by adhesive and will be described in the following text. If you have moldings that have been installed either by the dealer or at some other point in the vehicle's life, you will have to follow the procedures involving that particular type of side molding.*

1   To remove the molding, strip about 1.2 in (30 mm) of the molding at the edge with a scraper wrapped in protective tape.
2   Remove the remainder of the molding by cutting the adhesive with a special cutter or blade.
3   Take care not to damage the body paint during this step as it is a very critical operation.
4   Once the molding is removed, remove the remaining adhesive on the body with a scraper or sandpaper.
5   Clean the body molding installation area with solvent.
6   Heat the body contact area to about 86 to 122°F (30 to 50°C) with an infrared light.
7   Heat the molding to the same temperature. Make sure the molding is not heated excessively as it can be damaged.
8   Apply the primer T to the punched-out areas of the two-sided tape at both ends of the molding and allow it to set for at least 15 minutes.

24 Windshield wiper linkage – removal, inspection and installation

1   Remove the wiper arm and blade from the linkage on the outside of the vehicle.
2   Remove the knob retaining the wiper arm to the wiper link.
3   Remove the wiper link from the wiper motor as described in Chapter 11.
4   Remove the spring from the wiper links.
5   Remove the links from beneath the cowl area.
6   Inspect the wiper links for looseness, breakage or bending. If any of these conditions exist, replace the wiper links with new ones, as they are too fragile to be re-bent or re-shaped.
7   Installation is the reverse of removal. Make sure that the wipers are in the parked position before connecting the link to the wiper motor. Also make sure that the wiper motor is in its fully parked position before connecting the wiper links.
9   Apply adhesive to the punched-out areas of the two-sided tape at both ends of the molding.
10   Install the molding within 15 minutes after this adhesive has been applied.
11   Lift the molding release sheet from the base of the molding. Make sure that the body molding is put into the proper position and that no dirt or dust has fallen onto the contact area.

Conversion factors

Length (distance)

Inches (in)	X	25.4	= Millimetres (mm)	X 0.0394	= Inches (in)
Feet (ft)	X	0.305	= Metres (m)	X 3.281	= Feet (ft)
Miles	X	1.609	= Kilometres (km)	X 0.621	= Miles

Volume (capacity)

Cubic inches (cu in; in³)	X	16.387	= Cubic centimetres (cc; cm³)	X 0.061	= Cubic inches (cu in; in³)
Imperial pints (Imp pt)	X	0.568	= Litres (l)	X 1.76	= Imperial pints (Imp pt)
Imperial quarts (Imp qt)	X	1.137	= Litres (l)	X 0.88	= Imperial quarts (Imp qt)
Imperial quarts (Imp qt)	X	1.201	= US quarts (US qt)	X 0.833	= Imperial quarts (Imp qt)
US quarts (US qt)	X	0.946	= Litres (l)	X 1.057	= US quarts (US qt)
Imperial gallons (Imp gal)	X	4.546	= Litres (l)	X 0.22	= Imperial gallons (Imp gal)
Imperial gallons (Imp gal)	X	1.201	= US gallons (US gal)	X 0.833	= Imperial gallons (Imp gal)
US gallons (US gal)	X	3.785	= Litres (l)	X 0.264	= US gallons (US gal)

Mass (weight)

Ounces (oz)	X	28.35	= Grams (g)	X 0.035	= Ounces (oz)
Pounds (lb)	X	0.454	= Kilograms (kg)	X 2.205	= Pounds (lb)

Force

Ounces-force (ozf; oz)	X	0.278	= Newtons (N)	X 3.6	= Ounces-force (ozf; oz)
Pounds-force (lbf; lb)	X	4.448	= Newtons (N)	X 0.225	= Pounds-force (lbf; lb)
Newtons (N)	X	0.1	= Kilograms-force (kgf; kg)	X 9.81	= Newtons (N)

Pressure

Pounds-force per square inch (psi; lbf/in²; lb/in²)	X	0.070	= Kilograms-force per square centimetre (kgf/cm²; kg/cm²)	X 14.223	= Pounds-force per square inch (psi; lbf/in²; lb/in²)
Pounds-force per square inch (psi; lbf/in²; lb/in²)	X	0.068	= Atmospheres (atm)	X 14.696	= Pounds-force per square inch (psi; lbf/in²; lb/in²)
Pounds-force per square inch (psi; lbf/in²; lb/in²)	X	0.069	= Bars	X 14.5	= Pounds-force per square inch (psi; lbf/in²; lb/in²)
Pounds-force per square inch (psi; lbf/in²; lb/in²)	X	6.895	= Kilopascals (kPa)	X 0.145	= Pounds-force per square inch (psi; lbf/in²; lb/in²)
Kilopascals (kPa)	X	0.01	= Kilograms-force per square centimetre (kgf/cm²; kg/cm²)	X 98.1	= Kilopascals (kPa)
Millibar (mbar)	X	100	= Pascals (Pa)	X 0.01	= Millibar (mbar)
Millibar (mbar)	X	0.0145	= Pounds-force per square inch (psi; lbf/in²; lb/in²)	X 68.947	= Millibar (mbar)
Millibar (mbar)	X	0.75	= Millimetres of mercury (mmHg)	X 1.333	= Millibar (mbar)
Millibar (mbar)	X	0.401	= Inches of water (inH₂O)	X 2.491	= Millibar (mbar)
Millimetres of mercury (mmHg)	X	0.535	= Inches of water (inH₂O)	X 1.868	= Millimetres of mercury (mmHg)
Inches of water (inH₂O)	X	0.036	= Pounds-force per square inch (psi; lbf/in²; lb/in²)	X 27.68	= Inches of water (inH₂O)

Torque (moment of force)

Pounds-force inches (lbf in; lb in)	X	1.152	= Kilograms-force centimetre (kgf cm; kg cm)	X 0.868	= Pounds-force inches (lbf in; lb in)
Pounds-force inches (lbf in; lb in)	X	0.113	= Newton metres (Nm)	X 8.85	= Pounds-force inches (lbf in; lb in)
Pounds-force inches (lbf in; lb in)	X	0.083	= Pounds-force feet (lbf ft; lb ft)	X 12	= Pounds-force inches (lbf in; lb in)
Pounds-force feet (lbf ft; lb ft)	X	0.138	= Kilograms-force metres (kgf m; kg m)	X 7.233	= Pounds-force feet (lbf ft; lb ft)
Pounds-force feet (lbf ft; lb ft)	X	1.356	= Newton metres (Nm)	X 0.738	= Pounds-force feet (lbf ft; lb ft)
Newton metres (Nm)	X	0.102	= Kilograms-force metres (kgf m; kg m)	X 9.804	= Newton metres (Nm)

Power

Horsepower (hp)	X	745.7	= Watts (W)	X 0.0013	= Horsepower (hp)

Velocity (speed)

Miles per hour (miles/hr; mph)	X	1.609	= Kilometres per hour (km/hr; kph)	X 0.621	= Miles per hour (miles/hr; mph)

Fuel consumption*

Miles per gallon, Imperial (mpg)	X	0.354	= Kilometres per litre (km/l)	X 2.825	= Miles per gallon, Imperial (mpg)
Miles per gallon, US (mpg)	X	0.425	= Kilometres per litre (km/l)	X 2.352	= Miles per gallon, US (mpg)

Temperature

Degrees Fahrenheit = (°C x 1.8) + 32

Degrees Celsius (Degrees Centigrade; °C) = (°F - 32) x 0.56

It is common practice to convert from miles per gallon (mpg) to litres/100 kilometres (l/100km), where mpg (Imperial) x l/100 km = 282 and mpg (US) x l/100 km = 235

Index

HAYNES AUTOMOTIVE MANUALS

NOTE: New manuals are added to this list on a periodic basis. If you do not see a listing for your vehicle, consult your local Haynes dealer for the latest product information.

ALFA-ROMEO
531 **Alfa Romeo Sedan & Coupe** '73 thru '80

AMC
Jeep CJ – *see JEEP (412)*
694 **Mid-size models,** Concord, Hornet, Gremlin & Spirit '70 thru '83
934 **(Renault) Alliance & Encore** all models '83 thru '87

AUDI
162 **100** all models '69 thru '77
615 **4000** all models '80 thru '87
428 **5000** all models '77 thru '83
1117 **5000** all models '84 thru '88
207 **Fox** all models '73 thru '79

AUSTIN
049 **Healey 100/6 & 3000** Roadster '56 thru '68
Healey Sprite – *see MG Midget Roadster (265)*

BLMC
260 **1100, 1300 & Austin America** '62 thru '74
527 **Mini** all models '59 thru '69
*646 **Mini** all models '69 thru '88

BMW
276 **320i** all 4 cyl models '75 thru '83
632 **528i & 530i** all models '75 thru '80
240 **1500 thru 2002** all models except Turbo '59 thru '77
348 **2500, 2800, 3.0 & Bavaria** '69 thru '76

BUICK
Century (front wheel drive) – *see GENERAL MOTORS A-Cars (829)*
*1627 **Buick, Oldsmobile & Pontiac Full-size (Front wheel drive)** all models '85 thru '90
Buick Electra, LeSabre and Park Avenue; **Oldsmobile** Delta 88 Royale, Ninety Eight and Regency; **Pontiac** Bonneville
*1551 **Buick Oldsmobile & Pontiac Full-size (Rear wheel drive)**
Buick Electra '70 thru '84, Estate '70 thru '90, LeSabre '70 thru '79
Oldsmobile Custom Cruiser '70 thru '90, Delta 88 '70 thru '85, Ninety-eight '70 thru '84
Pontiac Bonneville '70 thru '86, Catalina '70 thru '81, Grandville '70 thru '75, Parisienne '84 thu '86
627 **Mid-size** all rear-drive **Regal & Century** models with V6, V8 and Turbo '74 thru '87
Skyhawk – *see GENERAL MOTORS J-Cars (766)*
552 **Skylark** all X-car models '80 thru '85

CADILLAC
Cimarron – *see GENERAL MOTORS J-Cars (766)*

CAPRI
296 **2000 MK I Coupe** all models '71 thru '75
283 **2300 MK II Coupe** all models '74 thru '78
205 **2600 & 2800** V6 Coupe '71 thru '75
375 **2800 Mk II** V6 Coupe '75 thru '78
Mercury in-line engines – *see FORD Mustang (654)*
Mercury V6 & V8 engines – *see FORD Mustang (558)*

CHEVROLET
*1477 **Astro & GMC Safari Mini-vans** all models '85 thru '90
554 **Camaro** V8 all models '70 thru '81
*866 **Camaro** all models '82 thru '89
Cavalier – *see GENERAL MOTORS J-Cars (766)*
Celebrity – *see GENERAL MOTORS A-Cars (829)*

625 **Chevelle, Malibu & El Camino** all V6 & V8 models '69 thru '87
449 **Chevette & Pontiac T1000** all models '76 thru '87
550 **Citation** all models '80 thru '85
*1628 **Corsica/Beretta** all models '87 thru '90
274 **Corvette** all V8 models '68 thru '82
*1336 **Corvette** all models '84 thru '89
704 **Full-size Sedans** Caprice, Impala, Biscayne, Bel Air & Wagons, all V6 & V8 models '69 thru '90
319 **Luv Pick-up** all 2WD & 4WD models '72 thru '82
626 **Monte Carlo** all V6, V8 & Turbo models '70 thru '88
241 **Nova** all V8 models '69 thru '79
*1642 **Nova and Geo Prizm** all front wheel drive models, '85 thru '90
*420 **Pick-ups '67 thru '87** – Chevrolet & GMC, all V8 & in-line 6 cyl 2WD & 4WD models '67 thru '87
*1664 **Pick-ups '88 thru '90** – Chevrolet & GMC all full-size (C and K) models, '88 thru '90
*831 **S-10 & GMC S-15 Pick-ups** all models '82 thru '90
*345 **Vans – Chevrolet & GMC,** V8 & in-line 6 cyl models '68 thru '89
208 **Vega** all models except Cosworth '70 thru '77

CHRYSLER
*1337 **Chrysler & Plymouth Mid-size** front wheel drive '82 thru '88
K-Cars – *see DODGE Aries (723)*
Laser – *see DODGE Daytona (1140)*

DATSUN
402 **200SX** all models '77 thru '79
647 **200SX** all models '80 thru '83
228 **B-210** all models '73 thru '78
525 **210** all models '78 thru '82
206 **240Z, 260Z & 280Z** Coupe & 2+2 '70 thru '78
563 **280ZX** Coupe & 2+2 '79 thru '83
300ZX – *see NISSAN (1137)*
679 **310** all models '78 thru '82
123 **510 & PL521 Pick-up** '68 thru '73
430 **510** all models '78 thru '81
372 **610** all models '72 thru '76
277 **620 Series Pick-up** all models '73 thru '79
235 **710** all models '73 thru '77
720 Series Pick-up – *see NISSAN Pick-ups (771)*
376 **810/Maxima** all gasoline models '77 thru '84
124 **1200** all models '70 thru '73
368 **F10** all models '76 thru '79
Pulsar – *see NISSAN (876)*
Sentra – *see NISSAN (982)*
Stanza – *see NISSAN (981)*

DODGE
*723 **Aries & Plymouth Reliant** all models '81 thru '88
*1231 **Caravan & Plymouth Voyager Mini-Vans** all models '84 thru '89
699 **Challenger & Plymouth Saporro** all models '78 thru '83
236 **Colt** all models '71 thru '77
419 **Colt (rear wheel drive)** all models '77 thru '81
610 **Colt & Plymouth Champ (front wheel drive)** all models '78 thru '87
*556 **D50 & Plymouth Arrow Pick-ups** '79 thru '88
234 **Dart & Plymouth Valiant** all 6 cyl models '67 thru '76
*1140 **Daytona & Chrysler Laser** all models '84 thru '88
*545 **Omni & Plymouth Horizon** all models '78 thru '89
*912 **Pick-ups** all full-size models '74 thru '90
*349 **Vans – Dodge & Plymouth** V8 & 6 cyl models '71 thru '89

FIAT
080 **124 Sedan & Wagon** all ohv & dohc models '66 thru '75
094 **124 Sport Coupe & Spider** '68 thru '78
087 **128** all models '72 thru '79
310 **131 & Brava** all models '75 thru '81
038 **850 Sedan, Coupe & Spider** '64 thru '74
479 **Strada** all models '79 thru '82
273 **X1/9** all models '74 thru '80

FORD
*1476 **Aerostar Mini-vans** all models '86 thru '88
788 **Bronco and Pick-ups** '73 thru '79
*880 **Bronco and Pick-ups** '80 thru '90
014 **Cortina MK II** all models except Lotus '66 thru '70
295 **Cortina MK III** 1600 & 2000 ohc '70 thru '76
268 **Courier Pick-up** all models '72 thru '82
789 **Escort & Mercury Lynx** all models '81 thru '90
560 **Fairmont & Mercury Zephyr** all in-line & V8 models '78 thru '83
334 **Fiesta** all models '77 thru '80
754 **Ford & Mercury Full-size,** Ford LTD & Mercury Marquis ('75 thru '82); Ford Custom 500, Country Squire, Crown Victoria & Mercury Colony Park ('75 thru '87); Ford LTD Crown Victoria & Mercury Gran Marquis ('83 thru '87)
359 **Granada & Mercury Monarch** all in-line, 6 cyl & V8 models '75 thru '80
773 **Ford & Mercury Mid-size,** Ford Thunderbird & Mercury Cougar ('75 thru '82); Ford LTD & Mercury Marquis ('83 thru '86); Ford Torino, Gran Torino, Elite, Ranchero pick-up, LTD II, Mercury Montego, Comet, XR-7 & Lincoln Versailles ('75 thru '86)
*654 **Mustang & Mercury Capri** all in-line models & Turbo '79 thru '90
*558 **Mustang & Mercury Capri** all V6 & V8 models '79 thru '89
357 **Mustang V8** all models '64-1/2 thru '73
231 **Mustang II** all 4 cyl, V6 & V8 models '74 thru '78
204 **Pinto** all models '70 thru '74
649 **Pinto & Mercury Bobcat** all models '75 thru '80
*1026 **Ranger & Bronco II** all gasoline models '83 thru '89
*1421 **Taurus & Mercury Sable** '86 thru '90
*1418 **Tempo & Mercury Topaz** all gasoline models '84 thru '89
1338 **Thunderbird & Mercury Cougar/XR7** '83 thru '88
*344 **Vans** all V8 Econoline models '69 thru '90

GENERAL MOTORS
*829 **A-Cars** – Chevrolet Celebrity, Buick Century, Pontiac 6000 & Oldsmobile Cutlass Ciera all models '82 thru '89
*766 **J-Cars** – Chevrolet Cavalier, Pontiac J-2000, Oldsmobile Firenza, Buick Skyhawk & Cadillac Cimarron all models '82 thru '89
*1420 **N-Cars** – Pontiac Grand Am, Buick Somerset and Oldsmobile Calais '85 thru '87; Buick Skylark '86 thru '87

GEO
Tracker – *see SUZUKI Samurai (1626)*
Prizm – *see CHEVROLET Nova (1642)*

GMC
Safari – *see CHEVROLET ASTRO (1477)*
Vans & Pick-ups – *see CHEVROLET (420, 831, 345, 1664)*

(continued on next page)

* Listings shown with an asterisk (*) indicate model coverage as of this printing. These titles will be periodically updated to include later model years — consult your Haynes dealer for more information.

Haynes Publications Inc., P.O. Box 978, Newbury Park, CA 91320 ● (818) 889-5400 ● (805) 498-6703

NOTE: New manuals are added to this list on a periodic basis. If you do not see a listing for your vehicle, consult your local Haynes dealer for the latest product information.

HONDA
- **138**   **360, 600 & Z** Coupe all models '67 thru '75
- **351**   **Accord CVCC** all models '76 thru '83
- ***1221**   **Accord** all models '84 thru '89
- **160**   **Civic 1200** all models '73 thru '79
- **633**   **Civic 1300 & 1500 CVCC** all models '80 thru '83
- **297**   **Civic 1500 CVCC** all models '75 thru '79
- ***1227**   **Civic** all models except 16-valve CRX & 4 WD Wagon '84 thru '86
- ***601**   **Prelude CVCC** all models '79 thru '89

HYUNDAI
- ***1552**   **Excel** all models '86 thru '89

ISUZU
- ***1641**   **Trooper & Pick-up**, all gasoline models '81 thru '89

JAGUAR
- **098**   **MK I & II,** 240 & 340 Sedans '55 thru '69
- ***242**   **XJ6** all 6 cyl models '68 thru '86
- ***478**   **XJ12 & XJS** all 12 cyl models '72 thru '85
- **140**   **XK-E** 3.8 & 4.2 all 6 cyl models '61 thru '72

JEEP
- ***1553**   **Cherokee, Comanche & Wagoneer Limited** all models '84 thru '89
- **412**   **CJ** all models '49 thru '86

LADA
- ***413**   **1200, 1300. 1500 & 1600** all models including Riva '74 thru '86

LANCIA
- **533**   **Lancia Beta** Sedan, Coupe & HPE all models '76 thru '80

LAND ROVER
- **314**   **Series II, IIA, & III** all 4 cyl gasoline models '58 thru '86
- **529**   **Diesel** all models '58 thru '80

MAZDA
- **648**   **626** Sedan & Coupe (rear wheel drive) all models '79 thru '82
- ***1082**   **626 & MX-6** (front wheel drive) all models '83 thru '90
- ***267**   **B1600, B1800 & B2000 Pick-ups** '72 thru '90
- **370**   **GLC Hatchback** (rear wheel drive) all models '77 thru '83
- **757**   **GLC** (front wheel drive) all models '81 thru '86
- **109**   **RX2** all models '71 thru '75
- **096**   **RX3** all models '72 thru '76
- **460**   **RX-7** all models '79 thru '85
- ***1419**   **RX-7** all models '86 thru '89

MERCEDES-BENZ
- ***1643**   **190 Series** all four-cylinder gasoline models, '84 thru '88
- **346**   **230, 250 & 280** Sedan, Coupe & Roadster all 6 cyl sohc models '68 thru '72
- **983**   **280 123 Series** all gasoline models '77 thru '81
- **698**   **350 & 450** Sedan, Coupe & Roadster all models '71 thru '80
- **697**   **Diesel 123 Series** 200D, 220D, 240D, 240TD, 300D, 300CD, 300TD, 4- & 5-cyl incl. Turbo '76 thru '85

MERCURY
See FORD Listing

MG
- **475**   **MGA** all models '56 thru '62
- **111**   **MGB** Roadster & GT Coupe all models '62 thru '80
- **265**   **MG Midget & Austin Healey Sprite** Roadster '58 thru '80

MITSUBISHI
Pick-up – *see Dodge D-50 (556)*

MORRIS
- **074**   **(Austin) Marina 1.8** all models '71 thru '80
- **024**   **Minor 1000** sedan & wagon '56 thru '71

NISSAN
- ***1137**   **300ZX** all Turbo & non-Turbo models '84 thru '86
- ***1341**   **Maxima** all models '85 thru '89
- ***771**   **Pick-ups/Pathfinder** gas models '80 thru '88
- ***876**   **Pulsar** all models '83 thru '86
- ***982**   **Sentra** all models '82 thru '90
- ***981**   **Stanza** all models '82 thru '90

OLDSMOBILE
- **Custom Cruiser** – *see BUICK Full-size (1551)*
- **658**   **Cutlass** all standard gasoline V6 & V8 models '74 thru '88
- **Cutlass Ciera** – *see GENERAL MOTORS A-Cars (829)*
- **Firenza** – *see GENERAL MOTORS J-Cars (766)*
- **Ninety-eight** – *see BUICK Full-size (1551)*
- **Omega** – *see PONTIAC Phoenix & Omega (551)*

OPEL
- **157**   **(Buick) Manta Coupe 1900** all models '70 thru '74

PEUGEOT
- **161**   **504** all gasoline models '68 thru '79
- **663**   **504** all diesel models '74 thru '83

PLYMOUTH
- **425**   **Arrow** all models '76 thru '80
- *For all other PLYMOUTH titles, see DODGE listing.*

PONTIAC
- **T1000** – *see CHEVROLET Chevette (449)*
- **J-2000** – *see GENERAL MOTORS J-Cars (766)*
- **6000** – *see GENERAL MOTORS A-Cars (829)*
- **1232**   **Fiero** all models '84 thru '87
- **555**   **Firebird** all V8 models except Turbo '70 thru '81
- ***867**   **Firebird** all models '82 thru '89
- **Full-size Rear Wheel Drive** – *see Buick, Oldsmobile, Pontiac Full-size (1551)*
- **551**   **Phoenix & Oldsmobile Omega** all X-car models '80 thru '84

PORSCHE
- ***264**   **911** all Coupe & Targa models except Turbo '65 thru '87
- **239**   **914** all 4 cyl models '69 thru '76
- **397**   **924** all models including Turbo '76 thru '82
- ***1027**   **944** all models including Turbo '83 thru '89

RENAULT
- **141**   **5 Le Car** all models '76 thru '83
- **079**   **8 & 10** all models with 58.4 cu in engines '62 thru '72
- **097**   **12 Saloon & Estate** all models 1289 cc engines '70 thru '80
- **768**   **15 & 17** all models '73 thru '79
- **081**   **16** all models 89.7 cu in & 95.5 cu in engines '65 thru '72
- **598**   **18i & Sportwagon** all models '81 thru '86
- **Alliance & Encore** – *see AMC (934)*
- **984**   **Fuego** all models '82 thru '85

ROVER
- **085**   **3500 & 3500S Sedan** 215 cu in engines '68 thru '76
- ***365**   **3500 SDI V8** all models '76 thru '85

SAAB
- **198**   **95 & 96 V4** all models '66 thru '75
- **247**   **99** all models including Turbo '69 thru '80
- ***980**   **900** all models including Turbo '79 thru '88

SUBARU
- **237**   **1100, 1300, 1400 & 1600** all models '71 thru '79
- ***681**   **1600 & 1800** 2WD & 4WD all models '80 thru '88

SUZUKI
- ***1626**   **Samurai/Sidekick and Geo Tracker** all models '86 thru '89

TOYOTA
- ***1023**   **Camry** all models '83 thru '90
- **150**   **Carina Sedan** all models '71 thru '74
- **229**   **Celica ST, GT & liftback** all models '71 thru '77
- **437**   **Celica** all models '78 thru '81
- ***935**   **Celica** all models except front-wheel drive and Supra '82 thru '85
- **680**   **Celica Supra** all models '79 thru '81
- **1139**   **Celica Supra** all in-line 6-cylinder models '82 thru '86
- **201**   **Corolla 1100, 1200 & 1600** all models '67 thru '74
- **361**   **Corolla** all models '75 thru '79
- **961**   **Corolla** all models (rear wheel drive) '80 thru '87
- ***1025**   **Corolla** all models (front wheel drive) '84 thru '88
- ***636**   **Corolla Tercel** all models '80 thru '82
- **230**   **Corona & MK II** all 4 cyl sohc models '69 thru '74
- **360**   **Corona** all models '74 thru '82
- ***532**   **Cressida** all models '78 thru '82
- **313**   **Land Cruiser** all models '68 thru '82
- **200**   **MK II** all 6 cyl models '72 thru '76
- ***1339**   **MR2** all models '85 thru '87
- **304**   **Pick-up** all models '69 thru '78
- ***656**   **Pick-up** all models '79 thru '90
- **787**   **Starlet** all models '81 thru '84

TRIUMPH
- **112**   **GT6 & Vitesse** all models '62 thru '74
- **113**   **Spitfire** all models '62 thru '81
- **028**   **TR2, 3, 3A, & 4A** Roadsters '52 thru '67
- **031**   **TR250 & 6** Roadsters '67 thru '76
- **322**   **TR7** all models '75 thru '81

VW
- **091**   **411 & 412** all 103 cu in models '68 thru '73
- **036**   **Bug 1200** all models '54 thru '66
- **039**   **Bug 1300 & 1500** '65 thru '70
- **159**   **Bug 1600** all basic, sport & super (curved windshield) models '70 thru '74
- **110**   **Bug 1600 Super** all models (flat windshield) '70 thru '72
- **238**   **Dasher** all gasoline models '74 thru '81
- ***884**   **Rabbit, Jetta, Scirocco, & Pick-up** all gasoline models '74 thru '89 & **Convertible** '80 thru '89
- **451**   **Rabbit, Jetta & Pick-up** all diesel models '77 thru '84
- **082**   **Transporter 1600** all models '68 thru '79
- **226**   **Transporter 1700, 1800 & 2000** all models '72 thru '79
- **084**   **Type 3 1500 & 1600** all models '63 thru '73
- **1029**   **Vanagon** all air-cooled models '80 thru '83

VOLVO
- **203**   **120, 130 Series & 1800 Sports** '61 thru '73
- **129**   **140 Series** all models '66 thru '74
- **244**   **164** all models '68 thru '75
- ***270**   **240 Series** all models '74 thru '90
- **400**   **260 Series** all models '75 thru '82
- ***1550**   **740 & 760 Series** all models '82 thru '88

SPECIAL MANUALS
- **1479**   **Automotive Body Repair & Painting Manual**
- **1654**   **Automotive Electrical Manual**
- **1480**   **Automotive Heating & Air Conditioning Manual**
- **482**   **Fuel Injection Manual**
- **299**   **SU Carburetors** thru '88
- **393**   **Weber Carburetors** thru '79
- **300**   **Zenith/Stromberg CD Carburetors** thru '76

See your dealer for other available titles

6-1-90

Over 100 Haynes motorcycle manuals also available

* Listings shown with an asterisk (*) indicate model coverage as of this printing. These titles will be periodically updated to include later model years — consult your Haynes dealer for more information.

Haynes Publications Inc., P.O. Box 978, Newbury Park, CA 91320 ● (818) 889-5400 ● (805) 498-6703

Printed by
J H Haynes & Co Ltd
Sparkford Nr Yeovil
Somerset BA22 7JJ England